THE PRESIDENCY

THE PRESIDENCY

CLASSIC AND CONTEMPORARY READINGS

Edited by

Jeffrey Cohen

Department of Political Science
Fordham University

David Nice

Department of Political Science
Washington State University

Boston Burr Ridge, IL Dubuque, IA Madison, WI New York
San Francisco St. Louis Bangkok Bogotá Caracas Kuala Lumpur
Lisbon London Madrid Mexico City Milan Montreal New Delhi
Santiago Seoul Singapore Sydney Taipei Toronto

McGraw-Hill Higher Education ⚛

A Division of The McGraw-Hill Companies

THE PRESIDENCY: CLASSIC AND CONTEMPORARY READINGS

Published by McGraw-Hill, a business unit of The McGraw-Hill Companies, Inc., 1221 Avenue of the Americas, New York, NY 10020. Copyright © 2003 by The McGraw-Hill Companies, Inc. All rights reserved. No part of this publication may be reproduced or distributed in any form or by any means, or stored in a database or retrieval system, without the prior written consent of The McGraw-Hill Companies, Inc., including, but not limited to, in any network or other electronic storage or transmission, or broadcast for distance learning.

Some ancillaries, including electronic and print components, may not be available to customers outside the United States.

This book is printed on acid-free paper.

1 2 3 4 5 6 7 8 9 0 QPF/QPF 0 9 8 7 6 5 4 3 2

ISBN 0-07-239041-7

Vice president and editor-in-chief: *Thalia Dorwick*
Publisher: *Lyn Uhl*
Sponsoring editor: *Monica Eckman*
Editorial coordinator: *Angela W. Kao*
Marketing manager: *Janise A. Fry*
Project manager: *Mary Lee Harms*
New book production supervisor: *Enboge Chong*
Senior media technology producer: *Lance Gerhart*
Lead designer: *Matthew Baldwin*
Cover Designer: *Joanne Schopler*
Cover Image: © *Getty Images*
Senior supplement producer: *David A. Welsh*
Compositor: *ElectraGraphics, Inc.*
Typeface: *10/12 Garamond*
Printer: *Quebecor World Fairfield, PA*

The credits section for this book begins on page 359 and is considered an extension of the copyright page.

Library of Congress Cataloging-in-Publication Data

Cohen, Jeffrey.
    The presidency : classic and contemporary readings / Jeffrey Cohen, David Nice.— 1st ed.
      p. cm.
    Includes index.
    ISBN 0-07-239041-7
     1. Presidents—United States. 2. United States—Politics and government. I. Nice, David.
  II. Title.

JK516 .C528 2003
973'.09'9—dc21

                        2002069631

www.mhhe.com

To Charlotte Josselsohn and
to Mary Nice

CONTENTS

PREFACE

Studying the presidency can be a rewarding enterprise, but it can also be frustrating. Presidents have been involved in many of the most important issues that the United States has faced over the years. When we examine the expansion of the United States after independence from England, the Civil War, the Great Depression, the World Wars, or the fight against terrorism, presidents have often been major participants. Moreover, the presidency has attracted a number of intriguing personalities, from George Washington and Thomas Jefferson to Abraham Lincoln and the two Roosevelts. We have not always been pleased with presidential actions—indeed, we often seem to be displeased with their action or their personalities. In a country as large and diverse as the United States, presidents often find that pleasing one group means angering another group.

We have also struggled with a number of difficulties in trying to make sense of the presidency. Researchers have often lacked good information regarding White House operations. The result has been more progress studying presidential interactions with other parts of the political system, such as Congress, because that information is easier to find. Presidents also arouse strong emotions, from admiration to hatred, and those emotions sometimes color people's judgments of presidents and presidential actions. Different presidents have faced different types of problems and different political contexts, both of which complicate our efforts to understand the office. Despite these difficulties, however, researchers have made major progress in understanding the presidency over the years.

In this book, we have assembled a number of readings from many different sources. The authors included here have examined the presidency from a variety of perspectives and used different approaches to understanding the office and its occupants. We have tried to avoid some of the more technical literature but have tried to include a range of opinions and analytical approaches. We have included works over a large span of time, from early discussions regarding the Constitution to recent works on the White House chiefs of staff to President George W. Bush's response to the September 11, 2001, terrorist attacks. We don't necessarily agree with everything the authors write, but we think their ideas are worth exploring.

We hope that these selections will encourage readers to explore the presidency further. Whether people are interested in the history of the presidency, presidential involvement in public policy making, presidential elections, or any other aspect of the presidency, a wealth of literature is waiting.

HOW TO USE
THIS READER

This reader is designed for use as the main supplement to our textbook, *The Presidency*. These icons from the textbook guide students to relevant selections in this reader, while discussion questions and key terms in the textbook also challenge students to apply concepts and ideas from a textbook to primary resource material. To avoid redundancy, this reader does not include additional student tools. Students will find that the selections in the reader will be more meaningful after they have read the related chapter in the textbook. Additionally, students should refer to the text website www.mhhe.com/cohennice when using the text and reader. Used together, students can test themselves, participate in simulations, read primary and secondary documents, and gain the maximum benefit from all three sources.

1

THE CONSTITUTIONAL NATURE OF THE PRESIDENCY

Federalist Papers

NUMBER 69

The Same View Continued, with a Comparison between the President and the King of Great Britain on the One Hand, and the Governor of New York on the Other

[Alexander Hamilton]

I PROCEED now to trace the real characters of the proposed executive, as they are marked out in the plan of the convention. This will serve to place in a strong light the unfairness of the representations which have been made in regard to it.

The first thing which strikes our attention is that the executive authority, with few exceptions, is to be vested in a single magistrate. This will scarcely, however, be considered as a point upon which any comparison can be grounded; for if, in this particular, there be a resemblance to the king of Great Britain, there is not less a resemblance to the Grand Seignior, to the khan of Tartary, to the Man of the Seven Mountains, or to the governor of New York.

That magistrate is to be elected for four years; and is to be re-eligible as often as the people of the United States shall think him worthy of their confidence. In these circumstances there is a total dissimilitude between him and a king of Great Britain, who is an hereditary monarch, possessing the crown as a patrimony descendible to his heirs forever; but there is a close analogy between him and a governor of New York, who is elected for three years, and is re-eligible without limitation or inter mission. If we consider how much less time would be requisite for establishing a dangerous influence in a single State than for establishing a like influence through-out the United States, we must conclude that a duration of four years for the Chief

Source: James Madison, Alexander Hamilton, and John Jay, The Federalist, or The New Constitution, 2 vols. (Chicago: Albert Scott & Company, 1894), pp. 396–402.

Magistrate of the Union is a degree of permanency far less to be dreaded in that office, than a duration of three years for a corresponding office in a single State.

The President of the United States would be liable to be impeached, tried, and, upon conviction of treason, bribery, or other high crimes or misdemeanors, removed from office; and would afterwards be liable to prosecution and punishment in the ordinary course of law. The person of the king of Great Britain is sacred and inviolable; there is no constitutional tribunal to which he is amenable; no punishment to which he can be subjected without involving the crisis of a national revolution. In this delicate and important circumstance of personal responsibility, the President of Confederated America would stand upon no better ground than a governor of New York, and upon worse ground than the governors of Virginia and Delaware.

The President of the United States is to have power to return a bill, which shall have passed the two branches of the legislature, for reconsideration; but the bill so returned is not to become a law unless, upon that reconsideration, it be approved by two thirds of both houses. The king of Great Britain, on his part, has an absolute negative upon the acts of the two houses of Parliament. The disuse of that power for a considerable time past does not affect the reality of its existence and is to be ascribed wholly to the crown's having found the means of substituting influence to authority, or the art of gaining a majority in one or the other of the two houses, to the necessity of exerting a prerogative which could seldom be exerted without hazarding some degree of national agitation. The qualified negative of the President differs widely from this absolute negative of the British sovereign and tallies exactly with the revisionary authority of the council of revision of this State, of which the governor is a constituent part. In this respect the power of the President would exceed that of the governor of New York, because the former would possess, singly, what the latter shares with the chancellor and judges; but it would be precisely the same with that of the governor of Massachusetts, whose constitution, as to this article, seems to have been the original from which the convention [has] copied.

The President is to be the "commander-in-chief of the army and navy of the United States, and of the militia of the several States, when called into the actual service of the United States. He is to have power to grant reprieves and pardons for offenses against the United States, except in cases of impeachment: to recommend to the consideration of Congress such measures as he shall judge necessary and expedient; to convene, on extraordinary occasions, both houses of the legislature, or either of them, and, in case of disagreement between them with respect to the time of adjournment, to adjourn them to such time as he shall think proper; to take care that the laws be faithfully executed; and to commission all officers of the United States." In most of these particulars, the power of the President will resemble equally that of the king of Great Britain and of the governor of New York. The most material points of difference are these:—First. The President will have only the occasional command of such part of the militia of the nation as by legislative provision may be called into the actual service of the Union. The king of Great Britain and the governor of New York have at all times the entire command of all the militia within their several jurisdictions. In this article, therefore, the power of the President would be inferior to that of either the monarch or the governor. Second. The President is to be the commander-in-chief of the army and navy of the United States. In this respect his authority would be nominally the same with that of the king of Great Britain, but in substance much inferior to it. It would amount to nothing more than the supreme command and direction of the military and naval forces, as first general and admiral of the Confederacy; while that of the British king extends to the declaring of war and to the raising and regulating of fleets and armies—all which, by the Constitution under consideration, would appertain to the legislature. The governor of New York, on the other hand, is by the constitution of the State vested only with the command of its militia and navy. But the constitutions of several of the States expressly declare their governors to be commanders-in-chief, as well of the army as navy; and it may well be a question whether those of New Hampshire and Massachusetts, in particular, do not, in this instance, confer larger powers upon their respective governors than could be claimed by a President of the United States. Third. The power of the President, in respect to pardons, would extend to all cases, except those of impeachment. The governor of New York may pardon in all cases, even in those of impeachment, except for treason and murder. Is not the power of the governor, in this article, on a calculation of political consequences, greater than that of the President? All conspiracies and plots against the government which have not been matured into actual treason may be screened from punishment of every kind by the interposition of the prerogative of pardoning. If a governor of New York, therefore, should be at the head of any such conspiracy, until the design had been ripened into actual hostility he could insure his accomplices and adherents an entire impunity. A President of the Union, on the other hand, though he may even pardon treason, when prosecuted in the ordinary course of law, could shelter no offender, in any degree, from the effects of impeachment and conviction. Would not the prospect of a total indemnity for all the preliminary steps be a greater temptation to undertake and persevere in an enterprise against the public liberty, than the mere prospect of an exemption from death and confiscation, if the final execution of the design, upon an actual appeal to arms, should miscarry? Would this last expectation have any influence at all, when the probability was computed that the person who was to afford that exemption might himself be involved in the consequences of the measure, and might be incapacitated by his agency in it from affording the desired impunity? The better to judge of this matter, it will be necessary to recollect that, by the proposed Constitution, the offense of treason is limited "to levying war upon the United States, and adhering to their enemies, giving them aid and comfort"; and that by the laws of New York it is confined within similar bounds. Fourth. The President can only adjourn the national legislature in the single case of disagreement about the time of adjournment. The British monarch may prorogue or even dissolve the Parliament. The governor of New York may also prorogue the legislature of this State for a limited time; a power which, in certain situations, may be employed to very important purposes.

The President is to have power, with the advice and consent of the Senate, to make treaties, provided two thirds of the senators present concur. The king of Great Britain is the sole and absolute representative of the nation in all foreign transactions. He can of his own accord make treaties of peace, commerce, alliance, and of every other description. It has been insinuated that his authority in this respect is not conclusive, and that his conventions with foreign powers are subject to the revision, and stand in need of the ratification, of Parliament. But I believe this doctrine was never heard of until it was broached upon the present occasion. Every jurist of that kingdom, and every other man acquainted with its Constitution knows, as an established fact, that the prerogative of making treaties exists in the crown in its utmost plenitude; and that the compacts entered into by the royal authority have the most complete legal validity and perfection, independent of any other sanction. The Parliament, it is true, is sometimes seen employing itself in altering the existing laws to conform them to the stipulations in a new treaty; and this may have possibly given birth to the imagination that its co-operation was necessary to the obligatory efficacy of the treaty. But this parliamentary interposition proceeds from a different cause: from the necessity of adjusting a most artificial and intricate system of revenue and commercial laws, to the changes made in them by the operation of the treaty; and of adapting new provisions and precautions to the new state of things, to keep the machine from running into disorder. In this respect, therefore, there is no comparison between the intended power of the President and the actual power of the British sovereign. The one can perform alone what the other can only do with the concurrence of a branch of the legislature. It must be admitted that in this instance the power of the federal executive would exceed that of any State executive. But this arises naturally from the exclusive possession by the Union of that part of the sovereign power which relates to treaties. If the Confederacy were to be dissolved, it would become a question whether the executives of the several States were not solely invested with that delicate and important prerogative.

The President is also to be authorized to receive ambassadors and other public ministers. This, though it has been a rich theme of declamation, is more a matter of dignity than of authority. It is a circumstance which will be without consequence in the administration of the government; and it was far more convenient that it should be arranged in this manner than that there should be a necessity of convening the legislature, or one of its branches, upon every arrival of a foreign minister, though it were merely to take the place of a departed predecessor.

The President is to nominate, and, with the advice and consent of the Senate, to appoint ambassadors and other public ministers, judges of the Supreme Court, and in general all officers of the United States established by law, and whose appointments are not otherwise provided for by the Constitution. The king of Great Britain is emphatically and truly styled the fountain of honor. He not only appoints to all offices, but can create offices. He can confer titles of nobility at pleasure, and has the disposal of an immense number of church preferments. There is evidently a great inferiority in the power of the President, in this particular, to that of the British king; nor is it equal to that of the governor of New York, if we are to interpret the meaning of the constitution of the State by the practice which has obtained under it. The power of appointment is with us lodged in a council, composed of the governor and four members of the Senate, chosen by the Assembly. The governor claims, and has frequently exercised, the right of nomination, and is entitled to a casting vote in the appointment. If he really has the right of nominating, his authority is in this respect equal to that of the President, and exceeds it in the article of the casting vote. In the national government, if the Senate should be divided, no appointment could be made; in the government of New York, if the council should be divided, the governor can turn the scale and confirm his own nomination. If we compare the publicity which must necessarily attend the mode of appointment by the President and an entire branch of the national legislature, with the privacy in the mode of appointment by the governor of New York, closeted in a secret apartment with at most four, and frequently with only two persons; and if we at the same time consider how much more easy it must be to influence the small number of which a council of appointment consists than the considerable number of which the national Senate would consist, we cannot hesitate to pronounce that the power of the chief magistrate of this State, in the disposition of offices, must, in practice, be greatly superior to that of the Chief Magistrate of the Union.

Hence it appears that, except as to the concurrent authority of the President in the article of treaties, it would be difficult to determine whether that magistrate would, in the aggregate, possess more or less power than the governor of New York. And it appears yet more unequivocally that there is no pretense for the parallel which has been attempted between him and the king of Great Britain. But to render the contrast in this respect still more striking, it may be of use to throw the principal circumstances of dissimilitude into a closer group.

The President of the United States would be an officer elected by the people for four years; the king of Great Britain is a perpetual and hereditary prince. The one would be amenable to personal punishment and disgrace; the person of the other is sacred and inviolable. The one would have a qualified negative upon the acts of the legislative body; the other has an absolute negative. The one would have a right to command the military and naval forces of the nation; the other, in addition to this right, possesses that of declaring war, and of raising and regulating fleets and armies by his own authority. The one would have a concurrent power with a branch of the legislature in the formation of treaties; the other is the sole possessor of the power of making treaties. The one would have a like concurrent authority in appointing to offices; the other is the sole author of all appointments. The one can confer no privileges whatever; the other can make denizens of aliens, noblemen of commoners, can erect corporations with all the rights incident to corporate bodies. The one can prescribe no rules concerning the commerce or currency of the nation; the other is in several respects the arbiter of commerce, and in this capacity can establish markets and fairs, can regulate weights and measures, can lay embargoes for a limited time, can coin money, can authorize or prohibit the circulation of foreign coin. The one has no particle of spiritual jurisdiction; the other is the supreme head and governor of the national church! What answer shall we give to those who would persuade us that things so unlike resemble each other? The same that ought to be given to those who tell us that a government, the whole power of which would be in the hands of the elective and periodical servants of the people, is an aristocracy, a monarchy, and a despotism.

PUBLIUS [Hamilton]

NUMBER 70

The Same View Continued in Relation to the Unity of the Executive, with an Examination of the Project of an Executive Council

Alexander Hamilton

THERE is an idea, which is not without its advocates, that a vigorous executive is inconsistent with the genius of republican government. The enlightened well-wishers to this species of government must at least hope that the supposition is destitute of foundation; since they can never admit its truth, without at the same time admitting the condemnation of their own principles. Energy in the executive is a leading character in the definition of good government. It is essential to the protection of the community against foreign attacks; it is not less essential to the steady administration of the laws; to the protection of property against those irregular and high-handed combinations which sometimes interrupt the ordinary course of justice; to the security of liberty against the enterprises and assaults of ambition, of faction, and of anarchy. Every man the least conversant in Roman history knows how often that republic was obliged to take refuge in the absolute power of a single man, under the formidable title of dictator, as well against the intrigues of ambitious individuals who aspired to the tyranny, and the seditions of whole classes of the community whose conduct threatened the existence of all government, as against the invasions of external enemies who menaced the conquest and destruction of Rome.

There can be no need, however, to multiply arguments or examples on this head. A feeble executive implies a feeble execution of the government. A feeble execution is but another phrase for a bad execution; and a government ill executed, whatever it may be in theory, must be, in practice, a bad government.

Source: James Madison, Alexander Hamilton, and John Jay, The Federalist, or The New Constitution, 2 vols. (Chicago: Albert Scott & Company, 1894), pp. 402–409.

Taking it for granted, therefore, that all men of sense will agree in the necessity of an energetic executive, it will only remain to inquire, what are the ingredients which constitute this energy? How far can they be combined with those other ingredients which constitute safety in the republican sense? And how far does this combination characterize the plan which has been reported by the convention?

The ingredients which constitute energy in the executive are unity, duration, an adequate provision for its support, and competent powers.

The ingredients which constitute safety in the republican sense are a due dependence on the people, and a due responsibility.

Those politicians and statesmen who have been the most celebrated for the soundness of their principles and for the justness of their views have declared in favor of a single executive and a numerous legislature. They have, with great propriety, considered energy as the most necessary qualification of the former, and have regarded this as most applicable to power in a single hand; while they have, with equal propriety, considered the latter as best adapted to deliberation and wisdom, and best calculated to conciliate the confidence of the people and to secure their privileges and interests.

That unity is conducive to energy will not be disputed. Decision, activity, secrecy, and dispatch will generally characterize the proceedings of one man in a much more eminent degree than the proceedings of any greater number; and in proportion as the number is increased, these qualities will be diminished.

This unity may be destroyed in two ways: either by vesting the power in two or more magistrates of equal dignity and authority, or by vesting it ostensibly in one man, subject in whole or in part to the control and co-operation of others, in the capacity of counselors to him. Of the first, the two consuls of Rome may serve as an example; of the last, we shall find examples in the constitutions of several of the States. New York and New Jersey, if I recollect right, are the only States which have intrusted the executive authority wholly to single men. Both these methods of destroying the unity of the executive have their partisans; but the votaries of an executive council are the most numerous. They are both liable, if not to equal, to similar objections, and may in most lights be examined in conjunction.

The experience of other nations will afford little instruction on this head. As far, however, as it teaches anything, it teaches us not to be enamored of plurality in the executive. We have seen that the Achaeans, on an experiment of two Praetors, were induced to abolish one. The Roman history records many instances of mischiefs to the republic from the dissensions between the consuls, and between the military tribunes, who were at times substituted for the consuls. But it gives us no specimens of any peculiar advantages derived to the state from the circumstance of the plurality of those magistrates. That the dissensions between them were not more frequent or more fatal is a matter of astonishment, until we advert to the singular position in which the republic was almost continually placed, and to the prudent policy pointed out by the circumstances of the state, and pursued by the consuls, of making a division of the government between them. The patricians engaged in a perpetual struggle with the plebeians for the preservation of their ancient authorities and dignities; the consuls, who were generally chosen out of the former body, were commonly united by the personal interest they had in the defense of the privileges of their order. In addition to this motive of union, after the arms of the republic had considerably expanded the bounds of its empire, it became an established custom with the consuls to divide the administration between themselves by lot—one of them remaining at Rome to govern the city and its environs, the other taking command in the more distant provinces. This expedient must no doubt have had great influence in preventing those collisions and rivalships which might otherwise have embroiled the peace of the republic.

But quitting the dim light of historical research, and attaching ourselves purely to the dictates of reason and good sense, we shall discover much greater cause to reject than to approve the idea of plurality in the executive, under any modification whatever.

Whenever two or more persons are engaged in any common enterprise or pursuit, there is always danger of difference of opinion. If it be a public trust or office in which they are clothed with equal dignity and authority, there is peculiar danger of personal emulation and even animosity. From either, and especially from all these causes, the most bitter dissensions are apt to spring. Whenever these happen, they lessen the respectability, weaken the authority, and distract the plans and operations of those whom they divide. If they should unfortunately assail the supreme executive magistracy of a country, consisting of a plurality of persons, they might impede or frustrate the most important measures of the government in the most critical emergencies of the state. And what is still worse, they might split the community into the most violent and irreconcilable factions, adhering differently to the different individuals who composed the magistracy.

Men often oppose a thing merely because they have had no agency in planning it, or because it may have been planned by those whom they dislike. But if they have been consulted, and have happened to disapprove, opposition then becomes, in their estimation, an indispensable duty of self-love. They seem to think themselves bound in honor, and by all the motives of personal infallibility, to defeat the success of what has been resolved upon contrary to their sentiments. Men of upright, benevolent tempers have too many opportunities of remarking, with horror, to what desperate lengths this disposition is sometimes carried, and how often the great interests of society are sacrificed to the vanity, to the conceit, and to the obstinacy of individuals, who have credit enough to make their passions and their caprices interesting to mankind. Perhaps the question now before the public may, in its consequences, afford melancholy proofs of the effects of this despicable frailty, or rather detestable vice, in the human character.

Upon the principles of a free government, inconveniences from the source just mentioned must necessarily be submitted to in the formation of the legislature; but it is unnecessary, and therefore unwise, to introduce them into the constitution of the executive. It is here too that they may be most pernicious. In the legislature, promptitude of decision is oftener an evil than a benefit. The differences of opinion, and the jarring of parties in that department of the government, though they may sometimes obstruct salutary plans, yet often promote deliberation and circumspection, and serve to check excesses in the majority. When a resolution too is once taken, the opposition must be at an end. That resolution is a law, and resistance to it punishable. But no favorable circumstances palliate or atone for the disadvantages of dissension in the executive department. Here they are pure and unmixed. There is no point at which they cease to operate. They serve to embarrass and weaken the execution of the plan or measure to which they relate, from the first step to the final conclusion of it. They constantly counteract those qualities in the executive which are the most necessary ingredients in its composition—vigor and expedition, and this without any counterbalancing good. In the conduct of war, in which the energy of the executive is the bulwark of the national security, everything would be apprehended from its plurality.

It must be confessed that these observations apply with principal weight to the first case supposed—that is, to a plurality of magistrates of equal dignity and authority, a scheme, the advocates for which are not likely to form a numerous sect; but they apply, though not with equal yet with considerable weight, to the project of a council, whose concurrence is made constitutionally necessary to the operations of the ostensible executive. An artful cabal in that council would be able to distract and to enervate the whole system of administration. If no such cabal should exist, the mere diversity of views and opinions would alone be sufficient to tincture the exercise of the executive authority with a spirit of habitual feebleness and dilatoriness.

But one of the weightiest objections to a plurality in the executive, and which lies as much against the last as the first plan is that it tends to conceal faults and destroy responsibility. Responsibility is of two kinds—to censure and to punishment. The first is the more important of the two, especially in an elective office. Men in public trust will much oftener act in such a manner as to render them unworthy of being any longer trusted, than in such a manner as to make them obnoxious to legal punishment. But the multiplication of the executive adds to the difficulty of detection in either case. It often becomes impossible, amidst mutual accusations, to determine on whom the blame or the punishment of a pernicious measure, or series of pernicious measures, ought really to fall. It is shifted from one to another with so much dexterity, and under such plausible appearances, that the public opinion is left in suspense about the real author. The circumstances which may have led to any national miscarriage or misfortune are sometimes so complicated that where there are a number of actors who may have had different degrees and kinds of agency, though we may clearly see upon the whole that there has been mismanagement, yet it may be impracticable to pronounce to whose account the evil which may have been incurred is truly chargeable.

"I was overruled by my council." "The council [members] were so divided in their opinions that it was impossible to obtain any better resolution on the point." These and similar pretexts are constantly at hand, whether true or false. And who is there that will either take the trouble or incur the odium of a strict scrutiny into the secret springs of the transaction? Should there be found a citizen zealous enough to undertake the unpromising task, if there happened to be a collusion between the parties concerned, how easy it is to clothe the circumstances with so much ambiguity as to render it uncertain what was the precise conduct of any of those parties.

In the single instance in which the governor of this State is coupled with a council—that is, in the appointment to offices, we have seen the mischiefs of it in the view now under consideration. Scandalous appointments to important offices have been made. Some cases, indeed, have been so flagrant that ALL PARTIES have agreed in the impropriety of the thing. When inquiry has been made, the blame has been laid by the governor on the members of the council, who, on their part, have charged it upon his nomination; while the people remain altogether at a loss to determine by whose influence their interests have been committed to hands so unqualified and so manifestly improper. In tenderness to individuals, I forbear to descend to particulars.

It is evident from these considerations that the plurality of the executive tends to deprive the people of the two greatest securities they can have for the faithful exercise of any delegated power, first, the restraints of public opinion, which lose their efficacy, as well on account of the division of the censure attendant on bad measures among a number as on account of the uncertainty on whom it ought to fall; and, second, the opportunity of discovering with facility and clearness the misconduct of the persons they trust, in order either to their removal from office or to their actual punishment in cases which admit of it.

In England, the king is a perpetual magistrate; and it is a maxim which has obtained for the sake of the public peace that he is unaccountable for his administration, and his person sacred. Nothing, therefore, can be wiser in that kingdom than to annex to the king a constitutional council, who may be responsible to the nation for the advice they give. Without this, there would be no responsibility whatever in the executive department—an idea inadmissible in a free government. But even there the king is not bound by the resolutions of his council, though they are answerable for the advice they give. He is the absolute master of his own conduct in the exercise of his office and may observe or disregard the counsel given to him at his sole discretion.

But in a republic where every magistrate ought to be personally responsible for his behavior in office, the reason which in the British Constitution dictates the propriety of a council not only ceases to apply, but turns against the institution. In the monarchy of Great Britain, it furnishes a substitute for the prohibited responsibility of the Chief Magistrate, which serves in some degree as a hostage to the national justice for his good behavior. In the American republic, it would serve to destroy, or would greatly diminish, the intended and necessary responsibility of the Chief Magistrate himself.

The idea of a council to the executive, which has so generally obtained in the State constitutions, has been derived from that maxim of republican jealousy which considers power as safer in the hands of a number of men than of a single man. If the maxim should be admitted to be applicable to the case, I should contend that the advantage on that side would not counterbalance the numerous disadvantages on the opposite side. But I do not think the rule at all applicable to the executive power. I clearly concur in opinion, in this particular, with a writer whom the celebrated Junius pronounces to be "deep, solid, and ingenious," that "the executive power is more easily confined when it is one"; that it is far more safe there should be a single object for the jealousy and watchfulness of the people; and, in a word, that all multiplication of the executive is rather dangerous than friendly to liberty.

A little consideration will satisfy us that the species of security sought for in the multiplication of the executive is unattainable. Numbers must be so great as to render combination difficult, or they are rather a source of danger than of security. The united credit and influence of several individuals must be more formidable to liberty than the credit and influence of either of them separately. When power, therefore, is placed in the hands of so small a number of men as to admit of their interests and views being easily combined in a common enterprise, by an artful leader, it becomes more liable to abuse, and more dangerous when abused, than if it be lodged in the hands of one man, who, from the very circumstance of his being alone, will be more narrowly watched and more readily suspected, and who cannot unite so great a mass of influence as when he is associated with others. The decemvirs of Rome, whose name denotes their number, were more to be dreaded in their usurpation than any ONE of them would have been. No person would think of proposing an executive much more numerous than that body; from six to a dozen have been suggested for the number of the council. The extreme of these numbers is not too great for an easy combination; and from such a combination America would have more to fear than from the ambition of any single individual. A council to a magistrate, who is himself responsible for what he does, are generally nothing better than a clog upon his good intentions, are often the instruments and accomplices of his bad, and are almost always a cloak to his faults.

I forbear to dwell upon the subject of expense; though it be evident that if the council should be numerous enough to answer the principal end aimed at by the institution, the salaries of the members, who must be drawn from their homes to reside at the seat of government, would form an item in the catalogue of public expenditures too serious to be incurred for an object of equivocal utility.

I will only add that, prior to the appearance of the Constitution, I rarely met with an intelligent man from any of the States who did not admit, as the result of experience, that the UNITY of the executive of this State was one of the best of the distinguishing features of our Constitution.

PUBLIUS [Hamilton]

2

ASSESSING THE
CONSTITUTIONAL
PRESIDENCY

The Strict Constructionist Presidency

William Howard Taft

While it is important to mark out the exclusive field of jurisdiction of each branch of the government, Legislative, Executive and Judicial, it should be said that in the proper working of the government there must be cooperation of all branches, and without a willingness of each branch to perform its function, there will follow a hopeless obstruction to the progress of the whole government. Neither branch can compel the other to affirmative action, and each branch can greatly hinder the other in the attainment of the object of its activities and the exercise of its discretion.

The true view of the Executive functions is, as I conceive it, that the President can exercise no power which cannot be fairly and reasonably traced to some specific grant of power or justly implied and included within such express grant as proper and necessary to its exercise. Such specific grant must be either in the Federal Constitution or in an act of Congress passed in pursuance thereof. There is no undefined residuum of power which he can exercise because it seems to him to be in the public interest, and there is nothing in the Neagle case and its definition of a law of the United States, or in other precedents, warranting such an inference. The grants of Executive power are necessarily in general terms in order not to embarrass the Executive within the field of action plainly marked for him, but his jurisdiction must be justified and vindicated by affirmative constitutional or statutory provision, or it does not exist. There have not been wanting, however, eminent men in high public office holding a different view and who have insisted upon the necessity for an undefined residuum of Executive power in the public interest. They have not been confined to the present generation. We may learn this from the complaint of a Virginia statesman, Abel P. Upshur, a strict

Source: William Howard Taft, *Our Chief Magistrate and His Powers* (New York: Columbia University Press, 1916), pp. 138–145.

constructionist of the old school, who succeeded Daniel Webster as Secretary of State under President Tyler. He was aroused by Story's commentaries on the Constitution to write a monograph answering and criticizing them, and in the course of this he comments as follows on the Executive power under the Constitution:

> The most defective part of the Constitution beyond all question, is that which is related to the Executive Department. It is impossible to read that instrument, without being struck with the loose and unguarded terms in which the powers and duties of the President are pointed out. So far as the legislature is concerned, the limitations of the Constitution, are, perhaps, as precise and strict as they could safely have been made; but in regard to the Executive, the Convention appears to have studiously selected such loose and general expressions, as would enable the President, by implication and construction either to neglect his duties or to enlarge his powers. *We have heard it gravely asserted in Congress that whatever power is neither legislative nor judiciary, is of course executive, and, as such, belongs to the President under the Constitution.* How far a majority of that body would have sustained a doctrine so monstrous, and so utterly at war with the whole genius of our government, it is impossible to say, but this, at least, we know, that it met with no rebuke from those who supported the particular act of Executive power, in defense of which it was urged. Be this as it may, it is a reproach to the Constitution that the Executive trust is so ill-defined, as to leave any plausible pretense even to the insane zeal of party devotion, for attributing to the President of the United States the powers of a despot; powers which are wholly unknown in any limited monarchy in the world.

The view that he takes as a result of the loose language defining the Executive powers seems exaggerated. But one must agree with him in his condemnation of the view of the Executive power which he says was advanced in Congress. In recent years there has been put forward a similar view by executive officials and to some extent acted on. Men who are not such strict constructionists of the Constitution as Mr. Upshur may well feel real concern if such views are to receive the general acquiescence. Mr. Garfield, when Secretary of the Interior, under Mr. Roosevelt, in his final report to Congress in reference to the power of the Executive over the public domain, said:

> Full power under the Constitution was vested in the Executive Branch of the Government and the extent to which that power may be exercised is governed wholly by the discretion of the Executive unless any specific act has been prohibited either by the Constitution or by legislation.

In pursuance of this principle, Mr. Garfield, under an act for the reclamation of arid land by irrigation, which authorized him to make contracts for irrigation works and incur liability equal to the amount on deposit in the Reclamation Fund, made contracts with associations of settlers by which it was agreed that if these settlers would advance money and work, they might receive certificates from the government engineers of the labor and money furnished by them, and that such certificates might be received in the future in the discharge of their legal obligations to the government for water, rent and other things under the statute. It became necessary for the succeeding administration to pass on the validity of these government certificates. They were held by Attorney-General Wickersham to be illegal, on the ground that no authority existed for their issuance. He relied on the Floyd acceptances in 7th Wallace, in which recovery was sought in the Court of Claims on commercial paper in the form of acceptances signed by Mr. Floyd when Secretary of War and delivered to certain contractors. The Court held that they were void because the Secretary of War had no statutory authority to issue them. Mr. Justice Miller, in deciding the case, said:

> The answer which at once suggests itself to one familiar with the structure of our government, in which all power is delegated, and is defined by law, constitutional or statutory, is, that to one or both of these sources we must resort in every instance. We have no officers in this government, from the President down to the most subordinate agent, who does not hold office under the law, with prescribed duties and limited authority. And while some of these, as the President, the Legislature, and the Judiciary, exercise powers in some sense left to the more general definitions necessarily incident to fundamental law found in the Constitution, the larger portion of them are the creation of statutory law, with duties and powers prescribed and limited by that law.

My judgment is that the view of Mr. Garfield and Mr. Roosevelt, ascribing an undefined residuum of power to the President is an unsafe doctrine and that it might lead under emergencies to results of an arbitrary character, doing irremediable injustice to private right. The mainspring of such a view is that the Executive is charged with responsibility for the welfare of all the people in a general way, that he is to play the part of a Universal Providence and set all things right, and that anything that in his judgment will help the people he ought to do, unless he is expressly forbidden not to do it. The wide field of action that this would give to the Executive one can hardly limit.

The Stewardship Presidency

Theodore Roosevelt

My view was that every executive officer, and above all every executive officer in high position, was a steward of the people bound actively and affirmatively to do all he could for the people, and not to content himself with the negative merit of keeping his talents undamaged in a napkin. I declined to adopt the view that what was imperatively necessary for the nation could not be done by the President unless he could find some specific authorization to do it. My belief was that it was not only his right but his duty to do anything that the needs of the nation demanded unless such action was forbidden by the Constitution or by the laws. Under this interpretation of executive power I did and caused to be done many things not previously done by the President and the heads of the departments. I

Source: Theodore Roosevelt, *The Autobiography of Theodore Roosevelt,* Centennial ed. (New York: Charles Scribner's Sons, 1913), pp. 197–200.

did not usurp power, but I did greatly broaden the use of executive power. In other words, I acted for the public welfare, I acted for the common well-being of all our people, whenever and in whatever manner was necessary, unless prevented by direct constitutional or legislative prohibition. . . .

The course I followed, of regarding the Executive as subject only to the people, and, under the Constitution, bound to serve the people affirmatively in cases where the Constitution does not explicitly forbid him to render the service, was substantially the course followed by both Andrew Jackson and Abraham Lincoln. Other honorable and well-meaning Presidents, such as James Buchanan, took the opposite and, as it seems to me, narrowly legalistic view that the President is the servant of Congress rather than of the people, and can do nothing, no matter how necessary it be to act, unless the Constitution explicitly commands the action. Most able lawyers who are past middle age take this view, and so do large numbers of well-meaning, respectable citizens. My successor in office took this, the Buchanan, view of the President's powers and duties.

For example, under my administration we found that one of the favorite methods adopted by the men desirous of stealing the public domain was to carry the decision of the secretary of the interior into court. By vigorously opposing such action, and only by so doing, we were able to carry out the policy of properly protecting the public domain. My successor not only took the opposite view, but recommended to Congress the passage of a bill which would have given the courts direct appellate power over the secretary of the interior in these land matters. . . . Fortunately, Congress declined to pass the bill. Its passage would have been a veritable calamity.

I acted on the theory that the President could at any time in his discretion withdraw from entry any of the public lands of the United States and reserve the same for forestry, for water-power sites, for irrigation, and other public purposes. Without such action it would have been impossible to stop the activity of the land-thieves. No one ventured to test its legality by lawsuit. My successor, however, himself questioned it, and referred the matter to Congress. Again Congress showed its wisdom by passing a law which gave the President the power which he had long exercised, and of which my successor had shorn himself.

Perhaps the sharp difference between what may be called the Lincoln-Jackson and the Buchanan-Taft schools, in their views of the power and duties of the President, may be best illustrated by comparing the attitude of my successor toward his Secretary of the Interior, Mr. Ballinger, when the latter was accused of gross misconduct in office, with my attitude toward my chiefs of department and other subordinate officers. More than once while I was President my officials were attacked by Congress, generally because these officials did their duty well and fearlessly. In every such case I stood by the official and refused to recognize the right of Congress to interfere with me excepting by impeachment or in other constitutional manner. On the other hand, wherever I found the officer unfit for his position, I promptly removed him, even although the most influential men in Congress fought for his retention. The Jackson-Lincoln view is that a President who is fit to do good work should be able to form his own judgment as to his own subordinates, and above all, of the subordinates standing highest and in closest and most intimate touch with him. My secretaries and their subordinates were responsible to me, and I accepted the responsibility for all their deeds. As long as they were satisfactory to me I stood by them against every critic or assailant, within or without Congress; and as for getting Congress to make up my mind for me about them, the thought would have been inconceivable to me. My successor took the opposite, or Buchanan, view when he permitted and requested Congress to pass judgment on the charges made against Mr. Ballinger as an executive officer. These charges were made to the President; the President had the facts before him and could get at them at any time, and he alone had power to act if the charges were true. However, he permitted and requested Congress to investigate Mr. Ballinger. The party minority of the committee that investigated him, and one member of the majority, declared that the charges were well-founded and that Mr. Ballinger should be removed. The other members of the majority declared the charges ill-founded. The President abode by the view of the majority. Of course believers in the Jackson-Lincoln theory of the presidency would not be content with this town-meeting majority and minority method of determining by another branch of the government what it seems the especial duty of the President himself to determine for himself in dealing with his own subordinate in his own department. . . .

The Prerogative Presidency
Letter to A. G. Hodges (April 4, 1864)
Abraham Lincoln

My dear Sir: You ask me to put in writing the substance of what I verbally said the other day in your presence, to Governor Bramlette and Senator Dixon. It was about as follows:

"I am naturally antislavery. If slavery is not wrong, nothing is wrong. I cannot remember when I did not so think and feel, and yet I have never understood that the presidency conferred upon me an unrestricted right to act officially upon this judgment and feeling. It was in the oath I took that I would, to the best of my ability, preserve, protect, and defend the Constitution of the United States. I could not take the office without taking the oath. Nor was it my view that I might take an oath to get power, and break the oath in using the power. I understood, too, that in ordinary civil administration this oath even forbade me to practically indulge my primary abstract judgment on the moral question of slavery. I had publicly declared this many times, and in many ways. And I aver that, to this day, I have done no official act in mere deference to my abstract judgment and feeling on slavery. I did understand, however, that my oath to preserve the Constitution to

Source: John Nicolay and John Hay, eds., *The Complete Works of Abraham Lincoln,* Vol. 10 (New York: Francis D. Tandy Co., 1894), pp. 65–68. (Albert G. Hodges was editor of the Frankfort, KY, *Commonwealth;* this letter was used as a campaign document in the 1864 election.)

the best of my ability imposed upon me the duty of preserving, by every indispensable means, that government—that nation, of which that Constitution was the organic law. Was it possible to lose the nation and yet preserve the Constitution? By general law, life and limb must be protected, yet often a limb must be amputated to save a life; but a life is never wisely given to save a limb. I felt that measures otherwise unconstitutional might become lawful by becoming indispensable to the preservation of the Constitution through the preservation of the nation. Right or wrong, I assume this ground, and now avow it. I could not feel that, to the best of my ability, I had even tried to preserve the Constitution, if, to save slavery or any minor matter, I should permit the wreck of government, country, and Constitution all together. When, early in the war, General Frémont attempted military emancipation, I forbade it, because I did not then think it an indispensable necessity. When, a little later, General Cameron, then Secretary of War, suggested the arming of the blacks, I objected because I did not yet think it an indispensable necessity. When, still later, General Hunter attempted military emancipation, I again forbade it, because I did not yet think the indispensable necessity had come. When in March and May and July, 1862, I made earnest and successive appeals to the border States to favor compensated emancipation, I believed the indispensable necessity for military emancipation and arming the blacks would come unless averted by that measure. They declined the proposition, and I was, in my best judgment, driven to the alternative of either surrendering the Union, and with it the Constitution, or of laying strong hand upon the colored element. I chose the latter. In choosing it, I hoped for greater gain than loss; but of this, I was not entirely confident. More than a year of trial now shows no loss by it in our foreign relations, none in our home popular sentiment, none in our white military force—no loss by it anyhow or anywhere. On the contrary it shows a gain of quite a hundred and thirty thousand soldiers, seamen, and laborers. These are palpable facts, about which, as facts, there can be no caviling. We have the men; and we could not have had them without the measure.

"And now let any Union man who complains of the measure test himself by writing down in one line that he is for subduing the rebellion by force of arms; and in the next, that he is for taking these hundred and thirty thousand men from the Union side, and placing them where they would be but for the measure he condemns. If he cannot face this case so stated, it is only because he cannot face the truth."

I add a word which was not in the verbal conversation. In telling this tale I attempt no compliment to my own sagacity. I claim not to have controlled events, but confess plainly that events have controlled me. Now, at the end of three years' struggle, the nation's condition is not what either party, or any man, devised or expected God alone can claim it. Whither it is tending seems plain. If God now wills the removal of a great wrong, and wills also that we of the North, as well as you of the South, shall pay fairly for our complicity in that wrong, impartial history will find therein new cause to attest and revere the justice and goodness of God. *Yours truly,*

A. Lincoln

3

THE EVOLUTION OF THE PRESIDENCY

Campaign Address, 1912

Woodrow Wilson

Ah, gentlemen, we are debating very serious things. And we are debating this: Are we going to put ourselves in a position to enter upon a great program of understanding one another and helping one another? I can't understand you unless you talk to me. I can't understand you by looking at you. I can't understand you by reading books. With apologies to the gentlemen in front of me, I couldn't even understand you by reading the newspapers. I can understand you only by what you know of your own lives and make evident in your own actions. I understand you only in proportion as you "hump" yourselves and take care of yourselves, and make your force evident in the course of politics. And, therefore, I believe in government as a great process of getting together, a great process of debate.

There are gentlemen on this platform with me who have seen a great vision. They have seen this, for example: You know that there are a great many foreigners coming to America and qualifying as American citizens. And if you are widely acquainted among them you will know that this is true: that the grown-up people who come to America take a long time in feeling at home in America. They don't speak the language and there is no place in which they can get together with the general body of American citizens and feel that they are part of them. But their children feel welcome. Where? In the schoolhouse. The schoolhouse is the great melting pot of democracy. And after the children of these men who have joined us in their desire for freedom have grown up and come through the processes of the schools, they have imbibed the full feeling of American life.

Now, somebody has said—somebody repeated to me the other day—the saying of one of these immigrants that when he went to a meeting or to a series of meetings in the evening in a schoolhouse where all the neighborhood joined to discuss the interests of the neighborhood, he for the first time saw America as he

(Buffalo, NY, Sept. 2), reprinted in Robert Isaak, *American Political Thinking,* Ft. Worth, Harcourt Brace, 1994.

had expected to see it. This [was] America as he had imagined it, this frank coming together of all the people in the neighborhood, of all sorts and conditions, to discuss their common interests. And these gentlemen to whom I have referred have devoted their lives to this: to make the schoolhouses of this country the vital centers of opportunity, to open them out of school hours for everybody who desires to discuss anything and for making them, among other things, the clearinghouses where men who are out of jobs can find jobs and where jobs who are out of men can find men. Why shouldn't our whole life center in this place where we learn the fundamentals of our life? Why shouldn't the schoolhouses be the constant year-in-and-year-out places of assembly where things are said which nobody dares ignore? Because, if we haven't had our way in this country, it has been because we haven't been able to get at the ear of those who are conducting our government. And if there is any man in Buffalo, or anywhere else in the United States, who objects to your using the schoolhouses that way, you may be sure that there is something he doesn't want to have discussed.

You know I have been considered as disqualified for politics because I was a school teacher. But there is one thing a school teacher learns that he never forgets, namely, that it is his business to learn all he can and then to communicate it to others. Now, I consider this to be my function. I have tried to find out how to learn things and learn them fast. And I have made up my mind that for the rest of my life I am going to put all I know at the disposal of my fellow citizens. And I know a good many things that I haven't yet mentioned in public which I am ready to mention at the psychological moment. There is no use firing it off when there is nobody to shoot at, but when they are present, then it is sport to say it. And I have undertaken the duty of constituting myself one of the attorneys for the people in any court to which I can get entrance. I don't mean as a lawyer, for while I was a lawyer, I have repented. But I mean in the courts of public opinion wherever I am allowed, as I am indulgently allowed today, to stand on a platform and talk to attentive audiences—for you are most graciously attentive—I want to constitute myself the spokesman so far as I have the proper table of contents for the people whom I wish to serve; for the whole strength of politics is not in the leader but in the followers. By leading I do not mean telling other people what they have got to do. I [mean] finding out what the interests of the community are agreed to be, and then trying my level best to find the methods of solution by common counsel. That is the only feasible program of social uplift that I can imagine, and, therefore, I am bound in conscience to fight everything that crystallizes things so at the center that you can't break in.

It is amazing to me that public-spirited, devoted men in this country have not seen that the program of the third party proclaims purposes and in the same breath provides an organization of government which makes the carrying out of those purposes impossible. I would rather postpone my sympathy for social reform until I had got in a position to make things happen. And I am not in a position to make things happen until I am part of a free organization which can say to every interest in the United States: "You come into this conference room on an equality with every other interest in the United States, and you are going to speak here with open doors. There is to be no whispering behind the hand. There is to be no private communication. What you can't afford to let the country hear had better be left unsaid."

What I fear, therefore, is a government of experts. God forbid that in a democratic country we should resign the task and give the government over to experts. What are we for if we are to be [scientifically] taken care of by a small number of gentlemen who are the only men who understand the job? Because if we don't understand the job, then we are not a free people. We ought to resign our free institutions and go to school to somebody and find out what it is we are about. I want to say I have never heard more penetrating debate of public questions than I have sometimes been privileged to hear in clubs of workingmen; because the man who is down against the daily problem of life doesn't talk about it in rhetoric; he talks about it in facts. And the only thing I am interested in is facts. I don't know anything else that is as solid to stand on. . . .

The Power to Persuade

Richard E. Neustadt

The limits on command suggest the structure of our government. The Constitutional Convention of 1787 is supposed to have created a government of "separated powers." It did nothing of the sort. Rather, it created a government of separated institutions *sharing* powers. "I am part of the legislative process," Eisenhower often said in 1959 as a reminder of his veto. Congress, the dispenser of authority and funds, is no less part of the administrative process. Federalism adds another set of separated institutions. The Bill of Rights adds others. Many public purposes can only be achieved by voluntary acts of private institutions; the press, for one, in Douglass Cater's phrase, is a "fourth branch of government." And with the coming of alliances abroad, the separate institutions of a London, or a Bonn, share in the making of American public policy.*

What the Constitution separates our political parties do not combine. The parties are themselves composed of separated organizations sharing public authority. The authority consists of nominating powers. Our national parties are confederations of state and local party institutions, with a headquarters that represents the White House, more or less, if the party has a President in office. These confederacies manage presidential nominations. All other public offices depend upon electorates confined within the states. All other nominations are controlled within the states. The President and congressmen who bear one party's label are divided by dependence upon different sets of voters. The differences are sharpest

*For distinctions drawn throughout between powers and power see note 1.

at the stage of nomination. The White House has too small a share in nominating congressmen, and Congress has too little weight in nominating presidents for party to erase their constitutional separation. Party links are stronger than is frequently supposed, but nominating processes assure the separation.

The separateness of institutions and the sharing of authority prescribe the terms on which a President persuades. When one man shares authority with another, but does not gain or lose his job upon the other's whim, his willingness to act upon the urging of the other turns on whether he conceives the action right for him. The essence of a President's persuasive task is to convince such men that what the White House wants of them is what they ought to do for their sake and on their authority. (Sex matters not at all; for *man* read *woman*.)

Persuasive power, thus defined, amounts to more than charm or reasoned argument. These have their uses for a President, but these are not the whole of his resources. For the individuals he would induce to do what he wants done on their own responsibility will need or fear some acts by him on his responsibility. If they share his authority, he has some share in theirs. Presidential "powers" may be inconclusive when a President commands, but always remain relevant as he persuades. The status and authority inherent in his office reinforce his logic and his charm.

Status adds something to persuasiveness; authority adds still more. When Truman urged wage changes on his secretary of commerce while the latter was administering the steel mills, he and Secretary Sawyer were not just two men reasoning with one another. Had they been so, Sawyer probably would never have agreed to act. Truman's status gave him special claims to Sawyer's loyalty or at least attention. In Walter Bagehot's charming phrase "no man can *argue* on his knees." Although there is no kneeling in this country, few men—and exceedingly few cabinet officers—are immune to the impulse to say "yes" to the President of the United States. It grows harder to say "no" when they are seated in his Oval Office at the White House, or in his study on the second floor, where almost tangibly he partakes of the aura of his physical surroundings. In Sawyer's case, moreover, the President possessed formal authority to intervene in many matters of concern to the secretary of commerce. These matters ranged from jurisdictional disputes among the defense agencies to legislation pending before Congress and, ultimately, to the tenure of the secretary, himself. There is nothing in the record to suggest that Truman voiced specific threats when they negotiated over wage increases. But given his formal powers and their relevance to Sawyer's other interests, it is safe to assume that Truman's very advocacy of wage action conveyed an implicit threat.

A President's authority and status give him great advantages in dealing with the men he would persuade. Each "power" is a vantage point for him in the degree that other men have use for his authority. From the veto to appointments, from publicity to budgeting, and so down a long list, the White House now controls the most encompassing array of vantage points in the American political system. With hardly an exception, those who share in governing this country are aware that at some time, in some degree, the doing of *their* jobs, the furthering of *their* ambitions, may depend upon the President of the United States. Their need for presidential action, or their fear of it, is bound to be recurrent if not actually continuous. Their need or fear is his advantage.

A President's advantages are greater than mere listing of his "powers" might suggest. Those with whom he deals must deal with him until the last day of his term. Because they have continuing relationships with him, his future, while it lasts, supports his present influence. Even though there is no need or fear of him today, what he could do tomorrow may supply today's advantage. Continuing relationships may convert any "power," any aspect of his status, into vantage points in almost any case. When he induces other people to do what he wants done, a President can trade on their dependence now and later.

The President's advantages are checked by the advantages of others. Continuing relationships will pull in both directions. These are relationships of mutual dependence. A President depends upon the persons whom he would persuade; he has to reckon with his need or fear of them. They too will possess status, or authority, or both, else they would be of little use to him. Their vantage points confront his own; their power tempers his.

Persuasion is a two-way street. Sawyer, it will be recalled, did not respond at once to Truman's plan for wage increases at the steel mills. On the contrary, the secretary hesitated and delayed and only acquiesced when he was satisfied that publicly he would not bear the onus of decision. Sawyer had some points of vantage all his own from which to resist presidential pressure. If he had to reckon with coercive implications in the President's "situations of strength," so had Truman to be mindful of the implications underlying Sawyer's place as a department head, as steel administrator, and as a cabinet spokesman for business. Loyalty is reciprocal. Having taken on a dirty job in the steel crisis, Sawyer had strong claims to loyal support. Besides, he had authority to do some things that the White House could ill afford. Emulating Wilson, he might have resigned in a huff (the removal power also works two ways). Or, emulating Ellis Arnall, he might have declined to sign necessary orders. Or he might have let it be known publicly that he deplored what he was told to do and protested its doing. By following any of these courses Sawyer almost surely would have strengthened the position of management, weakened the position of the White House, and embittered the union. But the whole purpose of a wage increase was to enhance White House persuasiveness in urging settlement upon union and companies alike. Although Sawyer's status and authority did not give him the power to prevent an increase outright, they gave him capability to undermine its purpose. If his authority over wage rates had been vested by a statute, not by revocable presidential order, his power of prevention might have been complete. So Harold Ickes demonstrated in the famous case of helium sales to Germany before the Second World War.

The power to persuade is the power to bargain. Status and authority yield bargaining advantages. But in a government of "separated institutions sharing powers," they yield them to all sides. With the array of vantage points at his disposal, a President may be far more persuasive than his logic or his charm could make him. But outcomes are not guaranteed by his advantages. There remain the counter pressures [*sic*] those whom he would influence can bring to bear on him from vantage points at their disposal. Command has limited utility; persuasion becomes give-and-take. It is well that the White House holds the vantage points it does. In such a business any President may need them all—and more.

———————— II ————————

This view of power as akin to bargaining is one we commonly accept in the sphere of congressional relations. Every textbook states and every legislative session demonstrates that save in times like the extraordinary Hundred Days of 1933—times virtually ruled out by definition at mid-century—a President will often be unable to obtain congressional action on his terms or even to halt action he opposes. The reverse is equally accepted: Congress often is frustrated by the President. Their formal powers are so intertwined that neither will accomplish very much, for very long, without the acquiescence of the other. By the same token, though, what one demands the other can resist. The stage is set for that great game, much like collective bargaining, in which each seeks to profit from the other's needs and fears. It is a game played catch-as-catch-can, case by case. And everybody knows the game, observers and participants alike.

The concept of real power as a give-and-take is equally familiar when applied to presidential influence outside the formal structure of the federal government. The Little Rock affair may be extreme, but Eisenhower's dealings with the governor— and with the citizens—became a case in point. Less extreme but no less pertinent is the steel seizure case with respect to union leaders, and to workers, and to company executives as well. When he deals with such people a President draws bargaining advantage from his status or authority. By virtue of their public places or their private rights they have some capability to reply in kind.

In spheres of party politics the same thing follows, necessarily, from the confederal nature of our party organizations. Even in the case of national nominations a President's advantages are checked by those of others. In 1944 it is by no means clear that Roosevelt got his first choice as his running mate. In 1948 Truman, then the President, faced serious revolts against his nomination. In 1952 his intervention from the White House helped assure the choice of Adlai Stevenson, but it is far from clear that Truman could have done as much for any other candidate acceptable to him. In 1956 when Eisenhower was President, the record leaves obscure just who backed Harold Stassen's efforts to block Richard Nixon from renomination as vice president. But evidently everything did not go quite as Eisenhower wanted, whatever his intentions may have been. The outcomes in these instances bear all the marks of limits on command and of power checked by power that characterize congressional relations. Both in and out of politics these checks and limits seem to be quite widely understood.

Influence becomes still more a matter of give-and-take when Presidents attempt to deal with allied governments. A classic illustration is the long unhappy wrangle over Suez policy in 1956. In dealing with the British and the French before their military intervention, Eisenhower had his share of bargaining advantages but no effective power of command. His allies had their share of counterpressures, and they finally tried the most extreme of all: action despite him. His pressure then was instrumental in reversing them. But had the British government been on safe ground at home, Eisenhower's wishes might have made as little difference after intervention as before. Behind the decorum of diplomacy—which was not very decorous in the Suez affair—relationships among allies are not unlike relationships among state delegations at a national convention. Power is persuasion, and persuasion becomes bargaining. The concept is familiar to everyone who watches foreign policy.

In only one sphere is the concept unfamiliar: the sphere of executive relations. Perhaps because of civics textbooks and teaching in our schools, Americans instinctively resist the view that power in this sphere resembles power in all others. Even Washington reporters, White House aides, and congressmen are not immune to the illusion that administrative agencies comprise a single structure, "the" executive branch, where presidential word is law, or ought to be . . . when a President seeks something from executive officials his persuasiveness is subject to the same sorts of limitations as in the case of congressmen, or governors, or national committeemen, or private citizens, or foreign governments. There are no generic differences, no differences in kind and only sometimes in degree. The incidents preceding the dismissal of MacArthur and the incidents surrounding seizure of the steel mills make it plain that here as elsewhere influence derives from bargaining advantages; power is a give-and-take.

Like our governmental structure as a whole, the executive establishment consists of separated institutions sharing powers. The President heads one of these; cabinet officers, agency administrators, and military commanders head others. Below the departmental level, virtually independent bureau chiefs head many more. Under midcentury conditions, federal operations spill across dividing lines on organization charts; almost every policy entangles many agencies; almost every program calls for interagency collaboration. Everything somehow involves the President. But operating agencies owe their existence least of all to one another—and only in some part to him. Each has a separate statutory base; each has its statutes to administer; each deals with a different set of subcommittees at the Capitol. Each has its own peculiar set of clients, friends, and enemies outside the formal government. Each has a different set of specialized careerists inside its own bailiwick. Our Constitution gives the President the "take-care" clause and the appointive power. Our statutes give him central budgeting and a degree of personnel control. All agency administrators are responsible to him. But they also are responsible to Congress, to their clients, to their staffs, and to themselves. In short, they have five masters. Only after all of those do they owe any loyalty to each other.

"The members of the cabinet," Charles G. Dawes used to remark, "are a president's natural enemies." Dawes had been Harding's budget director, Coolidge's vice president, and Hoover's ambassador to London; he also had been General Pershing's chief assistant for supply in World War I. The words are highly colored, but Dawes knew whereof he spoke. The men who have to serve so many masters cannot help but be somewhat the "enemy" of any one of them. By the same token, any master wanting service is in some degree the "enemy" of such a servant. A President is likely to want loyal support but not to relish trouble on his doorstep. Yet the more his cabinet members cleave to him, the more they may need help from him in fending off the wrath of rival masters. Help, though, is synonymous with trouble. Many a cabinet officer, with loyalty ill rewarded by his lights and help withheld, has come to view the White House as innately hostile to department heads. Dawes's dictum can be turned around.

A senior presidential aide remarked to me in Eisenhower's time: "If some of these cabinet members would just take time out to stop and ask themselves, 'What would I want if I were President?' they wouldn't give him all the trouble he's been having." But even if they asked themselves the question, such officials often could not act upon the answer. Their personal attachment to the President is all too often overwhelmed by duty to their other masters.

Executive officials are not equally advantaged in their dealings with a President. Nor are the same officials equally advantaged all the time. Not every officeholder can resist like a MacArthur, or like Arnall, Sawyer, Wilson, in a rough descending order of effective counterpressure. The vantage points conferred upon officials by their own authority and status vary enormously. The variance is heightened by particulars of time and circumstance. In mid-October 1950, Truman, at a press conference, remarked of the man he had considered firing in August and would fire the next April for intolerable insubordination:

> Let me tell you something that will be good for your souls. It's a pity that you . . . can't understand the ideas of two intellectually honest men when they meet. General MacArthur . . . is a member of the Government of the United States. He is loyal to that Government. He is loyal to the President. He is loyal to the President in his foreign policy. . . . There is no disagreement between General MacArthur and myself.

MacArthur's status in and out of government was never higher than when Truman spoke those words. The words, once spoken, added to the general's credibility thereafter when he sought to use the press in his campaign against the President. And what had happened between August and October? Near victory had happened, together with that premature conference on postwar plans, the meeting at Wake Island.

If the bargaining advantages of a MacArthur fluctuate with changing circumstances, this is bound to be so with subordinates who have at their disposal fewer powers, lesser status, to fall back on. And when officials have no powers in their own right, or depend upon the President for status, their counterpressure may be limited indeed. White House aides, who fit both categories, are among the most responsive men of all, and for good reason. As a director of the budget once remarked to me, "Thank God I'm here and not across the street. If the President doesn't call me, I've got plenty I can do right here and plenty coming up to me, by rights, to justify my calling him. But those poor fellows over there, if the boss doesn't call them, doesn't ask them to do something, what *can* they do but sit?"

Authority and status so conditional are frail reliances in resisting a President's own wants. Within the White House precincts, lifted eyebrows may suffice to set an aide in motion; command, coercion, even charm aside. But even in the White House a President does not monopolize effective power. Even there persuasion is akin to bargaining. A former Roosevelt aide once wrote of cabinet officers:

> Half of a President's suggestions, which theoretically carry the weight of orders, can be safely forgotten by a Cabinet member. And if the President asks about a suggestion a second time, he can be told that it is being investigated. If he asks a third time, a wise Cabinet officer will give him at least part of what he suggests. But only occasionally, except about the most important matters, do Presidents ever get around to asking three times.

The rule applies to staff as well as to the cabinet, and certainly has been applied *by* staff in Truman's time and Eisenhower's.

Some aides will have more vantage points than a selective memory. Sherman Adams, for example, as the assistant to the President under Eisenhower, scarcely deserved the appellation "White House aide" in the meaning of the term before his time or as applied to other members of the Eisenhower entourage. Although Adams was by no means "chief of staff" in any sense so sweeping—or so simple—as press commentaries often took for granted, he apparently became no more dependent on the President than Eisenhower on him. "I need him," said the President when Adams turned out to have been remarkably imprudent in the Goldfine case, and delegated to him, at least nominally, the decision on his own departure. This instance is extreme, but the tendency it illustrates is common enough. Any aide who demonstrates to others that he has the President's consistent confidence and a consistent part in presidential business will acquire so much business on his own account that he becomes in some sense independent of his chief. Nothing in the Constitution keeps a well-placed aide from converting status into power of his own, usable in some degree even against the President—an outcome not unknown in Truman's regime or, by all accounts, in Eisenhower's.

The more an officeholder's status and his powers stem from sources independent of the President, the stronger will be his potential pressure on the President. Department heads in general have more bargaining power than do most members of the White House staff; but bureau chiefs may have still more, and specialists at upper levels of established career services may have almost unlimited reserves of the enormous power which consists of sitting still. As Franklin Roosevelt once remarked:

> The Treasury is so large and far-flung and ingrained in its practices that I find it almost impossible to get the action and results I want—even with Henry [Morgenthau] there. But the Treasury is not to be compared with the State Department. You should go through the experience of trying to get any changes in the thinking, policy, and action of the career diplomats and then you'd know what a real problem was. But the Treasury and the State Department put together are nothing compared with the Na-a-vy. The admirals are really something to cope with—and I should know. To change anything in

the Na-a-vy is like punching a feather bed. You punch it with your right and you punch it with your left until you are finally exhausted, and then you find the damn bed just as it was before you started punching.

In the right circumstances, of course, a President can have his way with any of these people. Chapter 2 includes three instances where circumstances were "right" and a presidential order was promptly carried out. But one need only note the favorable factors giving those three orders their self-executing quality to recognize that as between a President and his "subordinates," no less than others on whom he depends, real power is reciprocal and varies markedly with organization, subject matter, personality, and situation. The mere fact that persuasion is directed at executive officials signifies no necessary easing of his way. Any new congressman of the Administration's party, especially if narrowly elected, may turn out more amenable (though less useful) to the President than any seasoned bureau chief "downtown." *The probabilities of power do not derive from the literary theory of the Constitution.*

─────────── III ───────────

There is a widely held belief in the United States that were it not for folly or for knavery, a reasonable President would need no power other than the logic of his argument. No less a personage than Eisenhower has subscribed to that belief in many a campaign speech and press-conference remark. But faulty reasoning and bad intentions do not cause all quarrels with Presidents. The best of reasoning and of intent cannot compose them all. For in the first place, what the President wants will rarely seem a trifle to the people he wants it from. And in the second place, they will be bound to judge it by the standard of their own responsibilities, not his. However logical his argument according to his lights, their judgment may not bring them to his view.

Those who share in governing this country frequently appear to act as though they were in business for themselves. So, in a real though not entire sense, they are and have to be. When Truman and MacArthur fell to quarreling, for example, the stakes were no less than the substance of American foreign policy, the risks of greater war or military stalemate, the prerogatives of Presidents and field commanders, the pride of a proconsul and his place in history. Intertwined, inevitably, were other stakes as well: political stakes for men and factions of both parties; power stakes for interest groups with which they were or wished to be affiliated. And every stake was raised by the apparent discontent in the American public mood. There is no reason to suppose that in such circumstances men of large but differing responsibilities will see all things through the same glasses. On the contrary, it is to be expected that their views of what ought to be done and what they then should do will vary with the differing perspectives their particular responsibilities evoke. Since their duties are not vested in a "team" or a "collegium" but in themselves, as individuals, one must expect that they will see things for themselves. Moreover, when they are responsible to many masters and when an event or policy turns loyalty against loyalty—a day-by-day occurrence in the nature of the case—one must assume that those who have the duties to perform will choose the terms of reconciliation. This is the essence of their personal responsibility. When their own duties pull in opposite directions, who else but they can choose what they will do?

When Truman dismissed MacArthur, the latter lost three posts: the American command in the Far East, the Allied command for the occupation of Japan, and the United Nations command in Korea. He also lost his status as the senior officer on active duty in the United States armed forces. So long as he held those positions and that status, though, he had a duty to his troops, to his profession, to himself (the last is hard for any man to disentangle from the rest). As a public figure and a focus for men's hopes he had a duty to constituents at home, and in Korea and Japan. He owed a duty also to those other constituents, the UN governments contributing to his field forces. As a patriot he had a duty to his country. As an accountable official and an expert guide he stood at the call of Congress. As a military officer he had, besides, a duty to the President, his constitutional commander. Some of these duties may have manifested themselves in terms more tangible or more direct than others. But it would be nonsense to argue that the last negated all the rest, however much it might be claimed to override them. And it makes no more sense to think that anybody but MacArthur was effectively empowered to decide how he himself would reconcile the competing demands his duties made upon him.

Similar observations could be made about the rest of the executive officials. . . . Price Director Arnall, it will be recalled, refused in advance to sign a major price increase for steel if Mobilization Director Wilson or the White House should concede one before management had settled with the union. When Arnall did this, he took his stand, in substance, on his oath of office. He would do what he had sworn to do in *his* best judgment, so long as he was there to do it. This posture may have been assumed for purposes of bargaining and might have been abandoned had his challenge been accepted by the President. But no one could be sure and no one, certainly, could question Arnall's right to make the judgment for himself. As head of an agency and as a politician, with a program to defend and a future to advance, he had to decide what he had to do on matters that, from his perspective, were exceedingly important. Neither in policy nor in personal terms, nor in terms of agency survival, were the issues of a sort to be considered secondary by an Arnall, however much they might have seemed so to a Wilson (or a Truman). Nor were the merits likely to appear the same to a price stabilizer and to men with broader duties. Reasonable men, it is so often said, *ought* to be able to agree on the requirements of given situations. But when the outlook varies with the placement of each man, and the response required in his place is for each to decide, their reasoning may lead to disagreement quite as well—and quite as reasonably. Vanity, or vice, may weaken reason, to be sure, but it is idle to assign these as the cause of Arnall's threat or MacArthur's defiance. Secretary Sawyer's hesitations, cited earlier, are in the same category. One need not denigrate such men to explain their conduct. For the responsibilities they felt, the "facts" they saw, simply were not the same as those of their superiors; yet they, not the superiors, had to decide what they would do.

Outside the executive branch the situation is the same, except that loyalty to the President may often matter *less*. There is no need to spell out the comparison with governors of Arkansas, steel company executives, trade union leaders, and the like. And when one comes to congressmen who can do nothing for themselves (or their constituents) save as they are elected, term by term, in districts and through party structures differing from those on which a President depends, the case is very clear. An able Eisenhower aide with long congressional experience remarked to me in 1958: "The people on the Hill don't do what they might *like* to do, they do what they think they *have* to do in their own interest as *they* see it." This states the case precisely.

The essence of a President's persuasive task, with congressmen and everybody else, is to induce them to believe that what he wants of them is what their own appraisal of their own responsibilities requires them to do in their interest, not his. Because men may differ in their views on public policy, because differences in outlook stem from differences in duty—duty to one's office, one's constituents, oneself—that task is bound to be more like collective bargaining than like a reasoned argument among philosopher kings. Overtly or implicitly, hard bargaining has characterized all illustrations offered up to now. This is the reason why: Persuasion deals in the coin of self-interest with men who have some freedom to reject what they find counterfeit.

——————— IV ———————

A President draws influence from bargaining advantages. But does he always need them? Suppose such sharp divergences are lacking, suppose most players of the governmental game see policy objectives much alike, then can he not rely on logic (or on charm) to get him what he wants? The answer is that even then most outcomes turn on bargaining. The reason for this answer is a simple one: Most who share in governing have interests of their own beyond the realm of policy objectives. The sponsorship of policy, the form it takes, the conduct of it, and the credit for it separate their interest from the President's despite agreement on the end in view. In political government the means can matter quite as much as ends; they often matter more. And there are always differences of interest in the means.

Let me introduce a case externally the opposite of my previous examples: the European Recovery Program of 1948, the so-called Marshall Plan. This is perhaps the greatest exercise in policy agreement since the Cold War began. When the then secretary of state, George Catlett Marshall, spoke at the Harvard commencement in June 1947, he launched one of the most creative, most imaginative ventures in the history of American foreign relations. What makes this policy most notable for present purposes, however, is that it became effective upon action by the eightieth Congress, at the behest of Harry Truman, in the election year 1948.

Eight months before Marshall spoke at Harvard, the Democrats had lost control of both houses of Congress for the first time in fourteen years. Truman, whom the secretary represented, had just finished his second troubled year as President-by-succession. Truman was regarded with so little warmth in his own party that in 1946 he had been urged not to participate in the congressional campaign. At the opening of Congress in January 1947, Senator Robert A. Taft, "Mr. Republican," had somewhat the attitude of a President-elect. This was a vision widely shared in Washington, with Truman relegated thereby to the role of caretaker-on-term. Moreover, within just two weeks of Marshall's commencement address, Truman was to veto two prized accomplishments of Taft's congressional majority: the Taft-Hartley Act and tax reduction. Yet scarcely ten months later the Marshall Plan was under way on terms to satisfy its sponsors, its authorization completed, its first-year funds in sight, its administering agency in being: all managed by as thorough a display of executive-congressional cooperation as any we have seen since the Second World War. For any President at any time this would have been a great accomplishment. In years before midcentury it would have been enough to make the future reputation of his term. And for Truman, at this time, enactment of the Marshall Plan appears almost miraculous.

How was the miracle accomplished? How did a President so situated bring it off? In answer, the first thing to note is that he did not do it by himself. Truman had help of a sort no less extraordinary than the outcome. Although each stands for something more complex, the names of Marshall, Vandenberg, Patterson, Bevin, Stalin tell the story of that help.

In 1947, two years after V-J Day, General Marshall was something more than secretary of state. He was a man venerated by the President as "the greatest living American," literally an embodiment of Truman's ideals. He was honored at the Pentagon as an architect of victory. He was thoroughly respected by the secretary of the Navy, James V. Forrestal, who that year became the first secretary of defense. On Capitol Hill, Marshall had an enormous fund of respect stemming from his war record as Army chief of staff, and in the country generally no officer had come out of the war with a higher reputation for judgment, intellect, and probity. Besides, as secretary of state, he had behind him the first generation of matured foreign service officers produced by the reforms of the 1920s, and mingled with them, in the departmental service, were some of the ablest of the men drawn by the war from private life to Washington. In terms both of staff talent and staff use, Marshall's years began a State Department "golden age" that lasted until the era of McCarthy. Moreover, as his under secretary, Marshall had, successively, Dean Acheson and Robert Lovett, men who commanded the respect of the professionals and the regard of congressmen. (Acheson had been brilliantly successful at congressional relations as assistant secretary in the war and postwar years.) Finally, as a special undersecretary Marshall had Will Clayton, a man highly regarded, for good reason, at both ends of Pennsylvania Avenue.

Taken together, these are exceptional resources for a secretary of state. In the circumstances, they were quite as necessary as they obviously are relevant. The Marshall Plan was launched by a lame-duck Administration "scheduled" to leave office in eighteen months. Marshall's program faced a congressional leadership traditionally isolationist and currently intent upon economy. European aid was viewed with envy by a Pentagon distressed and virtually disarmed through budget cuts, and by domestic agencies intent on enlarged welfare programs. It was not viewed with liking by a Treasury intent on budget surpluses. The plan had need of every asset that could be extracted from the personal position of its nominal author and from the skills of his assistants.

Without the equally remarkable position of the senior senator from Michigan, Arthur H. Vandenberg, it is hard to see how Marshall's assets could have been enough. Vandenberg was chairman of the Senate Foreign Relations Committee. Actually, he was much more than that. Twenty years a senator, he was the senior member of his party in the chamber. Assiduously cultivated by FDR and Truman, he was a chief Republican proponent of bipartisanship in foreign policy and consciously conceived himself its living symbol to his party, to the country, and abroad. Moreover, by informal but entirely operative agreement with his colleague Taft, Vandenberg held the acknowledged lead among Senate Republicans in the whole field of international affairs. This acknowledgment meant more in 1947 than it might have meant at any other time. With confidence in the advent of a Republican administration two years hence, most of the gentlemen were in a mood to be responsive and responsible. The war was over, Roosevelt dead, Truman a caretaker, theirs the trust. That the senator from Michigan saw matters in this light his diaries make clear. And this was not the outlook from the Senate side alone; the attitudes of House Republicans associated with the Herter Committee and its tours abroad suggest the same mood of responsibility. Vandenberg was not the only source of help on Capitol Hill. But relatively speaking his position there was as exceptional as Marshall's was downtown.

Help of another sort was furnished by a group of dedicated private citizens who organized one of the most effective instruments for public information seen since the Second World War: the Committee for the Marshall Plan, headed by the eminent Republicans whom FDR in 1940 had brought to the Department of War: Henry L. Stimson as honorary chairman and Robert P. Patterson as active spokesman. The remarkable array of bankers, lawyers, trade unionists, and editors, who had drawn together in defense of "internationalism" before Pearl Harbor and had joined their talents in the war itself, combined again to spark the work of this committee. Their efforts generated a great deal of vocal public support to buttress Marshall's arguments, and Vandenberg's, in Congress.

But before public support could be rallied, there had to be a purpose tangible enough, concrete enough, to provide a rallying ground. At Harvard, Marshall had voiced an idea in general terms. That this was turned into a hard program susceptible of presentation and support is due, in major part, to Ernest Bevin, the British foreign secretary. He well deserves the credit he has sometimes been assigned as, in effect, coauthor of the Marshall Plan. For Bevin seized on Marshall's Harvard speech and organized a European response with promptness and concreteness beyond the State Department's expectations. What had been virtually a trial balloon to test reactions on both sides of the Atlantic was hailed in London as an invitation to the Europeans to send Washington a bill of particulars. This they promptly organized to do, and the American Administration then organized in turn for its reception without further argument internally about the pros and cons of issuing the "invitation" in the first place. But for Bevin there might have been trouble from the secretary of the treasury and others besides.

If Bevin's help was useful at that early stage, Stalin's was vital from first to last. In a mood of self-deprecation Truman once remarked that without Moscow's "crazy" moves "we would never have had our foreign policy . . . we never could have got a thing from Congress." George Kennan, among others, had deplored the anti-Soviet overtone of the case made for the Marshall Plan in Congress and the country, but there is no doubt that this clinched the argument for many segments of American opinion. There also is no doubt that Moscow made the crucial contributions to the case.

By 1947 events, far more than governmental prescience or open action, had given a variety of publics an impression of inimical Soviet intentions (and of Europe's weakness) and a growing urge to "do something about it." Three months before Marshall spoke at Harvard, Greek-Turkish aid and promulgation of the Truman Doctrine had seemed rather to crystallize than to create a public mood and a congressional response. The Marshall planners, be it said, were poorly placed to capitalize on that mood, nor had the secretary wished to do so. Their object, indeed, was to cut across it, striking at the cause of European weakness rather than at Soviet aggressiveness, per se. A strong economy in Western Europe called, ideally, for restorative measures of continental scope. American assistance proffered in an anti-Soviet context would have been contradictory in theory and unacceptable in fact to several of the governments that Washington was anxious to assist. As Marshall, himself, saw it, the logic of his purpose forbade him to play his strongest congressional card. The Russians then proceeded to play it for him. When the Europeans met in Paris, Molotov walked out. After the Czechs had shown continued interest in American aid, a Communist coup overthrew their government while Soviet forces stood along their borders within easy reach of Prague. Molotov transformed the Marshall Plan's initial presentation; Czechoslovakia assured its final passage, which followed by a month the takeover in Prague.

Such was the help accorded Truman in obtaining action on the Marshall Plan. Considering his politically straitened circumstances he scarcely could have done with less. Conceivably some part of Moscow's contribution might have been dispensable, but not Marshall's or Vandenberg's or Bevin's or Patterson's or that of the great many other men whose work is represented by their names in my account. Their aid was not extended to the President for his own sake. He was not favored in this fashion just because they liked him personally or were spellbound by his intellect or charm. They might have been as helpful had all held him in disdain, which some of them certainly did. The Londoners who seized the ball, Vandenberg and Taft and the congressional majority, Marshall and his planners, the officials of other agencies who actively supported them or "went along," the host of influential private citizens who rallied to the cause—all these played the parts they did because they thought they had to, in their interest, given their responsibilities, not Truman's. Yet they hardly would have found it in their interest to collaborate with one another or with him had he not furnished them precisely what they needed from the White House. Truman could not do without their help, but he could not have had it without unremitting effort on his part.

The crucial thing to note about this case is that despite compatibility of views on public policy, Truman got no help he did not pay for (except Stalin's). Bevin scarcely could have seized on Marshall's words had Marshall not been plainly backed by Truman. Marshall's interest would not have comported with the exploitation of his prestige by a president who undercut him openly or subtly or even inadvertently at any point. Vandenberg, presumably, could not have backed proposals by a White House that begrudged him deference and access gratifying to his fellow partisans (and satisfying to himself). Prominent Republicans in private life would not have found it easy to promote a cause identified with Truman's claims on 1948—and neither would the prominent New Dealers then engaged in searching for a substitute.

Truman paid the price required for their services. So far as the record shows, the White House did not falter once in firm support for Marshall and the Marshall Plan. Truman backed his secretary's gamble on an invitation to all Europe. He made the plan his own in a well-timed address to the Canadians. He lost no opportunity to widen the involvements of his own official family in the cause. Averell Harriman, the secretary of commerce; Julius Krug, the secretary of the interior; Edwin Nourse, the Economic Council chairman; James Webb, the director of the budget—all were made responsible for studies and reports contributing directly to the legislative presentation. Thus these men were committed in advance. Besides, the President continually emphasized to everyone in reach that he did not have doubts, did not desire complications and would foreclose all he could. Reportedly his emphasis was felt at the Treasury, with good effect. And Truman was at special pains to smooth the way for Vandenberg. The senator insisted on "no politics" from the Administration side; there was none. He thought a survey of American resources and capacity essential; he got it in the Krug and Harriman reports. Vandenberg expected advance consultation; he received it, step by step, in frequent meetings with the President and weekly conferences with Marshall. He asked for an effective liaison between Congress and agencies concerned; Lovett and others gave him what he wanted. When the senator decided on the need to change financing and administrative features of the legislation, Truman disregarded Budget Bureau grumbling and acquiesced with grace. When, finally, Vandenberg desired a Republican to head the new administering agency, his candidate, Paul Hoffman, was appointed despite the President's own preference for another. In all these ways Truman employed the sparse advantages his "powers" and his status then accorded him to gain the sort of help he had to have.

Truman helped himself in still another way. Traditionally and practically, no one was placed as well as he to call public attention to the task of Congress (and its Republican leadership). Throughout the fall and winter of 1947 and on into the spring of 1948, he made repeated use of presidential "powers" to remind the country that congressional action was required. Messages, speeches, and an extra session were employed to make the point. Here, too, he drew advantage from his place. However, in his circumstances, Truman's public advocacy might have hurt, not helped, had his words seemed directed toward the forthcoming election. Truman gained advantage for his program only as his own endorsement of it stayed on the right side of that fine line between the "caretaker" in office and the would-be candidate. In public statements dealing with the Marshall Plan he seems to have risked blurring this distinction only once, when he called Congress into session in November 1947 asking both for interim aid to Europe and for peacetime price controls. The second request linked the then inflation with the current Congress (and with Taft), becoming a first step toward one of Truman's major themes in 1948. By calling for both measures at the extra session he could have been accused—and was—of mixing home-front politics with foreign aid. In the event no harm was done to the European program (or his politics). But in advance a number of his own advisers feared that such a double call would jeopardize the Marshall Plan. Their fears are testimony to the narrowness of his advantage in employing his own "powers" for its benefit.

It is symptomatic of Truman's situation that bipartisan accommodation by the White House then was thought to mean congressional consultation and conciliation on a scale unmatched in Eisenhower's time. Yet Eisenhower did about as well with opposition congresses as Truman did, in terms of requests granted for defense and foreign aid. It may be said that Truman asked for more extraordinary measures. But it also may be said that Eisenhower never lacked for the prestige his predecessor had to borrow. It often was remarked, in Truman's time, that he seemed a split personality, so sharply did his conduct differentiate domestic politics from national security. But personality aside, how else could he, in his first term, gain ground for an evolving foreign policy? The plain fact is that Truman had to play bipartisanship as he did or lose the game.

——————— V ———————

Had Truman lacked the personal advantages his "powers" and his status gave him, or if he had been maladroit in using them, there probably would not have been a massive European aid program in 1948. Something of the sort, perhaps quite different in its emphasis, would almost certainly have come to pass before the end of 1949. Some American response to European weakness and to Soviet expansion was as certain as such things can be. But in 1948 temptations to await a Taft plan or a Dewey plan might well have caused at least a year's postponement of response had the outgoing Administration bungled its congressional or public or allied or executive relations. Quite aside from the specific virtues of their plan. Truman and his helpers gained that year, at least, in timing the American response. As European time was measured then, this was a precious gain. The President's own share in this accomplishment was vital. He made his contribution by exploiting his advantages. Truman, in effect, lent Marshall and the rest the perquisites and status of his office. In return they lent him their prestige and their own influence. The transfer multiplied his influence despite his limited authority in form and lack of strength politically. Without the wherewithal to make this bargain, Truman could not have contributed to European aid.

Bargaining advantages convey no guarantees. Influence remains a two-way street. In the fortunate instance of the Marshall Plan, what Truman needed was actually in the hands of men who were prepared to "trade" with him. He personally could deliver what they wanted in return. Marshall, Vandenberg, Harriman, et al., possessed the prestige, energy, associations, staffs essential to the legislative effort. Truman himself had a sufficient hold on presidential messages and speeches, on budget policy, on high-level appointments, and on his own time and temper to carry through all aspects of his necessary part. But it takes two to make a bargain. It takes those who have prestige to lend it on whatever terms. Suppose that Marshall had declined the secretaryship of state in January 1947; Truman might not have found a substitute so well equipped to furnish what he needed in the months ahead. Or suppose that Vandenberg had fallen victim to a cancer two years before he actually did; Senator Wiley of Wisconsin would not have seemed to Taft a man with whom the world need be divided. Or suppose that the secretary of the treasury had been possessed of stature, force, and charm commensurate with that of his successor in Eisenhower's time, the redoubtable George M. Humphrey. And what if Truman then had seemed to the Republicans what he turned out to be in 1948, a formidable candidate for President? It is unlikely that a single one of these "supposes" would have changed the final outcome; two or three, however, might have altered it entirely. Truman was not guaranteed more power than his "powers" just because he had continuing relationships with cabinet secretaries and with senior senators. Here, as everywhere, the outcome was conditional on who they were and what he was and how each viewed events, and on their actual performance in response.

Granting that persuasion has no guarantee attached, how can a President reduce the risks of failing to persuade? How can he maximize his prospects for effectiveness by minimizing chances that his power will elude him? The Marshall Plan suggests an answer: He guards his power prospects in the course of making choices. Marshall himself, and Forrestal and Harriman, and others of the sort held office on the President's appointment. Vandenberg had vast symbolic value partly because FDR and Truman had done everything they could, since 1944, to build him up. The Treasury Department and the Budget Bureau—which together might have jeopardized the plans these others made—were headed by officials whose prestige depended wholly on their jobs. What Truman needed from these "givers" he received, in part, because of his past choice of men and measures. What they received in turn were actions taken or withheld by him, himself. The things they needed from him mostly involved his own conduct where his current choices ruled. The President's own actions in the past had cleared the way for current bargaining. His actions in the present were his trading stock. Behind each action lay a personal choice, and these together comprised his control over the give-and-take that gained him what he wanted. In the degree that Truman, personally, affected the advantages he drew from his relationships with other men in government, his power was protected by his choices.

By "choice" I mean no more than what is commonly referred to as "decision": a President's own act of doing or not doing. Decision is so often indecisive, and indecision is so frequently conclusive, that *choice* becomes the preferable term. "Choice" has its share of undesired connotations. In common usage it implies a black-and-white alternative. Presidential choices are rarely of that character. It also may imply that the alternatives are set before the choice maker by someone else. A President is often left to figure out his options for himself.

If Presidents could count upon past choices to enhance their current influence, as Truman's choice of men had done for him, persuasion would pose fewer difficulties than it does. But Presidents can count on no such thing. Depending on the circumstances, prior choices can be as embarrassing as they were helpful in the instance of the Marshall Plan. The incidents described in Chapter 2 include some sharp examples of embarrassment. Among others: Eisenhower's influence with Faubus was diminished by his earlier statements to the press and by his unconditional agreement to converse in friendly style at Newport. Truman's hold upon MacArthur was weakened by his deference toward him in the past.

Assuming that past choices have protected influence, not harmed it, present choices still may be inadequate. If Presidents could count on their own conduct to provide them enough bargaining advantages, as Truman's conduct did where Vandenberg and Marshall were concerned, effective bargaining might be much easier to manage than it often is. In the steel crisis, for instance, Truman's own persuasiveness with companies and union, both, was burdened by the conduct of an independent wage board and of government attorneys in the courts, to say nothing of Wilson, Arnall, Sawyer, and the like. Yet in practice, if not theory, many of *their* crucial choices never were the President's to make. Decisions that are legally in others' hands, or delegated past recall, have an unhappy way of proving just the trading stock most needed when the White House wants to trade. One reason why Truman was consistently more influential in the instance of the Marshall Plan than in the steel case or the MacArthur case is that the Marshall Plan directly involved Congress. In congressional relations there are some things that no one but the President can do. His chance to choose is higher when a message must be sent, or a nomination submitted, or a bill signed into law, than when the sphere of action is confined to the executive, where all decisive tasks may have been delegated past recall.

But adequate or not, a President's own choices are the only means in his own hands of guarding his own prospects for effective influence. He can draw power from continuing relationships in the degree that he can capitalize upon the needs of others for the Presidency's status and authority. He helps himself to do so, though, by nothing save ability to recognize the preconditions and the chance advantages and to proceed accordingly in the course of the choice making that comes his way. To ask how he can guard prospective influence is thus to raise a further question: What helps him guard his power stakes in his own acts of choice?

4

NOMINATING
AND ELECTING
PRESIDENTS

Progressive Ambition among United States Senators: 1972–1988[*]

Paul R. Abramson
Michigan State University

John H. Aldrich
University of Minnesota

David W. Rohde
Michigan State University

A rational-choice model is used to account for the decisions of United States Senators to run for president. The model predicts that senators will be more likely to run for president if their relative costs of running are low, if they have no political liabilities that might reduce their chances of winning, and if they have a propensity to take risks, which we measure by their past willingness to take risks in running for the Senate. The model works well in accounting for the decisions of Democrats to seek the presidency in 1972, 1976, and 1984, and can explain why few Republican senators ran in 1980. The model is used to predict which senators in the 99th Congress are relatively likely to run for president in 1988. The model works better in accounting for the past behavior of Democrats than Republicans, and also generates more plausible predictions about future Democratic presidential candidates. This partisan difference results largely from the different opportunity structures of the two parties. Finally, we discuss the changing dynamics of the nomination process and the implications of this change both for our model and for American electoral politics.

*We are grateful to Paul Brace, Thomas H. Hammond, Gary C. Jacobson, and Jack H. Knott for their comments on an earlier version of this article, to Brian Morris for suggestions, and to John Williams for his assistance. Referees for the *Journal* made extensive and helpful comments. We are especially grateful to Joseph A. Schlesinger for his insights.

An earlier version of this article was presented at the 1985 annual meeting of the American Political Science Association. The classification of senators relatively likely and unlikely to run for president was presented at that time. . . .

Politicians strive for office, and the highest office an American can achieve is the presidency. To win the presidency they must first win the nomination of their party. The McGovern-Fraser reforms, introduced after the 1968 elections, greatly increased the role of the electorate in the nomination process. Candidates who previously might have concluded that they had very little chance to win their party's nomination may well have thought that they had a better chance by appealing to the electorate. From 1972 on a large number of politicians have run for president. According to *Congressional Quarterly,* in the last four elections there have been a total of 35 "major" Democratic candidates and 13 "major" Republican candidates.[1]

While 48 candidates seem numerous, only a relatively small percentage of politicians ran for president. Two years before each of these presidential elections there were 50 governors, 100 U.S. Senators, and 435 members of the U.S. House of Representatives, the vast majority of whom were constitutionally eligible to serve as president. Over the course of these four elections they provided the basis for nearly 2340 candidacies. The pool of available candidates was even larger, since it included politicians who had left office, as well as other prominent Americans who had never held elective office.

In this article we attempt to explain why some U.S. Senators seek the presidency, while most do not. Our explanation is drawn from Joseph A. Schlesinger's (1966) theory of political ambition. Schlesinger accounts for office-seeking decisions by examining the type of ambition harbored by the politician and the relationship between that ambition and the opportunity structure that politician confronts. Politicians who seek higher office manifest what Schlesinger termed "progressive ambition." They advance up the informal ladder of political offices by seeking the best opportunity available that provides the greatest balance of benefits to costs in the light of the probability of success. This theory was formalized in rational choice theoretic terms by Gordon Black (1972), who cast the problem of office-seeking in the specific terms of expected utility maximization.

David W. Rohde (1979) extended these accounts in two ways. First, he argued that almost all politicians possess progressive ambition (at least at the relatively high level of U.S. Representative) in the sense that they would accept higher office if it were offered to them without cost or risk. Second, he paid explicit attention in his model to politicians who are more or less willing to put their political careers at risk. As Rohde demonstrates, a great deal can be learned about who runs for higher office by examining the risk-taking propensities of politicians, as revealed by their past office-seeking behavior.

Our basic assumption is the same as Rohde's. We assume that almost all elected officials (or, in this case, almost all U.S. Senators) are progressively ambitious and would accept the presidency if it were offered to them without cost or risk. The major consequence of this assumption is that we assume, in effect, that

---

[1]For the full list, see *Congressional Quarterly,* 1985, p. 378. We use this list of presidential candidates to define operationally those senators who ran for president between 1972 and 1984. We operationally classify any senator who entered a presidential primary outside of his or her own state as a presidential candidate, a procedure that is consistent with the *Congressional Quarterly* classification.

all hold a similar—and high—value for becoming president. In other words, there is little variation among senators in the benefit they place on the presidency, relative to the costs and risks involved. We assume, however, that as rational actors politicians recognize that the probability of attaining the presidency is low, and therefore are unlikely to run if circumstances reduce their chances of winning. We assume that politicians realize that a presidential candidacy is risky. Not only is it physically risky—as the candidacies of Robert F. Kennedy and George C. Wallace demonstrate—but it is risky politically as well. Therefore, if we can identify politicians who have been risk-takers in the past, we may predict better who will choose to run for president. Finally, we assume that politicians are less likely to run if circumstances raise the costs of running, whether those costs be actual or opportunity costs, such as foregoing the opportunity to remain in the Senate.

In principle our model could be applied to all politicians. In practice, however, we can safely reduce the number we study. We know, for example, that the House of Representatives has only once provided an electoral base for successfully seeking the presidency.[2] Of the 48 major candidates between 1972 and 1984, only seven have been incumbent members of the House of Representatives, even though there were nearly 1740 members who could have sought the White House. Only five candidates have been incumbent governors, even though some 200 could have sought the office. On the other hand, 17 incumbent U.S. Senators have sought their party's presidential nomination. Although the overall percentage of senators seeking the presidency was small (only 4.3 percent of the 396 constitutionally eligible to serve), U.S. Senators were more likely to run for president during this period than the holders of any other elective office, except for incumbent presidents.

In principle, we could analyze the total pool of ex-officeholders. Indeed, among the 48 candidates identified by *Congressional Quarterly,* 12 had left elective office (three by defeat). In principle, we could study all ex-governors and ex-senators, or even all ex-members of the U.S. House. Two other "major" candidates had never held elective office, although one of them (Sargent Shriver) had formerly run for vice-president. There is no practical way, however, to study all prominent Americans who might seek the presidency.

Studying incumbent senators clearly provides a reasonable test of our model. In fact, much of the groundwork for our analysis has been done in our prior research on progressive ambition. In Aldrich (1980, pp. 22–41), all the Democratic senators in the 94th Congress were studied to explain who among them sought the presidency in 1976. In Abramson, Aldrich, and Rohde (1983, pp. 274–79), we predicted which Democratic senators in the 98th Congress would seek the presidency in 1984.

This article will extend our research in five ways. First, we will improve the model, clarifying the formulation and modifying some of our measures. Second, we will provide a comprehensive analysis of all Democratic senators who could

---

[2]The one exception is James A. Garfield, who resigned his seat in the House after being elected president in 1880.

have sought the presidency in 1972, 1976, and 1984, as well as all Republican senators who could have run in 1980. In other words, we will examine the office-seeking choices of U.S. Senators when there was no incumbent president of their own party seeking the party nomination. Third, we will apply our model to the 99th Congress, and predict which senators are relatively likely to run for president in 1988. Our analysis will reveal that our model worked better for identifying Democratic candidates than Republicans, and that it generates more plausible predictions for Democratic senators than for their Republican counterparts. Our fourth task will be to explain these partisan differences, which result largely from the different opportunity structures of the two parties. Finally, we will show how the dynamics of the nomination process have changed, and discuss the implication of this change both for our model and for the future of American electoral politics.

The Success of the Model During the Last Four Elections

Our study begins by examining the decisions of senators to run for the presidency during the last four elections, and turns to predictions for the 1988 campaign. We limit our attention to this time period because of the vast changes in the presidential nomination process that began after the 1968 campaign. The reforms of the delegate selection process and of campaign financing were substantial and controversial (see, for example, Ranney, 1975; Polsby, 1983; and Crotty and Jackson, 1985).

The post-1968 reforms clearly altered the nature of the campaign process. More important for our purposes, they appear to have altered the opportunity structure for the presidency. The opportunity structure, as Schlesinger (1966) defines it, is a regularized, quasi-institutionalized patterning of offices that structures political careers. As such, the opportunity structure ordinarily changes slowly. With major institutional reform, however, the structure would be expected to change, and Schlesinger does find differences in the opportunity structure among the various states that result from different institutional patterns. The post-1968 nomination reforms caused a substantial alteration in the opportunity structure for seeking the presidency between 1968 and 1972. Aldrich (forthcoming), for instance, finds differences between the opportunity structure for the president in the 1952 to 1968 and in the post-1968 periods.[3] Indeed, the opportunity structure changed so much between 1968 and 1972 that our operational definition of running for president cannot be applied to the pre-1972 contests. Therefore, we limit our time frame to this most recent period. Our assumption is that the opportunity structure remains essentially constant over this period, although, as we shall see, there is some evidence that the structure does vary somewhat between the two parties.

---

[3]Aldrich (forthcoming) analyzed four different periods, chosen for their differences in the patterns of the nomination process. In addition to the two mentioned in the text, he examined the 1876–92 and the 1912–32 periods. He concluded that the opportunity structure was different in each period. Interestingly, he also found differences between the opportunity structure of the major parties within each period.

To test our model during the past four elections, we systematically classified all U.S. Senators who were constitutionally eligible to serve as president. Our model predicts that senators will be more likely to run for president if (a) their costs of running are relatively low, (b) they have no liabilities that reduce their chance of winning, and (c) if they are risk-takers.

The costs of running are very high if one chooses to challenge an incumbent president of one's own party. One risks the enmity of an incumbent president, and may be blamed by others for splitting the party. Moreover, the chances of winning are very low. No presidential candidate has ever won his party's nomination by challenging an incumbent of his own party who was seeking reelection. During the four elections we studied, Edward M. Kennedy was the only senator who challenged an incumbent president of his own party, although this option was open to 195 other senators. The remaining 16 who ran were among the 200 constitutionally eligible senators who did not face an incumbent of their own party. Since our model predicts that senators will not run against an incumbent of their own party, it made a correct negative prediction in 99.5 percent of the cases.[4]

We will place a more severe test on our model, however, by determining how well it worked when the differential costs and liabilities facing senators were less severe. We will examine the office-seeking choices of senators when they did not need to challenge an incumbent of their own party, focusing therefore on the Democratic senators in the 92nd, 94th, and 98th Congresses, and on the Republican senators in the 96th Congress. We have elsewhere classified 161 Democratic senators (or, to be more precise, 161 senatorial decisions) and 39 Republican senators according to the costs they faced, their liabilities (i.e., factors that lowered their probability of winning), and whether they had previously taken political risks. (See Abramson, Aldrich, and Rohde, 1985, tables A-1 through A-4, for the specific classification for each senator during this period.) Our analysis excludes three senators (one Democrat and two Republicans) who were constitutionally ineligible to serve as president. We also exclude Henry M. Jackson from our analysis of the 98th Congress because he died before the election year began.

Costs   Although it is always costly to run for president, the costs are higher if a senator is up for reelection.[5] At some stage, senators up for reelection may have to face the unenviable dilemma of choosing between a relatively safe run for their own Senate seats, or a much riskier race for the presidency. Even though senators will usually not have to give up defending their seats to seek the nomination,

---

[4]Eugene J. McCarthy and Robert F. Kennedy both challenged Lyndon B. Johnson in 1968. Their candidacies were possible because of the strong opposition to Johnson's Vietnam policies within the Democratic party. These exceptions serve to illustrate that only highly unusual circumstances are likely to lead senators to challenge incumbent presidents of their own party.

[5]In our earlier formulation, we considered being up for reelection a liability. It seems better, however, to classify being up for reelection as a cost. Being up for reelection does not diminish the chances that a senator will win either the party's nomination or the presidency. It does, however, increase the costs of running if the senator is unsuccessful.

senators will (with rare exceptions) be forced to give up defending their seats if they are nominated.[6] If senators run, but do not get nominated, an embarrassing loss may even reduce their chances of successfully defending their Senate seat. Over the course of the 1972, 1976, and 1984 elections, 50 Democratic senators were up for reelection. Three of them ran for president. Among the 111 who were not up for reelection, 11 ran for president. On the Republican side, however, being up for reelection was unrelated to running. Robert Dole was up for reelection; Howard H. Baker, Jr., was not.

Liabilities that Reduce the Probability of a Successful Candidacy

First-termers   The U.S. Senate provides a major electoral base for potential presidential candidates, offering them the opportunity for national visibility and the potential for building a national following. But gaining visibility and support takes time, and a first-term senator has had relatively little time to use his or her senatorial base. Moreover, a senator who has successfully defended his or her seat after six years in office gains additional electoral credibility. Among all the liabilities a senator may have, being a first-termer is the clearest and least ambiguous.

During the period we studied, 45 Democrats were first-termers when the presidential election year began; among these, only one (Lloyd M. Bentsen) ran for his party's presidential nomination. None of the 19 Republican first-termers ran for president.

There are several other liabilities that also reduce a senator's chances of gaining the presidential nomination. They are less clear-cut than being a first-termer, however, and we have modified or dropped some of the categories we employed in our earlier work.[7] Given that we made some minor changes in our previous operationalizations, we reanalyzed all our previous results, and we should stress that throughout this analysis we consistently apply the same measures for all four elections we studied. We consider the following characteristics to be liabilities:

Age   One senator during the period we studied was too young to serve as president. But even for senators who have reached, or will reach, 35 by inauguration day, being very young can be a liability. It is hard to know how old one must

---

[6]State law would usually prevent a senator from running for the Senate and the presidency within his or her own state. A senator could legally run for reelection to his or her Senate seat while running for president in the remaining 49 states and D.C. Barry Goldwater was offered the opportunity to run for both offices in 1964 by the Arizona legislature, but declined. In 1960 the Texas legislature passed a statute that allowed Lyndon B. Johnson to run simultaneously for senator and vice-president. That law would allow Texas senators today to run for both offices.

[7]In Aldrich (1980) any senator from the deep South was considered to have a political liability. Carter's election demonstrated that being a southerner was a liability that could be overcome. We would therefore not expect being a southerner to discourage senators from seeking the presidency after 1976. Rather than include this criterion for 1972 and 1976, but not for 1980 and 1984, we decided to drop this criterion in Abramson, Aldrich, and Rohde (1983) and in this article. We should emphasize that although we have changed some of our measurements of liabilities from those we used in our earlier work, in this article we use the same definitions throughout our analyses of all four elections.

be before youth ceases to be a disadvantage.[8] John F. Kennedy, the youngest person ever elected to be president, was only 43 when he was nominated, and only 42 when 1960 began. His youth and relative political inexperience, moreover, were issues he had to face in his campaign. We shall consider any senator who was not yet 42 years old when the election year began to have an electoral liability. During the period we studied, 15 Democrats were below this age, and only one of them (Fred Harris) ran for president. Most of these very young senators (12 of 15) were also first-termers, but their youth added a liability. Four Republican senators (all first-termers) were this young, and none ran for president.

Being too old is also a liability. Ronald Reagan's election has forced us to reconsider our definition of old age.[9] Alan Cranston, for example, was 69 years old when 1984 began, but he reminded voters that he was, and always would be, younger than Ronald Reagan. Reagan was 69 years old when first nominated, and 73 when renominated. We will consider any senator 70 years old or older when the election year began to have an electoral liability. During the period we studied, 19 Democrats and four Republicans were this old. None ran for president.

Minority or female status   All major party presidential nominees have been white, male, Christians. During the period we studied, there was only a single black senator, but he was no longer in the Senate when his party could not field an incumbent. Being Asian-American, Hispanic, or Jewish would, in our view, also be a liability. We classified 13 Democrats as having some minority status, as well as one Republican. None ran for president.

A woman senator, Margaret Chase Smith, did run for president in 1964. Her campaign was not treated seriously, at least partly because she was a woman. Two decades later, Geraldine A. Ferraro's nomination for vice-president was hailed as a breakthrough. It seems reasonable to view being female as a liability in seeking the presidency. During the period we studied, only a single woman senator had the chance to run without facing an incumbent of her own party. That woman, Nancy Landon Kassebaum, did not run in 1980, but she was also a first-termer.

Past political actions   Previous political actions can create a liability. Among these, a past failure to gain the presidency can weaken the ability of senators to gain support for a subsequent presidential bid. But classifying failures

---

[8]In Aldrich (1980) any senator born after 1929 was considered to have a liability. In other words, any senator who was not yet 46 years old when the election year began was considered to be too young. In Abramson, Aldrich, and Rohde (1983) we did not specifically employ youth as a criterion. Had we employed the youth criterion used in this article, four Democratic senators would have been considered as too young. However, none of these senators was predicted as likely to run in 1984, since three were first-termers and one was up for reelection.

[9]In Aldrich (1980) senators were considered to have a liability if they were born before 1910. In other words, any senator 66 years or older when the election year began was considered to be old. In Abramson, Aldrich, and Rohde (1983), we specified three senators as being over 75 years old. Had we employed the age criterion used in this article, Henry M. Jackson would have incurred an additional liability. Even without this age liability, however, Jackson was predicted as unlikely to run in 1984. As mentioned above, we did not include Jackson in our analysis of the 98th Congress, since he died before the election year began.

involves subjective judgment. Failure in the general election, especially when a candidate comes close to winning, has not been a bar to future nomination success, or even to future election. A strong nomination effort, especially when it is unexpected, may prove to be an asset. But an embarrassingly poor nomination effort may make it difficult to gain financial support for a subsequent presidential try. Some failures, such as Thomas F. Eagleton's forced resignation as the Democratic vice-presidential nominee in 1972, are truly *sui-generis*. We have also assigned an electoral liability to Harry F. Byrd, Jr., since he ran for reelection to the Senate in 1970 as an Independent. We have classified 13 Democrats as having incurred a political liability, mainly as a result of past political failures. Only one (Henry M. Jackson in 1976) ran for president. Two Republicans, Barry M. Goldwater and Strom Thurmond, are classified as having liabilities resulting from past political actions. Neither ran for president in 1980, but both were 70 years or older when the election year began. Goldwater was also up for reelection (a fact that did not dissuade him in 1964).

These various measures of liabilities are indicators of the variable probability of success that faces individual senators. As such, they are multiple indicators of a single construct, the relative chance of success of a presidential bid. It is therefore theoretically appropriate to combine them into a single index, which we do simply by adding up each liability. This simple index is sufficient, since these indicators are generally independent of each other (see note 14). Thus, the more liabilities a senator has, the less likely he or she should be to seek the presidency.[10]

In fact, the liabilities we measure do have a cumulative effect in reducing the likelihood that a senator will run for president. Seventeen Democrats had two liabilities, and none of them ran for president; among the 71 with one liability, only three ran; among the 73 with no liabilities, 11 ran for president. Twenty-three of the Republicans had one or more liabilities, and none of them ran for president. Both Baker and Dole were among the 16 with no liabilities.

Risk-Taking   Senators are more likely to run for president if their costs of running are relatively low and if they have no political liabilities. But even among those favorably situated only a small percentage actually run. Of the 53 Democrats who met these conditions, 11 ran for president. Among the 11 Republicans who met them, only one ran. A major reason that more do not run is because launching a presidential campaign is risky. Some senators are more prone to accept risks with their political careers than others, and we can improve our understanding of who runs for president if we can identify those who are willing to take risks.

---

[10]Given the detailed information we provide in Abramson, Aldrich, and Rohde (1985; tables A1 through A4), it would be possible to attempt to assess the relative impact of each liability separately. But given the small number of cases involved, as well as the fact that the decision to run for president is relatively rare even for U.S. Senators, examining the separate impact of each component is unrealistic.

The propensity to take risks is an attribute of individuals. In economics and in some applications in political science (e.g., Shepsle, 1972) decision makers are classified as risk acceptant, risk neutral, or risk averse, based upon the shape of their utility function, i.e., on how they value alternatives. (In particular, whether the utility function or indifference curve is concave, linear, or convex to the origin.) The propensity to take risks differs from risk acceptance, however. The propensity to take risks is a relative concept; one senator is more willing to take risks than another, even if both senators have utility functions that are technically risk averse. For example, Bartels (1986) has analyzed a spatial model of voter choice in which all voters are assumed to be risk averse but face candidates who offer risky alternatives (i.e., present a lottery over possible policy choices, much as in Shepsle, 1972; Enelow and Hinich, 1981). He deduces that the variance of the citizens' "uncertainty" about the candidates' policy positions enters into their choice as a variable in addition to its strict expected utility.

Our approach to risk-taking is also rooted in psychological theory. For many years, psychologists have studied individual decision makers (often in laboratory experiments) and have concluded consistently that individuals value risky alternatives such as gambles based in part on the expected value of the alternatives, but in part as well on the degree of risk involved. In one classic experiment, for example, Coombs and Pruitt (1960) found that subjects have preferences for the variance and skewness of gambles. Moreover, they found that there was substantial variation across individuals. Their subjects conveniently divided into thirds preferring high, intermediate, and low variance gambles, respectively. Most psychological models of individual choice include the variance of the gamble as a variable separate from its expected utility (see Wright, 1984, for a recent, extensive summary of these models). We follow this approach here by measuring risk-taking as a separate variable.

Obviously, we cannot use psychological measures to assess directly the risk-taking propensity of U.S. Senators. Fortunately, we can develop an indirect measure. Senators, like all politicians in democracies, leave a clear public record of their past attempts to seek office, and we can learn a great deal about their risk-taking propensities by observing their past office-seeking decisions. Some senators, in their quest for their senate seat, demonstrated a willingness to take risks. We classify senators as proven risk-takers if: (a) The *first* time they ran for the Senate they challenged an incumbent. A candidate may challenge an incumbent of his or her own party in a primary or run for the Senate when an incumbent of the opposite party is seeking reelection. We classify candidates as risk-takers if they would have expected to face an opposition-party incumbent at the time they sought their Senate seat, even if they did not wind up facing that incumbent in the general election.[11] We also classify senators as risk-takers (b) if they *first* ran for the Senate in a state that was relatively safe for the opposition party. We

---

[11]We employed this criterion in our previous analyses as well, but did not state it explicitly. In addition, we consider a senator to be a risk-taker only if he or she challenged an *elected* incumbent, since appointed senators are often vulnerable at the polls.

define a state as relatively safe for the opposition party if the opposition party averaged 57 percent of the vote in the four previous Senate elections.[12]

It is important to note that while risk-taking propensity is a psychological attribute of senators, our risk-taking measure depends on observation of the office-seeking behavior that is produced in part by that propensity. Senators who do not meet at least one of the . . . conditions may or may not have a propensity to take risks. But they are not proven risk-takers. A fairly large number of senators are proven risk-takers. Among both the Democrats and Republicans, just over half the senators we studied were proven risk-takers. Among the Democrats, proven risk-takers were a good deal more likely to run for president than those who were not. Twelve of the 83 proven risk-takers ran for president; only two of the 78 who were not proven risk-takers ran.[13] Among Republicans, however, there was no relationship between proven risk-taking and running. Baker was a proven risk-taker, Dole was not.

Our operational definition of risk-taking includes only the initial Senate campaign. In principle, one might want to extend the measurement to include risk-taking in other campaigns. Of course, the practical difficulties of doing so are substantial. Moreover, it is reasonable to focus only on the most proximate career decision prior to the presidential race. After all, while risk-taking propensity is likely to be a fairly stable, long-term attribute, it is unreasonable to suggest that it should be considered stable over what would be a period of several decades for many of the senators.

One could also argue that some senators we have not classified as risk-takers did in fact encounter risky situations in their first race for the Senate. For instance, some senators may have faced particularly strong opponents who were not incumbent senators—for example, popular incumbent governors who were trying to gain a Senate seat. Some candidates may have run despite holding policy positions that were unpopular with many members of their own party—for example, liberal Republicans who sought the Senate in a conservative Republican state. However, such extensions of our operational definition would require individual, subjective criteria. The question in any event is the relative degree of riskiness. Given that about half the senators are classified as risk-takers, further extending our definition to include more senators would weaken the utility of the risk-taking variable as we have operationalized it.

Despite the utility of our risk-taking variable, we recognize that we have measured risk-taking indirectly. Therefore, we cannot rule out the possibility that we are inadvertently capturing some propensity to run for president that is closely correlated with having run for the Senate in a particularly risky situation. For example, it is possible that charismatic or otherwise particularly attractive candidates run and win in risky situations and that these characteristics, in turn,

---

[12]We use this percentage to follow the decision rule employed by Rohde in his analysis of progressive ambition among members of the U.S. House of Representatives.

[13]On the other hand, the one senator who challenged an incumbent of his own party, Kennedy in 1980, was not a proven risk-taker by our measure.

contribute to running for president. Careful examination of who we have classi-fied as risk-takers makes charisma an unlikely explanation, but we cannot rule out all such alternative interpretations. Still, the strong and consistent findings in the psychological literature suggest that attitude toward risk should be relevant to decision makers facing this most risky situation.

The Cumulative Effect of Costs, Liabilities, and Risk-Taking   There is no reason in principle to expect any relationship between being up for reelection, having a liability that reduces one's chances of winning, and having a prior record as a proven risk-taker. Indeed, among both the 161 Democrats and 39 Republicans we studied, these attributes were only weakly related to each other.[14] However, these three factors should have an additive effect in predicting which senators will run. Running should be most frequent among senators who are not up for reelection, have no liabilities, and who are proven risk-takers. Senators who are up for reelection, who have liabilities, and who are not proven risk-takers may still seek their party's nomination, but the probability that they will run should be very low.

In table 1 we classify the 161 Democrats along these three basic dimensions, showing the actual number who ran for president and the number who did not. Table 2 classifies the 39 Republicans who could have sought the presidency in 1980. Each table is divided into four blocks. The first block represents our results according to the number of liabilities among proven risk-takers who were not up for reelection. The second block presents our results among proven risk-takers who were up for reelection. The third block presents our results for senators who were not proven risk-takers, and who were not up for reelection. The final block presents our results among senators who were not proven risk-takers and who were also up for reelection.

As table 1 shows, there were only 33 Democratic senators who were proven risk-takers who were not up for reelection and had no liabilities. Ten of the 14 Democrats who ran were drawn from this subset. Indeed, while only 20 percent of the Democrats met all three conditions, 71 percent of the candidates were from this group.

Since only two Republican senators ran in 1980, table 2 serves mainly to pre-sent the distribution of Republicans along these three basic dimensions. However, the table does show that one of the two Republicans who ran (Baker) was drawn from the very small subset of Republicans who were proven risk-takers, who were not up for reelection, and who had no liabilities. On the other hand, Dole was not a proven risk-taker and, moreover, was up for reelection. Our model clearly helps explain why few Republican senators ran. Our analysis of Demo-cratic senators reveals that running is most likely among senators who are proven

---

[14]We constructed a correlation matrix for both the Democratic and Republican senators in which we related all these variables to each other. The only strong relationship was between being young and being a first-termer.

TABLE 1
WHETHER DEMOCRATIC SENATORS RAN FOR PRESIDENT IN 1972, 1976, AND 1984,
BY NUMBER OF LIABILITIES, CONTROLLING FOR RISK-TAKING AND REELECTION STATUS

	Proven Risk-Takers; Not Up for Reelection		
Number of Liabilities:	None	One	Two
Ran for president	10	0	0
Did not run	23	21	5

	Proven Risk-Takers; Up for Reelection		
Number of Liabilities:	None	One	Two
Ran for president	0	2	0
Did not run	9	9	4

	Not Proven Risk-Takers; Not Up for Reelection		
Number of Liabilities:	None	One	Two
Ran for president	1	0	0
Did not run	19	24	8

	Not Proven Risk-Takers; Up for Reelection		
Number of Liabilities:	None	One	Two
Ran for president	0	1	0
Did not run	11	14	0

Source: Compiled by authors. For the classification of each Democratic senator in the 92nd, 94th, and 98th Congress, see Abramson, Aldrich, and Rohde (1985), tables A1 through A3.

risk-takers favorably situated by virtue of not being up for reelection and having no liabilities. As only four Republican senators met all these conditions, we would expect few GOP senators to have run.

To assess the relative importance of risk-taking, reelection status, and the presence of liabilities, we conducted a probit analysis for both the 161 Democrats and the 39 Republicans (see Aldrich and Nelson, 1984).[15] The dependent variable was scored as one if the senator ran for president, a zero if not. Risk-taking and reelection status were also scored as zero-one variables, where a score of one indicates that the senator was a risk-taker or that he or she was up for reelection that year, respectively. The liabilities variable was scored zero, one, or two, depending on the number of liabilities applicable. The results for the Democrats are presented in table 3, those for the Republicans in table 4.

[15]We also conducted a probit analysis for the combined list of Democratic and Republican senators. Not surprisingly, the results are very similar to those for the Democrats. Given that the Democratic and Republican parties have somewhat different opportunity structures, however, we believe on theoretical grounds that the results should be analyzed separately for each party.

TABLE 2
WHETHER REPUBLICAN SENATORS RAN FOR PRESIDENT IN 1980, BY NUMBER
OF LIABILITIES, CONTROLLING FOR RISK-TAKING AND REELECTION STATUS

Proven Risk-Takers; Not Up for Reelection			
Number of Liabilities:	None	One	Two
Ran for president	1	0	0
Did not run	3	10	2

Proven Risk-Takers; Up for Reelection			
Number of Liabilities:	None	One	Two
Ran for president	0	0	0
Did not run	3	1	1

Not Proven Risk-Takers; Not Up for Reelection			
Number of Liabilities:	None	One	Two
Ran for president	0	0	0
Did not run	7	2	4

Not Proven Risk-Takers; Up for Reelection			
Number of Liabilities:	None	One	Two
Ran for president	1	0	0
Did not run	1	2	1

Source: Compiled by authors. For the classification of each Republican senator in the 96th Congress, see
Abramson, Aldrich, and Rohde (1985), table A4.

TABLE 3
PROBIT ESTIMATES OF THE PROBABILITY OF PRESIDENTIAL CANDIDACIES
AMONG DEMOCRATIC SENATORS, 1972, 1976, AND 1984

Probability of Running for President:

Variable	Coefficient (M.L.E.)	Standard Error	t-Ratio (MLE/SE)
Reelection	−.030	.353	−0.08
Liabilities	−.684	.306	−2.24
Risk-taker	.836	.359	2.33
Constant	−1.592	.344	−4.63

−2xLLR (Chi-Square Goodness of Fit, 3 degrees of freedom) = 14.6

Source: Compiled by authors. For the classification of each Democratic senator in the 92nd, 94th, and
98th Congress, see Abramson, Aldrich, and Rohde (1985), tables A1 through A3. For the distribution of cases,
see table 1.
  The variables were scored as follows: Ran for president = 1, did not run = 0; Up for reelection = 1, not up for
reelection = 0; No liabilities = 0, 1 liability = 1, 2 liabilities = 2; Proven risk-taker = 1, not proven risk-taker = 0.

TABLE 4

PROBIT ESTIMATES OF THE PROBABILITIES OF PRESIDENTIAL CANDIDACIES
AMONG REPUBLICAN SENATORS, 1980

Probability of Running for President:

Variable	Coefficient (M.L.E.)	Standard Error	t-Ratio (MLE/SE)
Reelection	.488	.830	0.59
Liabilities	−4.462	239.468	−0.02
Risk-taker	.140	.818	0.17
Constant	−1.400	.669	−2.10

−2xLLR (Chi-Square Goodness of Fit, 3 degrees of freedom) = 4.1

Source: Compiled by authors. For the classification of each Republican senator in the 96th Congress, see Abramson, Aldrich, and Rohde (1985), table A4. For the distribution of cases, see table 2.

The variables were scored as follows: Ran for president = 1, did not run = 0; Up for reelection = 1, not up for reelection = 0; No liabilities = 0, 1 liability = 1, 2 liabilities = 2; Proven risk-taker = 1, not proven risk-taker = 0.

The Republican case can be dealt with briefly. There was too little variation in the dependent variable (i.e., only two senators ran) to provide the empirical evidence needed to provide reliable estimates. Two of the three signs are in the right direction, since having liabilities reduces one's chances of running while being a proven risk-taker increases them. The sign for reelection status is in the wrong direction. However, for all three variables the standard errors are large (even vast in the case of liabilities), and thus the model estimations cannot be trusted.

The Democratic case, with its larger number of cases and consequent greater incidence of senators running for president, provides the only feasible test of the probit model. In this case, the fit of the model is good, as the chi-squared goodness of fit test is significant beyond the .005 level. The reelection variable has the correct sign, but its effect is small and statistically insignificant. The two other variables have the correct sign, and their impact is significant and, in substantive terms, substantial.

Measuring the impact of a variable is complicated by the nonlinear relationship between independent variables in a probit model and the probability of a senator running for the presidency (i.e., the probability that the dependent variable is a one instead of a zero). Given the small number of possible values for our independent variables, however, we can measure the influence of the variables by constructing alternative scenarios. In all cases, we assume that the senator is not up for reelection, but, given the size of the reelection variable coefficient, the results are virtually identical for the case of a senator who is up for reelection. We first calculated the predicted probability that such a senator would run for president for all possible combinations of the two other variables. In part A of table 5, we report the probability of running among proven risk-takers with varying numbers of liabilities, while table 5B reports the same calculations for senators who did not demonstrate risk-taking behavior when they first ran for the Senate.

TABLE 5

PROBABILITY OF PRESIDENTIAL CANDIDACIES PREDICTED FROM PROBIT EQUATION
FOR DEMOCRATIC SENATORS, 1972, 1976, 1984

Part A: Proven Risk-Taker; Not Up for Reelection

Number of Liabilities	Probability of Running
None	.225
One	.075
Two	.017

Part B: Not Proven Risk-Taker; Not Up for Reelection

Number of Liabilities	Probability of Running
None	.061
One	.011
Two	.002

Source: Based upon the probit estimates in table 3.

As can be seen in the table, the probability of running for a Democratic senator who was a proven risk-taker with no liabilities was .23. Adding a single liability decreased that probability substantially to only [.08]. The addition of a second liability reduced that already low probability of candidacy even further, to barely more than one chance in a hundred. Conversely, a senator with no liabilities but who also was not a proven risk-taker had an estimated probability of running only .06, a substantial reduction from the .23 of a risk-taker who also had no liabilities. Adding liabilities to a non-risk-taker reduced the chances that the senator would run for president to .01 for one liability and to only one chance in 500 for a second liability.

The conclusions, therefore, are that the probit-estimated model of Republican senators must be disregarded due to lack of variance of the dependent variable, but that the model provides a reasonably good fit (given that running for president is still a rare event) for Democratic senators. All three independent variables had the expected sign. The variables tapping risk-taking propensities and factors that reduce the chances of winning (the liabilities variable) yield coefficients that are statistically significant and substantively large. In particular, only those most well situated to run for president in terms of these two variables were at all likely to run for president in these three elections. . . . Moreover, the two variables exert about comparable impacts on the probability of a candidacy.

As we saw, however, reelection status does not have a significant impact on the decision to run. This lack of impact raises the question of whether reelection status should be discarded from the model, and, in particular, whether a senator's reelection status should be used to predict his or her candidacy in future elections. In our view, it would be premature to discard this information. We do, after all, have theoretical reasons for predicting that senators who are up for reelection do face somewhat greater costs if they seek the presidency. There may, however, be circumstances when the costs of not running also seem to be high. It is note-worthy that two of the three Democrats who ran despite being up for reelection ran in 1976. A Democrat running in 1976 could expect to face either an unelected incumbent or a divided party that had refused him his party's nomination. Under these circumstances the Democratic nominee was likely to win, and a Democrat who did not run in 1976 would have to wait eight years to have another favorable opportunity to seek the party's nomination. To some senators the cost of waiting might have outweighed the cost of being up for reelection. Moreover, one of the two senators who ran, Lloyd Bentsen, would have been the beneficiary of the "Johnson rule" and could have run for both the presidency and his Senate seat. In addition, Fred Harris, the Democrat who ran for the 1972 nomination despite being up for reelection, may not have planned to defend his Senate seat. After withdrawing from the presidential race after a seven-week campaign, Harris did not run for reelection to the Senate. If Harris did not plan to defend his seat, he incurred no additional cost by being up for reelection.

Predicting Candidates for 1988

Since our model has worked well in the past, we can use it to attempt to predict future candidacies. In fact, we did use this model to predict which Democratic senators would be relatively likely to run in 1984, and our model worked remark-ably well. We predicted that 10 of the 46 Democrats in the Senate at the begin-ning of the 98th Congress would be the most likely to run, since they were proven risk-takers who were not up for reelection and had no liabilities.[16] Four of these senators ran. Among the 36 senators predicted as relatively less likely to run, none sought the presidency.[17]

Our predictions for 1984, as well as our postdictions for 1972, 1976, and 1980, were based upon the Senate as it was composed before the presidential election year. We therefore knew the results of the 1970, 1974, 1978, and 1982 midterm elections before making our postdictions or predictions. The predictions we are making in this article were originally presented at the 1985 annual meeting of the American Political Science Association, held between August 29 and September 1. We have not altered our predictions. Readers of this article will have the advan-tage of knowing the results of the 1986 midterm elections.

Scholars who apply our model after the 1986 midterm election may be able to improve on our predictions in three ways. First, given Reagan's age, the dangers inherent in the office, and the health problems he might face if complications arise from colon cancer, he might no longer be president. If Bush were the incumbent president, we would expect him to be challenged, but since the chances of defeat-

---

[16]Although we have made some minor modifications in our interpretation of the age criteria used to assign liabilities, none of these changes would have affected our overall prediction.

[17]We predicted that Jackson would be unlikely to run, but obviously could not include him in our present test.

ing an incumbent president for his own party's nomination are low, we would expect few contenders. We would, therefore, forego predicting which Republicans would run—just as we made no such predictions for the 1984 election.

Second, scholars who wait until after the 1986 midterm election to apply our model will gain additional information about the electoral strength of about one-fourth of the Senate. Senators who seek reelection in 1986, but who fail to hold their Senate seat, will demonstrate electoral weakness that will undercut their claims to the nomination. Moreover, the 1986 election will provide an opportunity to test the electoral strength of a large number of Republican first-termers. At the time our article went to press in mid-April 1986, there were 15 Republican first-terms seeking reelection in 1986, and none of them will be first-termers when the 100th Congress convenes. Our test assumes that all will be reelected. We realize that this assumption is implausible, and that the list of likely Republican presidential candidates may be smaller after the 1986 election.

Third, the 1986 election will have added to the total number of first-termers, for seven senators had already announced that they would not seek reelection as this article went to press. At least some of the remaining 27 senators who were up for reelection in 1986 may have lost office. Given that first-termers are unlikely to seek the presidency, scholars who apply our model may be able to marginally improve its predictive ability merely by classifying these first-terms as unlikely to run.

Although our predictions have been made early, they are in one sense complete. As . . . indicate[d], it is highly unlikely that any new senators will be added to our list of most likely presidential candidates.[18]

To make our predictions, we classified all 47 Democrats in the 99th Congress, as well as all 53 Republicans, except for Rudy Boschwitz, who is not constitutionally eligible to serve as president. . . .[19]

Turning first to the Democrats, we must begin by commenting on the additional liabilities incurred as a result of the 1984 nomination campaign. We assume that Alan Cranston, John Glenn, and Ernest F. Hollings all incurred liabilities by their poor performance in the 1984 race. Gary Hart, on the other hand, did far better than expected, and came close to upsetting Mondale, despite the latter's financial and organizational advantages, as well as new party rules that may have provided his winning margin.[20] Hart's failed candidacy may actually strengthen his position in 1988. But Hart poses another problem, since he decided not to defend his Senate seat in 1986. Hart will not be in the pool of incumbent senators in the 100th Congress, and thus our model would not identify him as a potential candidate

---

[18]A new senator could be added to our list if a former senator who was considered a risk-taker by virtue of his first Senate try reenters the Senate, and if that senator has no liabilities. (For example, we did not classify Hubert H. Humphrey as a first-termer in 1972 or 1976, even though he reentered the Senate in 1970.) Very few individuals could meet these conditions.

[19]Boschwitz was born in Berlin as a German citizen. Lowell P. Weicker, Jr., was born in Paris, but had an American father. He was born with dual U.S. and French citizenship, but renounced his French citizenship in the 1950s. We are grateful to Senator Weicker for providing us with this information about his citizenship status.

[20]For a discussion, see Abramson, Aldrich, and Rohde, 1986, chapter 1.

unless it [was] modified. Clearly, we do expect Hart to run for president. This potential anomaly raises a larger question that we will address in our conclusions.

Our empirical analysis demonstrated that Democratic presidential candidates are most likely to emerge from the subset of senators who are proven risk-takers and who have no liabilities. We have theoretical grounds for predicting that the costs of running will be higher for senators who are up for reelection. Seven Democrats emerge as most likely to seek the presidency in 1988. They are:

Joseph R. Biden, Jr., Delaware
Bill Bradley, New Jersey
Dale Bumpers, Arkansas
Wendell H. Ford, Kentucky
Gary Hart, Colorado
Patrick J. Leahy, Vermont
David Pryor, Arkansas

If we ignore reelection status, three additional senators would be added to the list of likely Democrats:

Daniel Patrick Moynihan, New York
Paul S. Sarbanes, Maryland
Jim Sasser, Tennessee

Given our view that being up for reelection does raise the costs of running for president, we would view the first seven as more likely to run than the remaining three, although we cannot dependably estimate the reduced likelihood that senators up for reelection will run.

Our model does not predict that all seven senators predicted as relatively likely to run will actually run or that none of the remaining 40 will seek the presidency. Indeed, during the period we studied even senators who had no liabilities, who were proven risk-takers, and who were not up for reelection ran only about one-fourth of the time. For any individual senator, therefore, the most likely prediction is that he or she will not run. However, our model predicts that the seven we have designated are more likely to run than the remaining 40. Our predictions may be wrong, but as of April 1986 they certainly appeared to be plausible. Among the seven we predict as relatively likely to run, Hart seems almost certain to run, although he will not be running as an incumbent senator. Joseph R. Biden, Jr., has often been discussed as a dark-horse prospect, and Bill Bradley has frequently been mentioned as a presidential prospect. Dale Bumpers seriously considered running in 1984, and may run in 1988. It seems highly unlikely that two Democratic senators from the same state would run, but David Pryor is a possibility if Bumpers does not.

Among the 40 senators predicted as relatively less likely to run there are few presidential possibilities, although Kennedy was clearly a possibility until he announced in December 1985 that he would not run for president—an announcement in which he also declared that he would run for reelection for his Senate seat in 1988.[21] Sam Nunn is occasionally mentioned as a long-shot possibility to seek the presidency. In our view, with the possible exception of Nunn, none of the 40 Democrats not on our primary list appears to be a likely contender, although the joint probability that none of them will run may be fairly low.

Although the small number of Republican senators in our analysis precluded any meaningful test of the model, we will apply the same model used to predict which Democrats are relatively likely to run. However, the list of Republicans predicted as relatively likely to seek the presidency is both large and implausible. Fully 18 Republican proven risk-takers emerge as well situated to seek the presidency. They are:

James Abdnor, South Dakota
William L. Armstrong, Colorado
Thad Cochran, Mississippi
William S. Cohen, Maine
Alfonse M. D'Amato, New York
Jeremiah Denton, Alabama
John P. East, North Carolina
Slade Gorton, Washington
Charles E. Grassley, Iowa
Jesse Helms, North Carolina
Gordon J. Humphrey, New Hampshire
Robert W. Kasten, Jr., Wisconsin
Paul Laxalt, Nevada
Charles McC. Mathias, Jr., Maryland
Mack Mattingly, Georgia
Frank H. Murkowski, Alaska
Bob Packwood, Oregon
Steven D. Symms, Idaho

If we ignore reelection status in our predictions, six additional Republicans would be added to our list. They are:

John H. Chafee, Rhode Island
John C. Danforth, Missouri
Dave Durenberger, Minnesota
Orrin G. Hatch, Utah
Richard G. Lugar, Indiana
Malcolm Wallop, Wyoming

---

[21]For the reasons we do not assign Kennedy a liability for losing to Jimmy Carter in the 1980 Democratic presidential nomination contest, see Abramson, Aldrich, and Rohde, 1983, p. 292. We realize that this decision is debatable, but it should be pointed out that it makes little difference in our analysis. Since Kennedy was not a proven risk-taker, he was predicted as relatively unlikely to run for president. Assigning a liability to Kennedy in 1984 marginally increases the explanatory power of the liabilities variable, but has little additional effect on our estimates.

Even though nine of the Republicans on our primary list were expected to seek reelection in 1986, and although this list may have been trimmed, it seems likely that few of the 18 on our primary list will run for president. Even if all were highly qualified presidential prospects, the very large list of potential contenders might discourage most from running. Moreover, the actual names on the list do not seem particularly plausible, since Armstrong and Laxalt are the only two of the 18 who have been discussed as a presidential prospect. (In August 1985 Laxalt announced that he would not defend his Senate seat in 1986, a decision that commentators suggested might facilitate a possible presidential bid.) Of course, several of these Republicans could run. All have taken political risks in the past, and they could take the risk of a presidential run in the future. Nonetheless, the list of Republicans generated by our model does not seem as reasonable as the list of Democrats.

While few of the 18 senators on our primary list are likely to run, most of the remaining 34 Republicans (excluding Boschwitz) also appear to be unlikely prospects. Dole, of course, is frequently mentioned as a possibility, despite his poor showing in 1980. As the leader of his party in the Senate, he may find it difficult to launch an effective campaign, however, a problem that plagued Baker in 1980. Our model will prove correct if the Republicans predicted as relatively likely to run do prove more likely to seek the presidency than those predicted as unlikely. But it seems to be a weak mechanism for identifying future Republican presidential candidates.

Both our comparison of past office-seeking, and a comparison of Democratic and Republican senators in the 99th Congress, strongly suggest that our model works better in accounting for the behavior of Democrats than Republicans. Given that we tested our model with a relatively small number of Republicans, part of this partisan difference may result from chance. In our view, however, this difference does not result primarily from chance but from systematic differences in the opportunity structure of the two parties.

Discussion

Two basic facts should be considered when comparing the Democrats and Republicans. First, there has been a Republican incumbent seeking reelection in three of the last four elections. Second, the past decade has been a period of Republican ascendancy in the Senate.

Since there was an incumbent Republican president seeking the party nomination in 1972, 1976, and 1984 relatively few Republicans have had a favorable opportunity to seek their party's presidential nomination. As a result, only one of the 52 Republicans has suffered a failed nomination campaign. Five of the 47 Democrats have incurred a liability as the result of a weak attempt to gain their party's nomination.

Second, this is an era of rapid Republican gains in the Senate, and a large percentage of Republicans in the present Senate are proven risk-takers. At the beginning of the 94th Congress (just after the Watergate election of 1974), there were only 38 Republicans in the Senate. Even with a loss of two seats in 1984, there were 53 Republican senators in the 99th Congress. A large part of the GOP gain came from defeating Democratic incumbents. Since many Republicans are in the Senate by virtue of defeating a Democratic incumbent, there are many Republican risk-takers.[22] Moreover, at the beginning of the 94th Congress, there were only six Republicans from the South. In the 99th Congress, 10 of the 22 senators from the states of the old Confederacy were Republicans, and two of them were risk-takers by virtue of coming from a state that, before their election, was heavily Democratic in prior Senate contests.

In the 99th Congress, 49 percent of the Democratic senators were proven risk-takers, while 58 percent of the Republicans were. Risk-taking proved an important variable in accounting for past office-seeking decisions, but the relatively large number of Republican risk-takers may make it less effective for identifying future Republican candidates than for identifying Democrats.

That the Republicans control the White House may also limit future Republican candidacies, for it means that Republican hopefuls may have to face a sitting vice-president. In all the years from 1840 through 1956, no sitting vice-president received a major-party nomination.[23] But sitting vice-presidents have received a major-party nomination in two of the last seven elections. For the last eight elections, the party in power has fielded either an incumbent president or vice-president. Although Bush certainly appears likely to face a strong challenge for the nomination, he enjoys a level of visibility that few other Republicans can match. If Bush raises a substantial amount of money, and if he depletes the potential pool of contributors for other presidential hopefuls, his presence as an incumbent vice-president may somewhat restrict the number of Republican senators who run.

Finally, senatorial incumbency may not be as much of an advantage for the Republicans as for the Democrats, for Republican party activists are very conservative. Senators, especially those in leadership positions, often must support moderate policies, and supporting moderate policies may aid senators who seek reelection. But in campaigning for the Republican presidential nomination, it is helpful to gain support from Republican activists, many of whom reject the conservative credentials of senators who compromise on issues conservatives view as important. For example, Baker's support of the Panama Canal Treaty as minority leader weakened his credibility among conservatives. But even senators who are not in leadership positions must cast public votes on many issues. Moreover, as long as the Republicans are the majority party in the Senate, Republican senators will be pressured to support legislation that can also win support in the Democrat controlled House.

Over the past century, presidential candidates have been more likely to emerge from the majority party in the Senate (see Aldrich, forthcoming). During the periods

---

[22]Our classification of risk-taking is based upon the first time the senator ran for the Senate, but, of course, a majority of those who are proven risk-takers succeeded on their first try.

[23]The only possible exception is John C. Breckinridge, who was the candidate of the Southern Democrats in 1860. However, Stephen A. Douglas is considered to be the candidate of the regular Democratic party.

when the Republicans dominated the Senate (1876–1892 and 1912–1932 in Aldrich's analysis), over a third of the Republicans who sought their party's presidential nomination were senators, while fewer than one in five Democratic candidates was a senator. This difference is not merely the result of the larger number of Republican senators during these years. In many respects, the Senate is a particularly appropriate forum for establishing the presidential credentials for the party that dominates national politics. That this may no longer be true for Republicans underscores a major difference between the present nomination system and the system that existed before 1972. The growing advantages of nonincumbency provide another striking difference. But while not being in office seems to have become an advantage in recent nomination campaigns, it may be even more of an asset for Republicans than for Democrats.

Although we have developed a model that accounts very well for the past office-seeking of U.S. Senators, and although it appears to generate reasonable predictions for future Democratic presidential candidates, the increasing advantages of nonincumbency have serious implications for our model. In the last three elections, the nonincumbent party has turned for its standard-bearer to a politician who was not in office. Jimmy Carter and Ronald Reagan left their governorships under favorable conditions. Walter Mondale left office through defeat, although the onus of the defeat fell upon Carter. Still, Mondale did not seek the opportunity to reestablish his electoral credentials by challenging an incumbent Republican in Minnesota in 1982. Rather, he spent nearly four years campaigning for the presidency.

Baker's resignation from the Senate provides another example of the potential advantages of nonincumbency. Part of the reason for Baker's failure to launch an effective campaign in 1980 was that he was too busy attending to his duties as minority leader. Baker's decision to give up his Senate seat in 1984 may have been motivated by many considerations, but one of them was probably gaining free time to run for the presidency. Laxalt's decision not to seek reelection in 1986 fueled speculation that he might seek the Republican presidential nomination. And Hart's decision not to defend his Senate seat in 1986 was almost certainly made to facilitate a bid for the presidency.

The calculus of candidacy has changed dramatically if incumbent senators are willing to give up the national platform and organizational resources provided by a Senate seat. Yet the presidential nomination campaign is now so long and time-consuming that the time and freedom gained by voluntarily choosing nonincumbency may be worth the trade-off. It is already clear that the nomination process is now so lengthy and burdensome that it is difficult for incumbent governors to seek the presidency. During the last two presidential contests, only a single incumbent governor (Jerry Brown in 1980) has sought his party's presidential nomination. But it is possible that even the lighter work load imposed by being a U.S. senator places too great a burden on a candidate.

These changed conditions can, of course, be incorporated into a rational choice model, for they result from the increased costs of candidacy. One modification of our prediction model can be made rather easily. In addition to predicting which members of the Senate will run, we can add to our pool of likely candidates proven risk-takers with no liabilities who have voluntarily left the Senate during the two previous congressional elections. This would not lead us to predict Baker, since he clearly incurred a liability as a result of his weak presidential bid in 1980. But it would lead us to predict that candidacies by Laxalt and Mathias are relatively likely, even though the latter candidacy seems highly implausible. And it would lead us to continue to predict a Hart candidacy, a prediction that seems remarkably plausible.

Two minor modifications to our model might also be necessary. We might continue to regard first-term senators who voluntarily leave the Senate as first-termers, since they will have never demonstrated that they had the electoral strength to win reelection. Likewise, we would assign a liability to senators who leave office for health reasons. Both these considerations would lead us to drop East from our list of likely Republicans.

We would drop from our list senators who leave office through defeat. Being defeated clearly creates a serious liability that erodes potential support for a presidential bid. Of course, as George S. McGovern demonstrated in 1984, even defeated senators can run. Under the new nomination system they do gain one advantage: they have more available time to campaign for their party's nomination.

The increasing advantages of nonincumbency have far more important implications, for they may affect the quality of American electoral politics. Elected officials, whether executives or legislators, have ongoing responsibilities and must develop a public record based upon actual policy decisions. Not only are they more likely to support responsible policies than politicians out of office, but the public can judge their actual behavior. Moreover, when politicians voluntarily choose to give up elected office, the nation may be deprived of the services of some of its most capable political leaders. And even with voluntary retirement, the chances of these politicians later becoming president remain low.

The American presidential system has always been atypical among democracies, for it has always provided substantial opportunities for nonincumbents to ascend to the nation's highest office. But, until recently, the system did not discourage politicians from seeking other elective office, or encourage them to give up office, to seek the presidency. A nomination system that encourages elected officials to give up office, and which may give advantages to defeated politicians, is not a fortuitous development for American democracy.

REFERENCES

Abramson, Paul R., John H. Aldrich, and David W. Rohde. 1983. *Change and Continuity in the 1980 Elections*, rev. ed. Washington: CQ Press.

———. 1985. Progressive Ambition among United States Senators: 1972–1988. Presented at the annual meeting of the American Political Science Association, New Orleans, LA.

———. 1986. *Change and Continuity in the 1984 Elections*. Washington: CQ Press.

Aldrich, John H. 1980. *Before the Convention: Strategies and Choices in Presidential Nomination Campaigns*. Chicago: University of Chicago Press.

_____ . Forthcoming. Methods and Actors: The Relationship of Process to Candidates. In Alexander Heard and Michael Nelson, eds., *Perspectives on Presidential Selection*. Durham, NC: Duke University Press.

Aldrich, John H., and Forrest D. Nelson. 1984. *Linear Probability, Logit, and Probit Models*. Beverly Hills, CA: Sage.

Bartels, Larry M. 1986. Issue Voting Under Uncertainty: An Empirical Test. *American Journal of Political Science,* 30:709–28.

Black, Gordon S. 1972. A Theory of Political Ambition: Career Choices and the Role of Structural Incentives. *American Political Science Review,* 66:144–59.

Congressional Quarterly, Inc. 1985. *Guide to U.S. Elections,* 2d ed. Washington: CQ Press.

Coombs, Clyde, and Dean C. Pruitt. 1960. Components of Risk in Decision Making: Probability and Variance Preferences. *Journal of Experimental Psychology,* 60:265–77.

Crotty, William, and John S. Jackson III. 1985. *Presidential Primaries and Nominations*. Washington: CQ Press.

Enelow, James, and Melvin J. Hinich. 1981. A New Approach to Voter Uncertainty in the Downsian Spatial Model. *American Journal of Political Science,* 25:483–93.

Polsby, Nelson W. 1983. *The Consequences of Party Reform*. New York: Oxford University Press.

Ranney, Austin. 1975. *Curing the Mischiefs of Faction: Party Reform in America*. Berkeley: University of California Press.

Rohde, David W. 1979. Risk-Bearing and Progressive Ambition: The Case of Members of the United States House of Representatives. *American Journal of Political Science,* 23:1–26.

Schlesinger, Joseph A. 1966. *Ambition and Politics: Political Careers in the United States*. Chicago: Rand McNally.

Shepsle, Kenneth A. 1972. The Strategy of Ambiguity: Uncertainty and Electoral Competition. *American Political Science Review,* 66:555–68.

Wright, George. 1984. *Behavioral Decision Theory: An Introduction*. Beverly Hills, CA: Sage.

The 2000 Presidential Election in Historical Perspective

Robert S. Erikson

The year 2000 presidential election was a unique historical event. With a very close popular vote, the outcome depended on Florida, where, whichever way the votes were counted, the outcome was the closest state election in memory, closer

Robert S. Erikson is professor of political science at Columbia University and a fellow of the Institute of Social and Economic Theory and Research, Columbia University. He is the co-author of *American Public Opinion* (with Kent Tedin), recently published in its sixth edition. His book *The Macro Polity* (co-authored with Michael B. MacKuen and James A. Stimson) is in press.

than if Florida voters were deciding by flipping fair coins.[1] Although Al Gore won the national popular vote, George W. Bush eventually won the contested Electoral College verdict with help from the U.S. Supreme Court.

Continuing the *Political Science Quarterly* tradition of following each presidential election with an early analysis in the spring issue after the election[2] this article attempts to put the 2000 election in perspective—to understand the electorate's 2000 verdict within the context of what we know about elections past. Fortunately, several resources are available to help with this task. For a start, there are the Voter News Service (VNS) exit polls of voters as they left their polling places on election day. Both national and state exit polls, with their breakdowns of the vote by attitudes and social characteristics, became available to all on the web immediately after the election. Another data source available from the web is the trial-heat poll results reported throughout the campaign. From election to election, the density of trial-heat polling has grown to the point that during the heat of the 2000 campaign, multiple surveys were reported every day. Still another resource is the rich pool of surveys conducted at the state level. During the fall 2000 campaign, there were more daily state surveys reported than national surveys. When the results of state surveys are adjusted for state effects, they can be used to assess national trends.[3]

Drawing on History: Past Elections as Models for 2000

One way to understand an election is to frame it in terms of its historical analogies. For example, the story-line of 1996 ("popular incumbent wins reelection easily in a wave of national prosperity") followed the familiar script from 1956 (Eisenhower reelected) and 1984 (Reagan reelected) among others.[4] For 2000,

---

[1]To understand how close the election in Florida was, consider the likely outcome if the approximately six million voters all were flipping coins. Over multiple trials of six-million coin flips, the median lead for heads or tails would be about 600 votes.

[2]For 1989, 1993, and 1997, the late Everett Carll Ladd wrote these election postmortems. I am grateful for being asked to try to follow in his footsteps. See Everett Carll Ladd, "The 1988 Election: Continuity of the Post-New Deal System," *Political Science Quarterly* 104 (Spring 1989), 1–18; Everett Carll Ladd, "The 1992 Vote for President Clinton: Another Brittle Mandate?" 108 (Spring 1993): 1–28; Everett Carll Ladd, "1996 Vote: The 'No Majority' Realignment Continues," *Political Science Quarterly* 112 (Spring 1997): 1–28.

[3]This article goes to press in March 2001, only four months after the election and three months after the final determination of its outcome. Thus it runs the risk of being premature. Future analysts will have information about the election and its voters not yet available in the election's immediate aftermath. This will include the rich survey data of the 2000 National Election Study, which is normally disseminated about six months after the election. And the exit polls will reveal more of their riches after their individual level data are released a year after the election. The exit poll information available on the web immediately after the election consists of reported bivariate relationships between certain predictors (social characteristics, attitudes, policy preferences) and the vote. Valuable though this information is, it allows for no multivariate analysis. At their most rigorous, voting studies examine the effects of several predictors on the vote while controlling for each other. This is possible only with individual-level data.

[4]We could add 1964 and 1972 to this list of landslide reelections under economic prosperity. Those elections are more remembered for the ideological "extremism" of losers Barry Goldwater (1964) and George McGovern (1972) than for being conducted under the aura of prosperity.

there was no shortage of scripts from elections past. At various times during the campaign and the extended post-election period, events appeared to follow one story-line from the past, only to veer off and follow another. The surprise ending was a variant of Hays-Tilden in 1876—the disputed election decided by the vote along partisan lines of a special congressional commission. At the start of the campaign, the obvious model from the past was 1988, with Gore playing the role of George Bush senior from twelve years before. But as the campaign progressed, other models followed.

1988—Bush Defeats Dukakis   For several months, the 2000 campaign was following the script of 1988 to the letter. In both 1988 and 2000:

• The vice president of a popular term-limited president was the obvious early front-runner for his party's nomination.
• The vice president had difficulty shaking hints of personal involvement in scandals from the previous administration (Iran-contra for Reagan-Bush, fundraising problems for Clinton-Gore).
• The vice president showed surprising weakness in the early primary phase, even appearing to be beatable by his persistent rival (Robert Dole in 1988, Bill Bradley in 2000). However, aided by the stronger political machine, the vice president emerged victorious in the New Hampshire primary and glided to the nomination.
• Still politically weakened and overshadowed by the president, the vice president found himself behind in the preconvention polls against an out-party governor.
• At the out-party national convention, the delegates muffled their ideological leanings, and the candidate gave a good speech. The polls showed the out-party candidate zooming to a lead as large as 17 points. The thought was in the air that the out-party had a good shot at returning to power.
• At the in-party national convention, the smell of defeat was in the air. Now as the party's nominee, the vice president needed to give the speech of his life. He did and then some. Almost immediately, the polls showed the vice president surging to the lead.
• The election seemed on course to be a triumph of economic determinism where despite some apprehensions the nation was not about to reject the party in power during a time of prosperity.
• Consistent with economic prosperity and contrary to many predictions, the vice president's lead did not dissipate as a temporary convention bounce. The lead, albeit a small one, persisted to Labor Day and then held through most of September.

As of late September, the analogy with 1988 ended, as Gore lost his lead. It was replaced by a different script that had been competing for attention: 1960, John F. Kennedy beats Richard Nixon.

1960—Kennedy Beats Nixon   As a close election according to the polls, the 2000 election was repeatedly called the closest since 1960 (Kennedy-Nixon) by campaign commentators. But this was not the only analogy between 1960 and 2000. In each instance:

- The vice president, though very knowledgeable politically, was an awkward or stiff campaigner.
- The vice president was surprisingly reluctant to enlist the help of his popular president, preferring to campaign on his own merits rather than his administration's past accomplishments.
- The public credited the vice president with an edge in experience and competence.
- The opposition candidate was personable, but was held suspect for his lack of experience and being an unknown quantity.
- In the debates, the opposition candidate held his own with the vice president, an experienced debater, thereby gaining stature with the voters.
- Throughout the campaign, the opinion polls were so close that no observer could honestly forecast how the election was going to turn out.

Following the 1960 model, the 2000 contest was so close at the end as to be in dispute. In both elections, the vice president lost to the less experienced opponent, at least in the final electoral vote tally. Not to be forgotten though, is that Bush led almost all trial-heat polls during the month leading up to the election. This suggests another model from history.

1948—Truman Beats Dewey The 1948 model has a prominent place in twentieth-century electoral history. Against all odds, with the final polls showing a decisive Thomas Dewey lead, Harry Truman was reelected in the upset of the century. How close did 2000 come to be a replay?

- As the election approached, one candidate (Dewey, Bush) led in all or virtually all the polls.
- Fighting for his political survival, the underdog (Truman, Gore) ran a populist campaign, appealing to his Democratic base to get out the vote.
- The underdog's prospects were exacerbated by a pesky leftist third-party candidate (Henry Wallace, Ralph Nader) who threatened to drain votes away in key states.
- The favored out-party candidate posed not as a representative of his party's ideological wing but as a pragmatic large-state governor who gets results.
- As Election Day approached, the favorite candidate operated on the illusion of easy victory, saying little of substance. Bush continued to take most Sundays off, and by the Thursday before the election, he stopped all internal polling.
- A late campaign event (Dewey's impromptu complaint about his train engineer, revelations about Bush's earlier drunk driving arrest) may have caused some voters to shift, although it is hard to say.
- In the crucial analogy, undecided voters surged to the underdog, handing him the popular vote by a whisker. Although there were no last minute polls to record 1948's event, the 2000 surge is amply documented.

If it were not for the ballot difficulties in Florida, the repeat of 1948 might have been the final story of 2000. The difference was that in 1948 the pollsters were not in the field to record Truman's late advance, which generated a true upset. In

2000, one could not blame the pollsters, whose tallies converged toward a prediction of a dead heat. Still, since the popular vote "tie" did not arise until election eve, the magnitude of Gore's surge was not heavily publicized. Since most voters were aware only of Bush's narrow lead over the final month, the final Gore popular vote victory presented a surprise. In an ironic twist, a popular vote/electoral vote disparity was widely anticipated, but with the wrong electoral model.

1888—Harrison Beats Cleveland   The 1888 contest served as a model because it was the last time the popular vote winner lost in the Electoral College. As the 2000 contest approached, many observers (myself included) forecast that although Bush was ahead in the polls, Gore had a good chance to win the Electoral College. The reasoning was that in the supposed battleground states where the election was to be decided, Gore was running about even with Bush and maybe a bit ahead. It seemed quite possible that Gore could lose the popular vote and still win narrowly in the battleground states, doing to Bush what Harrison did to Cleveland.

Apart from Florida, Gore won most of the battleground states. Had the votes in Florida been counted to Gore's liking, Gore would have won the Electoral College and with a higher percent of the electoral votes than of the popular votes. Still, the fact that Bush, not Gore, benefited from the electoral vote, popular vote disparity deserves discussion.

1876—Hays Beats Tilden   The story ends with the replay of the now familiar Hays-Tilden postelection dispute. Neither the original 1876 outcome nor the 2000 replay require additional attention here.

The 2000 Election and Past Scripts: A Summary   To recapitulate the chapters of the 2000 story, we start with Bush ahead throughout the conventions, followed by a reversal with Gore holding a narrow lead (a la 1988). By late September the race tightened further but with Bush regaining the lead after the first presidential debate (echoes of 1960). Meanwhile, Gore was holding his own in the battleground states, suggesting a possible Electoral College upset (as in 1888). Finally, Gore surged at the last minute for an upset popular vote win (harking back to 1948) but of course only to lose in the all important Electoral College (see 1876).

Forecasting the 2000 Election: What Went Wrong?

Similar to the easily accessible scripts from past elections, political scientists have developed their own models as prisms for interpreting elections. By the 2000 election, political science forecasting models earned attention both within the profession and in the mass media. The forecasting models base their predictions from a statistical analysis of past election results, where the input for the predictions are various measures of economic prosperity plus aspects of political satisfaction, best summarized by the president's approval rating.[5] For 2000, the augers pointed clearly in one direction. With twelve years of prosperity and a president with a record level of popularity for his eighth year in office, all signs pointed to a Gore victory by a comfortable margin.

If elections can be predicted from the economy and other variables, what is the role of the campaign? While many studies focus on the influence of campaign events and strategies on voter decision making,[6] an increasingly dominant school of thought sees elections largely shaped by forces beyond the control of the candidates and their campaign managers. According to this view, campaigns matter, but only to steer the vote toward the proper equilibrium, which can be foreseen in advance.[7]

Simplified to the point of caricature, current theorizing about campaigns goes something like this: Elections are easily predictable from variables such as economic conditions and the popularity of the president (whether or not he can succeed himself). Therefore, what candidates do during the course of the campaign is largely irrelevant to their fate. Candidates try their best and do run the best campaigns they can. But this only cancels out their equal and opposite effects. It is not that election outcomes are automatic, but that the long campaign moves voters only by providing the information so that they become aware of their interests.

The argument behind this new conventional wisdom is a thoughtful one and based on certain truths. On the eve of the formal election campaign—around Labor Day—elections are as predictable from economic and political variables as they are from available polls. And polls typically show only mild movement over the fall campaign period from Labor Day to election day, when the campaign is full-blown. It is at least arguable that when the polls show change over the campaign, it is in the direction predicted by the forecasting models.

Throughout the 2000 campaign, the polls cooperated only part of the time to confirm the political science wisdom of a probable Gore victory. To a political scientist with faith in forecasting models, it would matter little in the days before the Democratic convention that Bush actually led in the polls. This faith was soon vindicated with force when Gore surged ahead after the conventions. The template of 1988 (when Bush Sr. similarly surged ahead) seemed so right. However, this faith was then put to the test when Bush Junior regained the lead, and it had to be seriously questioned after the election, even as the late surge to Gore and his narrow

[5]See, for instance, the consensus of very accurate forecasts of the 1996 presidential election in James Campbell and James Garand, eds., *Before the Vote: Forecasting American National Elections* (Thousand Hills, CA: Sage, 2000).

[6]Milton Lodge, Marco Steenbergen, and Shawn Brau, "The Responsive Voter: Campaign Information and the Dynamics of Candidate Evaluation," *American Political Science Review* 89 (May 1995): 309–26; Daron R. Shaw, "A Study of Campaign Even Effects from 1952 to 1992," *Journal of Politics* 61 (May 1999): 387–422.

[7]Andrew Gelman and Gary King, "Why Are American Presidential Election Polls so Variable When Votes Are so Predictable?" *British Journal of Political Science* 23 (October 1993): 409–519; Thomas Holbrook, *Do Campaigns Matter?* (Thousand Oaks, CA: Sage, 1996): James E. Campbell, *The American Campaign: U.S. Presidential Campaigns and the National Vote* (College Station: Texas A&M Press, 2000).

popular vote victory provided some reason to sustain belief. How could the model be wrong? What about the role of the campaign in deciding the outcome?

Let us see how badly the forecasting models got it wrong and then figure out why. At the American Political Science Association convention in early September 2000, a panel of nine political scientist forecasters made their predictions. They agreed in the expectation that Gore should win decisively if not in a landslide. Their only debates seemed minor, like exactly which way the economy should be gauged and whether other variables should be included in the equation.

Typical for these forecasting models is one presented by Christopher Wlezien and me. For 2000, the Wlezien-Erikson model predicted a Gore victory with about 55 percent of the two-party vote.[8] Since it explained 82 percent of the variance in the vote over the twelve elections 1952–1996, the prediction of a Gore victory might have seemed bankable. What went wrong?

To put the forecast in perspective, it is helpful to present the information graphically. Figure 1 displays the incumbent-party vote (as percent of the two-party vote) on the Y-axis and the model's predictions on the X-axis, using 1952–1996 data. The 2000 forecast is shown in bold. To aid understanding, it is also helpful to display the information after converting the incumbent-party vote and the prediction to the vote share of the two-party vote going to the Democratic party. This is done in Figure 2.

Figures 1 and 2 show that the vote prediction was off in 2000 by five percentage points. Interestingly, this is not even a record-setting amount of error, as the 1972 out-of-sample forecast was slightly larger. The difference was that nobody noticed much, if the usual predictors underestimated the size of Nixon's landslide win over McGovern in 1972 by six points. The five-point overestimate of Gore's showing in 2000 stood out, because even though the forecast got the popular vote winner correctly, it missed who would enter the White House.

The forecasters' excuse is that their predictions were not intended as precision estimates. With 82 percent of the variance explained by the model, obviously 18 percent is unexplained in the error term. With this degree of prediction and only twelve cases (past elections) to work with, the degree of precision is far from perfect. If one treats the statistical model presented in equation 1 seriously and applies it to the facts of 2000, Gore wins but only with odds of about 4 to 1. So we can assume that the models are correct up to a point, but that the things they do not measure contribute as well. What would they be? In other words, what other factors contributed to throw the 2000 prediction off course? There are at least four possible explanations.

[8]This forecasting equation is

$$IPV = 33.49 + 7.56PCIG + 0.30PA$$
$$(3.05)\ (2.71)\qquad (0.07)$$

where IPV = the incumbent presidential party's percent of the two-party vote. $PCIG$ = quarterly per capita income growth through quarter 15 of the administration, weighted so each quarter counts 1.25 times the previous one, and PA = the president's Gallup approval rating in quarter 15. Standard errors are in parentheses. Adjusted R squared = .82; N = 12.

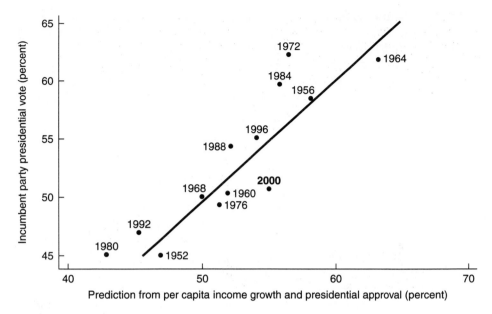

FIGURE 1
Incumbent Party Vote, Actual and Predicted, 1952–2000

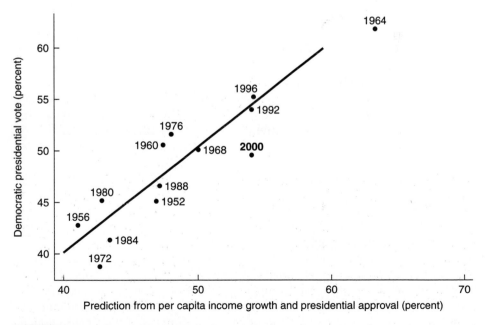

FIGURE 2
Democratic Presidential Vote, Actual and Predicted, 1952–2000

Explanation 1: Presidential Popularity Does Not Travel   One possible explanation is that when the president does not run again, perhaps neither the presidential approval rating nor economic record carry over fully to influence the reputation of the party's chosen successor. This idea is difficult to test empirically, not just because there are so few cases to work with statistically. Usually when the president does not run, the economy is in a middling position and the president's approval rating is mediocre. With no sitting president on the ballot, the result is usually a close election, which may or may not be due to the ambiguous forecasting cues from the past administration. Here, one historical example stands out. The 1952 election was conducted in an atmosphere of conflicting signals. Although outgoing President Truman was unpopular and the Korean War was continuing with no end in sight, the 1952 economy was surging. The electoral verdict was a landslide victory for the out-party's popular candidate, Dwight Eisenhower, former five-star general, the conqueror of Europe, who had promised "I will go to Korea." The voters saw the need for a change of parties after twenty years of Democratic rule. Thus, 1952 was one prior instance where a positive economy was no guide to the electoral verdict.

Explanation 2: Ralph Nader   A second explanation for model failure in 2000 is the Nader campaign. One aspect of this explanation is that while he won only 3 percent of the total vote, most of Nader's votes would have gone to Gore. Without Nader, one could image that 2000 would have provided Gore with at least a 51 percent vs. 49 percent win and a decisive Electoral College edge.

There is a second way that Nader may have helped Bush. This argument is more speculative. Possibly, fear of losing votes to Nader on the Left propelled Gore to campaign farther to the Left than he would have if Nader were not on the ballot. Had Gore campaigned explicitly as a centrist manager of economic prosperity (more or less Clinton's stance of 1996), he could have gained votes in the center of the spectrum but lost votes on the Left. Of course, it can only be an educated guess whether the left-leaning or the centrist strategy would have worked best for Gore once Nader was in the picture. But it is easy to imagine that whichever strategy could have garnered more votes, there would have been more votes for Gore without the Nader candidacy creating the dilemma.

Explanation 3: Bad (Good) Campaigning   A third way of accounting for the mistaken forecasting models in 2000 is simply to refer to the forecast error as the residue of the campaign's effect on the outcome. Although it can be debated whether campaigns generally move voters toward or away from the equilibrium outcome where voters "should" produce, campaigns do affect election outcomes. In 2000, it would appear that the campaign moved voters away from the equilibrium outcome. Put more colloquially, perhaps Gore did not get the votes he deserved because he ran a bad campaign. The reader can fill in the blanks to complete this argument. Gore failed because he would not enlist Clinton and could not effectively claim credit for the accomplishments of the Clinton administration. (See explanation 1. . . .) Gore failed because he ran too far to the left. (See explanation 2. . . .) Or Gore failed because he simply was a bad candidate

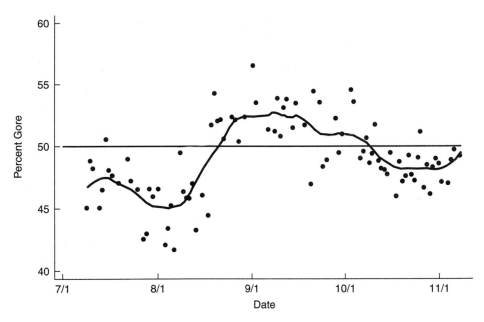

FIGURE 3
Daily Polls, July–November, 2000

who could not connect with voters. Importantly, we should keep in mind that to the extent candidates affect the outcome, both candidates are potentially responsible. One should be as willing to credit the quality of the Bush campaign as to blame Gore's mistakes and inadequacies as a campaigner.

The Polls and the 2000 Campaign

The wealth of poll data for 2000 makes it possible to trace the progress of the campaign on a virtually daily basis. Figure 3 presents a wide-angle view over a lengthy time span, revealing the progress of the trial-heat polls from July 2000 to election day. Each point represents the two-party vote estimated from the one or more polls with the particular date as the center of its polling period.[9]

Because the polls fluctuate more because of random sampling error than real trends, it is necessary to summarize the trajectory of the polls by some sort of moving average. This is done by using the well-established LOWESS procedure

---

[9]This graph is created from the polls reported at the website pollingreport.com. Each national presidential poll was coded by the middle date of its reported polling period. Where a poll was reported as conducted over an even number of dates, the later of the two middle dates was used. When, as often was the case, multiple polls were centered on a particular date, the date's observation represents the average—a poll of the polls. Where a particular poll series represented a daily tracking poll as a moving average over two, three, or four days, the daily samples were discounted by the number of polling dates. For example, the three-day Gallup tracking polls would each be counted, but each weighted by one-third.

(locally-weighted scatterplot smoothing) as devised by W. S. Cleveland.[10] The LOWESS line reveals clearly the presence of the major trends—Bush's early lead, Gore's postcampaign resurgence, the restoration of a slight Bush lead, and Gore's final comeback. This considerable movement contrasts with Clinton's stable lead in the 1996 race.[11]

Figure 4 zooms in for a close up picture of the fall horse-race, from 1 September to election day. We see the same features in close-up. With about 200 separate polls over the final campaign period of slightly more than two months, we have an average of over three fresh polls each day, representing multiple thousands of respondents.[12] But even with this density of polling, the moving picture of the horse race suffers from a certain degree of disappointing fuzziness. We see the major trends, but further details are elusive.

Ideally, the density of polling should be sufficiently thick—that is, with a large enough number of daily respondents—to allow short-term trends to become observable through the distortions caused by random sampling error. We would like, for example, to observe the effects of the series of presidential debates in October. But where can we find the data?

Starting with early September, it is possible to more than double the number of daily samples to an average of more than seven samples per day. This is accomplished by mingling state-level polls of the presidential race with national polls. Of course, to use the state polls for purposes of detecting national trends it is important to control for which state is being polled. Similarly, to compare state polls from different states, it is crucial to control for the dates the polls are conducted. To solve this problem, state and date effects were statistically estimated with each set of effects estimated while controlling for the other. This way, the date effects were estimated for each poll as if the poll were for the nation as a whole rather than the specific state.[13]

[10]See W. S. Cleveland, "Robust Locally Weighted Regression and Smoothing Scatterplots," *Journal of American Statistical Association* 74 (December 1979): 829–36. For political science discussions, see William G. Jacoby, *Statistical Graphics for Univariate and Bivariate Data* (Thousand Oaks, CA: Sage, 1997); and Nathaniel Beck and Simon Jackman, "Beyond Linearity by Default: Generalized Additive Models," *American Journal of Political Science* 42 (April 1998): 596–627. For an application of LOWESS to the 1996 campaign, see Robert S. Erikson and Christopher Wlezien, "Presidential Polls as a Time Series: The Case of 1996," *Public Opinion Quarterly* 63 (Summer 1999): 163–178.

[11]Christopher Wlezien and Robert Erikson, "Temporal Horizons and Presidential Elections," in *Before the Vote: Forecasting American National Elections,* eds. James Campbell and James Garand (Thousand Oaks, CA: Sage, 2000).

[12]The number 200 is approximate, with tracking polls weighted downward to reflect their rolling averages.

[13]The statistical technique employed is pooled cross-section time-series analysis using Least Squares Dummy Variable analysis (LSDV), pooling all surveys—national or state—conducted in September and October. Each date is a dummy variable. Similarly, each state is a dummy variable, with the base category being national polls. With the final date in October serving as the base category, the date coefficients represent differences from the horse-race on 31 October. Each state coefficient represents the difference between the particular state and the national polls. The key assumption underlying this use of state data to analyze national trends is that the movement of electoral preferences is uniform across states. For instance, if a candidate gains two points nationally, the assumption is that he gains the same two points in every state, or at least that national gains on average are reflected uniformly across states.

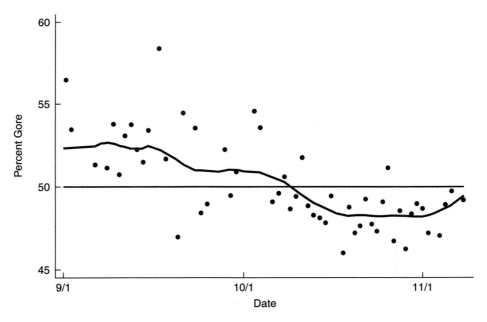

FIGURE 4
Daily Polls, September–November, 2000

The result of this exercise is Figure 5 which pools the estimates from national and state polls for September and October.[14] Like the two previous graphs, Figure 5 shows the daily observations of the poll of polls—this time including state-adjusted state polls—plus the LOWESS moving average. With the doubling of the number of daily samples, Figure 5 appears to show a series of real peaks and valleys over the fall campaign. We see Gore's rise through mid-September, the period when the Bush campaign had difficulty finding its bearings. We then see Gore's decline and Bush's gain in late September coinciding with Bush's appearance on the *Oprah* show and as Bush's attacks on Gore's "character" begin to take hold. We then see Gore rise again in early October (origin uncertain) only to plunge following the first of three presidential debates on 4 October. Just as the Bush momentum ceased, the second presidential debate on 13 October appeared to precipitate a further Gore plunge. The third, however on 24 October was followed by a Gore rally.

Attributing causes for small changes in the polls may be problematic. But whether we know the actual reasons, we can at least observe—or think we observe—periodic small changes in the nation's vote preferences over the campaign. Assuming these changes were real, whether they were only short-term blips or whether they represented a series of permanent shifts in the campaign landscape is a matter for further analysis.

[14]November data is not included for this figure.

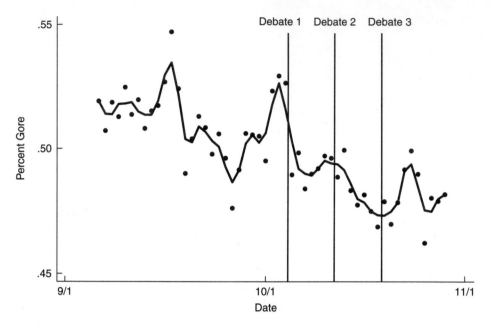

FIGURE 5
Daily National Preferences, Estimated from State and National Polls

The Final Days: The Gore Surge and the Electoral College Muddle

Around the end of October 2000, observers began to question whether the popular vote winner would win in the Electoral College. Based on the polls, one could foresee a narrow Bush win in the popular vote with a less certain outcome in the Electoral College. Thus, observers saw that conceivably Gore would win the Electoral College but without a popular vote mandate. This expectation turned out to be quite incorrect, as Gore won the popular vote while losing the Electoral College. How did this unexpected result come about?

Here I refer again to the multitude of state polls to draw a new lesson. Especially in the final weeks of a very close national election, state-level polling was particularly intense in the so-called battleground states where the presidential vote was expected to be the closest. Certainly with the Electoral College outcome being the election determiner, it made at least as much sense to follow the presidential trial heats in large battleground states such as Michigan, Pennsylvania, and Florida as it did to follow the national vote.

The late polls in the large battleground states told what appeared to be an amazing but largely hidden story. Even though Bush had the national lead, Gore led in most (but certainly not all) of the polls in the key battleground states. Given the wealth of information from state polls, especially in battleground states, it was possible to project expectations of the Electoral College outcome as a function of any possible movement of the popular vote. The one crucial assumption was that any swing of the national vote would be uniform across states. Given the polls through the end of October, although Bush led in the national popular vote by about four points, the projected Electoral College outcome was much closer. From the perspective of about 1 November, if Gore were to gain only a point or two in the popular vote, the projected Electoral College result would be a dead heat. (For further details, see the Appendix.) It follows that if Gore actually caught up to Bush in the popular vote, Gore would have been heavily favored to become the next president by virtue of a slight Electoral College advantage.

As it turned out, Gore surged to the popular vote lead but still lost the Electoral College. The question then shifts to why Bush had the Electoral College edge? The reason turned out to be that the surge to Gore was distributed unevenly across the states and in such a way that Gore gained the most in states where it did him the least good. Gore gained about 3 points in both safe-Gore states and safe-Bush states but only 1.3 points in the fifteen battleground states where the election was contested—only enough to set him roughly even in the Electoral College tally.

Figure 6 compares the states' actual vote outcomes with the projections from September and October state polls, assuming a uniform swing to a national tie in the popular vote, that is assuming all states move exactly the amount necessary to create a popular vote tie. The figure shows that predictions are good. Although not obvious to the naked eye, the safe states at the extremes were slightly more pro-Gore than predicted, while the battleground states in the middle were slightly less pro-Gore than predicted. The predicted and actual vote outcomes in the battleground states are shown in close-up in Figure 7. While the close fit overall is evidence that state polls are useful, the assumption of a uniform swing was wrong at the end of the campaign. Why?

We offer a speculative explanation for the concentration of Gore's gain in non-battleground states, which is interesting in its potential implications. Both campaigns focused their attention solely on the battleground states, leaving much of the nation with virtually no campaign ads or candidate appearances. By the final week, voters in the battleground states had enough information to figure out whom to vote for. Meanwhile, in the uncontested nonbattleground states, voters had little information. Many made up their minds at the last minute, generating late decisions for Gore.

For the electoral vote winner to be the popular vote loser is certainly a blemish on the Electoral College as an institution. The reason, however, is not that the Electoral College system was biased in favor of Bush or systematically biased in favor of Republicans generally.[15] The defect of the Electoral College is that as the

---

[15]The Electoral College has two sources of bias that cancel out. Small states gain extra representation from the fact that each state starts with two votes for each senator, and small states tend to vote Republican. Large states gain from their winner-take-all feature, and large states tend to vote Democratic. If the two votes per senator were taken away, the partisan advantage would go to the Democrats. If electoral votes were assigned proportionately rather than at-large, the advantage would go to the Republicans.

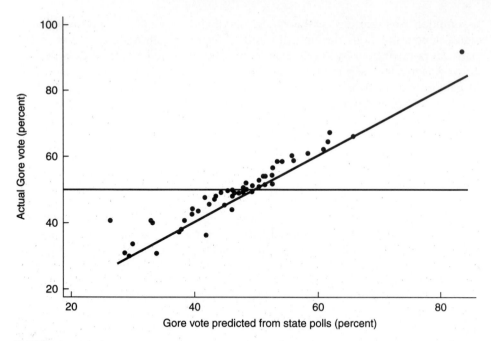

FIGURE 6
State's Gore Vote vs. Dead-Heat Predictions from State Polls

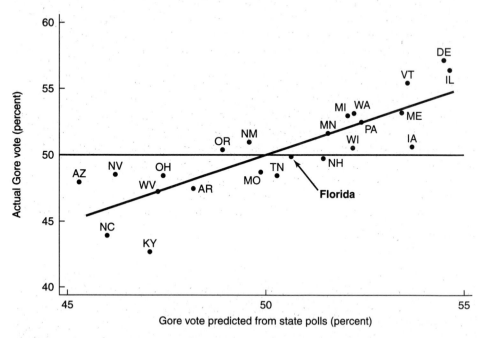

FIGURE 7
State's Gore Vote vs. Dead-Heat Predictions from State Polls, Battleground States Only

popular vote becomes extremely close, converging on a tie, the Electoral College outcome becomes increasingly arbitrary. But as the Florida story tells us, it is also true that as the vote gets close, the final count of the popular vote in the pivotal states becomes arbitrary as well. If a few hundred votes more were counted for Gore in Florida, the Electoral College and the popular vote would have been in their proper balance.

A Polarized Electorate

Ever since the concept was first refined by the authors of *The American Voter*,[16] election watchers have searched for signs of a new partisan realignment. The classic realignment occurred in the early 1930s, when the electorate changed from the decidedly Republican electorate of the 1920s to the Democratic electorate of the 1930s and thereafter. The Democratic majority stemming from the New Deal realignment was a coalition loosely comprised of the poor, Catholics and Jews, blacks, plus the Democrats' traditional base in the South. White southerners have since departed the coalition, but the other partisan divisions of rich vs. poor, Protestant vs. non-Protestant, and white vs. black have persisted in varying degrees up to the present.

Some degree of realignment has occurred, starting as early as the 1960s, as old economic issues of the New Deal were supplemented by partisan differences on civil rights and on social and cultural issues such as the emerging partisan divide on abortion. As new issues divided the parties, it became fashionable to claim that the old partisan cleavages from the New Deal era were eroding. A more accurate description of the change, however, was not that the old cleavages were disappearing but that they were supplemented by new sources of cleavage. Differences along lines of income, religion, and race persisted or even grew, while new partisan divisions sprouted, such as the famous "gender gap" between men and women. Party identification has become a stronger electoral force among the American electorate after a short period of seeming dealignment in the 1960s and 1970s. Ideological preferences have clearly become stronger determinants of peoples' partisan choices.[17]

These statements about stability and change are not new. They would have been valid if written a decade earlier. What is not so clear is whether the bases of peoples' presidential choices have shifted during the decade of the 1990s and into the beginning of the new millennium.

2000 Exit Polls   For a temporal perspective, let us examine the changes in the voting patterns over the twelve years from 1988, the year of George Bush's

---

[16]Angus Campbell, Philip E. Converse, Warren E. Miller, and Donald E. Stokes, *The American Voter* (New York: Wiley, 1960).

[17]For two recent accounts, see Larry Bartels, "Partisanship and Voting Behavior, 1952–1996," *American Journal of Political Science* 44 (January 2000): 35–50; and John H. Aldrich and Richard G. Niemi, "The Sixth Party System: Electoral Change 1952–1992" in Stephen C. Craig, ed., *Broken Contract? Changing Relationships between Americans and their Government* (Boulder, CO: Westview, 1996).

presidential victory, to 2000, the year of his son George W. Bush's presidential win. For a guide we have the exit polls conducted on the day of the election, in this case by ABC in 1988 and VNS in 2000. Table 1 shows some comparisons between these two election years. If we make allowances for the fact that Bush Sr. won by a 54-46 margin, while Bush Jr. actually lost the popular vote, the exit poll division shown for the two elections is remarkably similar. The forces that divided people into Bush and Michael Dukakis supporters were remarkably like those that divided people into Bush and Gore voters.

Consider party identification. In each election, Democrats had a slight 4 percentage point lead over Republicans in identification. In each contest, slightly over 90 percent of Republicans voted Republican, offsetting the more numerous Democrats with their slightly lower voter loyalty in the 80 percent + range. A similar stability is found for ideological identification. In 1988, about four in five liberals voted Democratic, while similarly about four in five conservatives voted Republican. We see these same ratios persisting in 2000. The one change in ideological preference was a slight decline in the conservatives' numerical advantage over liberals.

TABLE 1
STABILITY AND CHANGE IN THE ATTITUDINAL AND DEMOGRAPHIC BREAKDOWN
OF THE PRESIDENTIAL VOTE, 1988 TO 2000.

	1988			2000		
	%	Dukakis	Bush I	%	Gore	Bush II
Party Identification						
Democrats	42	82	15	39	86	11
Independents	18	42	45	27	45	47
Republicans	38	8	92	35	8	91
Ideological Identification						
Liberal	25	85	16	20	80	13
Moderate	52	54	45	50	52	44
Conservative	43	16	83	29	17	81
Race						
White	87	41	58	82	42	54
Black	8	88	10	10	90	8
Religion						
White Protestant	48	31	68	47	34	63
Catholic	28	51	49	26	49	47
Jewish	4	69	30	4	79	19
Income						
Top Third (88,>40K,00,>75K)	35	38	61	28	44	53
Middle Third	37	45	53	49	48	50
Bot. Third (88,<$20K,00<29K)	29	56	42	23	55	39
Gender						
Men	48	42	57	48	42	53
Women	52	49	50	52	54	43

Source: Compiled and extrapolated from 1988 ABC Exit Poll and 2000 VNS Exit Poll.

We also see from Table 1 that key demographic differences between the parties persisted with little change from 1988 to 2000. The income differential seemed to decline slightly, as high income voters were more attracted to Gore (despite his alleged populism) than to Dukakis in 1988. The Protestant vs. Catholic division declined very slightly, even as Jewish voters moved overwhelmingly to Gore. Meanwhile, the gender gap increased ever so slightly from 1988 to 2000 while the racial gap between blacks and whites also grew slightly—to its highest size ever.

Despite the stability of the electoral divisions across time, we can be on the lookout for new cleavages. For 2000, new cleavages emerged that had been given little notice a few years before. In 2000, the polls gave considerable treatment to divisions between married and unmarried voters, between churchgoers and those who attend few religious services, and between gun owners and nongun owners. Table 2 shows how these cleavages divided voters in the 2000 exit poll. For comparison, it also shows the 2000 electorate's divisions on religion, gender, and income. To facilitate comparison, each division is treated as a dichotomy.

What do we learn from this table? First, when expressed as dichotomies (women vs. men, Protestant vs. Catholic, rich vs. poor), we see that classical cleavages have about the same magnitudes. The gender gap (10 or 12 percent), the Protestant-Catholic gap (15 or 16 percent), and the rich half-poor half gaps (7 or 8 percent) are about the same size—a differential of about ten percentage points in voting.[18] These are visible differences, but not huge. Notably, the gender gap—unknown and unanticipated a quarter century ago—has caught up to the cleavages along income and religious lines in terms of general magnitude.

But what about the new cleavage along lines of marital status, religiosity, and guns? We see that by 2000, these cleavages have grown to as large if not larger than the traditional cleavages discussed. . . . By a point or so, the gap between married and unmarried voters (13 to 15 percent) is greater than the gender gap. The gap between frequent and infrequent churchgoers (16 percent) is virtually identical to that between Catholics and (white) Protestants. The division between gun owners and nongun owners is the largest of all, at 22 points! Without much notice, a new life-style division has developed. Analysts will be trying to sort out its meaning. Is it between traditionalists and modernists? A renewed cleavage between urban and rural?

Both the new and old social divisions are reflected in contemporary partisan divisions on the issues. Table 2 also shows how people on different sides of certain policy issues divide between Gore and Bush. On the classic issue of government involvement in the economy, we see proponents of big and little government lining up in the predictable directions, with pro-government types voting Democratic about 3 to 1 and antigovernment types voting Republican by almost the same 3 to 1 ratio. The 48 to 49 percent gap is clear evidence that the classic issue differences between the parties have by no means died.

---

[18]The gap sizes in parentheses are presented as variable, because the gaps in the Gore vote are not precisely the same as the gaps in the Bush vote.

TABLE 2
2000 EXIT POLLS—GORE VS. BUSH BY SELECTED VOTER CATEGORIZATIONS

	% of all Respondents	% Gore	% Bush
Income			
Under $50,000	47	52	44
$50,000 & Above	53	45	52
Protestant vs. Catholic			
White Protestant	47	34	63
Catholic	26	49	47
Gender			
Male	48	42	53
Female	52	54	43
Marital Status			
Married	65	44	53
Unmarried	35	57	38
Religious Attendance			
At least Once a Week	42	39	59
Less than Once a Week	56	55	43
Gun Ownership			
Gun in the House	48	36	61
No Gun	52	58	39
Role of Government			
Should do more to solve problems	43	74	23
Leave to businesses, individuals	53	25	71
Abortion Rights			
Should be legal all/most cases	56	65	32
Should be illegal all/most cases	40	27	71
Stricter Gun Legislation			
Support	60	62	34
Oppose	36	23	74

Source: Compiled and extrapolated from 2000 VNS Exit Poll.

Let us see how the big vs. little government division has been supplemented by new issues. Abortion is not a new issue, of course, but it is only within the past twenty years that it has become a partisan issue dividing people into Democrats and Republicans. We see from Table 2 that pro-choice vs. pro-life positions on abortion divide Americans in presidential choice with a 38 to 39 percent gap—almost as much as does the role of the government.

Finally, let us look at the gun control issue. In the 2000 campaign, the two major candidates offered only muted, nuanced distinctions on gun control. Still, with a 39 to 40 percent gap, the gun control issue divided Americans as much as did abortion rights. Further research must shed light on the source of this as a cultural division that increasingly separates rural and urban America.

2000 Exit Polls: A View from the States   The story told from the exit polls is of an increasingly polarized electorate. Although we have approached the limit of what we can learn about this phenomenon from bivariate relationships in the VNS national exit poll, we can exploit the fact that VNS also reports exit polls for the fifty states and the District of Columbia. Rather than repeat the survey analysis on a state-by-state basis, I aggregate state exit poll data on respondent party identification and respondent ideological identification to ascertain the mean party identification and mean ideological identification of each state's electorate.

The aggregate data from state exit polls give several signals of an increasingly polarized electorate. We know that two good predictors of individual votes are party identification and ideological identification. Yet as recently as 1988, state-level ideological identification and party identification were essentially uncorrelated ($r = -.08$): to know how Democratic or Republican a state's electorate was provided no clue regarding the state's ideological preferences and vice versa. By 2000 this has changed: the state-level correlation between the partisan and ideological indicators rose to $+.78$, meaning that they share 61 percent of the variance. Statistical evidence suggests that states are shifting their partisanship to reflect their ideology rather than the other way around.[19]

States have not only become more alike in their partisanship and ideology. In addition, the two indicators have become even stronger predictors of the states' presidential voting. In 1988, state ideology and state partisanship from state exit polls explained 50 percent of the variance in the two-part vote. By 2000, the explained variance reached 92 percent, with partisanship and ideology having equal weight in this vote equation.[20]

The strong relationship in 2000 between state partisanship and state ideology is shown in Figure 8. States closer to the bottom left corner have the partisan and ideological preferences typical of Republican voters; states closer to the upper right corner have the preferences indicative of Democratic voters. The graph in Figure 9 illustrates how strongly partisanship and ideology predict a state's presidential voting in 2000.[21] The state electorate's ideological and partisan preferences determine the state electorate's relative placement on the vote scale, with little left over for idiosyncratic variables to explain state voting.

---

[19]See Gerald C. Wright, John P. McIver, Robert S. Erikson, and David B. Hoolian, "Stability and Change in State Electorates, Carter through Clinton" (paper delivered at the meeting of the Midwest Political Science Association, Chicago, April, 2000).

[20]The exact OLS equation predicting the states' 2000 vote from exit poll partisanship and ideology is:

Percent Gore = 0.83 + 0.57 (percent Democrats) + 0.43 (percent Liberals)

where Percent Gore = Gore percent of the two-party vote in the state, percent Democrat = the Democratic percent of combined Republican and Democratic identifiers and percent Liberal = the liberal percent of combined liberal and conservative identifiers.

[21]See footnote 20 for exact equation.

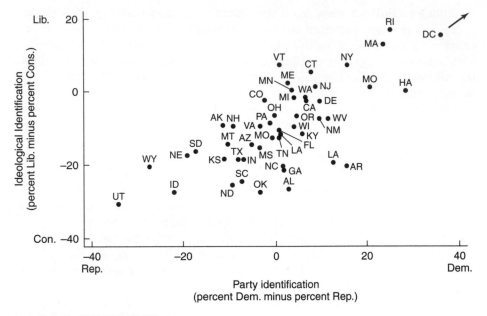

Data Source: VNS 2000 Exit Polls

Note: The following questions were asked in the exit polls.

No matter how you voted today, do you usually think of yourself as a:
Democrat
Republican
Independent

On most political matters, do you consider yourself:
Liberal
Moderate
Conservative

FIGURE 8
State Ideology by State Partisanship, 2000

Conclusions and Speculations

Can we conclude by speculating about the electoral future? Does their win in 2000 give the Republicans a leg up on 2004? Or does the closeness of 2000's verdict signal that the electorate will be in a mood to restore the Democrats in 2004? Despite the natural tendency to see each election as a harbinger of things to come, elections are remarkably difficult to forecast four years in advance. Knowing the vote in one election provides almost no leverage for forecasting the vote outcome in the next.

But, of course, we have more information than just the 2000 vote margin. The circumstances of this close election may provide the basis for a useful test of political science theories. One crucial fact is that although the electorate was evenly divided, power tilted to one party—the Republicans. This imbalance will

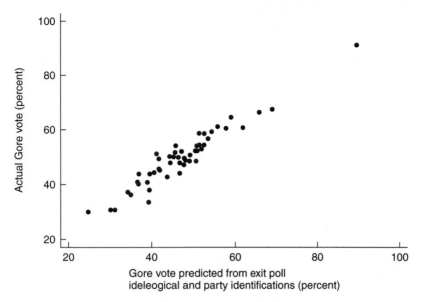

FIGURE 9
State Vote by Prediction from Exit Polls Ideology, Partisanship

provide a test of theories about the dynamic relationship between public opinion and policy. With power in the hands of the Republicans, will the electorate vote the Democrats back into control of Congress in 2002 as theories of ideological balancing behavior by voters would have us believe?[22] Will the Republican government follow through on its commitment to a conservative policy agenda even if polls show it to be unpopular? If they do, will it make the electorate turn more liberal and restore the Democrats to power? Or will the next presidential election be nothing more than a referendum on George W. Bush's presidential personality or on the state of the economy over which the president has little control?

The transfer of the presidency from Bill Clinton to George W. Bush is the seventh transfer of the presidency from one party to the other since World War II. Like 2000, most switches were close. But unlike 2000, one could find an underlying explanation for the electorate's change of leadership to provide the appearance of a policy mandate: fix the economy, end the war, or provide an ideological change of course. In five of the six previous transfers, the new president was reelected and reelected easily, as the economy improved, the war ended (or deescalated), and/or the nation was grateful for the ideological change. The exception was

[22]For one version of balance theory, see Alberto Alesina and Howard Rosenthal, *Partisan Politics, Divided Government, and the Economy* (Cambridge, UK: Cambridge University Press, 1995). Balance theory competes with the traditional thesis that withdrawn coattails contribute to the presidential party's midterm loss. There were no coattails in 2000 to withdraw in 2002.

Jimmy Carter's one-term presidency, a case that might provide still another historical model for 2000. When Carter got elected in 1976, the Vietnam war had ended, the economy was recovering, and the electorate was ideologically comfortable with the Ford presidency. Arguably, Carter was something of an accidental president, owing his victory to the Watergate scandals and to the fact that Ford was the first unelected president with no particular mandate other than to stay honest. On his watch, the world became more threatening, the economy went sour, and the electorate moved farther from the president ideologically—all contributing to the short four-year presidential tenure. We wait to see which path the Bush administration follows—the norm of eight or more years of power or the exception as when Reagan defeated Carter in 1980 after a single term.*

*I am greatly indebted to several coauthors on different projects. Without these joint intellectual enterprises, the current article could not have been written. The discussions of campaign dynamics and statistical models of elections borrow extensively from my collaboration with Christopher Wlezien. The discussions of the Electoral College and state-level campaign polls borrow from my collaboration with Karl Sigman. The discussion of rival statistical models borrows from joint work with Michael B. MacKuen and James A. Stimson. The discussion of state-level partisanship and ideology borrow from my collaboration with Gerald C. Wright, John P. McIver, and David Hoolian.

5

THE PERSON
IN THE OFFICE

The American Commonwealth

James Bryce

WHY GREAT MEN ARE NOT CHOSEN PRESIDENTS

Europeans often ask, and Americans do not always explain, how it happens that this great office, the greatest in the world, unless we except the Papacy, to which any man can rise by his own merits, is not more frequently filled by great and striking men? In America, which is beyond all other countries the country of a "career open to talents," a country, moreover, in which political life is unusually keen and political ambition widely diffused, it might be expected that the highest place would always be won by a man of brilliant gifts. But since the heroes of the Revolution died out with Jefferson and Adams and Madison some sixty years ago, no person except General Grant has reached the chair whose name would have been remembered had he not been President, and no President except Abraham Lincoln has displayed rare or striking qualities in the chair. Who now knows or cares to know anything about the personality of James K. Polk or Franklin Pierce? The only thing remarkable about them is that being so commonplace they should have climbed so high.

Several reasons may be suggested for the fact, which Americans are themselves the first to admit.

One is that the proportion of first-rate ability drawn into politics is smaller in America than in most European countries. This is a phenomenon whose causes must be elucidated later: in the meantime it is enough to say that in France and Italy, where half-revolutionary conditions have made public life exciting and accessible; in Germany, where an admirably-organized civil service cultivates and develops statecraft with unusual success; in England, where many persons of wealth and leisure seek to enter the political arena, while burning questions touch the interests of all classes and make men eager observers of the combatants, the total quantity of talent devoted to parliamentary or administrative work is far larger, relatively to the population, than in America, where much of the best ability, both for thought and for action, for planning and for executing, rushes into a field which is comparatively narrow in Europe, the business of developing the material resources of the country.

Another is that the methods and habits of Congress, and indeed of political life generally, seem to give fewer opportunities for personal distinction, fewer modes in which a man may commend himself to his countrymen by eminent capacity in thought, in speech, or in administration, than is the case in the free countries of Europe. This is a point to be explained in later chapters. I merely note here in passing what will there be dwelt on.

A third reason is that eminent men make more enemies, and give those enemies more assailable points, than obscure men do. They are therefore in so far less desirable candidates. It is true that the eminent man has also made more friends, that his name is more widely known, and may be greeted with louder cheers. Other things being equal, the famous man is preferable. But other things never are equal. The famous man has probably attacked some leaders in his own party, has supplanted others, has expressed his dislike to the crotchet of some active section, has perhaps committed errors which are capable of being magnified into offences. No man stands long before the public and bears a part in great affairs without giving openings to censorious criticism. Fiercer far than the light which beats upon a throne is the light which beats upon a presidential candidate, searching out all the recesses of his past life. Hence, when the choice lies between a brilliant man and a safe man, the safe man is preferred. Party feeling, strong enough to carry in on its back a man without conspicuous positive merits, is not always strong enough to procure forgiveness for a man with positive faults.

A European finds that this phenomenon needs in its turn to be explained, for in the free countries of Europe brilliancy, be it eloquence in speech, or some striking achievement in war or administration, or the power through whatever means of somehow impressing the popular imagination, is what makes a leader triumphant. Why should it be otherwise in America? Because in America party loyalty and party organization have been hitherto so perfect that any one put forward by the party will get the full party vote if his character is good and his "record," as they call it, unstained. The safe candidate may not draw in quite so many votes from the moderate men of the other side as the brilliant one would, but he will not lose nearly so many from his own ranks. Even those who admit his mediocrity will vote straight when the moment for voting comes. Besides, the ordinary American voter does not object to mediocrity. He has a lower conception of the qualities requisite to make a statesman than those who direct public opinion in Europe have. He likes his candidate to be sensible, vigorous, and, above all, what he calls "magnetic," and does not value, because he sees no need for, originality or profundity, a fine culture or a wide knowledge. Candidates are selected to be run for nomination by knots of persons who, however expert as party tacticians, are usually commonplace men; and the choice between those selected for nomination is made by a very large body, an assembly of over eight hundred delegates from the local party organizations over the country, who are certainly no better than ordinary citizens. How this process works will be seen more fully when I come to speak of those Nominating Conventions which are so notable a feature in American politics.

It must also be remembered that the merits of a President are one thing and those of a candidate another thing. An eminent American is reported to have said to friends who wished to put him forward, "Gentlemen, let there be no mistake. I should make a good President, but a very bad candidate." Now to a party it is more important that its nominee should be a good candidate than that he should turn out a good President. A nearer danger is a greater danger. As Saladin says in *The Talisman,* "A wild cat in a chamber is more dangerous than a lion in a distant desert." It will be a misfortune to the party, as well as to the country, if the candidate elected should prove a bad President. But it is a greater misfortune to the party that it should be beaten in the impending election, for the evil of losing national patronage will have come four years sooner. "B" (so reason the leaders), "who is one of our possible candidates, may be an abler man than A, who is the other. But we have a better chance of winning with A than with B, while X, the candidate of our opponents, is anyhow no better than A. We must therefore run A." This reasoning is all the more forcible because the previous career of the possible candidates has generally made it easier to say who will succeed as a candidate than who will succeed as a President; and because the wire-pullers with whom the choice rests are better judges of the former question than of the latter.

After all, too, and this is a point much less obvious to Europeans than to Americans, a President need not be a man of brilliant intellectual gifts. Englishmen, imagining him as something like their prime minister, assume that he ought to be a dazzling orator, able to sway legislatures or multitudes, possessed also of the constructive powers that can devise a great policy or frame a comprehensive piece of legislation. They forget that the President does not sit in Congress, that he ought not to address meetings, except on ornamental and (usually) nonpolitical occasions, that he cannot submit bills nor otherwise influence the action of the legislature. His main duties are to be prompt and firm in securing the due execution of the laws and maintaining the public peace, careful and upright in the choice of the executive officials of the country. Eloquence, whose value is apt to be overrated in all free countries, imagination, profundity of thought or extent of knowledge, are all in so far a gain to him that they make him "a bigger man," and help him to gain a greater influence over the nation, an influence which, if he be a true patriot, he may use for its good. But they are not necessary for the due discharge in ordinary times of the duties of his post. A man may lack them and yet make an excellent President. Four-fifths of his work is the same in kind as that which devolves on the chairman of a commercial company or the manager of a railway, the work of choosing good subordinates, seeing that they attend to their business, and taking a sound practical view of such administrative questions as require his decision. Firmness, common sense, and most of all, honesty, an honesty above all suspicion of personal interest, are the qualities which the country chiefly needs in its chief magistrate.

So far we have been considering personal merits. But in the selection of a candidate many considerations have to be regarded besides personal merits, whether they be the merits of a candidate, or of a possible President. The chief of these considerations is the amount of support which can be secured from different States or from different regions, or, as the Americans say, "sections," of the Union. State feeling and sectional feeling are powerful factors in a presidential election. The Northwest, including the States from Ohio to Dakota, is now the most populous region of the Union, and therefore counts for most in an election. It naturally conceives that its interests will be best protected by one who knows them from birth and residence. Hence *prima facie* a North-western man makes the best candidate. A large State casts a heavier vote in the election; and every State is of course more likely to be carried by one of its own children than by a stranger, because his fellow-citizens, while they feel honoured by the choice, gain also a substantial advantage, having a better prospect of such favours as the administration can bestow. Hence, *cœteris paribus,* a man from a large State is preferable as a candidate. New York casts thirty-six votes in the presidential election, Pennsylvania thirty, Ohio twenty-three, Illinois twenty-two, while Vermont and Rhode Island have but four, Delaware, Nevada, and Oregon only three votes each. It is therefore, parties being usually very evenly balanced, better worth while to have an inferior candidate from one of the larger States, who may carry the whole weight of his State with him, than a somewhat superior candidate from one of the smaller States, who will carry only three or four votes. The problem is further complicated by the fact that some States are already safe for one or other party, while others are doubtful. The North-western and New England States are most of them certain to go Republican: the Southern States are (at present) all of them certain to go Democratic. It is more important to gratify a doubtful State than one you have got already; and hence, *cœteris paribus,* a candidate from a doubtful State, such as New York or Indiana, is to be preferred.

Other minor disqualifying circumstances require less explanation. A Roman Catholic, or an avowed disbeliever in Christianity, would be an undesirable candidate. Since the close of the Civil War, any one who fought, especially if he fought with distinction, in the Northern army, has enjoyed great advantages, for the soldiers of that army, still numerous, rally to his name. The two elections of General Grant, who knew nothing of politics, and the fact that his influence survived the faults of his long administration, are evidence of the weight of this consideration. It influenced the selection both of Garfield and of his opponent Hancock. Similarly a person who fought in the Southern army would be a bad candidate, for he might alienate the North.

On a railway journey in the Far West in 1883 I fell in with two newspaper men from the State of Indiana, who were taking their holiday. The conversation turned on the next presidential election. They spoke hopefully of the chances for nomination by their party of an Indiana man, a comparatively obscure person, whose name I had never heard. I expressed some surprise that he should be thought of. They observed that he had done well in State politics, that there was nothing against him, that Indiana would work for him. "But," I rejoined, "ought you not to have a man of more commanding character. There is Senator A. Everybody tells me that he is the shrewdest and most experienced man in your party, and that he has a perfectly clean record. Why not run him?" "Why, yes," they answered, "that is all true. But you see he comes from a small State, and we have got that State already. Besides, he wasn't in the war. Our man was. Indiana's vote is worth having, and if our man is run, we can carry Indiana."

"Surely the race is not to the swift, nor the battle to the strong, neither yet bread to the wise, nor yet riches to men of understanding, nor yet favour to men of skill, but time and chance happeneth to them all."

These secondary considerations do not always prevail. Intellectual ability and force of character must influence the choice of a candidate, and their influence is sometimes decisive. They count for more when times are so critical that the need for a strong man is felt. Reformers declare that their weight will go on increasing as the disgust of good citizens with the methods of professional politicians increases. But for many generations past it is not the greatest men in the Roman Church that have been chosen Popes, nor the most brilliant men in the Anglican Church that have been appointed Archbishops of Canterbury.

Although several Presidents have survived their departure from office by many years, only one, John Quincy Adams, has played a part in politics after quitting the White House.[1] It may be that the ex-President has not been a great leader before his accession to office; it may be that he does not care to exert himself after he has held and dropped the great prize, and found (one may safely add) how little of a prize it is. Something, however, must also be ascribed to other features of the political system of the country. It is often hard to find a vacancy in the representation of a given State through which to re-enter Congress; it is disagreeable to recur to the arts by which seats are secured. Past greatness is rather an encumbrance than a help to resuming a political career. Exalted power, on which the unsleeping eye of hostile critics was fixed, has probably disclosed all a President's weaknesses, and has either forced him to make enemies by disobliging adherents, or exposed him to censure for subservience to party interests. He is regarded as having had his day; he belongs already to the past, and unless, like Grant, he is endeared to the people by the memory of some splendid service, he soon sinks into the crowd or avoids neglect by retirement. Possibly he may deserve to be forgotten; but more frequently he is a man of sufficient ability and character to make the experience he has gained valuable to the country, could it be retained in a place where he might turn it to account. They managed things better at Rome in the days of the republic, gathering into their Senate all the fame and experience, all the wisdom and skill, of those who had ruled and fought as consuls and prætors at home and abroad.

"What shall we do with our ex-Presidents?" is a question often put in America, but never yet answered. The position of a past chief magistrate is not a happy one. He has been a species of sovereign at home. He is received—General Grant was—with almost royal honours abroad. His private income may be insufficient

---

[1] J. Q. Adams was elected to the House of Representatives within three years from his presidency, and there became for seventeen years the fearless and formidable advocate of what may be called the national theory of the Constitution against the slaveholders.

to enable him to live in ease, yet he cannot without loss of dignity, the country's dignity as well as his own, go back to practice at the bar or become partner in a mercantile firm. If he tries to enter the Senate, it may happen that there is no seat vacant for his own State, or that the majority in the State legislature is against him. It has been suggested that he might be given a seat in that chamber as an extra member; but to this plan there is the objection that it would give to the State from which he comes a third senator, and thus put other States at a disadvantage. In any case, however, it would seem only right to bestow such a pension as would relieve him from the necessity of re-entering business or a profession.

We may now answer the question from which we started. Great men are not chosen Presidents, firstly, because great men are rare in politics; secondly, because the method of choice does not bring them to the top; thirdly, because they are not, in quiet times, absolutely needed. . . . I may observe that the Presidents, regarded historically, fall into three periods, the second inferior to the first, the third rather better than the second.

Down till the election of Andrew Jackson in 1828, all the Presidents had been statesmen in the European sense of the word, men of education, of administrative experience, of a certain largeness of view and dignity of character. All except the first two had served in the great office of secretary of state; all were well known to the nation from the part they had played. In the second period, from Jackson till the outbreak of the Civil War in 1861, the Presidents were either mere politicians, such as Van Buren, Polk, or Buchanan, or else successful soldiers,[2] such as Harrison or Taylor, whom their party found useful as figure-heads. They were intellectual pigmies beside the real leaders of that generation—Clay, Calhoun, and Webster. A new series begins with Lincoln in 1861. He and General Grant his successor, who cover sixteen years between them, belong to the history of the world. The other less distinguished Presidents of this period contrast favourably with the Polks and Pierces of the days before the war, but they are not, like the early Presidents, the first men of the country. If we compare the nineteen Presidents who have been elected to office since 1789 with the nineteen English prime ministers of the same hundred years, there are but six of the latter, and at least eight of the former whom history calls personally insignificant, while only Washington, Jefferson, Lincoln, and Grant can claim to belong to a front rank represented in the English list by seven or possibly eight names.[3] It would seem that the natural selection of the English parliamentary system, even as modified by the aristocratic habits of that country, has more tendency to bring the highest gifts to the highest place than the more artificial selection of America.

---

[2]Jackson himself was something of both politician and soldier, a strong character, but a narrow and uncultivated intellect.

[3]The American average would be further lowered were we to reckon in the four Vice-Presidents who have succeeded on the death of the President. Yet the English system does not always secure men personally eminent. Addington, Perceval, and Lord Goderich are no better than Tyler or Fillmore, which is saying little enough.

Rating the Presidents: Washington to Clinton

Arthur M. Schlesinger, Jr.

My father, the historian Arthur M. Schlesinger, started it all nearly half a century ago. In 1948 he asked fifty-five leading historians how they rated the American presidents. The results, published in *Life* magazine just before Harry Truman confounded the prophets and won reelection, excited much interest and also much controversy. In 1962 the *New York Times Magazine* prevailed upon my father to repeat the poll. Again much interest and much controversy.

In 1996 the *New York Times Magazine* asked a less eminent historian, Arthur M. Schlesinger, Jr., to replicate his father's poll. The results appeared in the issue of 15 December 1996 under the title "The Ultimate Approval Rating." Space limitations required the omission of much historical and methodological commentary. With the kind permission of the *New York Times Magazine,* here is the more complete report.

The Schlesinger polls asked historians to place each president (omitting William Henry Harrison and James A. Garfield because they died so soon after taking office) in one of five categories: Great, Near Great, Average, Below Average, and Failure.[1] The standard was not lifetime achievement but performance in the White House. As to how presidential performance was to be judged, the scholars were left to decide for themselves. It was assumed that historians would recognize greatness—or failure—when they saw it, as Justice Potter Stewart once proposed to recognize pornography.

Presidents might well have wondered (and some did): who are historians to arrogate to themselves the judging of presidential performance? Dwight D. Eisenhower, who did badly in the Schlesinger 1962 poll, accused the scholars of equating "an individual's strength of dedication with oratorical bombast; determination, with public repetition of a catchy phrase; achievement, with the exaggerated use of the vertical pronoun."[2] "History will treat me fairly," said Richard M. Nixon, drawing an odd distinction. "Historians probably won't. They are mostly on the left."[3]

Other presidents felt that people who had never been president could not possibly appreciate what presidents go through. "Trials and encouragement come to each president," wrote Calvin Coolidge in an unwonted lyrical outburst. "It is

---

[1]Mrs. Leonard Lyons, after reading the *New York Times Magazine* article, wrote the author, not without justice: "Some categories other than yours come to mind: Dope, Lucky Stiff, Bumbler, etc.—which makes me realize how resilient Americans are if they can survive such as these."

[2]Dwight D. Eisenhower to James C. Hagerty, 18 October 1966 in R. Gordon Hoxie, *Command Decision and the Presidency* (New York: Reader's Digest Press, 1977), 245.

[3]Richard M. Nixon on *Meet the Press,* 10 April 1988 (responding to a question by John Chancellor).

Arthur M. Schlesinger, Jr. recently retired as Schweitzer Professor in the Humanities at the City University of New York Graduate Center. He has written books on the presidential administrations of Andrew Jackson, Franklin D. Roosevelt, and John F. Kennedy as well as an overall analysis called *The Imperial Presidency.* He also served as special assistant to President Kennedy.

impossible to explain them. Even after passing through the presidential office, it still remains a great mystery. . . . Like the glory of a morning sunrise, it can only be experienced—it cannot be told."[4]

John F. Kennedy too came to doubt whether the quality of the presidential experience could be understood by those who had not shared it. My father sent his 1962 questionnaire to the historian who had written *Profiles in Courage* and *A Nation of Immigrants*. Kennedy started to fill it out; then changed his mind. "A year ago," he wrote my father, "I would have responded with confidence . . . but now I am not so sure. After being in the office for a year, I feel that a good deal more study is required to make my judgment sufficiently informed. There is a tendency to mark the obvious names. I would like to subject those not so well known to a long scrutiny after I have left this office."

He said to me later, "How the hell can you tell? Only the president himself can know what his real pressures and real alternatives are. If you don't know that, how can you judge performance?" Some of his greatest predecessors, he went on, were given credit for doing things when they could have done nothing else; only detailed inquiry could disclose what difference a president made by his individual contribution. War, he observed, made it easier for a president to achieve greatness. But would Abraham Lincoln have been judged so great a president if he had had to face the almost insoluble problem of Reconstruction?

For all his skepticism, Kennedy read the results of my father's 1962 poll with fascination. He was greatly pleased that Truman was voted a Near Great, nor was he displeased that Eisenhower came in twenty-second, near the bottom of the Averages. Later, jokingly or half-jokingly, he blamed Eisenhower's vigorous entry into the 1962 congressional elections on the historians. "It's all your father's poll," he said. "Eisenhower has been going along for years, basking in the glow of applause he has always had. Then he saw that poll and realized how he stood before the cold eye of history—way below Truman; even below Hoover. Now he's mad to save his reputation."[5]

Kennedy was surprised that the historians voted Woodrow Wilson a Great, placing him number four after Abraham Lincoln, George Washington, and Franklin D. Roosevelt, while ranking Andrew Jackson only number six and a Near Great. Though a fine speaker and writer, Wilson, in Kennedy's view, had failed in a number of cherished objectives. Why did professors admire him so much? (I suggested that he was, after all, the only professor to make the White House.)

Kennedy was surprised too by Theodore Roosevelt's ranking—number seven and a Near Great; TR had really got very little significant legislation through Congress. Why should Wilson and TR rate ahead of achievers like James K. Polk (number eight) or Truman (number nine)? For Kennedy, the measure of presidential success was evidently concrete accomplishment. Presidents who raised the consciousness of the nation without achieving their specific objectives ought,

[4]Calvin Coolidge, *Autobiography* (New York: Cosmopolitan Book Corp., 1929), 234, 194.
[5]The Kennedy quotes are from Arthur M. Schlesinger, Jr., *A Thousand Days: John F. Kennedy in the White House* (Boston: Houghton Mifflin, 1965), 674–675.

he seemed to think, to rate below those, like Polk and Truman, who achieved their objectives even if they did little to inspire or illuminate the nation. Ironically, historians feel that Kennedy himself comes off better when measured by the TR-Wilson rather than by the Polk-Truman standard.

There is force in the argument that only presidents can really understand the presidency. But by the Coolidge-Kennedy doctrine only presidents would have the qualifications to rate presidents. Alas, few presidents have claimed that right. Indeed, the only presidential list I know comes, not surprisingly, from that plain-speaking history buff Harry Truman. In 1953 he named his eight best Presidents—in chronological order, Washington, Jefferson, Jackson, Polk, Lincoln, Grover Cleveland, Wilson, and FDR—and his eight worst—Zachary Taylor, Franklin Pierce, James Buchanan, Ulysses S. Grant, Benjamin Harrison, Warren G. Harding, Coolidge, and Eisenhower.[6]

Meanwhile, scholars continued to play the rating game. Some felt that ratings on the Schlesinger basis were unduly impressionistic and subjective. Quantitative history was coming into vogue. Also political scientists, with their faith in typologies and models, were joining the fun. Would not the results be more "scientific" if presidents were given numerical scores against stated criteria? Then feed the figures into the computer.

So further polls were undertaken in the 1970s and 1980s with more pretentious methodologies. Some poll takers used only a few yardsticks: success in attaining objectives, for example; the relationship of objectives to the general welfare; the quality of political leadership; personal trustworthiness and integrity; impact on history. Others multiplied yardsticks. Thomas A. Bailey of Stanford, who regarded the Schlesinger polls as a Harvard-eastern elitist-Democratic plot, came up with no less than forty-three.

But the yardsticks were mostly too general to warrant mathematical precision or to escape subjective judgment. Their proliferation only produced lengthy and intimidating questionnaires. And, to judge by the results, the refinement of standards made little difference. However simple or complex the method, the final ratings turned out to be much the same. Even Bailey's own rankings were remarkably similar to the Schlesinger polls.

There have been nine Greats and Near Greats in nearly all the scholarly reckonings. Lincoln, Washington and F. D. Roosevelt are always at the top, followed always, though in varying order, by Jefferson, Jackson, Polk, Theodore Roosevelt, Wilson, and Truman. Occasionally John Adams, Cleveland, and Eisenhower join the top nine. The Failures have always been Grant and Harding, with Buchanan, Pierce, Fillmore, Taylor, and Coolidge always near the bottom.

The scholars' lists not seldom provoke popular as well as presidential indignation. For a long time FDR's top standing enraged many who had opposed his New Deal. "To rank him with Lincoln and Washington," the Detroit editor Malcolm Bingay wrote in 1948 about the first Schlesinger poll, "hits me as historical

---

[6]Harry S. Truman, "The Eight Best Presidents, the Eight Worst Presidents and Why," *Parade,* 3 April 1988.

sacrilege."[7] As late as 1982, Robert K. Murray of Penn State, a leading scholar of presidential ratings, polled 846 historians. When they placed Franklin Roosevelt slightly ahead of George Washington (though still behind Lincoln), Murray was deluged with angry letters, "many being from the fanatic right," he wrote me, "whose fulminations know no bounds."[8] People today forget that Roosevelt was the most hated as well as the best loved president of the twentieth century. But now that even Newt Gingrich pronounces FDR the greatest president of the century, conservatives accept FDR at the top with stoic calm.

The choice of best and worst presidents has remained relatively stable through the years. There is much more fluctuation in between. Some presidents—particularly J. Q. Adams, Buchanan, Andrew Johnson, and Cleveland—have declined in the later polls, but the most striking change has been the steady rise of Eisenhower from twenty-second place in the Schlesinger 1962 poll to twelfth in David Porter's 1981 poll, to eleventh in the poll taken by Robert Murray and Tim Blessing in 1982, to ninth in Steve Neal's *Chicago Tribune* poll the same year and ninth again in Neal's *Chicago Sun-Times* poll in 1996. Had he lived long enough, Eisenhower might have raged less over the verdicts of scholars.

Several factors account for Eisenhower's ascent. The opening of his papers showed that the mask of genial affability Ike wore in the White House concealed an astute, crafty, confident, and purposeful leader. As Nixon typically put it, Eisenhower was "a far more complex and devious man than most people realized, and in the best sense of those words."[9] Moreover, the FDR model and the yardsticks in earlier polls contained a bias in favor of an activist presidency. After Vietnam and Watergate showed that presidential activism could go too far, Eisenhower appeared in a better light. The peace and harmony sentimentally recollected from Ozzie-and-Harriet days shone well against the turbulence of the 1960s and 1970s. The more his successors got into trouble, the better Eisenhower looked. Presidents sometimes do more for the reputations of their predecessors than they do for their own.

Over the years it has been periodically suggested that I replicate my father's polls. But the difficulty of making overall judgments about some of the presidents since Eisenhower stumped me—in the cases of Kennedy and Gerald Ford, because of the brevity of their time in office; in the cases of Lyndon Johnson, Nixon, and George Bush, because their foreign and domestic records are so discordant. Scholars, for example, might be inclined to rate Johnson higher in domestic than in foreign affairs and do the reverse for Nixon and Bush. And the most recent presidents always seem more controversial and harder to classify. Still the passage of time permits appraisals to crystallize. So in 1996 *New York Times Magazine* took a new poll.

The question of disjunction still nags. "I find three cases," Walter Dean Burnham said, "which one could describe as having dichotomous or schizoid profiles.

[7]Malcolm Bingay, "Chides Historian for Hasty Appraisal of FDR As 'Great,'" *Akron Beacon-Journal,* 4 November 1948.

[8]Robert K. Murray to Arthur Schlesinger, Jr., 15 March 1983.

[9]Richard M. Nixon, *Six Crises* (Garden City, NY: Doubleday, 1962; Warner paperback, 1979), 189.

On some very important dimensions, both Wilson and L. B. Johnson were out-right failures in my view; while on others they rank very high indeed. Similarly with Nixon." Alan Brinkley said: "There are presidents who could be considered *both* failures *and* great or near great (for example, Wilson, Johnson, Nixon)." James MacGregor Burns observed of Nixon, "How can one evaluate such an idiosyncratic president, so brilliant and so morally lacking? . . . so I guess to average out he would be average."

Another source of confusion comes from the reluctance of some respondents to confine their judgments to White House performance. Several presidents—James Madison, J. Q. Adams, Grant, Herbert Hoover, Jimmy Carter—had pre- or post-presidential careers of more distinction than their presidencies; and this evidently affected some of the ratings.

Yet the 1996 poll still shows a high degree of continuing scholarly consensus. In nearly all the polls since 1948, the same nine men top the list. Lincoln, with a unanimous Great vote, comes in first in 1996. Washington and FDR, as usual, are next; each had one Near Great vote. The big three are followed, as usual, by the Near Greats—Jefferson, Jackson, Theodore Roosevelt, Wilson, Truman, and Polk. Steve Neal's 1996 poll, with five yardsticks (political leadership, foreign policy, domestic policy, character, impact on history) and fifty-eight respondents, came up with the same nine men, plus Eisenhower and Ronald Reagan, who edged out Polk.

Polk's high ranking is always a puzzle for laymen. "Of all our array of presidents," James Thurber once imprudently wrote, "there was none less memorable than James K. Polk."[10] But Polk at 49 was the youngest man up to that time, and the only Speaker of the House of Representatives ever, to make the White House. He specified his objectives early on—to reduce the tariff, establish the independent treasury system, settle the Oregon boundary question, and acquire California—and worked efficiently and relentlessly to achieve them. His objectives have been criticized but not his ability. Besides, he kept the most complete of presidential diaries, which endears him to scholars.

The next batch, the High Averages, are led in the 1996 Schlesinger poll by Eisenhower, whose one Great vote and ten Near Greats are outweighed by a host of Averages. The same fate befalls John Adams with ten Near Greats and Kennedy with nine. Lyndon Johnson receives fifteen Near Greats from scholars who seem to have forgotten about Vietnam, but low ratings and two Failures awarded by those who remember Vietnam bring his score down below Kennedy's. Monroe and McKinley complete the High Averages.

Most presidents fall into the Average class. Recent presidents, too close for historical perspective, are likely to rise or fall in polls to come. Carter has one Near Great and two Failures, with the rest of his votes in between. Some admire his accomplishment in putting human rights on the world's agenda; others deplore his political ineptitude and the absence of any clear direction in his handling of domestic affairs.

[10]James Thurber, *Let Your Mind Alone!* (New York: Harper, 1937), 141.

Reagan, on the other hand, has seven Near Great votes, including some from liberal scholars impressed by his success in restoring the prestige of the presidency, in negotiating the last phases of the cold war, and in imposing his priorities on the country. But he also receives nine Below Averages and four Failures from those who consider his priorities—his attack on government as the root of all evil and his tax reductions that increased disparities between rich and poor while tripling the national debt—a disaster for the republic.

His score averages out a shade below that of George Bush, who receives no Near Greats but more Averages than Reagan and only one Failure. Bush's skill in putting together the coalition that won the Gulf War outweighs for many his seeming lack of purpose in domestic policy. Some respondents thought it premature to judge Clinton, but two vote him Near Great and two more a Failure, and he ends up Average.

Some exception has been taken to Reagan's rating as number twenty-five, placing him between Bush and Arthur and below Clinton. According to the March-April 1997 *Policy Review,* this "low assessment" was "the most astonishing part of Schlesinger's poll." The Reagan rating, the magazine continued, "invites suspicion that participants were selected as much for the conclusions they were likely to reach as for their scholarly credentials."[11] *Policy Review* then picked its own panel, including William F. Buckley, Jr., Henry Kissinger, Jeane Kirkpatrick, George H. Nash, Joshua Muravchik, Michael Barone, and others—a group that invites the same suspicion roused in *Policy Review* by my panel—and they joined seven of my respondents in putting Reagan in the Near Great category. As for the suggestion of bias in the selection of my thirty-two, William J. Ridings, Jr., and Stuart B. McIver polled *seven hundred and nineteen* historians and political scientists for their 1997 book *Rating the Presidents,* published some months after the *New York Times Magazine* poll. The Ridings-McIver poll ranked Reagan even lower, number twenty-six, placing him between Hayes and Ford and below both Bush and Clinton.[12]

The list of Failures shows a slight shift from past polls. Harding and Grant are, as usual, favorite Failures. Do they really deserve it? They are marked down because of the scandal and corruption that disgraced their administrations. But they were careless and negligent rather than villainous. Their sin was excessive loyalty to crooked friends. "Harding was not a bad man," as Theodore Roosevelt's daughter, Alice Roosevelt Longworth, put it. "He was just a slob."[13] The president who commuted the prison sentence of the Socialist leader Eugene V. Debs after Wilson refused to do so hardly merits the bottom slot as the worst of all presidents. Scandal and corruption are indefensible, but they may injure the general welfare less than misconceived policies.

[11]Alvin S. Felzenberg, "'There You Go Again': Liberal Historians and the *New York Times* Deny Ronald Reagan His Due," *Policy Review,* March-April, 1997.

[12]William J. Ridings, Jr. and Stuart B. McIver, *Rating the Presidents: From the Great and Honorable to the Dishonest and Incompetent* (New York: Citadel Press, 1997).

[13]Alice Roosevelt Longworth, *Crowded Hours* (New York: Scribner's, 1933), 324–25.

In the new poll the ineffectual Franklin Pierce and the rigidly dogmatic Herbert Hoover tie with Grant as the best among the Failures. Next down the list comes Nixon. Most respondents, while recognizing Nixon's intelligence and drive, resolve the "schizoid profile" by concluding that his impressive ability is negated by his rather more impressive offenses against the Constitution. It is perhaps hard to demonstrate that the only president forced to resign from the office was not a Failure.

The nation's belated awakening to racial injustice explains why two presidents receive more Failure votes this time than in earlier polls: James Buchanan, whose irresolution encouraged the secession of the Confederate states; and Andrew Johnson, who, while a Unionist, was a stout believer in white supremacy. It seems reasonable to suggest that Buchanan, Andrew Johnson, Hoover, and Nixon damaged the republic a good deal more than did the hapless Grant and the feckless Harding.

Nine men, we have seen, have led the list from the first Schlesinger poll of historians nearly half a century ago. What do Washington, Jefferson, Jackson, Polk, Lincoln, Theodore Roosevelt, Wilson, Franklin Roosevelt, and Truman have in common? What do they, and Eisenhower too, who arrived too late for the 1948 poll, tell us about the qualities necessary for success in the White House?

Well, half were over six feet tall. The exceptions were Polk (5' 8"), Theodore Roosevelt (5' 10"), Wilson (5' 11"), Truman (5' 9"), and Eisenhower (5' 10½"). On the other hand, James Monroe, John Tyler, Buchanan, Chester A. Arthur, Taft, Harding, Kennedy, Lyndon Johnson, Gerald Ford, Reagan, Bush, and Clinton were also six feet or more; so height by itself is no guarantee of greatness in the White House. Nor is education. Nearly half the prize group—Washington, Jackson, Lincoln, and Truman—never attended college. As for age, the average age of the nine at inauguration or succession was 54 years; so youth is a comparative advantage.

Height and age are minor considerations. Intelligence helps, though Reagan—with his seven Near Greats—shows that an influential president need not have much. Maturity? The British ambassador called Theodore Roosevelt an arrested 11-year-old. Unflinching honesty? Deviousness is a presidential characteristic not confined to Eisenhower. Loyalty? This can be a presidential defect: remember Grant and Harding. Private virtues do not guarantee public effectiveness.

More to the point is the test proposed 125 years ago by our most brilliant historian, Henry Adams. The American president, he wrote, "resembles the commander of a ship at sea. He must have a helm to grasp, a course to steer, a port to seek."[14] The Constitution offers every president a helm, but the course and the port constitute the first requirement for presidential greatness. Great presidents possess, or are possessed by, a vision of an ideal America. Their passion is to make sure the ship of state sails on the right course.

If that course is indeed right, it is because they have an instinct for the dynamics of history. "A statesman may be determined and tenacious," de Gaulle once

---

[14]Henry Adams, "The Session, 1869–1870" in G. E. Hochfield, ed., *The Great Secession Winter of 1860–61 and Other Essays* (New York: Sagamore Press, 1958), 197.

observed, ". . . but, if he does not understand the character of his time, he will fail."[15] Great Presidents have a deep connection with the needs, anxieties, dreams of the people. "I do not believe," said Wilson, "that any man can lead who does not act . . . under the impulse of a profound sympathy with those whom he leads—a sympathy which is insight—an insight which is of the heart rather than of the intellect."[16]

"All our great presidents," said Franklin D. Roosevelt, "were leaders of thought at times when certain ideas in the life of the nation had to be clarified." So Washington embodied the idea of federal union, Jefferson and Jackson the idea of democracy, Lincoln union and freedom, Cleveland rugged honesty. Theodore Roosevelt and Wilson, said FDR, were both "moral leaders, each in his own way and his own time, who used the presidency as a pulpit."[17]

To succeed, presidents must have a port to seek and must convince Congress and the electorate of the rightness of their course. Politics in a democracy is ultimately an educational process, an adventure in persuasion and consent. Every president stands in Theodore Roosevelt's bully pulpit. National crisis widens his range of options but does not automatically make a man great. The crisis of rebellion did not spur Buchanan to leadership, nor did the crisis of depression turn Hoover into a bold and imaginative president. Their inadequacies in the face of crisis allowed Lincoln and the second Roosevelt to show the difference that individuals can make to history.

Of national crises, war is the most fateful, and all the top ten save Jefferson were involved in war either before or during their presidencies. As Robert Higgs has noted, five (Polk, Lincoln, Wilson, Franklin Roosevelt, and Truman) were commanders-in-chief when the republic was at war, and four more (Washington, Jackson, Theodore Roosevelt, and Eisenhower) made pre-presidential reputations on the battlefield. Military metaphors even accompanied nonmilitary crises. In summoning the nation to battle against the Great Depression, Franklin Roosevelt called on Americans to "move as a trained and loyal army" and asked Congress for "broad Executive power to wage a war against the emergency, as great as the power that would be given to me if we were in fact invaded by a foreign foe."[18]

Crisis helps those who can rise to it, and the association of war with presidential greatness has its ominous aspect. Still, two of the immortals, it should be noted, made their mark without benefit of first-order crisis. Jackson and Theodore Roosevelt forced the nation through sheer power of personality to recognize incipient problems—Jackson in vindicating the national authority against the state of South Carolina and against the Second Bank of the United States; the first Roosevelt in vindicating the national authority against the great corporations and against raids on the people's natural resources. As the historian Elting Morison

---

[15]Charles de Gaulle, *The Edge of the Sword* (New York: Criterion, 1960), 81.
[16]Woodrow Wilson, *Leaders of Men,* T. H. Vail Motter, ed. (Princeton, NJ: Princeton University Press, 1952), 53–54.
[17]Anne O'Hare McCormick, "Roosevelt's View of the Big Job," *New York Times Magazine,* 11 September 1932.
[18]Franklin D. Roosevelt, First Inaugural Address.

admirably described this quality of noncrisis leadership: "Theodore Roosevelt could get the attention of his fellow citizens and make them think. He knew how to put the hard questions a little before they became obvious to others; how to make the search for sensible answers exciting; how to startle the country into informing debate; and how to move people into their thinking beyond short-run self-interest toward some longer view of the general welfare."[19]

We hear much these days about the virtues of the middle of the road. But not one of the top nine can be described as a middle-roader. Middle-roading may be fine for campaigning, but it is a sure road to mediocrity in governing. The succession of middle-roaders after the Civil War inspired James Bryce to write the notorious chapter in *The American Commonwealth* entitled "Why Great Men Are Not Chosen President."[20] The middle of the road is not the vital center: it is the dead center.

The Greats and Near Greats all recognized, in the aphorism of Pierre Mendes-France, that "to govern is to choose." They all took risks in pursuit of their ideals. They all provoked intense controversy. They all, except Washington, divided the nation before reuniting it on a new level of national understanding.

Every president would like to be loved by everyone in the country, but presidents who sacrifice convictions to a quest for popular affection are not likely to make it to the top. Harding was an immensely popular president. His death provoked an outpouring of national grief that observers thought unmatched since the death of Lincoln. Scholars are unanimous in pronouncing him a Failure.

Presidents who seek to change the nation's direction know that they are bound to alienate those who profit from the status quo. Great presidents go ahead anyway. "Judge me," FDR said, "by the enemies I have made." Truman's approval rating at the end of his presidency was down to 31 percent. Look where he ranks now.

After his reelection, William Jefferson Clinton faces his rendezvous with history. Debarred by the 22nd Amendment from pursuing a third term, he must make his mark between now and 19 January 2001. This may not be easy. The 22nd Amendment, by turning reelected presidents into lame ducks, reduces their political potency. Second terms tend to be times of trouble: ask FDR, Eisenhower, Johnson, Nixon, Reagan. On the other hand, lame-duckery, by liberating presidents from the demands of reelection, does allow them to run political risks for national benefits.

Clinton brings to the bar of history a rare combination of talents and infirmities. He is a man of penetrating intelligence. He has impressive technical mastery of complicated issues. He has genuine intellectual curiosity and listens as well as talks. He is a skilled and resilient politician. When the spirit moves him, he is capable of real eloquence, and the spirit moves him most of all when he confronts the supreme American problem—race. Racial justice appears to be his most authentic concern.

[19]Elting Morison testifying before the Senate Foreign Relations Committee, 19 January 1978.
[20]James Bryce, *The American Commonwealth* (London: Macmillan, 1888), I, chap. 8.

Rating	Voting Breakdown*					
	Great	Near Great	Below Average	Average	Mean Failure	Score
GREAT						
Lincoln	32					4.00
Washington	31	1				3.97
Franklin D. Roosevelt	31	1				3.97
NEAR GREAT						
Jefferson	12	16	1			3.38
Jackson	11	17	1			3.34
Theodore Roosevelt	10	18	1			3.31
Wilson	11	17			1	3.21
Truman	6	21	3			3.10
Polk	2	17	8	1		2.71
HIGH AVERAGE						
Eisenhower	1	10	20	1		2.34
John Adams		10	17	1		2.32
Kennedy		9	21	1		2.29
Cleveland		8	2	1		2.24
Lyndon Johnson		15	12	3	2	2.21
Monroe	1	1	22	2		2.15
McKinley		5	20	2		2.11
AVERAGE						
Madison	1	2	20	5	1	1.83
John Quincy Adams		1	18	8		1.74
Harrison			14	7		1.67
Clinton		2	17	5	2	1.58
Van Buren			18	8	1	1.56
Taft			17	9	1	1.52
Hayes			16	10	1	1.48
Bush			16	12	1	1.45
Reagan		7	11	9	4	1.42
Arthur			13	11	1	1.40
Carter		1	15	12	2	1.37
Ford			6	20	2	1.00
BELOW AVERAGE						
Taylor			6	17	3	0.88
Coolidge			7	16	4	0.81
Fillmore			3	20	3	0.77
Tyler			6	17	5	0.68
FAILURE						
Pierce				15	12	−9
Grant				9	18	−9
Hoover			11	9	10	−9
Nixon		2	4	5	20	−21
Andrew Johnson			2	7	17	−23
Buchanan				6	22	−38
Harding			2		26	−48

*Not every respondent voted for all the presidents, hence the discrepancies in the total number of votes.

On the other hand, he lacks self-discipline. His judgment of people is erratic. His political resilience strikes many as flagrant opportunism. His reactions are instinctively placatory, perhaps from growing up in a household where the wrong words might provoke an alcoholic stepfather to violence. He rushes to propitiate the audience before him, often at his own long-term expense. His scandals and cover-ups are ripe for exploitation by a vindictive opposition. Who can tell how this combination of talents and infirmities will play out?

To make a mark on history, Clinton must liberate himself from polls and focus groups. Let him put his first-rate intelligence to work on the hard problems. Playing it safe, taking it easy, sticking to the middle of the road may make for a more comfortable second term. But following this course would put Clinton alongside William Howard Taft and Rutherford B. Hayes on the ratings list. Far better to anticipate the problems of the twenty-first century, to startle the country into informing debate, to move people into thinking beyond short-run self-interest toward some longer view of the general welfare and to propose remedies sufficient to the needs of the day. Only boldness and creativity, even if at times foiled and frustrated, will earn him a place among the immortals.

Schlesinger 1996 Poll

The score method of calculation: the following numbers were assigned to each category—Great = 4; Near Great = 3; Average = 2; Below Average = 1; Failure = –2. Failure seems such a drastic historical judgment as to require special weighting. Then each score was divided by the number of mentions.

PARTICIPANTS IN 1996 POLL

Samuel H. Beer, Harvard University
John Morton Blum, Yale University
Alan Brinkley, Columbia University
Douglas Brinkley, University of New Orleans
Walter Dean Burnham, University of Texas
James MacGregor Burns, Williams College
Mario Cuomo
Robert Dallek, Boston University
Robert H. Ferrell, Indiana University
Louis Fisher, Library of Congress
Eric Foner, Columbia University
George Frederickson, Stanford University
Doris Kearns Goodwin
Norman Graebner, University of Virginia
Henry Graff, Columbia University
Stephen Hess, Brookings Institution
Morton Keller, Brandeis University
Louis Koenig, New York University
William Leuchtenburg, University of North Carolina
David Levering Lewis, Rutgers University

Arthur Link, Princeton University
Forrest McDonald, University of Alabama
Merrill Peterson, University of Virginia
Richard M. Pious, Barnard College
Robert V. Remini, University of Illinois at Chicago
Donald A. Ritchie, Senate Historical Office
Robert Rutland, University of Virginia
Joel Silbey, Cornell University
Paul Simon, U.S. Senate
Stephen Skowronek, Yale University
Hans Trefousse, City University of New York
Sean Wilentz, Princeton University

6

PRESIDENTS, PARTIES, AND INTEREST GROUPS

GOP Missteps, Jeffords's Feelings About Agenda Led Toward Exit

Mike Allen and Ruth Marcus
Washington Post Staff Writers

When President Bush sat down in front of the Oval Office fireplace with Sen. James M. Jeffords on Tuesday afternoon, he posed the question directly. "Is there anything I or my administration has done to make you feel slighted?" Bush asked the Vermont Republican.

"No," Jeffords replied, according to White House aides.

But the truth was that Jeffords's slow-motion decision to leave the GOP, which he is expected to announce in his home state this morning, was the product of both the senator's increasing alienation from the policies of his party and miscalculations by Republicans in the Senate and the White House over how to handle him.

"This is a self-inflicted gunshot wound," a senior GOP official said yesterday of his party's fumbling.

Sen. Judd Gregg (R-N.H.) said: "I've been told that he just feels he doesn't have the friends up here he once had."

But if there were warning signs, the White House missed them. A top White House aide said Bush's high command did not realize until Tuesday—hours before the Oval Office meeting—that Jeffords could defect.

On Capitol Hill and in Vermont, associates of Jeffords said the problem was crystallized by the decision of the White House, after he had voted to scale back Bush's tax cut bill in a budget resolution, not to invite him to a Rose Garden ceremony honoring a Vermont social studies teacher last month.

The policy gulf between Jeffords and his party, combined with the administration's apparent decision to play hardball until it may have been too late, combined to help push the 67-year-old moderate over the edge—and the Senate to the brink of Democratic control.

For their part, Democrats have been wooing Jeffords since the election—and some Democrats have been mulling the prospect for even longer.

One Democrat recalled Sen. Harry M. Reid (D-Nev.) musing aloud in 1996 whether he could lure Jeffords to defect. Democratic sources said Reid played a critical role in persuading Jeffords it was finally time to leave the GOP, offering to relinquish his right to chair the Senate environment committee to Jeffords.

Over the past 24 hours, Republicans were engaged in a frenzy of "who lost Jeffords" finger-pointing. White House allies said they were blindsided by the failure of the Senate GOP leadership, particularly Majority Leader Trent Lott (R-Miss.), to recognize the scope of the problem. White House critics blamed political strategist Karl Rove, legislative liaison Nicholas Calio and others for mishandling Jeffords.

"Did the administration make some mistakes?" one Republican said. "Yes. It relied entirely on Lott to be their red-light warning system on Jeffords. Lott didn't sense the problems were serious."

Calio noted that education and tax cuts, the president's top two priorities, were on the floor at the same time. "Your focus is generally on the things that are most pressing," he said. As for the allegations about White House hardball, Calio said: "Categorically, there was no effort to punish Senator Jeffords."

A Jeffords aide, who refused to be named, said the senator's decision was based on "his whole comfort with the agenda" and not because he felt snubbed. "Anything else that people are bringing into it is not a part of how he made the decision," the aide said.

However, several lawmakers who talked to Jeffords yesterday said he had begun to feel beleaguered. Rep. Christopher Shays, a moderate Republican from Connecticut, criticized the Senate leadership. "Jim Jeffords is a good man, and he has been under a barrage of attacks by his own colleagues," Shays said.

Sen. Arlen Specter (R-Pa.) said he believes Jeffords was moved to leave the party for several reasons, largely having to do with the treatment of moderates by the conservative-dominated Senate GOP. "It's been hard to be a moderate in the caucus because there are so few of us," he said. "Sometimes, frankly, it gets fairly tough."

Others put the blame on the White House. "This is miscalculation upon miscalculation," said another Republican. "In a 50-50 Senate, are you supposed to go after people with guns? Of course not. This White House was too macho."

Vermont Gov. Howard Dean, a Democrat, called Jeffords "a very understated guy, but he has a real tough, principled core."

"He's not a guy you push around, and I think the White House pushed too far," Dean said.

The tensions between Jeffords and his party had been building over the past few months. The White House made Gregg their "go-to" person on the education bill because they did not want to have to deal with Jeffords.

SENATE SWITCHERS
Senators who have changed parties since the 1950s.

Senator	State	Party	Year
Bob Smith	New Hampshire	I to R	2000
Bob Smith	New Hampshire	R to I	1999
Ben Nighthorse Campbell	Colorado	D to R	1995
Richard Shelby	Alabama	D to R	1994
Phil Gramm	Texas	D to R	1983
Harry Byrd Jr.	Virginia	D to I	1971
Strom Thurmond	South Carolina	D to R	1964
Wayne Morse	Oregon	I to D	1955
Wayne Morse	Oregon	R to I	1952

Sources: Senate Library, Associated Press

"Jeffords didn't like the way Lott and Gregg pushed him aside during negotiations over the education bill," said one Republican. "It made him feel like, 'Gee, where's my place here?'"

On the other hand, administration and Senate leadership officials said Jeffords has been difficult and demanding, adding that they were unable to make deals with him that stuck. "They'd give him what he wanted, and then he'd say, 'Oh, I can't live with that,'" said an official involved in the process.

White House and leadership officials said relations with Jeffords began deteriorating irreparably on April 3, after an early evening meeting in the Capitol, where they negotiated the senator's demand for permanent funding for a program to help local school districts educate disabled children.

Administration officials said they agreed to $150 billion in funding over 10 years, with the stipulation that the program be changed in ways that they argued would make it more effective. They said Jeffords shook hands with them on the agreement and returned to his office. One official said that, shortly thereafter, a Jeffords aide called to renege, asserting that the senator had misunderstood the terms.

The next afternoon, Jeffords dropped by a news conference of moderate senators who were calling for a smaller tax cut package than what Bush had proposed. The first subject Jeffords mentioned was special education funding. "I finished my negotiations and unfortunately have not had an acceptable response," Jeffords said. He added pointedly: "I feel very comfortable here. First time in a while."

As Jeffords balked at the size of the tax cut, White House Chief of Staff Andrew H. Card Jr. called a Vermont radio station and a local reporter to argue that Jeffords should support Bush.

Three weeks later, Jeffords—who chairs the Senate education committee—was not invited to the White House teacher-of-the-year event. White House press secretary Ari Fleischer said yesterday that "nobody played hardball" with Jeffords and that a mid-level event planner could have left Jeffords off the guest list as a routine practice to keep the ceremony to a reasonable size.

One Republican said he was told that when Jeffords called the White House legislative affairs office on the morning of the event to inquire if his lack of an invitation had been an oversight, he was assured that no mistake had been made. Another called it a "stupid error," saying that if Jeffords's invitation was omitted by accident, it was "amiable duncehood," and "if it was punishment, then it was malicious stupidity."

Republicans also suggested that the administration would try to hurt Jeffords by opposing a dairy compact that benefits farmers. White House officials denied that.

Last week, "a senior GOP source" was quoted in the conservative magazine Weekly Standard as saying that the White House had "a one- or two-year plan to punish him for his behavior." White House officials said that is not true, but Jeffords allies said the report only fed the senator's feeling that he was an outcast in a party that he agreed with less and less often.

Indeed, some at the White House had been fretting for weeks about Jeffords's state of mind. Nancy Dorn, Vice President Cheney's legislative liaison, was warning others last month that the Jeffords situation could mushroom into a big problem, an official said.

But the real worrying among White House officials did not begin in earnest until over the weekend, with a flurry of concerned calls. By Monday evening, the decision was made that Cheney, who was heading to the Capitol for another meeting on Tuesday, needed to spend some time with Jeffords as well. But by then it was too late.

The Cheney meeting did not go well, and the White House called Jeffords's office to ask if he would come to meet with Bush. After that meeting, Bush officials were even gloomier. "The sense that we had was that his decision pretty much had been made," a senior aide said.

House GOP leaders and White House officials tried to minimize the damage a possible Jeffords defection would inflict on the party. House Speaker J. Dennis Hastert (R-Ill.) told a closed-door meeting of rank-and-file Republicans yesterday morning that they would have to stay even more united now that they face the prospect of a Democratic-controlled Senate.

"No matter what happens in the Senate, we have to keep positive and keep doing good things for the American people," Hastert said, according to participants.

Bush's counselor, Karen P. Hughes, organized a conference call yesterday afternoon with top communications aides to congressional GOP leaders, and she urged them to mute any criticism of either Jeffords or each other. One leadership aide paraphrased Hughes as saying, "Let's not go pointing fingers."

Staff writers David S. Broder, Helen Dewar and Juliet Eilperin contributed to this report.

7

THE MASS MEDIA
AND THE PRESIDENCY

Presidential Image-Makers on the Limits of Spin Control

Mark J. Rozell
Associate Professor of Political Science
Mary Washington College

Abstract

White House media strategists have an important vantage from which to view presidential press relations. This paper identifies the perceptions of these strategists regarding presidential efforts to manage and control the media. The perceptions of media strategists influence their evaluations of the president's actions and the development of their strategies. Based on personal interviews, oral history documents, and studies that draw from interview data, this study analyzes three central factors in presidential press relations: strategic, contextual, personal. The data reveal that, first, media strategists emphasize those factors that justify their actions and make their president look good in retrospect. Second, the view that the White House enjoys most of the advantages in its battles with the press is not accurate.

When Ronald Reagan became president in 1981, he did so not only with a 100 days plan put into place by a transition team but also with an acute understanding of the overriding importance of public and press relations to achieving policy goals. The former actor and his aides understood that imagery is an integral part of presidential leadership and that their White House predecessors had failed to effectively use public relations.

According to Mark Hertsgaard's (1988) content analysis of news coverage of Reagan's presidency, the White House achieved enormous success at media management. This success was acknowledged by such White House aides as Michael Deaver and David Gergen who offered numerous self-congratulatory assessments of their efforts at managing news content. During Reagan's tenure, the chief presidential spokesman Larry Speakes even so boldly kept a sign on his desk: "You don't tell us how to stage the news, we won't tell you how to cover it" (Hertsgaard

1988, 27). Hertsgaard's interviews with numerous Reagan White House media strategists revealed their perception that the administration masterfully managed its news coverage.

Not all media strategists can credibly claim such success. Interviews with the media strategists of Reagan's predecessors, Jimmy Carter and Gerald Ford, reveal the perception that an administration cannot script its own news coverage or deliberately manipulate journalists. Instead, according to this perspective, the president's press image usually is captive to events beyond the White House's control. According to Ron Nessen, "No White House can do much about a president's image."[1]

Interviews with modern White House media strategists reveal significantly different perceptions of what explains the nature of a president's press coverage. The reality perceived by Reagan's strategists is so different from that understood by Ford's and Carter's people.

This paper examines two central questions: (1) What factors explain the perceptions of White House media strategists of their president's press coverage? (2) How do the perceptions of these White House media strategists influence the development of presidential press strategies?

The primary value of the analysis is the presentation of White House media strategists' views of presidential news management. The interview data present the perceptions of witnesses to important events. Although the White House media strategists speak with understandable biases, their recollections of events reveal important information about the political realities perceived by these people and how such perceptions affect what they do in government.

A secondary value of the analysis is to provide much original data that counter the view that the White House maintains the advantage over the press in controlling news content by virtue of its ability to stage events, manipulate symbols, and dominate public discourse (Bennett 1988; Cronin 1974; Grossman and Kumar 1981, chapter 10; Hertsgaard 1988; Paletz and Entman 1980; Wolfson 1985, chapter 2; Zeidenstein 1984). Many factors bear on presidential press coverage (Entman 1989, 74). A president may succeed at achieving a good press for reasons completely unrelated to White House efforts at news management. Likewise, a president may receive poor press reviews despite intense White House efforts to generate favorable news coverage. A White House can influence press coverage through the use of public and press relations techniques and needs to do so to move its political and policy objectives forward. But success is never guaranteed, and no set of techniques will yield the same results for different presidencies.

Three Factors at Work

According to the media strategists of presidents Ford, Carter, and Reagan, there are three central factors that bear on an administration's press image: contextual, personal, and strategic. The perspectives of these people are analyzed through the use of personal interviews and through an examination of oral history transcripts, memoirs, and secondary sources.

1. *Contextual factors* are those surrounding the circumstances under which a president exercises leadership. Among these factors are the nature of the times, the collection of problems and issues facing the country, the partisan makeup of Congress, and the public's expectations for either policy change or continuity.

2. *Personal factors* concern the individual inclinations and media skills of the president and his public relations and press advisers. The ability and willingness of a president to use the media to move his objectives forward have significant influence on success at managing the news. The president also needs to surround himself with public relations advisers who know how to use the media.

3. *Strategic factors* involve the elements of the White House's news management plans. A White House may develop a press strategy based on many factors: the timing of news releases, cultivation of opinion elites, planned photo opportunities, presidential addresses, presidential travels at home and abroad, coordinating presidential themes and objectives.

The media strategists contend that the ability of the White House to manage the press generally depends upon each of these factors, but in varying degrees. No one of these factors alone can guarantee success. A president with great media skills, for example, may not be able to effect a good press relationship without a plan of action and a receptive environment. Excepting short-term circumstances, positive press relations involve a mixture of factors. White House media strategists care about these factors because journalistic portrayals of the president matter a great deal to an administration's ability to succeed. As Brody (1991) demonstrates, they have good reason to be concerned about the media evaluations of the president.

Contextual Factors   Gerald R. Ford became president under the most unusual circumstances in United States history. Ford's media strategists recalled that the leadership context created in light of President Richard M. Nixon's resignation provided both press relations advantages and disadvantages. As for advantages, Ford's press image for the first month in office benefited from the fact that he was not Nixon. Ford reaped the benefit of the national euphoria once Nixon departed the White House, according to presidential counsellor Robert Hartmann:

> During the first part of his presidency there was a national euphoria, a honeymoon that the press helped to create, all stemming in part from the fact that Ford was not Nixon and that he was a much more likeable personality meriting sympathy and support because of the difficult position he found himself in.[2]

During the first month in office Ford received what he described in his memoirs as "the kind of press coverage that every politician loves but almost never gets" (Ford 1987, 178). Journalists described Ford as open, honest, sincere, just about everything that Nixon wasn't.

The euphoria did not last. The pardon precipitated an immediate turnaround in Ford's press. Nonetheless, Ford's media strategists said that the pardon alone cannot explain the consistently negative press that he received throughout the rest of his term in office. The pardon occurred within the context of other events that severely hampered Ford's press image. The Deputy Press Secretary John Hushen commented that,

> There was great deal of suspicion within the press corps because of Watergate. They felt they couldn't trust what any government official said. That certainly influenced the events of Ford's presidency. The media viewed everything with a skeptical eye.[3]

The Assistant Press Secretary Louis M. Thompson, Jr. added that,

> What we were going through at that time was one of the strangest periods between the White House and the press, having come off of Watergate and Vietnam. There was extreme doubt about the veracity of official statements. And an attitude due to the way the Nixon people had treated the press. We were really caught in the aftermath of that.[4]

The Assistant Press Secretary John G. Carlson referred to the immediate post-Watergate years as the "anti-everything era" in which White House reporters believed that they had to be especially tough on Ford after having been beaten on the Watergate story by *Washington Post* "Metro" reporters Carl Bernstein and Bob Woodward.[5] President Ford said, "We inherited a very bad rapport between the White House press corps and the presidency as a result of Watergate and the Vietnam War. It was difficult to quickly change that negative attitude of the White House press corps."[6] And the Deputy Press Secretary William Greener added the following.

> I'm not sure that anybody, following Watergate and Vietnam, could have been successful. I was always surprised by the very thin veneer of trust that existed. It was there, but it was very thin. They were always ready to jump on you.[7]

Ford's press relations people also identified other contextual factors that negatively influenced his press relations. These included the lack of a presidential transition, the lack of a presidential mandate, the partisan composition of Congress. The Press Secretary Jerald terHorst noted other factors too.

> There was never a Ford coterie within the press, as there is with most new presidents, because Ford had never mounted a campaign for the office. . . . When reporters cover a candidate's campaign, they get to know the man's style, the players . . . Ford had none of that going in. He was a creature of Richard Nixon. So the whole effort had to be staff-driven because we didn't have any news media coalition out there. As a result, it was difficult to devise a strategy that would hold up over time. And it didn't hold up, partly for that reason, and partly because the press, after Nixon, had become a group that no longer would take the presidency at face value.[8]

From the perspectives of White House insiders, the leadership context also proved to be troublesome to President Jimmy Carter. A comprehensive content analysis of elite press coverage reveals that Carter fared even worse than his predecessor in press assessments of presidential leadership (Rozell 1989). Carter's White House staff offered substantially similar assessments of the leadership context as those presented by Ford White House staff, including the difficulty of developing affirmative press relations in the post-Watergate environment.

Succeeding Gerald Ford, Richard Nixon's Vice President, [Watergate] hadn't been that long, and there was still that real residual distrust which was obviously at one point very intensely felt throughout the country, but always . . . much more intensely felt in Washington. I can remember very much references to Watergate or Watergate-like actions in the transition period and that's part of the mix that we were competing with. . . .[9]

I found a real sensitivity among the press to being manipulated and questions were raised when we set up the radio operation and the media liaison office and [journalists] said, "You know this is just like something out of the Nixon press office. You know, going around the Washington press corps and manipulating the people."[10]

I came to the conclusion . . . that of all the institutions in our society, the press was probably the most traumatized by Watergate—and it probably took it longer to scab over than it did anything else. If you had to refine it more, I think that the White House press corps . . . were even more bloody and bruised from it than the press corps at large.[11]

They always went away giving you the impression of believing "I just know the SOB dodged or lied to me and later I'm going to be able to say that if they'd just answered my tough questions I would have caught it." There's always that sense that they're out to catch you. Very tiring at the end of the day. I'll tell you.[12]

Press Secretary Jody Powell (1984, 173) expressed the same sentiment. "The events of Watergate, Vietnam, and that whole turbulent decade of souring relations between press and government have created a residue of cynicism that is a serious and corrosive force." And White House Chief of Staff Hamilton Jordan (1982, 359) wrote the following.

I believe that Watergate and Vietnam pushed the American media from wholesome skepticism and doubt into out-and-out cynicism about the American political process generally and the Presidency specifically. Both Vietnam and Watergate had assumed that coloration of a struggle between the press and the President.

A number of White House staff also commented that the 1970s congressional reforms had created a new, more complex environment for presidential leadership. This perspective was reflected in the comment of a senior White House adviser that "even Lyndon Johnson wouldn't have had to cajole and twist [only] fifteen or twenty arms." This staff member and a member of the press secretary's office lamented this fact.

Twenty years ago if a President wanted to pass a bill to the Congress he'd get Speaker Sam Rayburn and Majority Leader Lyndon Johnson and George Meany and maybe someone from the business community. They could sit down in the Oval Office and write a tax bill and leave with a high degree of confidence that it would pass pretty much in the form they'd agreed upon. Our experience was that you could have the President and the Speaker and the committee chairs putting on a full court press on a piece of legislation on the Hill, and you could be defeated in subcommittee by a group of people whose names were barely recognizable to you.[13]

It is no longer possible to assemble a small group of congressional leaders in the family dining room at the White House or whatever and have a couple of drinks with them and reach some meeting of the minds and then be certain that the wheels will turn and that the thing will be produced at the other end of the legislative process.[14]

Carter's White House staff identified another aspect of the leadership environment: the nature of the late 1970s public policy agenda dominated by uncontrollable events and unmet demands and needs. They also noted that the president played a crucial role in creating a difficult environment for leadership by pushing "second term issues"—ones that a president emphasizes only after he does not have to worry about the electoral consequences of unpopular choices. The president dismissed staff advice to focus on programs that would be easier to move through the policy making process. Carter instead defined his policy priorities according to his own definition of the public good and exercised what Charles O. Jones (1988) has aptly called a "trusteeship" style of leadership. White House members commented as follows.

> If you back down the list of things, whether it's energy or civil service reform or nuclear proliferation or SALT or even the Mideast, the Camp David business, the Panama Canal, all of them were political liabilities for him in more than just the sense of well, you have a certain amount of capital to expend and you ration it, you expend it.[15]
>
> I asked [another White House staff member] last night if he could recall a specific bill, program or policy that we had advocated that was popular and helped us politically. We couldn't think of a single thing. Everything was politically a loser.[16]
>
> [So] many of the things that he tried to do and did both were really things that were behind the times. I mean they were things that should have been done twenty years ago, or ten years ago, or five years ago and the reasons they weren't done . . . were exactly the reasons we had such a hard time doing them. Good reasons. It was the political difficulty.[17]

Carter's "new kind of Democratic program" also resulted in negative press coverage. As Stephen Hess (1984) has shown, presidential news coverage coming from the Washington press corps tends to be funneled through Capitol Hill. Negative comments about a Democratic president from Democratic members of Congress accelerate unflattering press coverage of the chief executive's leadership. A congressional liaison staffer assessed that "our problem was that we were trying to build a Democratic party congressional majority for these very non-Democratic party ideas."[18] A member of the press secretary's office agreed.

> The programs the Carter Presidency was putting forward were certainly a new kind of Democratic program. It was more business management techniques—taking the available funds and targeting the citizen, not taking all the dollars there are in the world and throwing them at the problem. It caused the President, of course, to be disowned by his own party. You know, there's a Democrat sitting in the White House but he's not putting out Democratic bills and the coalition was falling apart.[19]

Carter's White House staff identified another contextual factor that created leadership problems: Carter campaigned for president as an "outsider" and met resistance from traditional Washington once in office. A senior staff member noted that Democratic leaders were never prepared to help Carter succeed.

> Carter came to Washington not particularly as the favorite of the Democratic establishment or the people in Congress. . . . We took a survey of news in the second year of

the administration . . . and found that 85% of the negative statements in *The Washington Post* about Carter were from members of his own party. It was really kind of ironic that Howard Baker was our best public supporter in the Congress from the day we came to Washington.[20]

Reagan White House advisers perceived a favorable leadership context. In relationship to the other factors influencing presidential-press relations—personal and strategic—the Reagan people did not place much emphasis on the environment for leadership as explanatory of the administration's relatively positive press coverage (Hertsgaard 1988). Nonetheless, some of Reagan's media advisers noted that the president had a built-in advantage because he followed presidents treated unfavorably by the press. According to the Director of the White House Office of Communications David Gergen,

> there was a feeling on the part of the press corps when Reagan came in that somehow they had been a participant in a lot of presidential hangings and that they wanted to stand back from the rope this time. . . . There is no question in my mind there was more willingness to give Reagan the benefit of the doubt than there was [for] Carter or Ford (Hertsgaard 1988, 101).
>
> I think a lot of the Teflon came because the press was holding back. . . . I don't think they wanted to go after him that toughly (Hertsgaard 1988, 203).

Presidential media adviser Michael Deaver also cited the importance of this contrast between Reagan and his predecessors.

> I think we were conscious of coming in after an administration that disliked the Washington media, the Washington aura and ambience, and jumping right in and enjoying it and becoming a part of it. . . . I think that made a big difference (Hertsgaard 1988, 44).

Gergen noted that the March 30, 1981, assassination attempt on the president gave a public relations lift to Reagan. The relevance of that tragic event to generating sympathy and support for the president cannot be ignored. Gergen recalled that the attempt on Reagan's life "gave us a second life, a second honeymoon. . . . [T]he March shooting transformed the whole thing. We had new capital" (Hertsgaard 1988, 116). Donald Regan wrote that "[Reagan] recovered from his wound stronger than ever in his leadership and in the affection in which the American people held him" (Regan, 1988, 190). And the Office of Management and Budget Director, David Stockman, wrote the following.

> From his remark to the First Lady in the emergency room of the George Washington University Hospital, "Honey, I forgot to duck," to his triumphant speech to the Congress on April 28, the momentum was all ours. Indeed, for a while the President acquired a heroic aura—and the polls reflected it (Stockman 1986, 173).

The leadership context represents the stage on which political actors play. It establishes important conditions on whether or not a president can develop a positive press image and lead effectively. The leadership context, and hence environment for press management, differs from administration to administration. Some aspects of the leadership context are uncontrollable. It is in the interest of the White House to make the most of the opportunities presented by contextual factors. Whether a White House does so, and its degree of success, are determined by the other factors: personal and strategic.

Personal Factors   The media skills of the president and his advisers, as well as their willingness to emphasize public relations, have a profound influence on a White House's success at news management. President Ford's media advisers said that these factors did not represent their strong suit in developing positive news coverage. Ford came to the presidency with an image problem. He had never sought national office and the press corps perceived him as lacking stature. Journalists ridiculed Ford as physically clumsy and not very intelligent. They oftentimes repeated a quip by former president Lyndon Johnson that Ford was so dumb he couldn't walk and chew gum at the same time. According to Ford White House staff, the president reinforced that image by the way that he spoke and presented himself to the public. Ford's Chief of Staff Richard Cheney (1988, 76) said that,

> The image was a problem, and I must say that Lyndon Johnson had contributed to its being rather negative. . . . That false image was strong enough so that when Ford came on board, it was something we had to deal with on a regular basis. I think it was accentuated by the President's speaking style. On occasion his remarks may have sounded less than articulate and I think that contributed to his problem.

The Assistant Press Secretary Larry Speakes more bluntly asserted that "Ford's manner of speaking was halting—he wasn't a great orator." Speakes added that,

> [Ford's speeches] contributed to the image problem, as well as the fall [in Austria and] bumping his head. In reality, he was a fine athlete, a war hero, a fellow who had a good academic record. Yet that never came across.[21]

The Assistant Press Secretary Louis M. Thompson, Jr., also noted that Ford entered the presidency lacking an effective speaking style. Ford "wasn't practiced at it at the time. He wasn't particularly good with delivery and he wasn't very good in the formal settings. . . . So we tried to deal with that problem, but I don't think we were especially successful."[22]

Press office staffers noted that Ford entered the presidency lacking the skills a president needs to command the media. Another problem concerned the media skills of some key White House figures. In particular, Ford's press secretaries— Jerald terHorst and Ron Nessen—lacked governmental experience. Each had an extensive journalistic background. As Hartmann explained, neither had ever served as a government information officer.

> [terHorst and Nessen] went directly from the White House press room to the White House press office. They had absolutely no experience in government, let alone a White House press office. They had no instincts that had in any way been conditioned to the differences between a press officer and a member of the press. It was difficult for them to establish where their allegiances were and whom they were supposed to please and serve.

Both of Ford's press secretaries contributed to the mistakes we made by not being themselves familiar enough with the process. We had a novice president working with a novice press secretary.[23]

John Hushen corroborated this view.

. . . unexpected problems develop when a press secretary is drawn directly out of the media without some kind of interim position. The transition of responsibilities is very difficult. A media person goes from being a free and independent spirit to that of a captive spokesman for a particular point of view.

. . . you just don't know what it's like if you've never been a government information officer. As a media person, you're trained to ask the tough questions, but answer none of them. Then you get on the other side of the fence and you suddenly realize that unless you've thought about your response beforehand, you're not prepared to answer questions for the President.[24]

Nessen in particular had a difficult relationship with the White House press corps. The Deputy Press Secretary William Greener said that "Ron didn't like the press corps even when he was a part of it. So he carried that antipathy over in some ways."[25] Another press office staffer told me that "Ron . . . would sometimes make fun of a newsman during a briefing, just ridicule him. Not a good way to develop a rapport with the media. They'll get you back one way or another."[26]

Nessen acknowledged that they did. "I think in terms of faulting myself for my own performance in the White House, I didn't have enough of a sense of humor. I think my skin was too thin. I took things too personally and I was too defensive of Ford."[27]

Larry Speakes commented that Ford had a number of successes and events that should have become public relations pluses, but did not because of the lack of any sustained effort to explain to the press what the administration was doing.[28] Perhaps the Ford White House did not place a great deal of emphasis on the public relations presidency (at least after the first month). When I asked Ford about the extent to which he considered public relations important to his presidency he immediately replied that his administration focused on the substance of his domestic and international policies. Ford did assert that he recognized the need for a good press strategy, but made it clear that public relations were not paramount to his presidency.[29]

According to Carter's communications advisers, the president downplayed the important role of public relations in creating and sustaining a leadership image. Carter had other priorities—managing the government, policy analysis. He did not expend the time and energy required to enhance his press image. Carter did not work closely with his speechwriters, nor did he believe that it was important to do so. He resisted selling his programs with slogans and simplifying explanations. Carter speechwriter James Fallows (1979, 6) explained the problem. "I think to a larger degree in this administration than most, it would not occur to Carter very often to ask, 'Well what's the [newspaper] lead going to be about this?' That's not the way his mind works." A member of the press secretary's office said, "President

Carter didn't spend a lot of time thinking about the press. . . . I wished at times that he was more interested in it and delighted in the game-playing aspects of it."[30]

Carter's advisers pointed out that the president disliked spending time on public persuasion skills. One senior White House adviser offered the following view.

> One of the greatest challenges of presidential leadership is the need for a president to be an effective communicator—the president as teacher. Carter was not enough of a showman. . . . I think we were long on content and substance—and short on dramatic flair and inspiration; long on policy and position—and short on passion.[31]
>
> If he had been a more artful, more dramatic articulator of what he was doing, we would have been more successful. He *does* lack a tendency to speak with fervor, force, inspiration, and rhetorical impact, which we all need.[32]
>
> He did not pay sufficient attention to the "presentational" aspect of what he was doing. That is a Carter characteristic. He is a man who loves to work more than he likes to politic. . . .[33]

A member of the White House public liaison team made a similar point.

> Jimmy Carter is an extremely bright and good man who refused to take a serious look at some of the communication techniques that are absolutely essential in an age of electronic media. . . . I don't believe President Carter worked very hard at improving his capacity to speak. . . . I had the impression that Jimmy Carter perceived studying a speech or studying the techniques of dealing with the media as a weakness, as plastic and something inconsistent with his personal view of being himself.[34]

Carter's resistance to slogans and simplifying themes made difficult the task of communicating a clear message. A chief Carter communications adviser pointed out that Reagan enhanced public relations with thematic addresses. "You don't have to give a list of regulations you're going to cut when you say 'I'm going to get the government off your back. . . .' Carter didn't like metaphors. Maybe he thought it was dishonest."[35]

Carter did not focus on creating a "line of the day" or "theme of the week." A speechwriter commented that "Carter never sent out directives, 'Let's stick to these themes the next two weeks. . . .' [We] never got any communication from Carter in terms of philosophy."[36] And "[Carter] simply resisted the idea of labeling himself in any way, shape or form."[37] Another speechwriter added that "we were not programmed . . . to create an image or even to deal with symbolism."[38]

Much of the administration's public and press relations problem derived from the fact that Carter could not act. A good actor-politician (e.g., Ronald Reagan) is capable of standing before a large public audience with whom he shares no common experiences and creating a believable sense of empathy with members of that audience. A poor actor-politician (e.g., Carter) is unable to create or fake emotions. A speechwriter said of Carter that, "there was nothing of the actor in that man."[39]

Another problem in the administration's press relations concerned a failure to cultivate personal relationships with leading journalists. Some of Carter's speechwriters faulted the president and his top advisers for not taking seriously enough this important "constituency" in the Washington community.

> Why didn't we ever give a *New York Times* ed board kind of speech? Why didn't we ever think we were looking at Meg Greenfield . . . and George Will and what would we say to them, and how would Carter explain himself?[40]
>
> By having contempt for those establishment media people, we set a time bomb each time we ignored them. I would even hear it said, "I don't care what so and so thinks."[41]
>
> They are a special constituency that need to be taken care of. When they have a complaint or their squeaky wheel starts up you've got to do something about it or otherwise they'll come back at you.[42]

Carter's communications advisers portrayed the president and his top White House aides as disinclined to cultivate public and press relations as well as not very skilled in these areas. Reagan's White House advisers presented a different view of their own experiences. In their view, Reagan conducted the most public relations oriented presidency in history. The president knew what skills he possessed, and he used them to move forward his policy agenda. Larry Speakes (1988, 116) linked leadership success to communications skills.

> What kind of man is Ronald Reagan? Above all, he is an actor, and we never apologized for his Hollywood background. Communicating is a key ingredient of leadership, I always maintained, and if being an actor made him a better communicator, then so be it.

The chief of staff Donald Regan (1988, 263) concurred.

> Nearly all politicians . . . are actors by nature. Reagan just happened to be a trained professional to whom the mechanics of the craft had become second nature through a lifetime of practice.
>
> No American President of the television age has combined the common touch with the unique ability to be everywhere at once in electronic form so successfully as Ronald Reagan (Regan 1988, 271).

And presidential speechwriter Peggy Noonan (1990, 154) wrote,

> He was to popular politics what Henry James was to American literature: He was the master. No one could do what he did, move people that way, talk to them so that they understood. A demagogue would have begged for that power.

Noonan (1990, 197) assessed that the press perception of Reagan as a "Great Communicator" often shielded the president from criticism. She recalled an example of a poor speech by the president that the press scored as a good speech. Reporters so much expected the "Great Communicator" to perform that they failed to recognize a poor speech when they heard one.

Deputy Assistant to the President Joanna Bistany offered an additional view. "A lot of what we've done [was] because of Ronald Reagan and his warm personality. . . . You can get away with a lot because he can then come up and diffuse the antagonism" (Hertsgaard 1988, 47). Deaver maintained that "90 percent of [Reagan's] success is the man himself" (Hertsgaard 1988, 48).

The Deputy White House Press Secretary Leslie Janka noted that Reagan and key presidential advisers knew the importance of public relations to achieving policy success.

The President, Deaver, Baker and those guys, when they do something, it's not an after-thought [to decide] who gets on the *Today* show, who are our spokesmen. This group understands that a policy, no matter how good it is, is not going to succeed if it isn't sold well (Hertsgaard 1988, 23).

The difference between Reagan and Carter is that Reagan fundamentally under-stands that politics is communication with leadership, and he probably puts communi-cation above substance. . . . Carter was just the flip-side of that. He put substance ahead of politics (Hertsgaard 1988, 38).

Donald Regan (1988, 271) pointed out that not only did the president benefit from "his physical appearance, his personality, and his long experience in front of the camera," but also from the nature of the times. In other words, the presi-dent's personal skills and inclinations suited well the leadership context. Nonetheless, to succeed at establishing effective press relations also requires a viable strategy for managing the news.

Strategic Factors   According to his White House advisers, a great disadvan-tage that President Ford brought to the presidency was a lack of a transition period to develop a press relations strategy. Jerald F. terHorst, the press secretary during Ford's first month in office, put it best when he said that "we never sat down and consciously devised what is called a 'media strategy' or a 'P.R. strategy.' There wasn't time for it, for one thing. We had to walk in there and hit the ground run-ning." terHorst described his "transition" to office as follows.

I had twenty minutes of briefing from [Nixon Press Secretary] Ron Ziegler, which was really, "here's the office, the men's room is around the corner, the safe is under my desk, here's the combination, if you need me give me a call in California—they're call-ing me to the helicopter now." That was the extent of the transition from one adminis-tration to another, as far as the press secretary was concerned.[43]

John W. Hushen and Larry Speakes also emphasized that the lack of a normal transition period made difficult the formulation of a press strategy.

Hushen: I think that one of the great complications for the Ford presidency was the fact that there was no regular transition period. Ford literally went from being Vice President of the United States to President of the United States overnight. So there was not time to give a lot of thought initially to press strategy.[44]

Speakes: Ford being thrust into the presidency as he was, there was not the usual time available to sit down and to plan a strategy. I think that was largely responsible for Ford's inability to get a good press for his initiatives. The first thirty days in the White House press office in 1974 are often compared to stand-ing by a railroad track and watching a freight train go by while trying to read the words on the boxcars. . . . There was no structure. Usually, in other White Houses there had been an office of communications or somebody, a chief of staff for example, who had an interest in looking at long-term strategy. We just didn't have that luxury in the Ford White House.[45]

Speakes contrasted his experiences dealing with press relations in the Ford and Reagan White Houses. In 1981 the Reagan White House had a "100 days" plan for setting the agenda that had been mapped out during the early stages of the 1980 presidential campaign. The Ford White House had to work out its agenda and means of communication on a day-to-day basis.[46]

Even without a regular transition period and press relations blue-print, White House advisers had ideas about how to establish good press relations. In the early days of Ford's presidency, the White House capitalized on the president's reputation for honesty and integrity—a major public relations asset in the wake of Watergate. To the extent that the White House had a press "strategy," it consisted of (1) the need to emphasize the change taking place in the nation's leadership, and (2) efforts to project the "open presidency" theme.

Greener: Generally speaking, the strategy was to be open and above board, and to answer [reporters'] questions as much as possible. And to make people available.[47]

Warren: If the Ford administration had any strategy at all, it was to impress upon the press corps that this . . . was not the Nixon administration. It was an administration under which things would be different. . . . And there was a press strategy to try to humanize the presidency. You may remember the President fixing his own breakfast and other such activities designed to humanize the presidency. . . . The other strategy . . . was to try to be as forthcoming as possible on all questions raised by journalists.[48]

terHorst: We wanted to convey that this administration would be an open place in a democratic, American fashion. It was important to make people once again proud of their president and proud of the White House. . . . [Ford] understood the need for what we were trying to do. . . . He did want to establish himself as a change from Richard Nixon. He may never have stated that publicly, but that was his personal view of the situation.[49]

terHorst identified steps adopted early by Ford to convey the themes of change and openness. Having been deprived for so long of a presidential press conference, members of the media clamored for an early Ford press conference. Ford agreed and, at terHorst's suggestion, the president entered the White House East Room press conference by walking down a long, open hallway to the simple podium that stood there before the press corps.

> I did not want Jerry Ford standing behind a huge bullet-proof podium with his back to the wall and that blue curtain, as Richard Nixon and Lyndon Johnson did. That set-up made them look like caged men surrounded by cameras and reporters with the press in a feeding frenzy, almost like sharks. Jerry Ford agreed to let me fashion something that would be different, more open. . . . It did indeed look open! The press liked it. It worked. It was cosmetic, but it also was symbolic. It reinforced Ford's promise to be an open, accessible president.[50]

terHorst also emphasized his accessibility to the president, another change from the practices of the Nixon White House. The press secretary wanted the press to be confident that when he announced a presidential directive or comment that the words actually came from Ford, not from some senior staffer speaking on behalf of the president.

One of Ron Ziegler's constant press problems was, "Ron, have you see the President? When was the last time you saw him? Or are you just talking with General Haig?" Which was often the case. . . . One of the first things I had to do was to demonstrate that I did have direct access to the President whenever I needed it so that questions could get answered. . . . We wanted to demonstrate that this President at least talked to his press secretary and the press secretary knew what he was saying. There was both an open door for the media through me, and an open door for me within the environs of the administration.[51]

terHorst explained that Ford directed him "to straighten out the press office." That meant taking off the payroll Nixon White House "holdovers" who did not work for the press secretary and staffers whom the press associated with the Nixon public relations apparatus.

We didn't have on my staff any room for such things as an "attack force" and a "defense force." I surely didn't need any of those offices. And I certainly didn't need those sorts of people. . . . The guard had changed.[52]

Ford adopted other symbolic changes to convey the theme of an open, unpretentious White House. These included replacing "Hail to the Chief" with the "Michigan Fight Song," referring to the White House as the "residence," and renaming the presidential plane "Air Force One" (rather than Nixon's usage, "The Spirit of '76"). Ford also dropped temporarily the name from the White House Office of Communications, Margita White explained, "largely because there was still a great deal of sensitivity to the impression of that office left by the Nixon White House. That office took on a very political role under Ken Clawson during the last days of Watergate."[53]

Carter's press strategy in many ways was similar to Ford's: stress an open, accessible presidency that differs from the practices of the Nixon White House. Nonetheless, despite having a transition period to plan, the Carter White House never developed a viable press strategy that would hold up over time. Early in the term the Carter White House did little to effectively articulate an agenda or sell to the public what the Carter presidency stood for. White House officials were not encouraged to speak with one voice, or to articulate broad themes. Public statements from administrative departments often were not coordinated.

Communications adviser Gregg Schneiders told John Anthony Maltese (1990, 2) that Carter White House staff meetings focused on "substantive" matters and lacked a "focused approach to communications." Deputy Press Secretary Walt Wurfel said that, "We didn't do very well at coordinating the departments at all" (Maltese 1990, 2). According to Schneiders "many people who wanted to support the President's programs didn't know what the right line was" (Maltese 1990, 2).

Carter's advisers noted that because the president eschewed political considerations and focused on policy substance, public relations strategy did not get much attention. Carter forthrightly addressed the nation's problems in public addresses and did not disguise the difficulties of trying to solve such problems. This forthrightness became a leadership liability. To the public, Carter identified problems, accepted responsibility, and then did not promise clear, immediate solutions. As a speechwriter noted, people associated what was wrong in their lives with Carter personally.[54] A White House media adviser and senior staff member identified the problems that created.

> I'm afraid what was happening and what happened a lot was that this president did decide to deliver a lot of the bad news and then cabinet members would deliver the good news, which is a reverse of [the Reagan administration].[55]
> Every time we would make a speech on inflation or energy, and the more we talked about it without being able ever to bring the little carrot of good news, people would more and more find Carter responsible for those things. We were more closely identified with the bad news the more we made speeches.[56]

In mid-1978 media adviser Gerald Rafshoon joined the Carter administration to coordinate White House communications. Rafshoon encouraged the White House to adopt some basic public relations techniques—coordinate the message, establish themes, orchestrate public appearances, and coordinate responses to criticisms. Trouble is, because the White House accepted the necessity of doing these things nearly by midterm, critics lambasted the effort as "media manipulation" and mockingly labeled it "Rafshoonery" (Maltese 1990). Had Carter initiated such a press game plan at the beginning of the term, few would have objected. But because Carter came to office promising to be different from other politicians, eschewing traditional politics and neglecting press strategy, the effort to develop a public relations plan later on generated much criticism. As Maltese noted, journalists subjected Carter to "the *charge* of trying to manipulate the media" (Maltese 1990, 16). The trick for any president is to learn how to manipulate the media without appearing to do so.

The Reagan White House, from the beginning of the first term, displayed no lack of interest in public relations. The chief of staff James Baker offered this comment.

> Implementing policy depends on getting your media operation and your political operation together, but so does running a successful presidential campaign. . . . A, you've got to have a message, and B, you've got to be able to sell that message. The only thing added to that once you move into the White House is that you've got to be able to sell it not just to the public but also on the Hill. But the key to selling it on the Hill is to sell it publicly (Hertsgaard 1988, 23).

Leslie Janka left no doubt about the extent to which the Reagan White House emphasized public relations.

> The whole thing was P.R. This was a P.R. outfit that became President and took over the country. And to the degree then to which the Constitution forced them to do things like make a budget, run foreign policy and all that, they sort of did. But their first, last and overarching activity was public relations (Hertsgaard 1988, 6).

Donald Regan (1988, 274, 277) offered a similar recollection when he noted that much of the president's inner circle perceived Reagan "as a sort of supreme anchorman whose public persona was the most important element of the Presidency."

> According to the rules of this school of political management, controversy was to be avoided at nearly any cost: every Presidential action must produce a positive public

effect. In practice, this meant stimulating a positive effect in the media, with the result that the press, not the people, became the president's primary constituency.

Every moment of every public appearance was scheduled, every word was scripted, every place where Reagan was supposed to stand was chalked with toe marks. The President was always being prepared for a performance.

And the former senior White House political strategist Lee Atwater told Hedrick Smith (1988, 398) that,

> I can't think of a single meeting I was at for more than an hour when someone didn't say, "How will this play in the media?" . . . Cabinet officers got run out of office because the White House couldn't manage the story in the media. You got it all the time. Major decisions were influenced by the media.

Janka described the White House public relations strategy that he said indeed enhanced press coverage.

> As opposed to Kissinger and Haldeman and that crowd, whose view was that you control the media by giving them bits and pieces [of information], the Reagan White House came to the totally opposite conclusion that the media will take what we feed them. . . . They've got to write their story every day. You give them their story, they'll go away. As long as you come in there [every] day, hand them a well-packaged, premasticated story in the format they want, they'll go away. The phrase is "manipulation by inundation." You give them the line of the day, you give them the press briefings, you give them the facts, access to people who will speak on the record. . . . And you do that long enough, they're going to stop bringing their own stories, and stop being investigative reporters of any kind, even modestly so (Hertsgaard 1988, 52).

According to Michael Deaver, the reporters take whatever the White House feeds them because they all stay too close to the White House and "beat on each other, and if they don't have a story, sure, they're going to take [ours]" (Hertsgaard 1988, 57).

David Gergen explained that one of his ploys to get the press to present the White House perspective was "frequent" phone calls to reporters working on stories. He made late afternoon phone calls to reporters, near story deadline time, to try to get the last say, or to leave the last impression. According to Gergen, the ploy was—if not innovative—remarkably effective for the Reagan administration (Hertsgaard 1988, 29). "The reporters respond to that. . . . They like it. They need it. And you could get them to change their feed" (Smith 1988, 405).

Another strategy that Gergen identified was the decision to be sure that the president publicly delivered good news, and Reagan's "lieutenants" delivered the bad news. Again, this strategy was not original with Reagan's White House, but according to Gergen—who also worked for presidents Nixon and Ford—it worked best for Reagan.

> it is terribly important that the President not be out on the line every day, particularly on bad news. . . . My theory on that is that you only have one four-star general in battle, but you've got a lot of lieutenants who can give blood. And if the going is getting hot and heavy, it is far better to have your lieutenants take the wounds than your general. Because once that happens to your President, it is very difficult to recover from it. One of the most destructive aspects of the Carter administration was that they continually let

him go out there and be the point man, on everything! A lot of our strategy had to do with *not* having the President out answering questions every day. . . .When we have something developed that we can go out and talk about in a positive way, then bring it back to the White House (Hertsgaard 1988, 32–33).

Gergen explained that the White House consciously made, for example, Interior Secretary James Watt the "point man" on environmental issues to deflect criticism from Reagan. On budgetary issues the Office of Management and Budget Director David Stockman consciously was put "out front" to deflect criticism. Gergen admitted that, "It was a conscious policy in terms of shaping the news" (Hertsgaard 1988, 33).

The most important aspect of Reagan's press strategy was to focus both the White House's agenda and statements. Gergen explained that "we molded a communications strategy around a legislative strategy. We very carefully thought through what were the legislative goals we were trying to achieve, and then formulated a communications strategy which supported them" (Hertsgaard 1988, 108).

Chief White House lobbyist to the House of Representatives Kenneth Duberstein noted that the White House coordinated the political and press strategies through the Legislative Strategy Group. "A high degree of coordination came out of there regarding our messages to the media, to the public, and so forth. . . . That's where the major linkages came together" (Hertsgaard 1988, 108).

Reagan's staff emphasized the importance of putting the legislative and communications strategies in place early in the first term. The point, according to James Baker, was to quickly establish the president's leadership.

The key to a successful presidency is that he be seen to be a leader—somebody who can convert his philosophy into policy goals. . . . And the way you do that is to pick your issues carefully, and make sure that once you pick them you win them. And also not to have the focus too diffuse. . . . If we had any success in those early years, it was because we were single-minded in our concentration on the economy that first year (Hertsgaard 1988, 107).

Duberstein, Deaver and Speakes added the following observations.

Duberstein: One of the critical points of that first year was to learn from the mistakes of the Carter administration, which had set a diverse initiative for the country when it set up several legislative initiatives [right away]. . . . If you can rivet public attention on one or two things, you have a less difficult time focusing the congressional mind-set. So the economic recovery program became *the* agenda. . . . The linkage between legislative priorities and communications priorities was exceedingly close that first year (Hertsgaard 1988, 107–108).

Deaver: In 1981 and through the first half of '82 I would not allow anything to be put on the [President's] schedule that didn't have to do with economic reform. . . . I just said, "That's all we're going to do" (Hertsgaard 1988, 107).

Speakes: Before we entered the White House we had decided that the sole focus of the first year was to be the President's economic program. . . . Almost no news item, no speech, no trip, no photo-op whatsoever was put on the President's schedule during 1981 unless it contributed to the President's economic program (1988, 301).

Conclusion: Presidential Press Strategies Reconsidered

Developing a favorable White House-press relationship is no simple task. It requires a president who knows how to communicate, a generally favorable political context, a susceptible press corps, and a White House staff skilled at public relations. White House media strategists identified three elements of a successful White House-press relationship.

Contextual Factors   The environment of press evaluations of a presidency is defined in large part by matters over which a White House has little or no control: the economic condition inherited by the president, international developments, the strength of the president's party in Congress, among others. Consequently, a president cannot control all of the outside events that bear upon the press assessments of his performance.

Ford's media strategists said that the situation that they inherited for the most part hurt their efforts to build a good press relationship. True, Ford succeeded a disgraced president and at first benefited from the inevitable press comparisons to his predecessor. But Ford also inherited a troubled economy, the end of U.S. involvement in South East Asia, a combative opposition-party led Congress, and a press corps left cynical by Watergate. He lacked a presidential transition period to build an agenda and a press strategy. He lacked an electoral mandate and needed to establish his legitimacy before the public.

Ford tried to reverse the trend toward increasingly sour White House-press corps relations, and did succeed somewhat in that endeavor. Yet for the most part, press cynicism remained resilient and carried over at least into Carter's term.

Carter's media strategists also stressed that their president had his hands full of problems over which he had little control. That Carter could not quickly turn around the economy or the energy problem resulted in negative press coverage. In his case, a significant improvement in economic and energy conditions could have resulted in better press treatment. A successful hostage rescue mission conceivably could have turned his presidency around completely.

Reagan's public and press image benefited from the 1980s period of economic growth. Reagan took advantage of the political context, exploiting opportunities created by the perception of a need for change in the White House's way of doing business in political Washington. Reagan's media strategists downplayed the importance of these contextual factors to his press image and instead largely attributed the White House's success to personal skills and strategies.

Personal Factors   The modern president cannot neglect the role of Communicator-in-Chief. Despite their claims of dislike of being "manipulated," journalists favorably evaluate a president who excels in the areas that they know best—public relations and the press. A president who eschews public relations likely will come under journalistic fire for so doing.

An emphasis on presidential communications does not guarantee success. Ford did not neglect public and press relations, but his lack of media savvy and his "halting manner of speaking" did not serve him well. Carter generally failed to place much emphasis on the public relations presidency and even Rafshoon's best efforts could not turn the president into a decent communicator. Reagan placed extraordinary emphasis on public relations and succeeded in part because of his personal skills. Unlike Ford and Carter, Reagan brought to the White House skills conducive to effecting a good image.

Strategic Factors   Personal skills and an agreeable political context may not suffice. A White House needs a press strategy, a plan. It is especially important to quickly establish a viable strategy, as early press evaluations have an enormous long-term influence on a president's reputation.

Ford's media strategists emphasized that they did not have a chance to establish early on a press relations plan. They said that they had to engage in an *ad hoc* process of developing press relations. Ford had short notice of Nixon's resignation and there was too little time to think about strategy.

Carter failed to establish a viable press plan early on that would include a means of communicating the White House's message in a clear, consistent fashion. The Carter White House did not integrate a press relations plan with a policy agenda strategy. When Rafshoon joined the White House in mid-1978 to help accomplish some fundamental tasks—coordinating statements, simplifying messages, connecting themes—it was too late to turn around Carter's negative press image. The press then portrayed Rafshoon's efforts as manipulative.

Reagan's media strategists said that they fared better than their predecessors at establishing a workable press strategy because they understood and cared about public relations. During the 1980 campaign Reagan had a transition team developing a 100-days plan and a press strategy in case of election. Reagan, to use James Pfiffner's (1988) description, "hit the ground running," both in terms of setting the agenda and coordinating the agenda with a press strategy. Reagan's advisers worked hard at developing and sustaining a press relations plan because they placed so much credence on the public presidency.

What emerges from the commentaries of White House media strategists are common perceptions of the elements of a president's press relationship: the *context* in which a president operates, the *personal* skills and inclinations of the man and his media strategists, the public relations *strategies* of these people. Although media strategists identify the same explanatory elements of a president's press relationship, they differ in degrees of emphasis.

White House media strategists emphasize those elements that justify their own efforts and make their president look as good as possible. Hence, Ford's media strategists emphasized that their poor press coverage could be explained by the difficulties engendered by the leadership context, the president's emphasis on policy problems over public relations, and the president's lack of background and skill at rousing national support. Carter's strategists also said that their president had to contend with a difficult leadership context caused by policy problems over which he had no control, and a post-Watergate independent minded Congress. They also stressed that Carter chose to focus on policy substance over public relations and rhetoric. By contrast, Reagan's media strategists emphasized that their success could be attributed to superior public relations personnel, presidential skill, and crafty White House strategies. They said relatively little about the leadership context.

The perceptions of the White House media strategists affect the development of an administration's media plans. In particular, media strategists are influenced by their perceptions of the leadership context and of the president's personal strengths and weaknesses. It is little wonder, then, why Reagan's media strategists emphasized an aggressive, act quickly public relations plan capitalizing on the honeymoon period and on the president's unique media-oriented skills. No such comparable effort was made to turn either Ford or Carter into a "great communicator." Ford's media people spent much time establishing their unelected president's legitimacy before the people, a task that had to predate any efforts to lead a policy agenda. Given a narrow electoral margin and public uncertainty over his leadership, Carter's media people put the president into various public relations formats early in the term. The White House for most of the remainder of the term downplayed public relations gimmickry, given the president's disinclination to expend much effort on such tasks and his desire to focus on policy substance (Hargrove 1989; Jones 1988; Rozell 1989, 1990).

The findings of this study show that first, not every White House attaches the same level of priority to public and press relations. Second, not every president and his advisers have the same media skills. Third, the leadership context, and hence environment for press management, differs from administration to administration.

Much of the literature emphasizes the advantages that a White House has in managing the press. From the perspectives of the White House insiders a different view emerges—one in which factors often beyond anyone's control establish the conditions for a president's press coverage. A White House, to be sure, can do some things to improve its image, and it should. The image of leadership today is an important part of its reality.

The perspectives of White House media strategists are pertinent to political scientists developing theories of presidential press relations. It appears that it may not be possible to develop a uniform set of guidelines on how to maximize favorable press coverage. Clearly some techniques work better than others, but it is difficult to control contextual and personal factors that set the stage for the development of White House strategies and for how journalists assess a presidency.

NOTES

1. Author interview with Ron Nessen (by telephone), July 5, 1990.
2. Author interview with Robert Hartmann (Bethesda, Maryland), December 15, 1989.
3. Author interview with John W. Hushen (Washington, D.C.), May 14, 1990.

*This essay is based on a paper presented at the annual meeting of the Western Political Science Association, Seattle, Washington, March 22, 1991.

4. Author interview with Louis M. Thompson, Jr. (Washington, D.C.), November 20, 1990.
5. Author interview with John G. Carlson (by telephone), May 2, 1990.
6. Author interview with President Gerald R. Ford (by telephone), December 13, 1989.
7. Author interview with William Greener (by telephone), January 23, 1990.
8. Author interview with Jerald F. terHorst (Washington, D.C.), June 27, 1990.
9. White Burkett Miller Center of Public Affairs, University of Virginia, Charlottesville, Virginia. Project on the Carter Presidency (hereafter cited as CPP), Vol. 10, p. 15.
10. CPP, Vol. 10, p. 16.
11. CPP, Vol. 10, p. 17.
12. CPP, Vol. 10, p. 18.
13. CPP, Vol. 7, p. 10.
14. CPP, Vol. 10, p. 90
15. CPP, Vol. 10, p. 111.
16. CPP, Vol. 7, p. 77.
17. CPP, Vol. 10, p. 114.
18. CPP, Vol. 4, p. 99.
19. CPP, Vol. 10, p. 93
20. CPP, Vol. 21, pp. 12–13.
21. Author interview with Larry Speakes (by telephone), February 6, 1990.
22. Thompson interview.
23. Hartmann interview.
24. Hushen interview.
25. Greener interview.
26. Interview with Ford White House press office staffer.
27. Nessen interview.
28. Speakes interview.
29. Ford interview.
30. CPP, Vol. 10, p. 78.
31. CPP, Vol. 3, p. 95.
32. CPP, Vol. 3, p. 97.
33. CPP, Vol. 3, p. 101.
34. CPP, Vol. 1, pp. 119–120.
35. CPP, Vol. 21, p. 23.
36. CPP, Vol. 8, p. 130.
37. CPP, Vol. 8, p. 84.
38. CPP, Vol. 8, p. 21.
39. CPP, Vol. 8, p. 14.
40. CPP, Vol. 8, p. 37.
41. CPP, Vol. 8, p. 38.
42. CPP, Vol. 8, p. 39.
43. terHorst interview.
44. Hushen interview.
45. Speakes interview.
46. *Ibid.*
47. Greener interview.
48. Author interview with former deputy press secretary Gerald Warren (by telephone), March 5, 1990.

49. terHorst interview.
50. *Ibid.*
51. *Ibid.*
52. *Ibid.*
53. Author interview with Margita White (by telephone), July 7, 1990.
54. CPP, Vol. 8, p. 138.
55. CPP, Vol. 21, p. 9.
56. CPP, Vol. 21, p. 32.

REFERENCES

1. Brody, Richard A. 1991. *Assessing the President: The Media, Elite Opinion, and Public Support.* Stanford: Stanford University Press.
2. Bennett, W. Lance. 1988. *News: The Politics of Illusion,* 2d ed. New York: Longman.
3. Cheney, Richard B. 1988. "Forming and Managing an Administration," in *The Ford Presidency: Twenty-Two Intimate Perspectives of Gerald R. Ford,* ed. Kenneth W. Thompson. Lanham, Maryland: University Press of America.
4. Cronin, Thomas E. 1974. "The Presidency Public Relations Script," in *The Presidency Reappraised,* eds. Rexford G. Tugwell and Thomas E. Cronin. New York: Praeger, 168–186.
5. Entman, Robert M. 1989. *Democracy Without Citizens: Media and the Decay of American Politics.* New York: Oxford University Press.
6. Fallows, James. 1979. "Rhetoric and Presidential Leadership," in White Burkett Miller Center Research Project on Presidential Rhetoric, University of Virginia, Charlottesville, Virginia.
7. Ford, Gerald R. 1987. *A Time to Heal.* Norwalk, Connecticut: Easton Press.
8. Grossman, Michael B. and Kumar, Martha J. 1981. *Portraying the President: The White House and the News Media.* Baltimore: Johns Hopkins University Press.
9. Hargrove, Erwin. 1989. *Jimmy Carter as President: Leadership and the Politics of the Public Good.* Baton Rouge: Louisiana State University Press.
10. Hertsgaard, Mark. 1988. *On Bended Knee: The Press and the Reagan Presidency.* New York: Farrar, Straus, and Giroux.
11. Hess, Stephen. 1984. *The Washington Reporters.* Washington, D.C.: The Brookings Institution.
12. Jones, Charles O. 1988. *The Trusteeship Presidency: Jimmy Carter and the United States Congress.* Baton Rouge: Louisiana State University Press.
13. Jordan, Hamilton. 1982. *Crisis: The Last Year of the Carter Presidency.* New York: Berkeley Books.
14. Maltese, John Anthony. 1990. "'Rafshoonery': The Effort to Control the Communications Agenda of the Carter Administration." Presented at the Hofstra University 8th Presidential Conference—"Jimmy Carter: Keeping Faith," Hempstead, New York.
15. Noonan, Peggy. 1990. *What I Saw at the Revolution: A Political Life in the Reagan Era.* New York: Ballantine Books.
16. Paletz, David L. and Entman, Robert M. 1980. "Presidents, Power, and the Press." *Presidential Studies Quarterly* 10:416–426.
17. Pfiffner, James. 1988. *The Strategic Presidency: Hitting the Ground Running.* Chicago: Dorsey Press.

18. Powell, Jody. 1984. *The Other Side of the Story*. New York: William Morrow.
19. Regan, Donald T. 1988. *For the Record: From Wall Street to Washington*. New York: St. Martin's Press.
20. Rozell, Mark J. 1990. "President Carter and the Press: Perspectives from White House Communications Advisers." *Political Science Quarterly* 105:419–434.
21. Rozell, Mark J. 1989. *The Press and the Carter Presidency*. Boulder, Colorado: Westview Press.
22. Smith, Hedrick. 1988. *The Power Game: How Washington Works*. New York: Ballantine Books.
23. Speakes, Larry. 1988. *Speaking Out: The Reagan Presidency from Inside the White House*. New York: Avon Books.
24. Stockman, David A. 1986. *The Triumph of Politics: Why the Reagan Revolution Failed*. New York: Harper and Row.
25. Wolfson, Lewis W. 1985. *The Untapped Power of the Press*. New York: Praeger.
26. Zeidenstein, Harvey G. 1984. "News Media Perceptions of White House News Management." *Presidential Studies Quarterly* 14:391–398.

US Presidents and the Mass Media

David Morgan

In the United States the presidency normally has more the appearance of power than the reality. The Founding Fathers never intended a powerful presidency and, when depression or wars in the mid-twentieth century seemed to conspire to produce one, the recoil in the 1970s, rooted in public opinion and congressional resentment at its own overshadowing, was relatively quick and effective. The Imperial Presidency had its wings clipped, and scholarly students of the presidency have charted the consequences not only for the office-holder but also in Congress and the bureaucracy. Curbing the White House evolved into curbing the federal government in general, certainly in domestic politics. Ronald Reagan in 1981 proclaimed: 'Government is not the solution; government is the problem.' Exactly as intended by the Founding Fathers, a President, except during a clearly perceived foreign or domestic crisis, has to compete to set the national agenda against Congress, the Supreme Court, federal agencies and departments, states and interest groups of all kinds.

Presidents are far from powerless but daily have to create and sustain coalitions of interest in Washington and the country if White House priorities are to prevail. Presidents are held responsible for a privately run economy and head an administration which does not fix interest rates or the money supply, does not control parts of the Executive branch, is constitutionally at odds with the legislature and supervised by the Supreme Court over which it has very limited influence. Added are cyclical swings of popular mood—now demanding intrusive government, now rebelling against seemingly all government and collective activity. Little wonder that President Truman said of Eisenhower: 'He'll say do this and do that—and nothing will happen. Poor Ike, it won't be a bit like the army.' It is clear that to succeed a President must establish priorities and work at generating supportive opinion for them.[1]

Building popular support is therefore critical and, seen from the White House, mass media can be potent allies or obstructive, constitutionally protected but unelected enemies. Mass media are themselves big business and must be seen as part of the large corporate business world currently going through major restructuring in search of greater profitability—a process which has led to major retrenchment in television. Hence employees have no interest in economic recession and a direct interest in sustained growth which generates advertising, sales and profits. Presidents are expected to ensure that growth occurs and are judged accordingly. Of course, media corporations also claim to operate in the public interest, a claim which makes complex demands on the White House. Presidents are routinely expected to have views on virtually all matters and proposals on most; White House silences are neither expected nor welcomed.

Media coverage gives salience to some and not other issues and, except where individual experience contradicts it, helps frame voter attitudes and involvement. In domestic affairs individual knowledge and beliefs can frame the perceptions of reporters and editors, but in foreign affairs this is often markedly less true and gives Presidents much more room to manoeuvre. The Vietnam war is a classic case in which that room was used and abused and, in the 1980s, the Grenada and Lebanon interventions saw similar examples of news management. In the recent Gulf War, the lengths to which the White House and Pentagon were prepared to go to manage reporters were very visible. The rivalries between media and between reporters were used by government news sources to plant stories to ensure that coverage had the required slant.[2]

In the face of all this, Presidents have to assume that media relations are a crucial part of White House activity and, on average, over a hundred staff members are directly employed in such relations. Indirectly engaged, of course, are all White House staff and the President since it is their business to produce policies which generate popular consent. The strategies and tactics used not only in the White House, but also in other parts of the federal government, repay examination. Journalistic attitudes—often derided by officials—are only understandable if government efforts at news and agenda setting are fully grasped.

[1]See Bert Rockman, *The Leadership Question. The Presidency and the American System,* New York: Praeger, 1984; Theodore Lowi *The Personal President, Power Invested, Promise Unfulfilled,* Ithaca and London, Cornell University Press, 1985 and Samuel Kernell *Going Public. New Strategies of Presidential Leadership,* Washington DC: CQ Press, 1986.

[2]See Shanto Iyengar and Donald R. Kinder, *News that Matters,* Chicago: Chicago University Press, 1987 and Stephen Ansolebehere, Ray Behr and Shanto Iyengar, *The Media Game. American Politics in the Television Age.* New York: Macmillan 1993.

By way of introduction, however, a brief outline of the US media system is necessary. The US has 1,800 daily newspapers, 8,800 weeklies and 10,000 magazines of all types. The country has 10,000 radio and 900 television stations. America thus has large numbers of media outlets but, in fact, relatively few owners—more than half the dailies and a third of radio and television stations, are owned by chains or conglomerates, and the trend is increasing. The country has four large commercial television networks—American Broadcasting Corporation, Columbia Broadcasting System, National Broadcasting Corporation, Fox Television—and the publicly-owned Public Broadcasting System, modeled in part on the BBC. By 1992, 67% of households had cable television and Cable Network News now reaches 50 million households in the US. In total, the US has scores of thousands of people engaged in newsgathering of all kinds, of whom perhaps 40,000 would be regarded as working journalists, and of these 10% are registered with the United States Senate and constitute the Washington press corps. Within that large number, however, relatively few work in Washington as *political* reporters for the thirty leading newspapers and magazines (perhaps 400) or in Washington and New York City for television and radio networks (perhaps 600) or for the two main news services—Associated Press and United Press International (perhaps 400). If these numbers seem small, it must be remembered that the average number of reporters at the daily White House briefings is about 90, while those at the State Department and Pentagon average about the same number.

Thus the US media scene has large numbers of outlets and reporters but relatively few reporters in the front line. Even major newspapers like the *New York Times* and *Wall Street Journal* have less than 30 reporters in their Washington bureaus. These numbers are not unimportant. Seen from the White House Press Secretary's office, the front line of the American news industry consists of perhaps 500 key players in Washington and New York City. Given the hierarchic nature of the industry—newspaper reporters and editors are very far from equal—the White House will see these as a vitally important small group of opinion leaders.

For the White House Press Secretary the prime focus is political news, but no one is more aware that such news has become ever more broadly defined. Almost any news which impacts on the popular standing of a government may now be taken as political news. Economic news obviously, but from time to time news of sport, society, religious affairs; all seem to impinge on governmental reputation. When government action is proposed, whether by office holders or outsiders, then clearly such proposals become political and must be addressed. For most purposes the political component of news is defined by reporters as that calling for governmental involvement either immediately, or in the foreseeable future.

What, then, constitutes national political news in the US? Briefly, television and radio focus some 70% of their coverage on the White House and Congress. In the leading American newspapers, advertisements take up on average 60% of the newspaper, leaving 40% for all other major news categories such as business, sport, general features—and politics. On average, the latter is given less than 20% of the space in this 'newshole', that is 8% of the total. This category covers local, state, national and international news, the last two usually taking up some 70% of the total. Strictly speaking, American national political news then comprises about 35% of all political news. Even when international news is of a kind likely to demand government action, the total of its coverage rarely exceeds 50% of all political news. For readers, significant political news of the national government will be less than half of all political news and be spread across news of the three branches of government, elections, scandals, interest group demands and anything unforeseen on many fronts.

Numbers, however, can deceive. National political news of domestic and foreign origin can still routinely make the front page and sometimes dominate it. Presidents who are wise will wish to influence lead stories even if they involve trenchant criticism of their policies. As Jimmy Carter found in the late 1970s, being off the front page is to risk being marginalised and quickly suffer disapproval from voters. Popular expectations do not allow much presidential silence. 'Everyone', as President Truman observed, 'thinks the man in the White House can do something about everything.' Most of his successors begin by thinking that and, sometimes too late, wish they had not done so. Presidents have to work to get favourable front page, lead story coverage.[3]

White House Strategies

What images of the President do his staff seek to portray through his Press Secretary and, more generally, by activities which form part of a cohesive communications strategy? Firstly, staff will try to portray the President's personal qualities. The incumbent, after all, is head of state as well as chief executive and his election was, in part, a judgement on his personal qualities. From at least the 1830s and Andrew Jackson, 'the man of the people' theme has been part of nearly every presidential campaign, and the advent of radio, then television has intensified this. Thus Eisenhower's golf, the Kennedy family softball games, Nixon's baseball enthusiasm, were all genuinely enjoyed activities but were also used to show the President's tastes—he was a 'regular guy' despite his high office. Carter carried this a stage further by walking from the Capitol to the White House after his Inauguration and, for a while, giving televised 'Fireside Chats' on the Roosevelt model—wearing an open cardigan. He also continued to wear jeans off duty and was probably genuinely surprised by the public and journalistic interest in this. Ronald Reagan was rich and western, hence his image maker exploited activities such as horse riding, wood chopping and land clearing at his luxurious ranch. He himself portrayed his political views as those of 'ordinary Americans' too long ignored by the 'elite, Eastern media'. President Clinton, likewise, has sought to exploit his ordinariness, presenting his marriage troubles as commonplace in mainstream America.

Presidential ordinariness is further sold via 'the family man' image. Thus Hillary Clinton is but the current spouse in a line of spouses exploited to add to the President's appeal. Eleanor Roosevelt provided a model for Democratic wives by

[3]See my *The Flacks of Washington. Government Information and the Public Agenda,* Westport CT: Greenwood Press, 1986.

creating an independent and more liberal identity—sometimes to the consternation of those around her husband. Jackie Kennedy, Lady Bird Johnson, Rosalyn Carter and now Hillary Clinton had to acquire similar independent but complementary interests. Republican incumbent's wives seemed less inclined to follow the model—Mamie Eisenhower, Pat Nixon and Betty Ford all found the First Lady role very stressful, and their behaviour and health suffered. Nancy Reagan, too, found the role difficult, acquired public 'causes' but seemed never able to satisfy the press corps and may well have hurt rather than helped her husband. Not only wives but children, too, have been pressed into service. John Kennedy's son John, Nixon's daughter Julie, Carter's daughter Amy, and now Chelsea Clinton—all had to endure media attention of a kind hitherto thought improper. It is fair to say that the 'family' angle easily backfires—Mamie Eisenhower's alcoholism, Pat Nixon and Nancy Reagan's 'frozen' public personae, Jimmy Carter's brother with his Libyan connections and, more recently, Hillary Clinton's visibility on health care policies, all created real public relations problems for incumbents. Journalists had been ready to collaborate in this White House image-making, but only up to a point. When the worm turned, the acerbic comments that followed clearly indicated long concealed resentments within the press corps.

Presidents have to be seen to be leaders and their behaviour in office becomes very important. Jet aircraft have, of course, enabled foreign travel to be frequent and brief. Hence Presidents have taken to being their own Secretaries of State, directly conducting negotiations and presiding over summits of allies and enemies. Indeed, presidential absence from such events is now a news story. Recognition by foreign leaders has been an ingredient of presidential power since Woodrow Wilson's long visit to the Versailles Conference after the first world war. Kennedy in Berlin, Johnson in Vietnam, Nixon on the Great Wall of China in 1972, Ford at the Helsinki Summit, Carter in Berlin, Reagan at Normandy and Moscow follow the pattern. At home, a variety of strategies are used. The President is Commander in Chief and hence photo opportunities against a backdrop of military power (warships, combat troops) have become routine. As chief executives, Presidents must appear to be personally very capable and not merely a tool of subordinates. Thus sacking subordinates—examples are Truman and General MacArthur, Nixon and Special Prosecutor Archibald Cox—is one tactic. Avoiding appointing a subordinate is another device—Ford's refusal to appoint Kissinger is a classic since US foreign policy had become identified with him. Clinton's refusal to appoint Jessie Jackson is another case. Presidents must also appear to be expert, capable of assessing specialist advice when it is given. Kennedy, Carter and Bush, as examples, traded on their military background; in contrast, Reagan and Ford claimed no particular expertise and, in Reagan's case, proudly so.

Presidents are expected to be policy makers and to offer to Congress and the public a coherent programme. The President, after all, is the only nationally elected politician and Presidents have traded heavily on their supposed authoritative overview of national needs. When compared with members of Congress or state Governors, Presidents have the advantage of using speeches to Congress (State of the Union, State of the economy) and appearances on network television to project their policy programmes. Inevitably, all travel and every ceremonial and working occasion—greeting ambassadors and briefing members of Congress—is used for projection purposes. The use by Franklin D. Roosevelt of radio to circumvent an unsympathetic press was not lost on his successors—all have used, even overused, television. The live press conference for a time looked like becoming the equivalent of the House of Commons Question Time—and a field day for reporters. Hence Presidents varied in their enthusiasm for the event—Republicans Nixon, Ford and Reagan being noticeably unenthusiastic and Johnson calling conferences at short notice so as to avoid the secondary questions he came to fear.[4]

Media Responses

All the foregoing are the strategies Presidents use in all they do and especially with the press corps. What tactics do they use to try to ensure that it is their agendas which are reported? This is a complex matter and the very core of the presidential-press relationship, since a plethora of other actors—members of Congress, agencies and departments, interest group leaderships—have access to the media and every intention of projecting their own agendas. Moreover, from a reporters' viewpoint, conflict between news sources is the stuff of news and the essence of their job as they see it. The capacity of others to set the agenda will depend on journalistic perceptions both of their importance and the timing of their interventions.

Presidents are usually given a honeymoon during which time the media feel duty bound to 'get the President's message out'. After that time, the message in all its parts is examined critically, and it is at this time that other actors can be most effective as critical sources for journalists. The White House usually sees some of this switch to new sources as rank hostility and behaves accordingly. Favoured reporters are given scoops, while those who are less than supportive are frozen out if at all possible. If reporters find alternative sources, the White House finds alternative outlets—at this time the national press corps finds scoops being given to the regional local press and television and, worse, attempts being made to exploit public hostility to mass media. Both Johnson and Carter did this; Nixon and Reagan raised such tactics to high art and were not averse to adding in the soupçon of intimidation of individual reporters if opportunity offered. In the cases of television journalists Dan Rather and Daniel Schorr under Nixon, the FBI was ordered to investigate their official sources, while strenuous and illegal attempts were made to plug leaks in the administration.

The White House, however, often finds that the Executive Branch itself is almost as reluctant simply to follow a White House line as is Congress. Agencies and departments have their own missions and Congressional supporters, to say nothing of their Congressionally-approved budgets. Despite the presence of White House-appointed leaders in agencies, inertia and disagreement over goals

---

[4]See Ronald Berkman and Laura Kitch, *Politics in the Media Age,* New York: McGraw Hill, 1981.

and policies often lead to discreet opposition being voiced through leaks to the media or to Congressional supporters. A President often finds that he prefers open disagreement to silent disobedience and virtual sabotage of parts of his programme. As Richard Neustadt observed: 'A presidential order has only the force of a strong suggestion not two blocks from the White House.'

The relationship between the media and federal agencies is a very important inhibitor of the President's power to lead, to be successful and to be seen to be successful. Though reporters in Washington are much less organised around single agencies than they used to be, it is still the case that officials work steadily to cultivate the reporters who regularly cover their news. Such regulars are seen as knowledgeable outlets for the official view. Some reporters, indeed, will be on very good terms with senior officials and easily able to go behind a line being pushed by the White House-appointed Cabinet member when this differs from the traditional agency view.

Where agency officials themselves find their programmes being threatened by White House-dictated changes, the regulars on the press corps are the vital conduit for discreet signals of dissent, not merely to a mass audience but also to the White House, to Congress and to other Washington actors. Very importantly, such journalists alert clientele groups in the larger society. These will subsequently be informed in greater detail by means of agency house journals which go out very regularly, but for securing fast responses of support the mass media, especially television, are vital. A Cabinet member will be pressing the White House line only to find it being derided, and the President embarrassed, by informed agency leaks coming out via Congress or interest group spokesmen all over the country. Reporters are well aware of the frequent use of mass media as in-house communications systems in Washington. Contending agency leaders will use their regulars and other reporters to signal qualified support or outright opposition to proposals emanating not only from the White House but from anywhere in the political arena.

The official leak is a key part of the Washington scene. Richard Nixon in the early 1970s entertained sweeping plans for departmental reorganisation—so, too, did Ronald Reagan in the 1980s. On both occasions the Washington air was full of clearly inspired leaks defending departmental autonomy and programmes hallowed by years of Congressional support. Nowhere has the role of mass media and the power of the leak been put better than by Morton Halperin. He noted that media information plays a major role in shaping presidential decisions and that some information is put into circulation by participants seeking to influence presidential decisions. So pervasive is the leak, he went on to argue, that '. . . an option under consideration will be rejected on the grounds that it could not be implemented before it was leaked'. The biggest leakers in Washington, he asserted, were the White House staff, or even the President himself.[5]

[5]Morton Halperin, *Bureaucratic Politics and Foreign Policy,* Washington DC: Brookings Institution 1973, pp. 174–5, pp. 192–3.

White House Responses

After 1978, Jimmy Carter's attempts to make the US more conservation-minded on energy provoked many examples of leaks from within the Washington bureaucracy and Congress. Indeed, the steady attrition of Carter's reputation among reporters and the public was owed in part to leaking of this kind and contributed directly to his electoral failure. A prominent columnist, reflecting on his steady decline during 1979, accepted that media coverage had been very important—'we personalise success or failure but the President is expected to overcome opposition.' Some of the reasons for Carter's inability to do so, a leading reporter argued, originated in the fact that 'special interests in Washington are not paid enough attention by the press'. Media coverage of Carter, he said, became 'a Hill view of the White House'.

After 1980, Ronald Reagan's efforts to promote a new agenda in several areas of major policy—defence, welfare, foreign policy and energy—exemplified this process both in official leaks and official efforts to plumb the leaks. The administration, but the President particularly, became thoroughly exasperated with this situation and made systematic efforts to restrict the release of information and to seek out leakers. The Reagan staff were admirers of the British Official Secrets Acts and contemplated regulation of a similar kind, adding the dimension of lie detector tests. When, however, White House staff realized that they themselves would have to undergo such tests, the idea was hurriedly dropped.

The President was, however, more successful at curtailing government-provided information. Budgets for information programmes in the agencies were steadily reduced and some hitherto declassified information was reclassified. The National Security Agency began to vet drafts of academic writings on codes and code-breaking while, at the White House after 1984, James Baker insisted that officials clear media appearances on any subject with him. Friends of the Administration in the Senate pressed amendments to the Freedom of Information Act and, by increasing fees, made using its provisions ever more difficult, so much so that journalists came to feel there was little point in asking their employers to use an Act which then became, as one reporter noted, a vehicle 'for rich corporations to spy on each other'.

At the foreign policy level, the Administration could point to several successes in the area of media management. To begin, there was the establishing of a new frame of reference. Capitalising particularly on Soviet advances in missile technology, the intervention in Afghanistan and the Iranian hostage crisis, the President successfully relaunched the Cold War and reasserted American autonomy in foreign relations. Confrontation with Libya, the invasion of Grenada, the intervention in Lebanon and the threat of intervention in Nicaragua—all were portrayed as vital if America was to be seen as the leader of resistance to Soviet or Soviet-proxy expansion. In this context, tight control of access by reporters was given a high priority—the British example of media control during the Falklands War being much admired. Television networks and newspapers might protest but were unable to change this policy for a long time.[6]

[6]Morgan, *Flacks*, Chapters 6, 8.

The Geneva and Reykjavik Summits in 1985 and 1986 were very successful examples of media management. Reagan's over-eagerness and limited understanding of arms control at Reykjavik nearly produced a rift both with Gorbachev and with American conservatives. Only through highly sophisticated and pre-emptive 'spin control' by the White House Press Office under Larry Speakes were rifts avoided. Speakes' memoirs document Soviet collaboration in manufacturing quotes of mutual convenience for the communiqués which helped mould opinion. At Geneva he had been amazed at the willingness of the press corps to accept a news blackout until the final communiqué. He put that down to the fear of being scooped being more potent than the hope of getting a scoop.

Speakes had long played favourites among the press, singling out Sam Donaldson of ABC, whose text was not edited by the network and whose audience was large. Much later, he regretted not favouring public television, since its audience for news took in more opinion leaders than the commercial networks. At the White House the 'Irangate Affair' was a secret not only from Speakes, but also from other high level officials. When it became public knowledge in 1986, it eroded his position and he left the White House early in 1987.[7]

Not until Irangate did Reagan's grip on public esteem weaken sufficiently to allow reporters to file the stories they had earlier written on the President's incompetence and duplicity. Both he and his advisors had relied on his mastery of set-piece television appearances to offset elite critics of his policies. The slow unveiling of the details of his duplicity illuminated the difficulty of managing media, since each revelation justified yet another critical journalistic bout of retrospection on Reagan's years in office. No 'spin control' from the White House, no Congressional support from conservatives or pleas of ignorance from Reagan himself could prevent the erosion of public support. The nonstick Teflon President had come badly unstuck as his popular approval ratings sank by 4% a month after August 1986. By March 1987, 33% of the electorate agreed that the President should resign. There was a recovery of sorts in his poll standing, but Reagan was never the same again— 'reigning rather than ruling' as the press put it.

Bush never enjoyed the personal likeability ratings of Reagan and, except for the period before and after the Gulf War, never enjoyed high general approval. As with his predecessors, he had to endure leaks and ever greater Congressional resistance to what in fact was a meagre domestic agenda. Though he might reasonably have expected a second term, his poor campaigning in 1992, on top of his poor personal ratings and a recovering but weak economy, ensured his decisive defeat. Like his predecessor, he, too, left office with unanswered questions on Irangate hanging over him.

The Washington bureaucracy is simply too large and complex to police easily. If military and intelligence secrets are frequently leaked in inter-service or inter-agency battles over budgets and policy, it may be expected that non-military 'secrets' stand little chance of being kept for long. Building leaks into the policy process is thus routinised in Washington. Leaks are countered by other, often pre-emptive leaks;

---

[7]Larry Speakes, *Speaking Out. The Reagan Presidency from Inside the White House,* New York: Avon Books, 1988.

little wonder that received wisdom among reporters in that 'every leak is a plant'. Leaks are used to fly trial balloons, to head off policy changes by giving early notice of serious resistance and, not least, to try to get policy decisions overturned. The latter, particularly, is associated with leaks from Congress, a source second only to the White House in terms of significance. Strategic leaking by committee staffs—not always with committee permission—is the stuff of much Congressional news, and this means that much White House news is Congressionally inspired. Frequently the White House is put on the defensive by the leaking of a story the subject of which is not widely known among White House staff, who then have to defend a 'decision' which is not in fact a 'decision' but an option.

A President, therefore, who wishes to keep the policy initiative, to dominate the national agenda, is engaged in daily battles to find allies in the bureaucracy and Congress who will champion his ideas and help the White House combat damaging leaks, whether accurate or inaccurate. All recent Presidents have found the task immensely difficult, calling for more time and resources than the White House or Executive Office can always find. Only by the tightest security at the highest level can the obedience of lower levels within the White House and agencies be kept and the initiative in policy retained. A first-term President whose public approval ratings and Congressional relations are at a low ebb—Jimmy Carter—will find less and less obedience and collaboration as, of course, will Presidents in their last months in office—Ronald Reagan and George Bush are examples. Central clearance of White House proposals, and consultation with interested parties, will avail such a President little if he is no longer seen as a real player on the Washington scene. Even when loyalty and consensus exist, the White House will find its proposals being modified by subordinates in agencies in ways the White House may not be able to check.

Toward Conclusions

All of which brings up the question of what constitutes success or failure in media management and, by extension, a capacity to maintain popular support. Presidents normally find it impossible to maintain the latter, seemingly losing popular support almost whatever they do. Considering incumbents since 1963, all seem to have had a 'good press' for the first 18 months in office and then found the tide turning against them. John Kennedy's assassination spared him the worst of this, but after the initially impressive months of Johnson, opinion turned, with the Vietnam War the principal cause after 1966. Richard Nixon benefited from a reluctantly admiring press corps as he wound down Vietnam, rescued the economy and opened the diplomatic door to China. Watergate ruined his second term, and the reputation of his nominated successor, Gerald Ford, never recovered from the Nixon pardon. Jimmy Carter began well in press esteem, faded over the Bert Lance affair in 1977 and then came back strongly after the Camp David 1978 Summit on the Middle East. This glow, however, did not last and the crises in Afghanistan and Iran intensified a steady decline. Ronald Reagan's reputation stood up well at first, faded during the 1982–83 recession, bounded back with the pre-election recovery and saw him reelected. Reagan's popularity was more personal than a vote of confidence in his presidency, and the Irangate crisis after the autumn of 1986 revealed this. The President, however, never totally lost his personal likeability rating. Bush began moderately, faded, and then came back strongly over the Gulf Crisis but resumed a decline in approval ratings thereafter.

In the case of the current incumbent, the post-election glow dimmed so promptly as to suggest that there was no honeymoon period. Disputes within the White House over gays in the military, economic policy, appointments and the early tensions over the Whitewater Affair—all eroded public confidence. The appointment of Republican David Gergen in 1993 to 'manage the message' seemed to steady things and the passage of the NAFTA agreement in Congress promised a recovery. Subsequently, however, media coverage of foreign policy failures and of the bogging down in Congress of White House proposals on health care contributed to the erosion of the President's popular standing and hence his capacity to mould a recovery in public confidence. The occupation of Haiti seems to promise some gain, but with very severe losses in the mid-term elections Clinton may yet become a one term President.

What seems clear is that media treatment of a President has an influence in amplifying success or failure as measured by opinion polls. Media coverage reflects media perceptions of popular approval. The White House media relations staff appears able to do no more than marginally effect a President's fortunes. Despite its strenuous efforts, the Vietnam War helped ruin Johnson, Watergate Nixon, Afghanistan and Iran Carter, while Irangate and the economy blighted Reagan and ruined Bush. This suggests that presidential capacity to manage the news is much less than supposed and a lot less than Presidents begin by believing.

Behind the falling approval ratings of Presidents lies the effect of many factors, both personal and political. At the personal level there are characteristics which become less appealing as time passes. Examples would be a regional accent or effusiveness which television exaggerates—Johnson, Carter, and Clinton have all suffered for their 'Southerness'. A wife can offend by her manner, examples are Pat Nixon's 'frozen smile' or Hillary Clinton's unconcealed ambition and confidence. There are again, damaging allegations of pre-election behaviour—as with Clinton—or illegal behaviour in office—as with Nixon and Reagan; neither help.

At the political level there is a range of factors. A serious presidential failure to accommodate Congressional political sensibilities—Carter and Clinton, both former Governors, are prime examples—is very damaging. A thoroughgoing attempt to run Executive Agencies creates difficulties—Nixon and Carter both suffered for this. A real failure to include Congressional leaderships in policy making from the outset contains the seeds of presidential disaster—Nixon, Carter and Clinton must be taken as examples here. Nixon arrogantly chose to confront a Democrat-dominated Congress, while Carter and Clinton claimed both superior knowledge and the high moral ground. Not for either was the pragmatic, horse-trading style of the majority of Congressional members. One may point also to a failure to try to govern from the centre of their parties and in ways which recognised Congressional bipartisanship—Carter, Clinton, but also Bush to some extent, suffered for this. Of course, none of these should be allowed to overshadow the fact of mistaken policies or behaviour. Failing wars or impotence in foreign affairs, scandalous behaviour by Presidents and, critically, a less than successful economy; the effects of these cannot be massaged away by media manipulation and may be intensified by such efforts.

When these personal and policy failings first become apparent, the mass media serve a real purpose in publicising them. In his California days as Governor, Reagan showed that he could learn from criticism and altered his behaviour. Carter, Bush and Clinton seemed to find learning difficult, and the consequences for all three were obvious and painful. Reagan, in his seeming revival of the Imperial Presidency, did something else. He demonstrated the power of prioritisation. Presidents are faced not only with a plethora of news sources but many centres of power. Only by concentrating Congressional and public attention on two or three generally acceptable public policy questions and subordinating all other matters to them can a President hope to overcome the inbuilt obstacles inherent in the US system.

8

PUBLIC OPINION
AND THE PRESIDENCY

Myth of the Presidential Mandate

Robert A. Dahl

On election night in 1980 the vice president elect enthusiastically informed the country that Ronald Reagan's triumph was

> . . . not simply a mandate for a change but a mandate for peace and freedom; a mandate for prosperity; a mandate for opportunity for all Americans regardless of race, sex, or creed; a mandate for leadership that is both strong and compassionate . . . a mandate to make government the servant of the people in the way our founding fathers intended; a mandate for hope; a mandate for hope for the fulfillment of the great dream that President-elect Reagan has worked for all his life.[1]

I suppose there are no limits to permissible exaggeration in the elation of victory, especially by a vice president elect. He may therefore be excused, I imagine, for failing to note, as did many others who made comments in a similar vein in the weeks and months that followed, that Reagan's lofty mandate was provided by 50.9 percent of the voters. A decade later it is much more evident, as it should have been then, that what was widely interpreted as Reagan's mandate, not only by supporters but by opponents, was more myth than reality.

In claiming that the outcome of the election provided a mandate to the president from the American people to bring about the policies, programs, emphases, and new directions uttered during the campaign by the winning candidate and his supporters, the vice president elect was like other commentators echoing a familiar theory.

---

[1]Stanley Kelley, Jr., *Interpreting Elections* (Princeton, N.J.: Princeton University Press, 1983), 217.

Robert A. Dahl is Sterling Professor Emeritus of Political Science at Yale University and past president of the American Political Science Association. He is the author of numerous books on democratic political theory and American politics, including the prizewinning *Who Governs?* and the recently published *Democracy and Its Critics*.

Origin and Development

A history of the theory of the presidential mandate has not been written, and I have no intention of supplying one here. However, if anyone could be said to have created the myth of the presidential mandate, surely it would be Andrew Jackson. Although he never used the word mandate, so far as I know, he was the first American president to claim not only that the president is uniquely representative of all the people, but that his election confers on him a mandate from the people in support of his policy. Jackson's claim was a fateful step in the democratization of the constitutional system of the United States—or rather what I prefer to call the pseudodemocratization of the presidency.

As Leonard White observed, it was Jackson's "settled conviction" that "the President was an immediate and direct representative of the people."[2] Presumably as a result of his defeat in 1824 in both the electoral college and the House of Representatives, in his first presidential message to Congress, in order that "as few impediments as possible should exist to the free operation of the public will," he proposed that the Constitution be amended to provide for the direct election of the president.[3]

> "To the people", he said, "belongs the right of electing their Chief Magistrate: it was never designed that their choice should, in any case, be defeated, either by the intervention of electoral colleges or by . . . the House of Representatives."[4]

His great issue of policy was the Bank of the United States, which he unwaveringly believed was harmful to the general good. Acting on this conviction, in 1832 he vetoed the bill to renew the bank's charter. Like his predecessors, he justified the veto as a protection against unconstitutional legislation; but unlike his predecessors in their comparatively infrequent use of the veto he also justified it as a defense of his or his party's policies.

Following his veto of the bank's charter, the bank became the main issue in the presidential election of 1832. As a consequence, Jackson's reelection was widely regarded, even among his opponents (in private, at least), as amounting to "something like a popular ratification" of his policy.[5] When in order to speed the demise of the bank Jackson found it necessary to fire his treasury secretary, he justified his action on the ground, among others, that "The President is the direct representative of the American people, but the Secretaries are not."[6]

Innovative though it was, Jackson's theory of the presidential mandate was less robust than it was to become in the hands of his successors. In 1848 James Polk explicitly formulated the claim, in a defense of his use of the veto on matters of policy, that as a representative of the people the president was, if not more representative than the Congress, at any rate equally so.

---

[2]Leonard D. White, *The Jacksonians: A Study in Administrative History, 1829–1861* (New York: Free Press, 1954), 23.
[3]Quoted in ibid., 23.
[4]Cited in James W. Ceaser, *Presidential Selection: Theory and Development* (Princeton, N.J.: Princeton University Press, 1979), 160, fn. 58.
[5]White, *Jacksonians*, 23.
[6]Ibid., 23.

"The people, by the constitution, have commanded the President, as much as they have commanded the legislative branch of the Government, to execute their will. . . . The President represents in the executive department the whole people of the United States, as each member of the legislative department represents portions of them. . . ." The President is responsible "not only to an enlightened public opinion, but to the people of the whole Union, who elected him, as the representatives in the legislative branches . . . are responsible to the people of particular States or districts. . . ."[7]

Notice that in Jackson's and Polk's views, the president, both constitutionally and as representative of the people, is on a par with Congress. They did not claim that in either respect the president is superior to Congress. It was Woodrow Wilson who took the further step in the evolution of the theory by asserting that in representing the people the president is not merely equal to Congress but actually superior to it.

Earlier Views   Because the theory of the presidential mandate espoused by Jackson and Polk has become an integral part of our present-day conception of the presidency, it may be hard for us to grasp how sharply that notion veered off from the views of the earlier presidents.

As James Ceaser has shown, the Framers designed the presidential election process as a means of improving the chances of electing a *national* figure who would enjoy majority support. They hoped their contrivance would avoid not only the populistic competition among candidates dependent on "the popular arts," which they rightly believed would occur if the president were elected by the people, but also what they believed would necessarily be a factional choice if the president were chosen by the Congress, particularly by the House.[8]

In adopting the solution of an electoral college, however, the Framers seriously underestimated the extent to which the strong impulse toward democratization that was already clearly evident among Americans—particularly among their opponents, the anti-Federalists—would subvert and alter their carefully contrived constitutional structure. Since this is a theme I shall pick up later, I want now to mention only two such failures that bear closely on the theory of the presidential mandate. First, the Founders did not foresee the development of political parties nor comprehend how a two-party system might achieve their goal of insuring the election of a figure of national rather than merely local renown. Second, as Ceaser remarks, although the Founders recognized "the need for a popular judgment of the performance of an incumbent" and designed a method for selecting the president that would, as they thought, provide that opportunity, they "did not see elections as performing the role of instituting decisive changes in policy in response to popular demands."[9] In short, the theory of the presidential mandate not only cannot be found in the Framers' conception of the Constitution; almost certainly it violates that conception.

---

[7]Ibid., 24.

[8]Although Madison and Hamilton opposed the contingent solution of a House election in the event that no candidate received a majority of electoral votes, Gouverneur Morris and James Wilson accepted it as not too great a concession. Ceaser, *Presidential Selection,* 80–81.

[9]Ibid., 84.

No president prior to Jackson challenged the view that Congress was the legitimate representative of the people. Even Thomas Jefferson, who adeptly employed the emerging role of party leader to gain congressional support for his policies and decisions

> was more Whig than . . . the British Whigs themselves in subordinating [the executive power] to "the supreme legislative power". . . . The tone of his messages is uniformly deferential to Congress. His first one closes with these words: "Nothing shall be wanting on my part to inform, as far as in my power, the legislative judgment, nor to carry that judgment into faithful execution."[10]

James Madison, demonstrating that a great constitutional theorist and an adept leader in Congress could be decidedly less than a great president, deferred so greatly to Congress that in his communications to that body his extreme caution rendered him "almost unintelligible"[11]—a quality one would hardly expect from one who had been a master of lucid exposition at the Constitutional Convention. His successor, James Monroe, was so convinced that Congress should decide domestic issues without presidential influence that throughout the debates in Congress on "the greatest political issue of his day . . . the admission of Missouri and the status of slavery in Louisiana Territory," he remained utterly silent.[12]

Madison and Monroe serve not as examples of how presidents should behave but as evidence of how early presidents thought they should behave. Considering the constitutional views and the behavior of Jackson's predecessors, it is not hard to see why his opponents called themselves Whigs in order to emphasize his dereliction from the earlier and presumably constitutionally correct view of the presidency.

Woodrow Wilson   The long and almost unbroken succession of mediocrities who succeeded to the presidency between Polk and Wilson for the most part subscribed to the Whig view of the office and seem to have laid no claim to a popular mandate for their policies—when they had any. Even Abraham Lincoln, in justifying the unprecedented scope of presidential power he believed he needed in order to meet secession and civil war, rested his case on constitutional grounds, and not as a mandate from the people.[13] Indeed, since he distinctly failed to gain a majority of votes in the election of 1860, any claim to a popular mandate would have been dubious at best. Like Lincoln, Theodore Roosevelt also

---

[10]Edward S. Corwin, *The President: Offices and Powers, 1789–1948*, 3rd. ed. (New York: New York University Press, 1948), 20.

[11]Wilfred E. Binkley, *President and Congress* (New York: Alfred A. Knopf, 1947), 56.

[12]Leonard D. White, *The Jeffersonians: A Study in Administrative History, 1801–1829* (New York: Free Press, 1951), 31.

[13]Lincoln drew primarily on the war power, which he created by uniting the president's constitutional obligation "to take care that the laws be faithfully executed" with his power as commander-in-chief. He interpreted the war power as a veritable cornucopia of implicit constitutional authority for the extraordinary emergency measures he undertook during an extraordinary national crisis. (Corwin, *The President*, 277ff.)

had a rather unrestricted view of presidential power; he expressed the view then emerging among Progressives that chief executives were also representatives of the people. Yet the stewardship he claimed for the presidency was ostensibly drawn—rather freely drawn, I must say—from the Constitution, not from the mystique of the mandate.[14]

Woodrow Wilson, more as political scientist than as president, brought the mandate theory to what now appears to be its canonical form. His formulation was influenced by his admiration for the British system of cabinet government. In 1879, while still a senior at Princeton, he published an essay recommending the adoption of cabinet government in the United States.[15] He provided little indication as to how this change was to be brought about, however, and soon abandoned the idea without yet having found an alternative solution.[16] Nevertheless, he continued to contrast the American system of congressional government, in which Congress was all-powerful but lacked executive leadership, with British cabinet government, in which parliament, though all powerful, was firmly led by the prime minister and his cabinet. Since Americans were not likely to adopt the British cabinet system, however, he began to consider the alternative of more powerful presidential leadership.[17] In his *Congressional Government,* published in 1885, he acknowledged that "the representatives of the people are the proper ultimate authority in all matters of government, and that administration is merely the clerical part of government."[18] Congress is "unquestionably, the predominant and controlling force, the center and source of all motive and of all regulative power." Yet a discussion of policy that goes beyond "special pleas for special privilege" is simply impossible in the House, "a disintegrate mass of jarring elements," while the Senate is no more than "a small, select, and leisurely House of Representatives."[19]

---

[14]"Every executive officer, in particular the President, Roosevelt maintained, 'was a steward of the people bound actively and affirmatively to do all he could for the people. . . .' He held therefore that, unless specifically forbidden by the Constitution or by law, the President had 'to do anything that the needs of the nation demanded. . . .' 'Under this interpretation of executive power,' he recalled, 'I did and caused to be done many things not previously done. . . . I did not usurp power, but I did greatly broaden the use of executive power,'" See John Morton Blum, *The Republican Roosevelt* (New York: Atheneum, 1954), 108.

[15]Woodrow Wilson, *Cabinet Government in the United States* (Stamford, Conn.: Overbrook Press, 1947), orig. publication in *International Review,* 1879.

[16]"He seems not to have paid much attention to the practical question of how so radical an alteration was to be brought about. As far as I know, Wilson's only published words on how to initiate the English system are in the article, *Committee or Cabinet Government,* which appeared in the *Overland Monthly* for January, 1884." His solution was to amend Section 6 of Article I of the Constitution to permit members of Congress to hold offices as members of the Cabinet, and to extend the terms of the president and representatives. See, Walter Lippmann, *Introduction to Congressional Government* (New York: Meridian Books, 1956), 14–15.

[17]Wilson's unfavorable comparative judgment is particularly clear in *Congressional Government: A Study in American Politics* (New York: Meridian Books, 1956; reprint of 1885 ed.), 181. Just as Jackson had proposed the direct election of the president, in his first annual message Wilson proposed that a system of direct national primaries be adopted. See Ceaser, *Presidential Selection,* 173.

[18]Wilson, *Congressional Government,* 181.

[19]Ibid., 31, 72–73, 145.

By 1908, when *Constitutional Government in the United States* was published, Wilson had arrived at strong presidential leadership as a feasible solution. He faulted the earlier presidents who had adopted the Whig theory of the Constitution.

> . . . (T)he makers of the Constitution were not enacting Whig theory. . . . The President is at liberty, both in law and conscience, to be as big a man as he can. His capacity will set the limit; and if Congress be overborne by him, it will be no fault of the makers of the Constitution,—it will be from no lack of constitutional powers on its part, but only because the President has the nation behind him, and Congress has not. He has no means of compelling Congress except through public opinion. . . . (T)he early Whig theory of political dynamics . . . is far from being a democratic theory. . . . It is particularly intended to prevent the will of the people as a whole from having at any moment an unobstructed sweep and ascendancy.

And he contrasted the president with Congress in terms that would become commonplace among later generations of commentators, including political scientists:

> Members of the House and Senate are representatives of localities, are voted for only by sections of voters, or by local bodies of electors like the members of the state legislatures.[20] There is no national party choice except that of President. No one else represents the people as a whole, exercising a national choice. . . . The nation as a whole has chosen him, and is conscious that it has no other political spokesman. His is the only national voice in affairs. . . . He is the representative of no constituency, but of the whole people. When he speaks in his true character, he speaks for no special interest. . . . (T)here is but one national voice in the country, and that is the voice of the President.[21]

Since Wilson, it has become commonplace for presidents and commentators alike to argue that by virtue of his election the president has received a mandate for his aims and policies from the people of the United States. The myth of the mandate is now a standard weapon in the arsenal of persuasive symbols all presidents exploit. For example, as the Watergate scandals emerged in mid-1973, Patrick Buchanan, then an aide in the Nixon White House, suggested that the president should accuse his accusers of "seeking to destroy the democratic mandate of 1972." Three weeks later in an address to the country Nixon said:

> Last November, the American people were given the clearest choice of this century. Your votes were a mandate, which I accepted, to complete the initiatives we began in my first term and to fulfill the promises I made for my second term.[22]

If the spurious nature of Nixon's claim now seems self-evident, the dubious grounds for virtually all such pretensions are perhaps less obvious.[23]

---

[20]The Seventeenth Amendment requiring a direct election of senators was not adopted until 1913.
[21]Woodrow Wilson, *Constitutional Government in the United States* (New York: Columbia University Press, 1908), 67–68, 70, 202–203.
[22]Kelley, *Interpreting Elections,* 99.
[23]For other examples of claims to a presidential mandate resulting from the election, see William Safire, *Safire's Political Dictionary* (New York: Random House, 1978), 398; and Kelley, *Interpreting Elections,* 72–74, 126–129, 168.

Critique of the Theory

What does a president's claim to a mandate amount to? The meaning of the term itself is not altogether clear.[24] Fortunately, however, in his excellent book *Interpreting Elections,* Stanley Kelley has "piece[d] together a coherent statement of the theory."

> Its first element is the belief that elections carry messages about problems, policies, and programs—messages plain to all and specific enough to be directive. . . . Second, the theory holds that certain of these messages must be treated as authoritative commands . . . either to the victorious candidate or to the candidate and his party. . . . To qualify as mandates, messages about policies and programs must reflect the *stable* views both of individual voters and of the electorate. . . . In the electorate as a whole, the numbers of those for or against a policy or program matter. To suggest that a mandate exists for a particular policy is to suggest that more than a bare majority of those voting are agreed upon it. The common view holds that landslide victories are more likely to involve mandates than are narrow ones. . . . The final element of the theory is a negative imperative: Governments should not undertake major innovations in policy or procedure, except in emergencies, unless the electorate has had an opportunity to consider them in an election and thus to express its views."[25]

To bring out the central problems more clearly, let me extract what might be called the primitive theory of the popular presidential mandate. According to this theory, a presidential election can accomplish four things. First, it confers constitutional and legal authority on the victor. Second, at the same time, it also conveys information. At a minimum it reveals the first preferences for president of a plurality of votes. Third, according to the primitive theory, the election, at least under the conditions Kelley describes, conveys further information: namely that a clear majority of voters prefer the winner because they prefer his policies and wish him to pursue his policies. Finally, because the president's policies reflect the wishes of a majority of voters, when conflicts over policy arise between president and Congress, the president's policies ought to prevail.

While we can readily accept the first two propositions, the third, which is pivotal to the theory, might be false. But if the third is false, then so is the fourth. So the question arises: Beyond revealing the first preferences of a plurality of voters, do presidential elections also reveal the additional information that a plurality (or a majority) of voters prefer the policies of the winner and wish the winner to pursue those policies?

In appraising the theory I want to distinguish between two different kinds of criticisms. First, some critics contend that even when the wishes of constituents can be known, they should not be regarded as in any way binding on a legislator.

---

[24]See "mandate" in *Oxford English Dictionary* (Oxford, England: Oxford University Press, 1971, compact edition); Safire, *Political Dictionary,* 398; Jack C. Plano and Milton Greenberg, *The American Political Dictionary* (New York: Holt, Rinehart and Winston, 1979), 130; Julius Gould and William L. Kolb, *A Dictionary of the Social Sciences* (New York: The Free Press, 1964), 404; Jay M. Shafritz, *The Dorsey Dictionary of American Government and Politics* (Chicago: The Dorsey Press, 1988), 340.
[25]Kelley, *Interpreting Elections,* 126–128.

I have in mind, for example, Edmund Burke's famous argument that he would not sacrifice to public opinion his independent judgment of how well a policy would serve his constituents' interests, and the argument suggested by Hanna Pitkin that representatives bound by instructions would be prevented from entering into the compromises that legislation usually requires.[26]

Second, some critics, on the other hand, may hold that when the wishes of constituents on matters of policy can be clearly discerned, they ought to be given great and perhaps even decisive weight. But, these critics contend, constituents' wishes usually cannot be known, at least when the constituency is large and diverse, as in presidential elections. In expressing his doubts on the matter in 1913, A. Lawrence Lowell quoted Sir Henry Maine: "The devotee of democracy is much in the same position as the Greeks with their oracles. All agreed that the voice of an oracle was the voice of god, but everybody allowed that when he spoke he was not as intelligible as might be desired."[27]

It is exclusively the second kind of criticism that I want now to consider. Here again I am indebted to Stanley Kelley for his succinct summary of the main criticisms.

> Critics agree that 1) some particular claim of a mandate is unsupported by adequate evidence; 2) most claims of mandates are unsupported by adequate evidence; 3) most claims of mandates are politically self-serving; or 4) it is not possible in principle to make a valid claim of a mandate, since it is impossible to sort out voters' intentions.[28]

Kelley goes on to say that while the first three criticisms may well be valid, the fourth has been outdated by the sample survey, which "has again given us the ability to discover the grounds of voters' choices." In effect, then, Kelley rejects the primitive theory and advances the possibility of a more sophisticated mandate theory according to which the information about policies is conveyed not by the election outcome but instead by opinion surveys. Thus the two functions are cleanly split: presidential elections are for electing a president, opinion surveys provide information about the opinions, attitudes, and judgments that account for the outcome.

However, I would propose a fifth proposition, which I believe is also implicit in Kelley's analysis:

> 5) While it may not be strictly impossible *in principle* to make a reasoned and well-grounded claim to a presidential mandate, to do so *in practice* requires a complex analysis that in the end may not yield much support for presidential claims.

But if we reject the primitive theory of the mandate and adopt the more sophisticated theory, then it follows that prior to the introduction of scientific sample surveys, no president could reasonably have defended his claim to a mandate. To put a precise date on the proposition, let me remind you that the first presidential election in which scientific surveys formed the basis of an extended and systematic analysis was 1940.[29]

---

[26]Cited in ibid., 133.
[27]Cited in ibid., 134.
[28]Ibid., 136.
[29]Paul F. Lazarsfeld, Bernard Berelson, and Hazel Gaudet, *The People's Choice* (New York: Columbia University Press, 1948).

I do not mean to say that no election before 1940 now permits us to draw the conclusion that a president's major policies were supported by a substantial majority of the electorate. But I do mean that for most presidential elections before 1940 a valid reconstruction of the policy views of the electorate is impossible or enormously difficult, even with the aid of aggregate data and other indirect indicators of voters' views. When we consider that presidents ordinarily asserted their claims soon after their elections, well before historians and social scientists could have sifted through reams of indirect evidence, then we must conclude that before 1940 no contemporary claim to a presidential mandate could have been supported by the evidence available at the time.

While the absence of surveys undermines presidential claims to a mandate before 1940, the existence of surveys since then would not necessarily have supported such claims. Ignoring all other shortcomings of the early election studies, the analysis of the 1940 election I just mentioned was not published until 1948. While that interval between the election and the analysis may have set a record, the systematic analysis of survey evidence that is necessary (though perhaps not sufficient) to interpret what a presidential election means always comes well after presidents and commentators have already told the world, on wholly inadequate evidence, what the election means.[30] Perhaps the most famous voting study to date, *The American Voter,* which drew primarily on interviews conducted in 1952 and 1956, appeared in 1960.[31] The book by Stanley Kelley that I have drawn on so freely here, which interprets the elections of 1964, 1972, and 1980, appeared in 1983.

A backward glance quickly reveals how empty the claims to a presidential mandate have been in recent elections. Take 1960. If more than a bare majority is essential to a mandate, then surely Kennedy could have received no mandate, since he gained less than 50 percent of the total popular vote by the official count—just how much less by the unofficial count varies with the counter. Yet "on the day after election, and every day thereafter," Theodore Sorenson tells us, "he rejected the argument that the country had given him no mandate. Every election has a winner and a loser, he said in effect. There may be difficulties with the Congress, but a margin of only one vote would still be a mandate."[32]

By contrast, 1964 was a landslide election, as was 1972. From his analysis, however, Kelley concludes that "Johnson's and Nixon's specific claims of meaningful mandates do not stand up well when confronted by evidence." To be sure, in both elections some of the major policies of the winners were supported by large majorities among those to whom these issues were salient. Yet "none of these policies was cited by more than 21% of respondents as a reason to like Johnson, Nixon, or their parties."[33]

[30]The early election studies are summarized in Bernard R. Berelson and Paul F. Lazarsfeld, *Voting* (Chicago: University of Chicago Press, 1954), 331ff.
[31]Angus Campbell et al., *The American Voter* (New York: Wiley, 1960).
[32]Quoted in Safire, *Political Dictionary,* 398.
[33]Kelley, *Interpreting Elections,* 139–140.

In 1968, Nixon gained office with only 43 percent of the popular vote. No mandate there. Likewise in 1976, Carter won with a bare 50.1 percent. Once again, no mandate there.

When Reagan won in 1980, thanks to the much higher quality of surveys undertaken by the media, a more sophisticated understanding of what that election meant no longer had to depend on the academic analyses that would only follow some years later. Nonetheless, many commentators, bemused as they so often are by the arithmetical peculiarities of the electoral college, immediately proclaimed both a landslide and a mandate for Reagan's policies. What they often failed to note was that Reagan gained just under 51 percent of the popular vote. Despite the claims of the vice president elect, surely we can find no mandate there. Our doubts are strengthened by the fact that in the elections to the House, Democratic candidates won just over 50 percent of the popular vote and a majority of seats. However, they lost control of the Senate. No Democratic mandate there, either.

These clear and immediate signs that the elections of 1980 failed to confer a mandate on the president or his Democratic opponents were, however, largely ignored. For it was so widely asserted as to be commonplace that Reagan's election reflected a profound shift of opinion away from New Deal programs and toward the new conservatism. However, from this analysis of the survey evidence, Kelley concludes that the commitment of voters to candidates was weak; a substantial proportion of Reagan voters were more interested in voting against Carter than for Reagan; and despite claims by journalists and others, the New Deal coalition did not really collapse. Nor was there any profound shift toward conservatism. "The evidence from press surveys . . . contradicts the claims that voters shifted toward conservatism and that this ideological shift elected Reagan." In any case, the relation between ideological location and policy preferences was "of a relatively modest magnitude."[34]

In winning by a landslide of popular votes in 1984, Reagan achieved one prerequisite to a mandate. Yet in that same election, Democratic candidates for the House won 52 percent of the popular votes. Two years earlier, they had won 55 percent of the votes. On the face of it, surely the 1984 elections gave no mandate to Reagan.

Before the end of 1986, when the Democrats had once again won a majority of popular votes in elections to the House and had also regained a majority of seats in the Senate, it should have been clear and it should be even clearer now that the major social and economic policies for which Reagan and his supporters had claimed a mandate have persistently failed to gain majority support. Indeed, the major domestic policies and programs established during the thirty years preceding Reagan in the White House have not been overturned in the grand revolution of policy that his election was supposed to have ushered in. For eight years, what Reagan and his supporters claimed as a mandate to reverse those policies was regularly rejected by means of the only legitimate and constitutional processes we Americans have for determining what the policies of the United States government should be.

[34]Ibid., 170–172, 174–181, 185, 187.

What are we to make of this long history of unsupported claims to a presidential mandate? The myth of the mandate would be less important if it were not one element in the larger process of the pseudodemocratization of the presidency— the creation of a type of chief executive that in my view should have no proper place in a democratic republic.

Yet even if we consider it in isolation from the larger development of the presidency, the myth is harmful to American political life. By portraying the president as the only representative of the whole people and Congress as merely representing narrow, special, and parochial interests, the myth of the mandate elevates the president to an exalted position in our constitutional system at the expense of Congress. The myth of the mandate fosters the belief that the particular interests of the diverse human beings who form the citizen body in a large, complex, and pluralistic country like ours constitute no legitimate element in the general good. The myth confers on the aims of the groups who benefit from presidential policies an aura of national interest and public good to which they are no more entitled than the groups whose interests are reflected in the policies that gain support by congressional majorities. Because the myth is almost always employed to support deceptive, misleading, and manipulative interpretations, it is harmful to the political understanding of citizens.

It is, I imagine, now too deeply rooted in American political life and too useful a part of the political arsenal of presidents to be abandoned. Perhaps the most we can hope for is that commentators on public affairs in the media and in academic pursuits will dismiss claims to a presidential mandate with the scorn they usually deserve.

But if a presidential election does not confer a mandate on the victor, what does a presidential election mean, if anything at all? While a presidential election does not confer a popular mandate on the president—nor, for that matter, on congressional majorities—it confers the legitimate authority, right, and opportunity on a president to try to gain the adoption by constitutional means of the policies the president supports. In the same way, elections to Congress confer on a member the authority, right, and opportunity to try to gain the adoption by constitutional means of the policies he or she supports. Each may reasonably contend that a particular policy is in the public good or public interest and, moreover, is supported by a majority of citizens.

I do not say that whatever policy is finally adopted following discussion, debate, and constitutional processes necessarily reflects what a majority of citizens would prefer, or what would be in their interests, or what would be in the public good in any other sense. What I do say is that no elected leader, including the president, is uniquely privileged to say what an election means—nor to claim that the election has conferred on the president a mandate to enact the particular policies the president supports.

The Democratization of the Presidency

It was inevitable that the executive designed by the Framers would be fundamentally altered in response to the powerful influence of democratizing impulses.

If the Framers had intended a chief executive whose election and capacity for governing would not require him to compete for popular approval and who therefore would not depend on "the popular arts" of winning public support,[35] they seriously underestimated both the strength of the democratic impulses among their fellow citizens and its effects on the presidency. Nothing reveals this more clearly than the amazing speed with which the Framers' design for the executive was replaced by a presidency dependent on popular election and popular approval.

The consequences of democratization were evident almost at once and gained strength with the passage of time. I have already described one aspect of this process of democratization in some detail: the invention of the theory of the presidential mandate. Jackson's invention was, however, preceded by decades of democratization that gave plausibility to the theory.

By Jackson's time the presidency had long since become an office sought by partisan candidates in popular elections. Though political parties had existed in Britain and Sweden as elite organizations in systems with a severely limited suffrage, under the leadership of Jefferson and Madison the Republican party became an instrument by which popular majorities could be organized, mobilized, and made effective in influencing the conduct of government. Henceforth a president would combine his role as a presumably nonpartisan chief executive with his role as a national leader of a partisan organization with a partisan following.[36]

If the presidential office was to be attained by partisan contestation, then in order to reach that office a serious presidential candidate would ordinarily need to gain the endorsement and support of a political party. Though the story of the evolution of the presidential nominating process has often been told, it so vividly reveals the impact of democratizing impulses that I want to summarize it briefly.

The Nominating Process   The first organized system for nominating candidates for president and vice president was the congressional caucus, which both the Republicans and the Federalists introduced in 1800.[37] Yet given the emerging strength of democratic ideology, a system so obtrusively closed to participation by any but a small group of congressional politicians was clearly vulnerable. Democratic sentiments we would find familiar in our own time were expressed in a resolution passed in the Ohio legislature in 1823:

---

[35]Ceaser, *Presidential Selection,* 47ff.

[36]As Ceaser remarks, *Presidential Selection,* 88, 90: "The nonpartisan selection system established by the Founders barely survived a decade. By the election of 1796, traces of partisanship were already clearly in evidence, and by 1800 the contest was being fought on strictly partisan lines." Like many other innovations, Jefferson's had unintended consequences. "Jefferson . . . had an abiding distrust of national elections and, except in the case of his own election, never regarded them as the proper forum for making decisive changes. . . . The paradox of Jefferson's election in 1800 was that while he was chosen for partisan reasons, he did not intend to institute a system of permanent party competition."

[37]Noble E. Cunningham, Jr., *The Jeffersonian Republicans: The Formation of Party Organization, 1789–1801* (Chapel Hill: University of North Carolina Press, 1957), 163–165.

The time has now arrived when the machinations of the *few* to dictate to the *many* . . . will be met . . . by a people jealous of their rights. . . . The only unexceptional source from which nominations can proceed is the people themselves. To them belongs the right of choosing; and they alone can with propriety take any previous steps.[38]

By 1824, when the candidate of the congressional caucus of Democratic Republicans trailed a bad fourth in the election behind Jackson, John Quincy Adams, and Henry Clay, who all ran without benefit of a blessing by the caucus, the outrage to democratic sentiments was easily exploited, most notably by Jackson and his supporters. The congressional nominating caucus came to an end.[39]

In an obvious extension of democratic ideas, which by then had thoroughly assimilated the concept of representation, in 1831 and 1832 the nominating convention came into existence. But in due time,

[j]ust as once the democratic passions of the people were roused against the Congressional caucus, so now they were turned against the convention system. . . . Away therefore with the delegates, who can never be trusted, and back to the people![40]

So in a further obvious extension of democratic ideas to the nominating process, from 1901 onward the direct primary was introduced, initially for state and congressional nominations, and soon for presidential candidates. The presidential primary system was in turn subjected to the democratizing impulse. "By the election of 1972," Ceaser remarks, "the election process had been transformed into what is essentially a plebiscitary system."[41]

Reducing Intermediate Forces   The democratization of the nominating process is instructive for many reasons—among others because after almost two centuries of trials employing three major forms with many variations, a sensible method of nominating presidential candidates still seems beyond the reach of Americans. The present system has its defenders no doubt, but they seem to be rapidly diminishing.

The democratization of the nominating process is also instructive because it shows how the relations between the public and presidents or presidential candidates have become increasingly direct. Jeffrey Tulis has described the enormous change that has taken place in the way presidents address the public—presidential speech, if you like. The view that prevailed during the early years of the republic, and for much of the nineteenth century, tended to follow "two general prescriptions for presidential speech." First, proposals for laws and policies would be written and directed principally to Congress; although public, they would be fashioned

---

[38]M. Ostrogorski, *Democracy and the Party System in the United States* (New York: Macmillan, 1926), 12, fn. 1.

[39]Though Jackson gained more votes than Adams, both popular and electoral, he was denied victory in the House of Representatives.

[40]Ostrogorski, *Democracy,* 342.

[41]Ceaser describes three phases in the evolution of the presidential selection process since the introduction of the primaries: 1912–1920, a period of the expansion of the primaries and the "plebiscitary model"; 1920–1960s, which saw the decline of primaries and the resurgence of parties; and the period since 1972. See *Presidential Selection,* 215ff.

for congressional needs and not necessarily for general public understanding or approval. Second, when presidential speech was directed primarily to the people at large it would address general principals rather than specific issues.

> The inaugural address, for example, developed along lines that emphasized popular instruction in constitutional principle and the articulation of the general tenor and direction of presidential policy, while tending to avoid discussion of the merits of particular policy proposals.[42]

Presidents rarely directly addressed the general public, except possibly on official occasions. From Washington through Jackson, no president gave more than five speeches a year to the general public, a total that was not exceeded by half the presidents from Washington through William McKinley. When they did address the general public the early presidents rarely employed popular rhetoric or discussed their policies.[43] The great exception was Andrew Johnson, who however scarcely served as a model for his successors.[44] Moreover, Gil Troy has recently discovered that until Woodrow Wilson no president had ever "stumped on his own behalf." Until the 1830s, even presidential candidates did not make stump speeches. "Such behavior," Troy has written, "was thought undignified—and unwise. Presidential candidates, especially after nomination, were supposed to stand, not run, for election."[45]

What we now take as normal presidential behavior is a product of this century. The innovators were Theodore Roosevelt and to an even greater extent Woodrow Wilson.[46] Since their day and particularly in recent decades, the task of shaping presidential speech to influence and manipulate public opinion—if necessary by appealing over the heads of Congress in order to induce the Congress to support the president's policies—has become a central element in the art and science of presidential conduct.

The President and the Constitutional System

Thus the presidency has developed into an office that is the very embodiment of the kind of executive the Framers, so far as we can discern their intentions, strove to avoid.

They did not wish an executive who would be a tribune of the people, a champion of popular majorities; who would gain office by popular election; who as a consequence of his popular election would claim a mandate for his policies; who in order to mobilize popular support for his policies would appeal directly to the people; who would shape the language, style, and delivery of his appeals so as best to create a public opinion favorable to his ambitions; and who whenever it

---

[42]Jeffrey K. Tulis, *The Rhetorical Presidency* (Princeton, N.J.: Princeton University Press, 1987), 46–47.

[43]Ibid., 64, table 3.1 and 66, table 3.2

[44]Ibid., 87ff.

[45]*New York Times,* 17 January 1988.

[46]On Theodore Roosevelt, see Tulis, *Rhetorical Presidency,* 95–116; on Wilson, see ibid., 118–137.

seemed expedient would by-pass the members of the deliberative body in order to mobilize public opinion and thereby induce a reluctant Congress to enact his policies. That is, however, a fair description of the presidency that emerged out of the intersection of the Framers' design with the strongly democratic ideology that came to prevail among politically active Americans.

One response to this kind of presidency is to argue that these developments are, on the whole, good. They are good, it might be said, because democracy is good, more democracy is better than less democracy, and a more democratized presidency is better than a less democratized presidency. In the immortal cliché of the 1970 McGovern-Fraser Commission, "the cure for the ills of democracy is more democracy."[47] Yet this response does not seem to quiet the fears of a growing number of critics. In Arthur Schlesinger's now popular term, the presidency was transformed into the imperial presidency.[48] James Ceaser, Theodore Lowi, and others have referred to development of the plebiscitary presidency.[49] Lowi has also dubbed it the personal presidency, remarking that "the new politics of the president-centered Second Republic can best be described as a plebiscitary republic with a personal presidency."[50] Jeffrey Tulis calls the presidency that was seeded by Wilson and cultivated by his successors the rhetorical presidency.[51]

In criticisms of the modern presidency I want to distinguish several different perspectives. From one, what is lamentable is the break with the doctrines, intentions, and designs of the Founders. A rather different perspective, one more pragmatic and functional, emphasizes that the presidency is simply no longer working satisfactorily in its existing constitutional setting. For example, a president claiming a mandate for his policies may be blocked in one or both houses of Congress by a majority of members who in effect also claim a mandate for their policies. The result is not constructive compromise but deadlock or contradictions in policies. Examples are the recent conflicts over the deficit and over American policies in Central America.

From a third perspective, however, the presidency has come to endanger the operation of democratic processes. It is this perspective that I want to emphasize here.

I have alluded to the developments over the past two centuries as the *pseudodemocratization* of the presidency. I have no wish, much less any hope of adding to the other epithets another even more cumbersome and more ugly; but the term does speak directly to my concerns. By *pseudodemocratization* I mean a change taken with the ostensible and perhaps even actual purpose of enhancing the democratic process that in practice retains the aura of its democratic justification and yet has the effect, intended or unintended, of weakening the democratic process.

[47]Ceaser, *Presidential Selection*, 275.
[48]Arthur Schlesinger, Jr., *The Imperial Presidency* (Boston: Houghton Mifflin, 1973).
[49]Ceaser, *Presidential Selection*, 5; Theodore J. Lowi, *The Personal President: Power Invested, Promise Unfulfilled* (Ithaca, N.Y.: Cornell University Press, 1985), 97ff, 134ff.
[50]Lowi, *Personal President*, xi.
[51]Tulis, *Rhetorical Presidency*.

In the case of the presidency, I have two adverse consequences in mind. One, the more obvious, is a loss of popular and congressional control, direct and indirect, over the policies and decisions of the president. A president endowed with the mystique of a mandate—which may sometimes be deepened in a democratic country by the majesty and mystery generated by his popularity and his capacity to evoke and reflect popular feelings, yearnings, and hopes—may encounter resistance to a particular policy in Congress, perhaps even in the public. So the president exploits all the resources of his office to overcome that resistance: his rhetorical resources, his unique capacity to influence or even manipulate public opinion, and all the power and authority derived properly or factitiously from the Constitution—including his power as commander-in-chief, his unique authority over foreign affairs, his right or claim to executive privilege and secrecy, his authority and influence over officials in the executive branch, over the objectives they are obliged or induced to seek, and over the moneys and other resources necessary to reach those objectives. Whatever term we may wish to apply to an executive like this, we can hardly call it democratic.

The other consequence, though more elusive and not wholly independent of the first, is equally important. Now on one view—which I would describe as either simplistic or hostile—democracy means rule by public opinion. This view is mistaken both historically and theoretically. Democracy cannot be justified, I think, and its advocates have rarely sought to justify it as no more than the triumph of raw will. It can be and is justified because more than any feasible alternative it provides ordinary people with opportunities to discover what public policies and activities are best for themselves and for others, and to insure that collective decisions conform with—or at least do not persistently and fundamentally violate—the policies they believe best for themselves and for others.

I cannot undertake to explicate the complexities in the notion of discovering what is best for themselves and for others, nor do I need to. For it is obvious that discovering what is best for oneself or others requires far more than announcing one's raw will or surface preferences. Imagine this extreme situation. Suppose we were called upon to vote in a national plebiscite on a proposed treaty governing nuclear weapons that had been secretly negotiated between the president and the leader of the Soviet Union. Suppose further that the plebiscite is to be held one day after the agreement between the two leaders, and that we are to vote yes or no. The very perversity of this example serves to emphasize the crucial importance of opportunities for *understanding* as a requirement in the democratic process and illustrates why in the absence of such opportunities we should speak instead of a pseudodemocratic process.

Many writers have stressed the importance of *deliberation*. While some associate it with classical republicanism, deliberation is surely central to the idea of a democratic decision making. What I have referred to elsewhere as enlightened understanding is an essential criterion for the democratic process. Deliberation is one crucial means, though I think not the only means, to enlightened understanding. Others include systematic research and analysis, experimentation, consultation with experts, orderly discussion, casual and disorderly discussion, day-dreaming, and self-inquiry.

The modern presidency all too often impairs not only deliberation but also other means to a more enlightened understanding by citizens and the Congress. Nelson Polsby's conclusions about the presidential selection process should be extended to the presidency as a whole. The increasing directness of relationships between a candidate or president and the public means that the traditional "intermediation processes," to use his term, have become less effective. Face-to-face groups, political parties, and interest groups are less autonomous and now rely heavily on the mass media.[52] For example, some nice experiments have recently shown that in assessing the relative importance of different issues, citizens are strongly influenced by television news.[53] I share Polsby's judgment that not only are deliberative processes weak in the general public's consideration of candidates and presidents, but they are also insufficiently subject to extensive review and appraisal by their peers.[54] I also share his judgment that "the directness of direct democracy in a very large scale society seems . . . illusory."[55]

Conclusion

How serious a matter is the pseudodemocratization of the presidency? What, if anything, can and should we do about it? To answer those questions responsibly would obviously take us far beyond the slender limits of an article. Among friends and colleagues I think I detect rather sharply differing perspectives. Let me list several.

First, the problem is not serious.

Second, though the problem is serious, the solution is to elect one more great president.

Third, the problem is serious but there isn't much we can do about it.

Fourth, the problem is serious but can be corrected by fairly modest incremental changes, possibly including a constitutional amendment, say one providing for an American equivalent to the question hour in the British or Canadian parliaments.

Last, the problem is so profoundly built into the interaction between the constitutional framework and democratic ideology that it cannot be solved without a fundamental alteration in one or the other. This is the conclusion to which I find myself increasingly drawn.

However, given that conclusion, a solution—assuming one is attainable—could require either that Americans transform their constitutional framework or give up their democratic beliefs. I think some critics may hope that Americans will reject their democratic ideology in favor of what these critics believe to be eighteenth-century republican doctrines that would restore the Constitution to its

[52]Nelson W. Polsby, *Consequences of Party Reform* (New York: Oxford University Press, 1983), 134, 170–172.

[53]Shanto Iyengar and Donald R. Kinder, *News That Matters: Television and American Opinion* (Chicago: University of Chicago Press, 1987).

[54]Polsby, *Consequences,* 134, 170–172.

[55]Ibid., 147.

pristine condition in the form the Framers presumably intended. I think this alternative is not only morally wrong but politically and historically illusory.

A goal more suitable to the democratic beliefs of Americans would be to begin the arduous task of rethinking constitutional needs in order to determine whether they may not design a form of government better adapted to the requirements of democracy and less conducive to pseudodemocratization. Among other rethinking, Americans need to consider how to create better opportunities for deliberation and other means by which citizens might gain a more enlightened understanding of their political goals.

To achieve the daunting goal of rethinking the Constitution will not be easy and no one should believe that, properly done, it can be accomplished quickly. But begun now, it might be achieved before this century is over. It would be an appropriate undertaking to commence now that the bicentennial of the American Constitution is behind us.*

*This article is based on *The Tanner Lectures on Human Values,* vol. 10, edited by Grethe B. Peterson, University of Utah Press.

Polling and the White House: Public Opinion and Presidential Behavior*

Robert Y. Shapiro
Department of Political Science
Columbia University
New York, NY 10027

and

Lawrence R. Jacobs
Department of Political Science
The University of Minnesota
Minneapolis, MN 55455

Revised December 10, 2000

Introduction

In our book, *Politicians Don't Pander: Political Manipulation and the Loss of Democratic Responsiveness* (Jacobs and Shapiro, 2000), we assert that there has been a decline in democratic responsiveness at the very top of American national government. The book raises a host of questions about present-day American

*An earlier version of this chapter was presented at the annual meeting of the American Political Science Association, Washington, D.C., August 30–September 3, 2000. We thank the Pew Charitable Trusts for research support. The responsibility for all analysis and interpretations is our own.

politics and about presidential behavior in particular, specifically concerning the causal effect (or lack thereof) of public opinion on the policymaking process. This chapter reviews what is known about the relationship between public opinion and presidential policymaking. While American presidents have paid increasing attention to public opinion with the institutionalization of polling and public opinion analysis in the White House, it should by no means be presumed that policymaking has become more responsive to public opinion. Recent political developments have provided presidents and both parties in Congress increasing incentives and opportunity to attempt to lead or manipulate public opinion. Evidence from the Clinton years described in *Politicians Don't Pander* most strikingly demonstrates this. We are only now beginning to learn about the relationship between presidents and the polling and public opinion analysis that has gone on in presidential administrations since the 1960s. Our working hypothesis is that the Reagan years are pivotal in understanding recent and future developments regarding the relationship between public opinion and presidential behavior.

Politicians Don't Pander: The Contemporary Puzzle

We begin with a contemporary puzzle: Public opinion polls are everywhere. The media report them without stop and political activists of all kinds—from candidates in election contests to political parties and interest groups—pump millions of dollars into focus groups and polls. The flood of polls has fuelled the nearly unquestioned assumption among observers of American politics that elected officials "pander" to public opinion. Politicians, it is charged, tailor their significant policy decisions to polls and other indicators of public opinion.

That politicians succumb to public opinion has been accepted not only by the press and political elites but also by some scholars (Quirk and Hinchliffe, 1998; Geer, 1996). While research (including our own) over the years has found substantial evidence of government responsiveness in the United States, perhaps the strongest recent claim that politicians incessantly follow public opinion comes from the work of James Stimson, Michael MacKuen, and Robert Erikson (1994 and 1995; see also Shapiro and Jacobs, 1989, 1999; Jacobs and Shapiro, 1994b). They tracked government decisions on domestic policies since the 1950s (like legislation enacted by Congress) and constructed global measures of liberalism and conservatism for each year. The researchers then asked: Did changes in government policy in a liberal or conservative direction correspond to changes in public support for more or less government? They report that government policy followed public opinion as it moved in a liberal direction in the 1960s, in a conservative direction around 1980, and then back toward a liberal course in the late 1980s (Stimson, et al., 1995). They concluded that politicians behave "[l]ike antelopes in an open field" (559): "When politicians perceive public opinion change, they adapt their behavior to please their constituency. . . ." (545).

While Stimson, Erikson, and MacKuen offer a compelling account, their reliance on global measures has missed the widening gulf between the specific policy decisions of politicians and the preferences of the American people toward individual issues. Recent American politics sports a long list of policies that failed to mirror public opinion: the impeachment of Clinton, campaign finance reform, tobacco legislation, Clinton's proposals in his first budget for an energy levy and a high tax on Social Security benefits (despite his campaign promises to cut middle class taxes), the North American Free Trade Agreement (at its onset), strict gun control, as well as congressional Republican proposals after the 1994 elections for a "revolution" in policies toward the environment, education, Medicare, and other issues.

A growing body of research provides evidence that this list is not a quirk of recent political developments; the policy decisions of presidents and members of Congress have apparently become less responsive to the substantive policy preferences of the average American since the 1970s. Alan Monroe's (1998; cf. 1979) research shows that government policies in the 1980–93 period were less consistent with the preferences of a *majority* of Americans than during 1960–79. He found that the consistency of government policies with majority public preferences on over 500 issues declined from 63% in the period 1960–79 to 55% in 1980–93 (with the most dramatic drop in opinion-policy consistency occurring for social welfare, economic and labor issues, and, especially, political reform).

Monroe's study is partly confirmed by our own preliminary study. We compared *changes* of public preferences toward social policies and congruent *changes* in government policy, and found a noticeable decline in correspondence in opinion and policy changes during the 1980s and especially the 1990s than found during earlier periods (Jacobs and Shapiro, 1997; Page and Shapiro, 1983). While this analysis is very preliminary, it does contrast with an increase in responsiveness that apparently occurred during the 1960–1979 period (see Shapiro, 1982; Page and Shapiro, 1983).

In a particularly eye-opening study, Ansolabehere et al (1998) examined the responsiveness of members of the House of Representatives between 1874 and 1996. They used the Republican share of the presidential two party vote within each congressional district as an indicator of constituency opinions, and compared it to the ideological position of each party's candidates for the House of Representatives. They found that the candidates' ideological responsiveness to opinion within their districts was weak prior to the 1930s, steadily rose between 1934 and its peak in the early 1970s, then declined into the 1990s (precipitously among Republican candidates). In short, the conventional wisdom that politicians habitually respond to public opinion when making major policy decisions is wrong.

Politicians Don't Pander develops three points, which we briefly summarize here. First, it provides an intensive and in-depth study of deliberations behind closed doors by conducting case studies of social policy making by the Clinton administration (1993–96) and the first Gingrich Congress (1995–96).

Consider Clinton's formulation of his health care reform proposal in 1993–94. Confidential White House records, interviews with high-level policy makers, and other evidence suggest that public opinion did not drive decisions on President Clinton's plan. Administration officials repeatedly insisted that their "plan [was] constructed by the policy people" and that "polling didn't drive the policy decision"

(Jacobs and Shapiro, 2000). They fully accepted that "the most compelling features of our package in policy terms may not yield the highest public support."[1]

The influence of public opinion on the Clinton White House's formulation of its health care plan was limited for three reasons. First, centrist opinion was less influential on White Ho e decisions than the policy goals that arose from Clinton's own philosophy a   policy preferences, interest group pressure, and White House judgments on "what would sell in Congress" to its various ideological factions. Advisers who were both defensive and critical of the administration agreed that the President's New Democratic philosophy and economic considerations regarding universal coverage and other issues were "uppermost in Clinton's mind." Even in those cases in which Americans supported a White House decision, public opinion was not the cause of the decision. This is important because it is tempting to infer from polls showing support for aspects of the health care reform proposal that public opinion drove its decisions. Appeasing interest groups and Democratic Party constituents substantially drove White House decisions. Long-term care and drug benefits were added to "make the Medicare and Medicaid savings possible for the American Association of Retired Persons [and other senior and disability groups] to support"; the early retiree discounts were created to "solidify large business, labor, senior and state and local government support"; and numerous other policies were designed to curry favor with small businesses, urban areas, provider groups, and single payer advocates.[2] Even on the issue of comprehensive benefits for which Stanley Greenberg's, Clinton's White House pollster's research reported strong national support, several administration officials suggested that aggregate public opinion was not as influential as "a lot of pressure from a lot of seniors." "We knew," one political adviser recalled, "that if we didn't have long-term care we wouldn't get the AARP."

The second factor that limited public opinion's influence was that many policy decisions were neither examined in polls nor were matters on which Americans had opinions. White House documents described hundreds of detailed issues that the public could not offer clear opinions on because it had hardly thought or known about them. Third, the White House decided to ignore or contradict public preferences on important policy issues (such as government regulation and payroll taxation) because of its judgments about the quality of public opinion and the role polls should have in policymaking. Officials argued that it was inappropriate and "wrong" to allow polling and public opinion to "drive the process." The President was elected, one White House official explained, "not to follow public opinion, necessarily, but to lead by making decisions about the best way to get to an ultimate end point." This was hardly the common lore about Bill Clinton at the time (or since). In short, the policy preferences of interest groups, party activists, and politicians themselves largely drove policy formulation; the mass public's preferences were persistently discounted.

Our book's second point is that the extensive public opinion research that President Clinton and other politicians used were devoted to finding the language, arguments, and symbols that would win public support and unify Washington elites behind the President's managed competition proposal. Polls and focus groups were an aid to leadership, identifying—as White House memos explained—"how best to sell a health care reform plan that is constructed by the policy people."[3]

Our argument flips the widespread image of politicians as "pandering" to public opinion on its head. The influence of public opinion on policy decisions is declining, whereas politicians' own policy goals are increasingly driving major policy decisions and public opinion research, which is used to identify the language, symbols, and arguments to "win" public support for their policy objectives. Responsiveness to public opinion and manipulation of public opinion are not mutually exclusive; politicians manipulate public opinion by tracking public thinking to select the actions and words that resonate with the public.

The book's third point is that the declining responsiveness of politicians since the 1970s is connected to two of the most widely debated and worrisome trends in American politics: the mass media's preoccupation with political conflict and strategy, and the record proportion of Americans' who distrust politicians—convinced that they no longer listen to them (see Kull and Destler, 1999).

Policy Responsiveness and Global Responsiveness

Our and others' findings of policy makers' declining responsiveness to the public's specific policy preference would seem to contradict the analysis of highly aggregated liberal-conservative trends in public mood and national policy by Stimson, Erikson, and MacKuen (1995). On the one hand, these authors study political representation by reducing policy decisions and national public opinion to a single dimension of ideological conservatism and liberalism and then comparing the public's liberal-conservative "mood" to their overarching policy measures. They argue that a focus on global measures is more realistic than a policy-specific approach: citizens tend to form highly generalizable policy attitudes and "usually fail" to develop specific preferences. Moreover, "it is the general public disposition, the mood, which policy makers must monitor" to reliably identify the public's thinking (Stimson et al., 1994, p. 30–31). Our contrasting view is that the public can and does develop preferences regarding specific policy issues and that policymakers and the press typically track these separate opinions and incorporate them into their actions.

On the other hand, the global approach presents a useful addition to the study of political representation; the use of global ideological measures offers the possibility of providing and tracking system-wide evidence (see especially Erikson, MacKuen, and Stimson [2001, forthcoming]). Further, it may well capture the longer-term patterns of government policies and global ideological shifts in public opinion.

Our policy-specific approach to studying political representation leads us to focus on the *processes* leading up [to] presidential decisions and congressional action. The political processes of formulating policies and balancing policy and electoral goals are often highly-charged. For this reason, we study policymakers' attentiveness to public opinion early in the policymaking process before presidential decisions or roll call votes are taken; this pre-vote process includes the setting of agendas, the formulation of the details of policies, and the attempts to construct supportive coalitions.

Our analysis (and those of others) indicates that public opinion toward specific proposals apparently moved in different directions since the 1980s and that policy-makers' responsiveness on some issues cancelled out unresponsiveness on others through important micro-level processes. The complex behavior and strategies of politicians to move public opinion is beyond the scope of an approach that ana-lyzes highly aggregated liberal-conservative trends in public mood and national policy. The study of global ideological trends may also unintentionally include in its estimation of responsiveness what we refer to as "simulated responsiveness"—cases in which politicians (with the inadvertent aid of the mass media) change public opinion in order to create the *appearance* of responsiveness to public opin-ion. In other words, the global approach may miss the simultaneity of politicians' efforts to manipulate public opinion and to respond to this changed opinion.

Last, as to theory and causal mechanism, the global approach uses the median voter theory to explain the motivations of politicians—namely, the personal ben-efits politicians expect from pursuing policies favored by most voters. The limita-tion of this account is that it is not in a position to explain any identifiable general or short-term increase or decrease in responsiveness. It also does not allow for strategic behavior by elites to attempt to change (and not simply accept) centrist opinion.

What is needed is a conditional and dynamic model of political motivation. The starting place is to acknowledge that politicians face enormous incentives to pursue their own policy goals and those of their partisan supporters, interest groups, or other policymakers in government. This policy-oriented account challenges the widespread presumption among political observers that public opinion mainly drives policy decisions; instead, it suggests that these decisions are driven when-ever politically possible by the policy objectives of politicians and their core sup-porters. Presidents and legislators attempt to minimize the electoral risk of pursuing their policy goals by developing strategies to shield their decisions from the scrutiny of voters. The policy-oriented model needs to be augmented in order to explain politicians' comparatively high responsiveness to public opinion in the past and during election periods.

In *Politicians Don't Pander,* we argue that the motivations of politicians are dynamic and conditional on political and institutional developments. Specifically, the increase since the early 1970s of the institutional independence of govern-ment officials, the strength of incumbency, and, most importantly, ideological polarization within Washington and among congressional districts has elevated the perceived benefits to politicians of pursuing the policy goals that they and their narrow group of supporters favor. Compromising policy goals in favor of centrist national opinion has become more costly to politicians since the 1970s. The approach of elections, however, still raises (over the short-term) the costs to politicians of discounting centrist opinion, thereby temporarily creating incentives to heed the public.

Politicians' perception of the costs and benefits of their behavior affects their strategy. The priority they attach to policy goals has prompted politicians to attempt to lower the potential electoral costs of discounting centrist opinion by *crafting* their arguments, rhetoric, and symbols. Thus presidents and legislators carefully track public opinion in order to identify the words, arguments, and symbols that are most likely to be effective in attracting favorable press coverage and ultimately "winning" public support for their desired policies. Politicians' attempts to change public sentiment toward their favored position convinces them that they can pursue their policy objectives while minimizing the risks of electoral punishment. The irony of contemporary politics is that politicians both slavishly track public opinion and, contrary to the myth of "pandering," studiously avoid simply conforming policy to what the public wants. Another irony here is that the increase in ideological polarizations has led to high levels of often visible political conflict, but while this has led to greater attention to, and importance of, public opinion, it has not led to the greater responsiveness that Schattschneider (1960; cf. Key, 1961), for example, anticipated as political debate expanded the "scope of conflict."

We leave it to readers, at this point, to evaluate further the analysis offered in *Politicians Don't Pander*. Whether they agree with it or not, the book lays out a research agenda for the further study of democratic responsiveness and representation. A critical focus of future research should be on tracking and accounting for historical variations in responsiveness to public preferences toward specific policies. The research by Monroe (1998), Ansolabehere et al (1998), Page and Shapiro (Shapiro, 1982; Page and Shapiro, 1983), as well as that found in *Politicians Don't Pander* show significant ebbs and flows in responsiveness over the past century. What explains these variations? Accounting for variations in responsiveness over time requires an appropriate political and institutional theory of policymaking. It also requires systematic study of politics, institutions, and policymaking over time.

In the rest of this paper, we first review important methodological considerations in attempting to study and disentangle particularly relevant causal relationships. We then examine briefly the recent political history concerning the relationship between presidents and the polling and public opinion analysis that has gone on in presidential administrations since the 1960s. As we currently see it, the Reagan years are pivotal in understanding recent and future developments regarding the relationships between public opinion and presidential behavior.

Presidents and Polling: Studying the Causal Connection

To trace precisely the *processes* by which public opinion and policymaking are causally related, historical and in-depth case study research is needed. While this analysis of specific cases may lack the generalizability of research encompassing a large number ("N") of cases, only it can provide the essential evidence needed to disentangle causal processes and mechanisms. This type of research takes longer to do, requiring archival, interview, and secondary analyses, as well as other ways of gathering evidence that will directly allow us to track how policymakers learn about and respond to public opinion. The case studies that have been done in both foreign policy as well as domestic policy have helped complement and supplement the research that has already been described. These include, for example, Lawrence Jacobs's (1992a, 1992b, 1993) study of what he called a government "public opinion apparatus." His analysis of health care policymaking in Britain and the U.S. uncovered a "recoil effect" in which political leaders' efforts to manipulate public opinion led them to track *and* respond to mass opinion in order to more effectively influence it. Studies of specific foreign policy issues and processes, which do not lend themselves easily to global liberal/conservative ideological conceptualization, have confirmed that public opinion has mattered notably (subject to different interpretations concerning the speed or degree of responsiveness) in U.S.-Chinese relations (Kusnitz, 1984), in U.S. policymaking toward the Contras in Nicaragua (Sobel, 1993), and in foreign policymaking during the Carter (Katz, 1998) and Reagan-Bush years (Hinckley, 1992).

A still better strategy, however, beyond single case studies of individual issues and particular time periods, is one that attempts to synthesize in-depth research in order to unravel *historical trends* in the causal relationship between public opinion and policy. This strategy requires finding trends over time in the extent to which policymakers seek out or otherwise get information on public opinion, and respond to, or are otherwise affected by this information. Jacobs (1993) did this in the case of health care policy, and Thomas Graham (1989, 1994), did the same for nuclear arms control from the beginning of the Cold War to the 1980s. In foreign policymaking in particular, Powlick (1991, 1995) found that there has been an increase in serious and responsive attention to public opinion in the State Department, representing a change in what Bernard Cohen (1973) had found earlier; but the most recent trend he found was for the Reagan and Clinton administrations to place more institutional emphasis in foreign policymaking on *leading* than following public opinion.

In an important book-length treatment of this subject, again in the area of foreign policymaking, Douglas Foyle (1999) also emphasizes that, overall, presidents from Truman to Clinton have tended to behave as "realist" (in contrast to Wilsonian "liberal") theorists in international relations have posited they should: they have tended to choose to lead, not respond to public opinion in foreign policymaking. However, this tendency to lead has varied from president to president in ways that show this to be a characteristic of the individual president, not of the office or institution of the presidency. Specifically, Foyle emphasizes how the extent to which presidents choose to lead or follow public opinion depends on their beliefs about the appropriate role of public opinion in foreign policymaking and the context in which a foreign policy choice has to be made (Foyle, 1999, Preface). While his research focused on the Eisenhower administration, he included case studies involving later presidents. While realist decision-making occurred in a number of cases, some presidents at certain times, most notably President Clinton in the case of the withdrawal of American troops from Somalia, were clearly more receptive than others to the public's input into policymaking.

Overall, then, the in-depth historically oriented research that has focused on finding out how presidents and others *directly used information about public opinion,* suggests that there is a *reciprocal* relationship between public opinion and policymaking, with evidence showing government efforts to respond to, as well as lead, public opinion (see also Heith, 1998a, 1998b, 2000). Clearly, it is necessary to track these processes over time in order to see if particular trends or tendencies have emerged, or if, as Foyle argues, the influences at work hinge on the highly specific beliefs and decision-making contexts of individual presidents.

In this spirit, looking at the institutional and political history that led up to the Clinton years examined in *Politicians Don't Pander,* we have been examining through primary source research the increasing institutionalization of public opinion analysis by American presidents. Our focus has been somewhat different from that of others who have focused on different presidents or different aspects or issues of presidential politics or decision-making (see especially Heith, 1998a, 1998b, 2000; Waller, 2000; Katz, 1998). We started our research with the Kennedy administration and have completed substantial work through the Nixon presidency, followed by Reagan and Clinton. We have found that the opinion-policy process that has evolved is one in which presidents have increasingly assembled and analyzed their own information on public opinion. Specifically, only since Kennedy has the entire process been routinized into the institutional functioning of the presidency. The driving forces are electoral goals as presidents once in office strive to be reelected, and policy goals as they work to establish their "place in history." Presidents started to use their own pollsters and public opinion consultants or staff during their campaigns, with private polls being paid for by the political parties or other non-governmental sources. The history of this is described in Jacobs (1993), Jacobs and Shapiro (1995a) and Heith (1998a, 1998b, 2000; see also Waller, 2000, and Murray, 1999). In these histories the most important data are the numbers of polls that Johnson, Nixon and later presidents conducted, and most notably in our judgment (though we have not yet examined all the available data), the figures for Reagan and Clinton during their two terms in office (especially during the *governing* period, not just during election campaigns), which show that the level of this polling has become substantial indeed. At this writing, the attention to public opinion during Clinton's 1996 election campaign and perhaps continuing into his second term, may well put him in the lead (but cf. Murray, 1999).

In addition to the clear electoral objectives of presidents, the other important aspect of the process is that since the Carter administration, the scope of the sharing and deliberation over public opinion information within the administration has expanded (Heith, 1998a, 2000; Waller, 2000). The result is that the White House has become increasingly better positioned than in the past to respond to, or to attempt to lead—or manipulate—public opinion.

What patterns, then, if any, have emerged? Thus far we have found striking evidence for government responsiveness to public opinion, for opinion leadership, and cases of presidents working opposite the public's wishes for particular reasons. Responsiveness occurred on salient issues, especially those that clearly had immediate or potential electoral consequences. For example, as Kennedy ran for the presidency in 1959–1960, his pollster and consultant, Louis Harris, provided public opinion data that enabled Kennedy's campaign to use issues to heighten Kennedy's image as the candidate who could "get America on the move at home and abroad" (Jacobs and Shapiro, 1994a, p. 531). His emphasis on keeping national defense strong and being vigilant abroad rang true with the American public, but Kennedy did take what he knew to be an unpopular position supporting foreign aid. His purpose for taking a position on foreign aid that was not widely supported was motivated by his need to establish credibility in elite circles and to attempt to educate the public about a policy that advanced the nation's interests (p. 534).

While Harris did not follow Kennedy into the White House, he continued to provide the President with poll data. Although this was not a formal relationship, it revealed that there was in fact an increased need for this kind of information in a routinized manner in modern politics. Responding to public opinion based on polls early in his administration, Kennedy emphasized his support for the Peace Corps, better relations with allies, strengthening the United Nations, and ameliorating the country's balance of payments (Jacobs and Shapiro, 1992).

After Kennedy, White House polling and analysis of public opinion became a regular part of the Johnson and Nixon administrations, with Johnson having available to him information obtained by pollster Oliver Quayle, and Nixon (privately and through the Republican party) commissioning full polls regarding his public image, support, and policy proposals. During the Johnson administration, the 1964 election provided an important juncture in how the president used information on public opinion. Concerned about being reelected, Johnson at first tended to respond to the public's wishes, emphasizing the popular desire to pursue world disarmament and peace in sharp contrast to the widely perceived positions of his Republican opponent, Barry Goldwater. Based on his polling reports, Johnson made sure to distinguish himself regarding the use of U.S. military force, including the use of nuclear weapons in Vietnam. But Johnson, like Kennedy, attempted to lead, rather than respond to the public on the issue of foreign aid. Johnson's apparent strategy of responding to public opinion was particularly pronounced on domestic issues as well (see Jacobs and Shapiro, 1993). Johnson continued this responsive behavior even after it became clear he would easily defeat Goldwater. He did so in order to solidify his public support for purposes of leading the public on his racial and social policy agenda *after* the election. (Jacobs and Shapiro, 1993).

Our systematic quantitative analysis of the relationship between Johnson's policy positions and objectives and his private polling information reveals that beginning after the election, in 1965, Johnson did indeed choose to *lead,* not follow the public. His forceful leadership on domestic proposals, especially the War on Poverty, had not been demanded by the public, but the public came to change its views and support this effort. In the case of foreign policy, the Vietnam war became an issue of extreme contention and here Johnson had no intention of letting the public influence his actions. There was a clear break in this opinion-policy relationship between 1964 and 1965–66, with responsiveness declining and leadership increasing from the first to the second period, with Vietnam being the dominant issue in foreign policy (Jacobs and Shapiro, 1993). In the end, however, after 1965–66, the failure to respond to what Johnson knew to be public opinion on particular aspects of the Vietnam war had increasingly adverse effects on his presidency, which raised normative questions for realist arguments about public opinion and foreign policymaking (Jacobs and Shapiro, 1999). On the other hand, another lesson that could be learned was that while polling could provide important information about the need to respond to public opinion, polling might also provide insights about the best means to move the public in directions presidents might want.

The Nixon administration greatly expanded the institutional organization and sophistication of White House-directed polling and public opinion analysis. Despite his claims that political leaders should not be influenced by polls, Nixon and his advisors used polling data to avoid taking unpopular positions and to enhance their ability to lead the public on policies that they wanted to pursue, especially in the area of foreign policy in which Nixon clearly wanted to leave his historical mark. The archival evidence shows that Nixon ultimately responded to public opinion in a manner consistent with the trends in public opinion and the withdrawal of troops from Vietnam (see Katz, 1998; Shapiro and Jacobs, 1999). Clearly, the Vietnam war was regarded as a crucial election issue in 1972.

While our research and analysis of Nixon are not complete (see Jacobs and Shapiro, 1995a; 1995–96), we have found that the Nixon administration was persistent in tracking public opinion on a wide range of policy and political concerns (especially approval of the president). Thus it is not surprising that the opinion-policy correlation described earlier was higher during the Nixon administration than in previous periods (see Shapiro, 1982; Page and Shapiro, 1983). Indeed, the White House itself not only had a veritable warehouse of its own private polls, but it also possessed the same publicly available opinion data on which such academic analyses were based (see Shapiro, 1982; Page and Shapiro, 1983). The private data, however, were more explicitly and better defined for political purposes (see Jacobs and Shapiro, 1995a, 1995–96, 2000). An especially impressive case of both opinion responsiveness and leadership in foreign policy concerned the admission of China to the United Nations, paving the way for the U.S.'s formal recognition of China. Archival evidence clearly shows that Nixon and his advisors had seen the softening of the public's hostility toward China, making it more receptive to efforts to lead it further in a less belligerent direction. The result was Nixon's trip to China and China's admission to the U.N., which Nixon and his administration did not finalize until they found further public support for it in their own polling data (based on our research in progress; see Kusnitz, 1984). Nixon increased the salience of this issue for the public in a way that enhanced his and his party's electoral appeal.

Thus, during this period through the Nixon administration there is evidence for significant presidential responsiveness to public opinion. This responsiveness occurred in ways associated with actual or anticipated electoral advantages, during a period in U.S. history in which Cold War foreign policies as well as domestic issues could become major election-year issues. As the Cold War ended, however, we might expect this to change: foreign policy issues might no longer arise as critical election issues as the Korean war, Vietnam, and the 1979–80 Iran and

Afghanistan crises had been. Further, while polling, public opinion analysis, and the institutionalization of public relations activities within the presidency might provide the means for responding to public opinion and gaining the public's favor, these tools and institutions also offered the means to try to direct, not respond to, public opinion.

While we have emphasized the reciprocal relationship between public opinion and presidential policymaking and have cited examples of responsiveness to public opinion, we have reason to believe that the dominant trend since the 1970s has been toward less presidential responsiveness and greater efforts at leading or manipulating public opinion. We do not think that this has solely to do with the personal characteristics of presidents whom Americans choose to elect but rather with processes of institutionalization of the means to track public opinion, and of *learning* how to use these means as political resources to lead and manipulate, and not necessarily respond to, public opinion.

From a theoretical and practical perspective, there are obvious limitations on presidents' efforts to lead public opinion. For presidents and their political parties (who pay for the political polling) electoral motivations create pressing incentives to be responsive to public opinion, in order to avoid falling too far out of line with the median voter (see Downs, 1957, and especially Geer, 1996).

But election campaign periods aside, there is in fact a fairly long period during which presidents have the freedom and opportunity to act without worrying immediately about electoral repercussions from the public. Come the next election, voters memories may fade concerning government actions that they did not support, especially as other issues supercede and eclipse the issues of the not so distant past. The president may have time to explain and even claim credit for actions that the public had not supported, as, for example, Bill Clinton did in the cases of the U.S.'s invasion of Haiti and intervention in Bosnia (in which there was, ultimately, probably supportive but divided public opinion; cf. Sobel, 1996). Further, the electoral incentives for presidents are likely to wane for themselves, though not for their parties, during their second terms in office.

To examine trends toward or away from presidential responsiveness to public opinion, the critical starting point is the Carter administration. Carter was the first president to have a publicly visible pollster, Patrick Caddell, who was brought in from Carter's successful presidential campaign. Caddell was the institutional successor to the relatively effective polling analysis operation of the Nixon administration. While the Ford administration has not yet been fully studied from this vantage point (but see Waller, 2000), President Ford inherited the polling and public opinion arrangements that Nixon had through the Republican party involving pollster and consultant Robert Teeter, but he did not benefit, as Nixon and later presidents did, from continuing relationships that began during election campaigns and that continued and evolved for presidents while in office.

Did the Carter presidency try to be responsive to public opinion? Our answer appears: not as much as expected (cf. the work by Heith and Waller cited above). This is particularly surprising for a president who believed it was desirable for public opinion to have some influence on foreign policy. As noted by Foyle (1999), Carter thought public involvement in open decision making would benefit foreign policymaking by preventing mistakes that might occur in a policy formed in secret. That said, it is not obvious that Carter would use polling and public opinion analysis to facilitate this, and the Carter White House clearly did not do the continuous polling of the sort done by later administrations that would have been required for this purpose. The most widely prevalent conclusion about Carter is that he was a "trustee" president, more concerned with acting effectively on behalf of the people but not taking direct "delegate"-style guidance from them (see Jones, 1988; Hargrove, 1988; Shapiro and Jacobs, 1999).

As Heith (1998b, for Carter and other presidents) and we (Jacobs and Shapiro, 1993, 1994a, for other presidents) have noted elsewhere, polling may affect what issues presidents push to the top of their political agenda, but actual policymaking is a different story. And presidents can independently raise issues that the public will then take up as their own (see Jacobs and Shapiro, 1993). Carter was influenced by the actual issues the nation faced and by his own personal assessments of them, and he acted accordingly (cf. Katz, 1998; Heith, 2000; Foyle, 1999; Graham, 1989, 1994). Thus, in practice Carter was not especially responsive to public opinion. Further, when it came to using information about public opinion to gain public support in foreign policy, he was ineffective at this. Later presidents, beginning with Ronald Reagan, in essence picked up where the Nixon administration left off and became better at it. What is striking about Carter is that a president who was not personally inclined toward tracking and analyzing public opinion, paid so much attention to it. Presidential attention to public opinion may reflect institutional rather than simply personal influences or needs.

Our working historical hypothesis is that the Reagan administration is the most informative reference point for future research on public opinion and presidential policymaking. Our preliminary analysis, based on archival evidence from the Reagan Library, is consistent with this and suggests that the main purpose of public opinion analysis was to enhance the White House's ability to shape and persuade public opinion (this will be examined further below). The behavior of the Clinton administration in domestic policymaking summarized above and at length in *Politicians Don't Pander* represents the current point in an evolutionary process. And it applied to foreign policymaking as well—perhaps more so. In the cases of U.S. intervention in Somalia and Bosnia, there was noticeable public opposition early on regarding Bosnia, and in the case of Somalia public opinion began moving against further intervention *before* American soldiers were killed, wounded, and humiliated in the unsuccessful effort to capture the enemy clan leader there (see Jacobs and Shapiro, 1995b, p. 203–6). The important point to be made here is that this type of behavior was informed by apparently well orchestrated polling and public opinion analysis that had not begun with the Clinton administration.

The Reagan Administration

In short, as a window into the future study of presidents, polling, and public opinion, the Reagan years were propitious: Public opinion was regularly monitored in the Reagan White House, and Richard Wirthlin and his firm, Decision

Making Information (DMI), conducted most of Reagan's public opinion analysis. (We have identified at least 184 privately commissioned surveys in the Reagan archival papers; we believe that more remain buried in papers which have yet to be publicly released.)

The President's polls were considered a major political resource and were usually controlled by the chief of staff, who would select sections to distribute to the appropriate administration officials. Reagan's team carefully tracked polls in published materials; it was quite concerned with monitoring how the public and elites were *perceiving* the state of public opinion. The White House carefully evaluated the public's reaction to the President's speeches in order to pinpoint the most effective language or presentations: e.g., small groups of 50 adults were regularly assembled to view Reagan speeches and to use hand held devices to record on a five point scale (from very positive to very negative) their reaction to the President's message, style, and delivery. This "pulseline" analysis was conducted, for instance, on the President's foreign policy speeches related to peace and national security in 1986 and the Venice Summit in June 1987. This analysis provided a detailed evaluation of what the audience found appealing or distressing in each section of the President's address. For instance, DMI's analysis of Reagan's nationally televised 1986 address on peace and national security issues reported "negative reaction" to early sections of the speech because of "anticipation that Reagan is going to ask for more money for defense" and suspicion that the military purchases of new fighters is characterized by "waste and fraud." But the report found that Reagan's claim in his speech that a sustained military buildup would allow the U.S. to bargain from strength and produce a "secure peace" was favorably received because it offered "hope of real progress."[4] These analyses were apparently incorporated into preparing future presidential addresses.

One main component of the White House's analysis of public opinion was Wirthlin's "big monthly surveys" on a variety of topics. These were labeled "Flash Results" and typically used identically worded questions to compile trends of attitudes and detect changes or stability in public opinion. Major new issues also received attention and, if they persisted, were added to the pool of questions that were consistently asked. The regular foreign policy topics in Wirthlin's monthly surveys included international trade, the strategic defense initiative, terrorism, and Central America (aid to the Nicaraguan rebels and policies regarding El Salvador and Mexico). Wirthlin used his analysis to identify potential weaknesses in public support for the President's arms control policy among different subgroups (e.g., 18–24 year olds who were unusually critical and consistently listed foreign policy as their top national concern).[5] In addition to probing public preferences on specific issues, DMI tracked the public's approval or disapproval of Reagan's performance on a range of foreign policy issues including the Persian Gulf, arms control, Central America, relations with the Soviet Union, terrorism, and international trade. Two foreign policy issues that received particular attention were aid for the Nicaraguan rebels and the Iran-Contra scandal. The White House carefully monitored the public's reaction to the administration's support for Nicaraguan aid. In this case the administration's policy was largely opposed by the public, and the administration was monitoring the public to see how—and ultimately, as it turned out, how long—it could maintain a policy at odds with public opinion (for further discussion of this important case, see Sobel, 1993, and Shapiro and Jacobs, 2000). The White House also conducted extensive daily tracking surveys during the Iran-Contra scandal. The data showed the White House that the public would not be sympathetic to blaming the media; majorities believed the press had been both accurate and responsible.[6]

In short, the White House devoted the time and money to commissioning and analyzing public opinion research because, according to Wirthlin, the public's evaluations and support represented the President's "most valuable of all political resources."[7] In recognizing the political significance of public support, the Reagan White House did not accept public opinion as a given. Rather, it attempted to shape it to support the positions the administration already favored. Although further archival and other research is required, it appears that the White House's extensive public opinion analysis was often used to design the presentation of already decided policies. We have found little evidence thus far that the Reagan White House's public opinion research systematically led to decisions that were responsive to public opinion on major issues (as opposed to how already decided policies were presented publicly; cf. Murray, 1999). For instance, Wirthlin repeatedly reported to the White House that aiding the Nicaraguans was consistently unpopular. The pollster's best hope was simply to distance Reagan from a major public campaign that reminded Americans of the President's distance from their views.

Our brief account here of the Reagan years is preliminary and it emphasizes the extent to which polling and public opinion analysis was used to attempt to lead or manipulate, rather than respond to, public opinion. It contrasts with the useful and important accounts that Heith (1998a, 1998b, 2000) and Murray (1999) have provided. Heith and Murray confirm that the polling and public opinion analysis and apparatus of the Reagan administration was extensive; indeed, Murray's (1999) estimate is that the Reagan administration's spending on this through the Republican party may well have surpassed that of the Clinton administration (through the Democratic party). More important, Murray and Heith emphasize the other uses of polling and public opinion analysis, including ways that ultimately led Reagan, contrary to popular belief, to be responsive to public opinion on certain issues. The point here is that the jury is just hearing testimony toward deliberation about the changes that we think occurred in the relationship between presidents and public opinion beginning in the Reagan years.

Increasing Opportunity to Lead or Manipulate Public Opinion?

Compared to much of the research literature of the past twenty years on the relationship between public opinion and policymaking (to which we, to be sure, have also contributed), our discussion of how presidents have used polling and public opinion information downplays presidents' responsiveness to public opinion in making policy decisions. Of course, the opinion-policy literature has acknowledged the complexity of drawing inferences about the widespread correlation between measures of public preferences and government policymaking (see Sharp, 1999), and, as we have described, about drawing explicitly causal inferences. However, we think the pattern of presidential behavior that we have described will continue. Presidents will continue to use polling and public opinion analysis to attempt to lead or manipulate public opinion, though the approach of imminent presidential elections will provide at least one pressing mechanism for restraining this.

Our analysis of the Reagan administration is clearly preliminary and driven by a particular hypothesis. The underlying theory and evidence during the Clinton years on which the hypothesis is based is described at length in *Politicians Don't Pander*. Further, while we have offered arguments and presented a variety of evidence for a decline in the responsiveness of policymakers and government policies to public opinion, the evidence is not so overwhelming or convincing for the jury to reach a final verdict on this either. There is other circumstantial evidence that we can cite that also points in the direction of less rather than more democratic responsiveness: this would include evidence of declining public attentiveness and interest in politics, particularly among new young adult cohorts, and also, in the area of foreign policy, the end of the urgency of the Cold War and the frame of reference the Cold War provided the public for understanding foreign affairs. Further, there are indications that the end of the Cold War has led to a decline in the news media's coverage of foreign affairs and foreign policymaking (on the preceding points, see Shapiro and Jacobs, 2000, and the references they cite). While such evidence is suggestive, it will take more directly persuasive large-scale statistical studies combined with historical case studies based on archival and interview evidence to confirm that the patterns and changes in political behavior that we have described have in fact occurred. In this respect, then, we consider the analysis of democratic responsive versus political manipulation in *Politicians Don't Pander* as the beginning (rather than ending) of a provocative and ambitious research agenda for us and others.

REFERENCES

Ansolabehere, Stephen D., James M. Snyder Jr., and Charles Stewart III. 1998. "Candidate positioning in U.S. House elections." Working paper, 29 July. Department of Political Science, Massachusetts Institute of Technology.

Cohen, Bernard C. 1973. *The Public's Impact of Foreign Policy*. Boston: Little, Brown.

Downs, Anthony. 1957. *An Economic Theory of Democracy*. New York: Harper & Row.

Erikson, Robert S., Michael B. MacKuen, and James A. Stimson, 2001. *The Macro Polity*. New York: Cambridge University Press, forthcoming.

Foyle, Douglas C. 1999. *Counting the Public In: Presidents, Public Opinion, and Foreign Policy*. New York: Columbia University Press.

Geer, John G. 1996. *From Tea Leaves to Opinion Polls: A Theory of Democratic Leadership*. New York: Columbia University Press.

Graham, Thomas W. 1989. *The Politics of Failure: Strategic Nuclear Arms Control, Public Opinion and Domestic Politics in the United States, 1945–1985*. Ph.D. dissertation, Massachusetts Institute of Technology.

Graham, Thomas. 1994. "Public Opinion and U.S. Foreign Policy Decision Making," in *The New Politics of American Foreign Policy* ed. by David A. Deese. New York: St. Martin's Press.

Hargrove, Erwin. 1988. *Jimmy Carter as President: Leadership and the Politics of the Public Good.* Baton Rouge: Louisiana State University Press.

Heith, Diane J. 1998a. "Staffing the White House Public Opinion Apparatus, 1969–1988." *Public Opinion Quarterly* 62 (Spring): 165–89.

Heith, Diane J. 1998b. "The Public Opinion Apparatus and the Presidential Agenda." Paper presented at the annual meeting of the American Political Science Association, Boston, September 3–6, 1998.

Heith, Diane J. 2000. "Presidential Polling and the Potential for Leadership." In Robert Y. Shapiro, Martha J. Kumar, and Lawrence R. Jacobs, eds., *Presidential Power: Forging the Presidency for the 21st Century.* New York: Columbia University Press, forthcoming.

Hinckley, Ronald H. 1992. *People, Polls, and Policymakers: American Public Opinion and National Security.* New York: Lexington Books.

Jacobs, Lawrence R. 1992a. "The Recoil Effect: Public Opinion and Policy Making in the United States and Britain." *Comparative Politics* 24 (January): 199–217.

_____ . 1992b. "Institutions and culture: Health policy and public opinion in the U.S. and Britain." *World Politics* 44 (January): 179–209.

Jacobs, Lawrence R. 1993. *The Health of Nations: Public Opinion and the Making of American and British Health Policy.* Ithaca, N.Y.: Cornell University Press.

Jacobs, Lawrence R. and Robert Y. Shapiro. 1992. "Public Decisions, Private Polls: John F. Kennedy's Presidency." Prepared for delivery at the 1992 Annual Meeting of the Midwest Political Science Association, Chicago.

Jacobs, Lawrence R. and Robert Y. Shapiro. 1993. "The Public Presidency, Private Polls, and Policymaking: Lyndon Johnson." Presented at the 1993 Annual Meeting of the American Political Science Association, Washington, D.C., September 2–5.

Jacobs, Lawrence R. and Robert Y. Shapiro, 1994a. "Issues, Candidate Image, and Priming: The Use of Private Polls in Kennedy's 1960 Presidential Campaign." *American Political Science Review* 88 (September): 527–40.

Jacobs, Lawrence R. and Robert Y. Shapiro. 1994b. "Studying Substantive Democracy: Public Opinion, Institutions, and Policymaking." *PS: Political Science and Politics* 27 (March): 9–17.

Jacobs, Lawrence R. and Robert Y. Shapiro. 1995a. "The Rise of Presidential Polling: The Nixon White House in Historical Perspective." *Public Opinion Quarterly* 59 (Summer): 163–95.

Jacobs, Lawrence R. and Robert Y. Shapiro. 1995b. "Public Opinion and President Clinton's First Year: Leadership and Responsiveness." In Stanley A. Renshon, ed., *The Clinton Presidency: Campaigning, Governing, & the Psychology of Leadership.* Boulder, Col.: Westview Press.

Jacobs, Lawrence R. and Robert Y. Shapiro. 1995–96. "Presidential Manipulation of Polls and Public Opinion: The Nixon Administration and the Pollsters." *Political Science Quarterly* 110 (Winter): 519–38.

_____ . 1997. "The myth of the pandering politician." *The Public Perspective* 8 (April/May): 3–5.

Jacobs, Lawrence R. and Robert Y. Shapiro. 1999. "Lyndon Johnson, Vietnam, and Public Opinion: Rethinking Realist Theory of Leadership." *Presidential Studies Quarterly* 29 (September): 592–616.

Jacobs, Lawrence R. and Robert Y. Shapiro. 2000. *Politicians Don't Pander: Political Manipulation and the Loss of Democratic Responsiveness*. Chicago: University of Chicago Press.

Jones, Charles O. 1988. *The Trusteeship Presidency*. Baton Rouge: Louisiana State University Press.

Katz, Andrew Z. 1998. "Public Opinion and the Contradictions of President Carter's Foreign Policy." Unpublished paper. Denison University.

Key, V. O., Jr. 1961. *Public Opinion and American Democracy*. New York: Alfred A. Knopf.

Kull, Steven, and I. M. Destler. 1999. *Misreading the Public: The Myth of a New Isolationism*. Washington, D.C.: Brookings Institution Press.

Kusnitz, Leonard A. 1984. *Public Opinion and Foreign Policy: America's China Policy, 1949–1979*. Westport, Conn.: Greenwood Press.

Monroe, Alan D. 1979. "Consistency Between Public Preferences and National Policy Decisions." *American Politics Quarterly* 7 (January): 3–19.

———. 1998. "Public Opinion and Public Policy, 1980–1993." *Public Opinion Quarterly* 62 (Spring): 6–28.

Murray, Shoon Kathleen. 1999. "The Reagan Administration's Use of Private Polls." Presented at the 1999 annual meeting of the American Political Science Association, Atlanta, GA, September.

Page, Benjamin I., and Robert Y. Shapiro. 1983. "Effects of Public Opinion on Policy." *American Political Science Review* 77 (March): 175–90.

———. 1992. *The Rational Public: Fifty Years of Trends in Americans' Policy Preferences*. Chicago: University of Chicago Press.

Powlick, Philip J. 1991. "The Attitudinal Bases of Responsiveness to Public Opinion among American Foreign Policy Officials." *Journal of Conflict Resolution* 35: 611–41.

Powlick, Philip J. 1995. "Public Opinion in the Foreign Policy Process: An Attitudinal and Institutional Comparison of the Reagan and Clinton Administrations." Paper presented at the annual meeting of the American Political Sciences Association, Chicago, September 1–4, 1995.

Quirk, Paul J. and Joseph Hinchliffe, 1998. "The rising hegemony of mass opinion." *Journal of Policy History*. 10 (1): 19–50.

Schattschneider, E. E., 1960. *The Semisovereign People: A Realist's View of Democracy in America*. Hinsdale, Illinois: The Dryden Press.

Shapiro, Robert Y. 1982. *The Dynamics of Public Opinion and Public Policy*. Doctoral dissertation, University of Chicago.

Shapiro, Robert Y., and Lawrence R. Jacobs. 1989. "The Relationship Between Public Opinion and Public Policy: A Review." In Samuel Long, ed., *Political Behavior Annual. Volume 2*. Boulder, Col.: Westview Press.

Shapiro, Robert Y., and Lawrence R. Jacobs, 1999. "Chapter 9. Public Opinion and Policymaking." In Carroll J. Glynn, Susan Herbst, Garrett J. O'Keefe, and Robert Y. Shapiro. *Public Opinion*. Boulder, Col.: Westview Press.

Shapiro, Robert Y., and Lawrence R. Jacobs, 2000. "Who Leads and Who Follows? U.S. Presidents, Public Opinion, and Foreign Policy." In Brigitte L. Nacos, Robert Y. Shapiro, and Pierangelo Isernia (eds.), *Decisionmaking in a Glass House: Mass Media, Public Opinion, and American and European Foreign Policy in the 21st Century*. Boston: Rowman and Littlefield Publishers, forthcoming.

Sobel, Richard, ed. 1993. *Public Opinion in U.S. Foreign Policy: The Controversy over Contra Aid*. Lanham, MD: Rowman and Littlefield.

Sobel, Richard. 1996. "U.S. and European Attitudes toward Intervention in the Former Yugoslavia: Mourir pour la Bosnie." In Richard H. Ullman, ed. *The World and Yugoslavia's Wars.* New York: Council on Foreign Relations.

Stimson, James A., Michael B. MacKuen, and Robert S. Erikson. 1994. "Opinion and policy: A global view." *PS: Political Science and Politics* 27 (March): 29–35.

Stimson, James A., Michael B. MacKuen, and Robert S. Erikson. 1995. "Dynamic Representation." *American Political Science Review* 89 (September): 543–65.

Waller, Wynne Pomeroy. 2000. *Presidential Leadership and Public Opinion: Polling in the Ford and Carter Administrations.* Doctoral dissertation, Columbia University.

NOTES

1. Memo to First Lady from Boorstin and David Dreyer (copies to McLarty, Rasco and Magaziner), 1/25/93.
2. Memo to the President and First Lady from Magaziner regarding where we are positioned, 10/1/93; "Long-Term Care: Political Context," 6/2/93, by Magaziner.
3. Memo to First Lady from Boorstin and Dreyer (copies to McLarty, Rasco and Magaziner), 1/25/93.
4. Reagan Library, PR15, "Analysis of the President's Peace and National Security Address," DMI, March 1986 attached to cover note from David Chew to President, 3/4/86.
5. Reagan Library, PR15, "Flash Results, #3084–01," DMI, 4/9–11/85.
6. PR15, "American Attitudes toward the Iranian Situation," DMI, 1/14/87 (#459046).
7. Reagan Library, PR15, Letter to President from Wirthlin, 4/10/85.

October 7, 2001, New York Times magazine, Sunday

The 2,988 Words That Changed a Presidency: An Etymology

By D. T. Max

The president could not find the right words. Soon after the World Trade Center and the Pentagon were attacked on Sept. 11, he tried to articulate his response. In one week he gave more than a dozen speeches and remarks to comfort, rally and then—when he'd rallied too much—calm the country. To some, his language seemed undisciplined. He called the terrorists "folks" and referred to the coming battle as a "crusade." He called for "revenge," called Osama bin Laden the "prime suspect" and asked for him "dead or alive." He said "make no mistake" at least eight times in public remarks. When Bush didn't seem lost, he often seemed scared. When he didn't seem scared, he often seemed angry. None of this soothed the public. "It was beginning to look like 'Bring Me the Head of Osama bin Laden,' starring Ronald Colman," one White House official remembered.

In a time of national crisis, words are key to the presidency. Too many and people tune out; too few and they think he is hiding. The president knew he had not yet said the right things. He returned from Camp David the weekend after the attacks with an intense desire to make a major speech. His aides agreed. The president needed to reassure Americans while conveying a message of resolve to the world.

Shaping a successful speech wouldn't be easy. Karen P. Hughes, the counselor to the president, helped write the straightforward statement the president gave on the night of the attack. The speech, delivered from the Oval Office, was poorly received; it felt too slight, too brief for the great events. Three days later, the president's speechwriting team, led by Michael Gerson, came up with an eloquent meditation on grief and resolution, which the president read at the National Cathedral. "We are in the middle hour of our grief," it began. But the beautiful speech sounded borrowed coming from Bush's mouth. The tone was too literary. The president's next speech had to be grand—but it also had to sound more like him.

The White House also had to decide where to give it. Among the choices the president and his advisers had was an address to Congress, which had invited him to speak before a joint session. There is no greater backdrop for a president. But some advisers were reluctant. The president couldn't march up Pennsylvania Avenue without something new to say. And according to his advisers, Bush wasn't sure yet what the administration's response to the attack would be. Some advisers suggested a second Oval Office speech, which would be more intimate and controlled than an address to Congress. Others suggested speaking at a war college. He would look strong there. Karl Rove, the president's chief political adviser, felt strongly that the president did better with a big audience. Applause revved him up. Congress, he thought, was ideal: it would build a sense of national unity. That was important. The speech was a huge political opportunity for Bush. War had given the president a second chance to define himself, an accidental shot at rebirth. Bush's first eight months had been middling. To many, he seemed a little slight for the job. His tax cut had gone through, but the education initiative, the defense transformation and the faith-based initiative were not moving forward well. Americans had still not embraced him as a leader. A strong speech could revive Bush's presidency.

The president decided to speak to Congress. But he wasn't sure yet what to say. The main focus of the speech was tricky to define. "He had to speak to multiple audiences," his national security adviser, Condoleezza Rice, later told me. "He was speaking to the American people, foreign leaders, to the Congress and to the Taliban."

Karen Hughes met Bush at the White House residence Sunday afternoon to discuss what ground the speech might cover. She jotted down notes: Who are they? Why they hate us? What victory means? How will it be won? On Monday morning, Bush talked to Hughes again. According to Hughes, he told her how to deal with the fact that military action might come anytime. "If we've done something, discuss what we have done," he told Hughes. "If not, tell people to get ready." He told her he wanted a draft quickly. Hughes called Michael Gerson and told him that he had until 7 P.M. to come up with something.

Gerson does not write alone. He has five other writers, two of whom he works closely with, Matt Scully and John McConnell. Scully is wiry and ironic, like a comedy writer. McConnell is more earnest. They help bring Gerson down to earth. Gerson, 37, is an owlish man who fills yellow pads with doodles when you ask him a question. He says he believes that social justice must be central in Republican thought. "The great stories of our time," he told me, "are moral stories and moral commitments: the civil rights movement, the War on Poverty." He and the president get along well. The president calls Gerson "the scribe." They share an intensely felt Christianity.

Gerson had written speeches with Scully and McConnell during the campaign. They worked well together. Since then, Gerson has moved up a notch: he now has an office in the basement of the West Wing. The office is prestigious but not great for writing. It is claustrophobic and illuminated by artificial light. McConnell and Scully were in the Old Executive Office Building. If the West Wing, with its plush carpeting and secretaries in heels, resembles a Sun Belt office suite, the O.E.O.B. is by comparison a funky hotel. Every office, no matter how small, has its own couch, yet no office had a matching set of chairs. It was a good place to brainstorm. So Gerson crossed West Executive Avenue to see McConnell and Scully. The three writers sat around the computer in McConnell's office, Gerson in one of the gray suits he wears, bouncing nervously, Scully's feet up on the couch. They began to write, adopting the magisterial tone of presidential speechwriting. These were great events. They deserved great sentiments, a lofty style that Don Baer, a communications director in the Clinton administration, called "reaching for the marble." The three wrote as a team, trying out sentences on each other: "Tonight we are a country awakened to danger. . . ." They went quickly. They knew there would be time to change things and plenty of hands to do it. They assumed that one of the widows of the heroes of United Airlines Flight 93 would be there, so they put in Lyzbeth Glick, the widow of Jeremy Glick, one of the men who apparently fought with the hijackers. (In fact it would be Lisa Beamer, whose husband, Todd, had also been on the plane.) They knew little for certain, and knowing little increased their natural tendency to sound like Churchill, whose writing they all liked. Gerson tried out: "In the long term, terrorism is not answered by higher walls and deeper bunkers." The team kept going: "Whether we bring our enemies to justice or bring justice to our enemies, justice will be done." The computer screen filled with rolling triads. "This is the world's fight; this is civilization's fight; this is the fight of all who believe in progress and pluralism, tolerance and freedom." Words tumbled out.

"They were just sitting there, jamming," said Juleanna Glover Weiss, the vice president's press secretary, whose office is next door. "There was a sort of one-upsmanship to it." Gerson wrote, "Freedom is at war with fear." Together, they tweaked it: "Freedom and fear are at war." They worked steadily, getting meals from the White House mess to keep them going.

The patriotic riffs were falling in place. But what, and how much, could they tell the country about the administration's plans for bin Laden and Afghanistan? They received some help from John Gibson, another speechwriter. Gibson writes foreign-policy speeches for the president and the National Security Council and regularly attends meetings with Condoleezza Rice, the national security adviser, and Stephen Hadley, her deputy. Gibson has the odd job of writing public words about the government's most private decisions. He has top-secret security clearance; his hard drive is stored in a safe.

Getting good information is always a problem for White House speechwriters. The most important officials keep it away from them for the obvious reason that they are writers: they have friends at newspapers; they eventually write memoirs. When sensitive policy is made, the principals close the door. Since the attack, information, as they say in the intelligence community, had become "stovepiped." Gibson's meeting with Rice and Hadley was canceled, and he couldn't get through to them.

Fortunately, Gibson had made contact with Richard A. Clarke, the counterterrorism director for the N.S.C. Clarke is a white-haired, stocky man who has been in the job for nearly a decade. He speaks very loudly. "Even his e-mails are blustery," one White House employee told me. Whatever the meetings were, he was still going to them. Gibson e-mailed Clarke questions that unintentionally echoed Hughes's original discussion with Bush: Who is our enemy? What do they want?

The e-mailed answer came in a bulleted memo. Who is our enemy? "Al Qaeda." What do they want? "That all Christians and Jews must be driven out of a vast area of the world," and "that existing governments in Islamic countries like Egypt and Saudi Arabia should be toppled. They have issued phony religious rulings calling for the deaths of all Americans, including women and children." Gibson liked the tone and authority of the response. He handed over an edited version to Gerson.

Using Gibson's edit, Gerson, Scully and McConnell began on the Taliban. Scully started: "We're not deceived by their pretenses to piety." Gerson wrote: "They're the heirs of all the murderous ideologies of the 20th century. By sacrificing human life to serve their radical visions, by abandoning every value except the will to power, they follow in the path of Fascism and Nazism and imperial Communism." Scully added, "And they will follow that path all the way to where it ends." They paused. Where would it end? They didn't know. But there were plenty of ready-made phrases around. McConnell threw out five or six, like crumbs from his pocket. They liked the idea of predicting the end of the Taliban's reign of terror. "You know, history's unmarked grave," McConnell said. The group bounced the phrase around until McConnell came up with: "It will end in discarded lies." Gerson liked that, too. So the line read, "history's unmarked grave of discarded lies."

But if the Taliban were going to wind up on the ash heap of history, then someone had to suggest how this would be accomplished. Would we attack tomorrow? Would we mount a land invasion of Afghanistan? Would we take on Iraq as well? No one knew. Policy and prose work their way on separate tracks at the White House, only meeting at higher levels. Speechwriters sometimes sit around with finished speeches, waiting for the policy person to call and let them know what the whole thing is for. Not knowing what the president was going to announce, Gerson and his team couldn't come up with the right tone for an ending. But they had done what they could, written a joint-session speech in a day. They sent it off to Hughes.

Late Monday night, Karen Hughes told Gerson that the president found the draft promising but thought it needed a lot of work. Hughes herself was already considering changes. Like Bush, she is a Texan who looks to the heartland. She is the person who reads with the president's eyes. "I can hear his voice," she said, "the way he likes to inflect and speak and the rhythm of his words."

Gerson and his team gave Hughes notes for a suggested ending. Hughes gave the draft a critical read. Speechwriters like beautiful phrases, the "marble." But this president stumbles over ornate writing. It makes him seem small. When he has time to edit, he cuts adjectives. "I've always described the president's style as eloquent simplicity," Hughes said. "There's a poetry, but it's a minimalist poetry." Some of this was image and some was reality and some was reality imitating image. The walls of the West Wing are lined with pictures of the president on the range in his jeans, pulling out trees by their roots. After two years of national exposure, the public had a certain expectation.

The way Hughes saw it, the speech needed to be vivid. "I felt strongly the need for new images to replace the horrible images we'd all seen," she said. It had to have sound bites. That was also her department: she had at one point been a TV reporter before going to work for Bush's first gubernatorial campaign. The White House press secretary, Ari Fleischer, would distribute a summary of the speech to the press beforehand so it could alert their listeners what to listen for. And the language couldn't be too flowery. Hughes felt the way to reach the vast middle ground was to explain things as if you were talking to a friend. The speechwriters were writing for history, but she just wanted it to be an informative conversation. She began making additions to the text: "Al Qaeda is to terror what the Mafia is to crime."

Meanwhile, the answer to what America was going to do next had been decided. Meeting at Camp David, the president's war cabinet among them Rice; Secretary of Defense Donald Rumsfeld; Rumsfeld's deputy, Paul Wolfowitz; and Secretary of State Colin Powell—spread out maps and charts of Central Asia before they began discussing strategy. Not everyone had a firm sense of the geography of places like Tajikistan. One question was how the United States would define victory. Obviously, capturing bin Laden wasn't enough. But should the United States go after every state that had ever harbored terrorism in the Middle East? Syria, Iraq and Iran were all on the State Department's state-sponsored terrorism list. Powell argued for a narrow targeting of the terrorists; Wolfowitz argued for a broader statement, one that would include Iraq. Powell prevailed. The president subsequently sided with him at a National Security Council meeting. "We decided we'd start with O.B.L., his lieutenants and Al Qaeda and then take it from there," a senior administration official recalled. For a president who had surprised many Americans in his first eight months with his hard-line conservatism, it was a turn toward the center.

At the same time, it was agreed that the speech would have flexible language that would give the military free license to win a war. There would be no pledge made not to bomb Kabul or Baghdad.

Under Powell's guidance, the State Department drafted the language of the goals. Condoleezza Rice walked them into the Oval Office. There, Bush was saying that he liked the speech but the ending wasn't right; the speechwriters and Hughes scribbled notes as he spoke. Bush was enormously excited, Hughes recalled. The speech shouldn't end reflectively, he said. It should end with him leading. Rice then read aloud the demands Powell sent over: deliver the leaders of Al Qaeda to the United States; release detained foreign nationals and protect those in Afghanistan; close the terrorist camps. Give the United States full inspection access. Bush liked the points. Calling on the Taliban to give up bin Laden in front of Congress would be a moment of some power. He told the speechwriters to translate them from bureaucratese. Rice left her notes with the speechwriters.

Bush still wasn't sure whether to give the speech or not. Andrew Card, his chief of staff, told Bush that Congress was eager for a decision. Bush said he still needed time.

The speechwriters went back to work. They laid more marble: "This is not, however, just America's fight. And what is at stake is not just America's freedom. This is the world's fight. This is civilization's fight." Meanwhile, Rice and Hughes wondered if the speech conveyed the Taliban's evil well enough. Rice sent Dick Clarke and Zalmay Khalilzad, another N.S.C. member, who is Afghan born, to Hughes to help punch up the section. Clarke and Khalilzad told her how men could be punished if their beards were too short, how women weren't allowed to go to school, how movies were illegal. Hughes took notes and put them into her copy of the speech. She was thinking domestically: these were wrongs Americans could understand. Hughes also amplified language that Gerson's team had written expressing compassion for the Afghan people. What had helped Bush become president were the overtures of compassion in his conservatism. In the days after the attack, he'd been so bellicose that his father called to tell him to tone it down. It was time to bring back the candidate.

Gerson, Scully, McConnell and Hughes sat down in Hughes's office on Wednesday at 11 A.M. They grouped around Hughes's computer. In front of her was a little plaque quoting Churchill: "I was not the lion, but it fell to me to give the lion's roar." New material kept coming in. Vice President Dick Cheney sent up a short text with McConnell defining the new cabinet position, director of homeland security. Hughes felt that the speech didn't make the point clearly enough about America's respect for Muslim Americans. The president's rush visit to a mosque had gotten a good response on Monday; it was important to highlight that theme. Hughes changed the phrase "Tonight I also have a message for Muslims in America" to "I also want to speak tonight directly to Muslims throughout the world. We respect your faith." She helped write the sentence "The United States respects the people of Afghanistan." Hughes was taking the speech out of marble and making it concrete. She added "I ask you to live your lives and hug your children." Rove stopped by; as a result of his input, the speechwriters added the line "I know many citizens have fears tonight, and I ask you to be calm and resolute." Rice's deputy, Stephen Hadley, who had to worry about more terrorism, suggested reminding people that there might be more terrorism to come. "Even in the face of a continuing threat" was added to the sentence.

All week, the president worked on the speech at night in the residence. He likes his speeches to make a point and for the point to be clear. He hates redundancies. He took a course in American oratory at Yale and remembers how a speech divides into an introduction, main body, peroration. (He once annotated a speech with phrases like "tugs at heartstrings" and "emotional call to arms.") Bush writes his notes with a black Sharpie pen. His edits tend to simplify. He is a parer. "Bush favors active verbs and short sentences," Rove said.

The president had strong feelings about the speech's ending. Although they had not yet found a place for it, the writers had suggested including a quote from Franklin Delano Roosevelt in the speech's conclusion: "We defend and we build a way of life, not for America alone, but for all mankind." The president didn't want to quote anyone else. He'd said this to them in emphatic terms at a meeting the day before, explaining that he saw this as a chance to lead. "I was scribbling notes as fast as I could," Gerson said.

The team worked on an ending that would be all Bush. They revisited the phrase "freedom and fear are at war" and gave it a providential spin: "We know that God is not neutral between them." Without hitting it too hard, a religious note would be sounded.

At 1 P.M., Gerson's team met with Bush and Hughes. They pulled up their chairs around the desk in the Oval Office. "You all have smiles on your faces; that's good," Bush said. Then, wearing his glasses, he began reading the speech aloud, stopping only for a few edits. He read the new ending aloud. "It is my hope that in the months and years ahead, life will return almost to normal," it said. "Even grief recedes with time and grace." But these comforting words were not all. "I will not forget the wound to our country and those who inflicted it," the speech went on. "I will not yield. I will not rest. I will not relent in waging this struggle for freedom and security for the American people." It echoed William Lloyd Garrison ("And I will be heard!"), but it was his own. Here was his peroration, and it tugged on your heartstrings and called you to arms. The final "freedom and fear" image worked, too. The president said: "Great speech, team. Let's call the Congress." He would give the speech the next night, on Thursday the 20th.

Although the main building blocks of the speech were in place and the speech would definitely be given, a lot had still to be nailed down. Other agencies had yet to be heard from. Speeches are sent out for comment to all the interested parties in the administration. Sometimes this encompasses much of the executive branch, speeches being like a ligament that binds together the administration. "The process of writing the speech forces the policy decisions to be finalized," Hughes said. In the case of a speech as big as a joint-session address, nearly everyone is involved, from the secretary of state to the chief of staff. People drop by and read a draft late in the process to make sure nothing has changed. They call with suggestions and send their emissaries.

Predictably, the State Department wanted emphasis on the coalition building that Powell was working on. Language went in. Defense was worried that the speech would focus on the wrong things. "Their point of view," one official remembered, "was that you could put a concrete dome over every stadium in the country and we still wouldn't be safe. The best defense is a good offense." These jostlings were the last echo of the arguments over the map at Camp David. They were an attempt to affect policy through minute changes in the text. Motivating it was the fact that a president's words receive enormous scrutiny overseas. Bin Laden had already thrown back some of Bush's most ill-chosen remarks, promising his jihad would beat Bush's "crusade." As Karl Rove told me: "In a crisis there's a gravity to each sentence. It's an awesome time and an awesome responsibility."

So the text got an extraordinary going-over. Language suggesting that Islamic organizations in the United States should be more aggressive in denouncing terrorism had earlier been tabled. Now "imperial Communism" was deleted from the list of ideologies that McConnell had put on the unmarked grave of discarded lies. According to one participant, the worry was about offending Russia, whom the alliance was courting. (The generic "totalitarianism" replaced it.) Some things that were in the text for no reason anyone could understand were cut. At one point, Hughes had put in that in Afghanistan you could be jailed for watching "movies like 'Gone with the Wind.'" It seemed odd to everyone, including Hughes, so it went out. Surprisingly to some, Hughes's Mafia line was not cut by Rove, who expended much effort courting American Catholics. Fact checking led to more changes. Someone realized that it was not true, as the speech asserted, that "Americans have known wars. But for the past 136 years they have been wars on foreign soil." What about Pearl Harbor? Pearl Harbor was added. History was history. But "sneak attack" became a "surprise attack." We were friends of the Japanese now and hoped to remain so. The staff collated the changes.

It was amazing how many countries you had to be nice to. The phrase "there are thousands of these terrorists concealed in more than 60 countries" lost the word "concealed." The terrorist organizations linked to Osama bin Laden were limited strategically to the Egyptian Islamic Jihad and the Islamic Movement of Uzbekistan—two, as one White House official noted, "of the most obscure terrorist organizations in the world." The Hezbollah, the Fatah and the Muslim brotherhood never got in. The Middle East was a fragile place. Still, that wasn't enough. An N.S.C. official flagged the phrasing of a sentence that read, "Any nation that harbors or supports terrorism will be regarded by the United States as 'hostile.'" What about Syria? The wording became "any nation that continues to harbor," giving the country, as one official said, "another chance to straighten up and fly right." Such softening was inevitable, but America still had to stand strong. Bush needed one hard phrase to lean on. It became this: "You're either with us, or with the terrorists."

Rice got one last look at the speech. If something misguided slipped in, it would be her problem first. She signed off. Policy and prose were now in place.

The president had to rehearse. It was the first thing he'd thought of after deciding to do the speech. The more time he practices, the better his speeches come off. The downward furl of his mouth relaxes. His tendency to end every phrase with an upward cadence diminishes. The first teleprompter rehearsal was at 6:30 Wednesday night. The president came out in his blue track suit with his baseball cap on. His dog, Spot, ran around the room, nuzzling the writers as they sat listening. The president weighed the sounds in his mouth. He came to lines about the administration's domestic legislative agenda, lines that had been slowly piling up—the energy plan, the faith-based initiative, the patients' bill of rights. "This isn't the time," he said and cut them. Hughes agreed. This was the time for Bush to assert his credentials on foreign policy and not retreat into the domestic sphere.

The president made more cuts. When he saw how many billions of bailout dollars the speech promised for the airline industry, he insisted the line be deleted. "We're still negotiating that," he said. He put in little things for sound. After "The United States respects the people of Afghanistan," he inserted the phrase "After all" to begin the next sentence, "we are currently its largest source of humanitarian aid." It would give him a chance to breathe. Hughes coached him: "Give the ear time to catch up," she advised.

Thursday morning, the day of the speech, Bush rehearsed again. He didn't like the clunky paragraph that contained the list of our allies: the Organization of American States and the European Union, among others. It was too much of a mouthful. They would no longer hear their names spoken. State lost that round.

The president took a nap at 4:30, was awakened by an aide and rehearsed one more time. At 5:15 Hughes told Gerson the name of the new director of homeland security. It was Bush's old friend, the governor of Pennsylvania, Tom Ridge. The news had been held back so it wouldn't leak. Tony Blair, the British prime minister, was late arriving for dinner, and the president was offered a chance to rehearse again but said he was ready. The communications office prepared a list of sound bites and distributed them to the press: "The enemy of America is not our many Muslim friends." "Be ready." "Freedom and fear are at war."

The president got into his motorcade and went to the Capitol. The vice president stayed behind so they would not be in the Capitol together. It was an unprecedented security move. It meant that every time the camera showed Bush, you would think about the meaning of Cheney's absence. You would remember the crisis. Bush walked into the Capitol, a president in wartime. He wore a pale blue tie. He began: "Mr. Speaker, Mr. President pro tempore, members of Congress and fellow Americans." He was interrupted for applause 31 times.

A week after the speech, the flag at the White House was back at full mast, waving in the wind. Karen Hughes wore a metal American flag on her lapel, upward streaming too. Was the speech a success? For the president, yes. "He told me he felt very comfortable," Hughes said. "I told him he was phenomenal." Bush had wanted to steady the boat, and he had done it. He had shown leadership. The Congress felt included. "The president's speech was exactly what the nation needed—a message of determination and hope, strength and compassion," Ted Kennedy said. For the writers, there was catharsis: Gerson felt that by working on the speech, he had become connected to "the men digging with shovels in New York." Pundits wrote that the president had said just the right thing in a time of crisis. The Uzbeks were pleased. The Syrians were not enraged. Only the Canadians, of all people, were piqued: their mention, as part of O.A.S., had been cut so the speech wouldn't sag. Even professional speechwriters, tough critics of one another, were impressed. "It was a good, strong speech," said Ted

Sorensen, who wrote speeches for John F. Kennedy. "I'm not sure 'freedom versus fear' means much. But it had a nice ring to it, and you can be sure we're on the side of freedom."

Hughes quoted to me an e-mail message she had gotten from a journalist, saying that after the speech he'd been able to sleep again. It made sense. The speech reassured, even in the way it alternated its soaring Gersonian moments and its Hughesian explanations. America was mad but not too mad, mindful and not weak. Courage, compassion, civility and character were all there too—the values that Bush ran on and that Gerson helped articulate in the campaign. After months of placating the right wing and days of disarray, the president had returned to the political and emotional center. The very act of the speech suggested that civilized life would continue.

The president had just sat around a big war map at Camp David—but instead of first doing something violent, he turned to words. Some of those words were bland. Many were vague. Other than the demands to the Taliban, there was little policy in it. "This was a strategic speech, not tactical," admitted a senior White House official.

This wasn't a State of the Union address. It wasn't a moment to look ahead. Bad news could wait. New presidents are terrified of looking indecisive, but this one realized it would be worse to be rash. Who are they? Where are they? How can we strike back? The coming challenge is enormous. By delivering a speech that emphasized reason over wrath, Bush bought himself some time until someone could draw a real map for the first war of the 21st century.

9

THE PRESIDENCY
AS AN INSTITUTION

Constrained Diversity: The Organizational Demands of the Presidency

Bruce Buchanan
Associate Professor of Government
The University of Texas at Austin

Abstract

Two characteristics in particular distinguish the presidency from most other complex organizations: the proportion of organizational energy and resources that must be devoted to coping with the unexpected, and the pervasive impact of its central figure—the president—on the manner and tone of organizational functioning. These features limit the strategies likely to be effective in the management of such an enterprise. The first demands flexibility, and discourages excessively formalistic procedures as too unresponsive for a turbulent environment. The second points up the futility of trying to impose any management system, however sound theoretically, on a president who finds it uncongenial.

It is in this light that the recent consensus in favor of "one best way" to organize the White House—a strong, hierarchically dominant chief of staff system—requires challenge. Various problems with the strong chief system are noted, and an alternative organizational model—the first Reagan system— is described and evaluated.

Presidents need help, and by our traditions, they generally get it on their own terms. Still, certain essential services—badly needed by every chief executive— must be provided.[1] The manner of their provision is up to the president, as is the choice concerning who will provide the help. But the services, listed below, must be there, in one form or another.

Help in Pushing the Discretionary Agenda This initiative-taking dimension of the presidency emphasizes creativity and forethought, as well as coordination and orchestration of strategic components in keeping with timetables. In the effort to set and dominate the national policy agenda, the president requires assistance in such matters as devising policy proposals, drafting legislation, conceiving political strategy, contending with the media, identifying potential appointees to executive branch positions, controlling bureaucracy, influencing congress, and the like. For each of these and other matters, information must be assembled and options identified for presidential decision-making, speech-making and other proactive, discretionary action.

Help in Coping with the Unexpected   This concerns the reactive dimension of the presidency; issues, problems and crises which emerge on their own, without presidential initiative or choice, but which require presidential decision or other action with potentially very adverse consequences, and long-term significance, often under severe time constraints, and with imperfect information. The prototype for this dimension of presidential responsibility is a foreign policy crisis, such as the Cuban Missile Crisis. But less portentous issues fit too. Those like the breakdown of the nuclear reactor at Three Mile Island during the Carter Administration, the inability of a cabinet officer, Secretary of State Alexander Haig, to work effectively with the White House Staff, or the sudden disclosure, by the Iranian government to a Beirut newspaper, of secret agreements involving trades of armaments for hostages struck between it and the United States, illustrate other unexpected and unwanted problems for which the president is not prepared and with which he suddenly and unexpectedly needs help.

One characteristic of such problems which distinguishes them from those in the first category is the usual lack of time for "staffing out" options; that is, for involving all the regular experts and planners and procedures normally consulted and followed prior to a more routine proactive decision. Another characteristic, urgency, is particularly pronounced in foreign policy crises, where modern communications technology involves the president in the micro-management of the unfolding crisis, forced to make decisions formerly made by officials on the scene. Alexander Haig explains:

> . . . the fact (is) that the president is exposed instantaneously through modern technology, satellite, with data that the other echelons below him are not getting, and wants answers and must have them . . . because modern technology also brings the American public immediately abreast of the crisis . . . and the presidents simply have to have answers.[2]

To whom does a president turn when confronted with the unexpected? Accessible personal advisors, generalists retained for their intelligence, poise, experience, good political instincts, and enjoyment of the personal trust of the president, rather than technical experts, tend to be sought out for whatever advice the president has time or stomach to consider in these circumstances.

Help in Fitting the President to the Job   Speaking before a national television audience as a member of the Tower Commission, charged with assessing the origins of the Iran-contra fiasco during the second Reagan term, General Brent Scowcroft, while by no means absolving President Reagan from the ultimate responsibility for the transgressions reported, nonetheless made a telling point of special relevance here. It was that it is the staff and the staff structure that is responsible for accommodating the management style of the president, not the president's responsibility to accommodate himself to some abstract staffing ideal.[3]

The traditions of the office mean that each new president literally starts over, *tabula rasa,* imposing new procedures, new assumptions, and a new atmosphere, or culture. In this sense, each new president is a founder. The White House Office is surely the most flexible organization in the executive branch of government. Because of his personal role in achieving his station, his considerable constitutional power, together with the ongoing importance of his personal presence to success in office, each incumbent continues to exert a dominant, and highly idiosyncratic impact on how the work of the White House is done. If his inevitable human shortcomings and flaws are not to consume him and undermine his regime, then others must fill the necessary gaps. The need is for others to help adjust the fit between a particular president and those job related problems which stem from his personal way of doing things: compensating for weaknesses, showcasing strengths, accommodating personal quirks, providing moral and emotional support, personal guidance, and the like, as he pursues his agenda and copes with the unexpected.[4]

Ronald Reagan, for example, was said to require a tranquil environment, a restful pace, and assistance in reconciling his ideological principles with the need for pragmatic compromise. Only thus can he retain the buoyant optimism and firm conviction which make it possible for him to do what he does best: communicate sincerity to the mass audience. The tranquil environment, we are told,[5] required a sort of mood management and schedule control, which had been the responsibility of Nancy Reagan and, during the first term, Michael Deaver. The restful pace demanded that others—variously James Baker, Donald Regan, Howard Baker, and Kenneth Duberstein, as respective chiefs of staff,—arrange for the policy analysis, and do the work scheduling and choice-framing, with Reagan usually involved only at the point of final decision. And the important work of preserving Ronald Reagan's belief that his compromises were actually consistent with his ideological convictions required that his staff make to him what one Cabinet official termed "Reagan arguments;" soothing assurances that the president is not breaking faith with his values, despite seeming to do so.[6]

Other presidents have of course required very different forms of handling, stroking, or help aimed at compensating for their personal shortcomings.[7] But every one requires some sort of highly personal accommodation, supplied by those who specialize in molding themselves to the presidential needs of the moment.

A Staffing Typology

Any president's organization and management system must accommodate itself to the fact that a diversity of human talent will be required to supply the necessary help. Typically, presidents have arrayed four classes of assistants across the three sorts of duties just described: process managers, experts, wise heads, and kids.[8] We will see that all four types may do one or more of the chores described, but there does seem to be some degree of specialization.

1. ***Process Manager*** John F. Kennedy and Lyndon Johnson reputedly assumed most of the responsibility for generating information and formulating

decision options themselves, but other recent presidents deployed management talent like Sherman Adams, H.R. Haldeman, or James Baker to coordinate and direct such processes as decision management, strategic planning, staff supervision, work assignments, and allocation of access to the president. These are the kinds of activities which are said to require a strong chief of staff. The complexity of the presidency does require a good deal of system and order, and the specialized talent able to impose it, but exactly why a single powerful agent, second only to the president, and perched atop a formal hierarchy, is the best instrument for delivering these services is not clear and will be debated later in this paper. As Richard Neustadt contends, there have been only two really strong chiefs in the modern era: during Eisenhower's recuperation from his heart attack and during the second Reagan administration. Most presidents employed a "big three or four" who shared process management duties rather than a single dominant advisor.[9]

2. **Wise Heads**   These are people whose counsel is sought not so much for their technical expertise (although they may have it), as for their wisdom and judgment. As suggested, they tend to 'specialize' in the unexpected crisis problems, during which they assist in thinking the problem through and devising a course of action. Wise heads are typically people whom the president regards as peers because of longstanding close association of one sort or another, or because of comparable age, impressive experience, achievement, special insight, unflappability, or some other quality which the president admires, respects, and is comforted by. They serve by helping the president maintain balance, perspective, accurate perception and understanding, composure, and confidence in himself in the face of circumstances which threaten to upset his equanimity and distort his judgment.

The titles and activities of such counselors vary widely. They may, for example, be in or outside the official White House staff. Kennedy's brother Robert (Attorney General) or his alter ego Theodore Sorensen (Special Counsel to the President) are cases in point, as are Charles Kirbo (Friend) and Rosalynn Carter (Wife) for Jimmy Carter; Donald Regan (Treasury Secretary and Chief of Staff), Michael Deaver (Deputy Chief of Staff), Stuart Spencer (outside political adviser) and Edwin Meese (Counsellor and Attorney General) for Reagan. During normal times, such people are engaged in other activities in or outside the presidential orbit. But in the crunch the president seeks their help in understanding his situation and his choices.

3. **Experts**   The national security adviser, the members of the Council of Economic Advisers, pollsters, campaign strategists, media specialists, the legal counselor, speechwriters and the domestic policy staff illustrate the range of technical expertise on which presidents routinely must call, usually for help in pushing the programmed agenda, occasionally for coping with the unexpected. Typically, these individuals bring a specialized knowledge of a policy domain plus familiarity with the history of policy experimentation within the domain, to bear in framing the technical dimensions of presidential decision options. For some advisers, politics is the technical specialty.[10] For others, the extent to which political (as opposed to purely technical) considerations are incorporated into the

analysis of decision options may depend on the proximity of the adviser to the president. In some presidential management systems, mid and low level advisers have exclusively technical responsibilities, with political considerations incorporated only after the staff work moves up the hierarchy for screening by political specialists.

The major contribution made by those possessing substantive expertise can be described as education. For a wide range of issues in all of which no president can hope to be knowledgeable, he must still somehow be brought 'up to speed;' made sufficiently acquainted with the background of a problem so that he can recognize the signs of serious debate, and distinguish the workable options from the implausible ones. He must know enough to discern when it is time to turn away from experts and let his own political instincts take over, and when such a turning away would be premature or otherwise mistaken. Many contemporary choices confronting presidents contain formidable technical complexity: the comparative value of alternative weapons systems, (Stealth v. B-1 bomber, for example), or the feasibility of a technological project like the 'star wars' (SDI) system. How much of the intricacies of aggregate economics must one know in order to intelligently assess alternative strategies for reducing the budget deficit? Other choices require detailed, hard to obtain information if they are to be addressed intelligently: how likely, for example are the 'moderates' in Iran to gain control of that government after the Ayatolla passes from the scene? Or what is the probable impact of economic sanctions on the government of South Africa? The question of how much a president needs to know in order to decide responsibly continues to be hotly debated.[11] Still, it is clear that even a minimally engaged president will need to assimilate, analyze and reflect on a great deal of complex, sometimes technical information. The experts are there to help him do it by putting the requisite information into a form he finds congenial.

Unsurprisingly, many of the most esteemed specialists whose expertise is relevant to the presidency have worked in both Republican and Democratic camps. A prominent recent example is Henry Kissinger, who first labored in the Kennedy administration, then became liberal Republican presidential candidate Nelson Rockefeller's foreign policy advisor before joining Rockefeller's archrival Nixon as National Security Advisor and eventually Secretary of State. This reflects both the scarcity of top talent and the pragmatic willingness of some candidates and presidents to sacrifice a measure of political loyalty in order to gain access to such talent.

4. **Kids**   In a discussion of what he terms the executive entourage, Matthew Holden points out that a significant majority of the aides closest to presidents since Abraham Lincoln have been considerably younger than their principals. Why do presidents tend to rely in part on such (comparative) youngsters? One obvious reason is the relatively greater willingness of youth to "do anything you ask and do it quickly;" particularly the kinds of chores that more senior and seasoned associates would find demeaning.[12] But service as errand runners, messengers and bringers of fresh coffee does not complete the list of the contributions made by bright, ambitious juniors. Twenty-nine year old Bill Moyers was more of a "wise head" than a "gofer" for Lyndon Johnson, and the youthful Theodore

Sorensen was all that and more to John Kennedy. What these two highly talented young men had in common was a willingness (and the freedom from other, conflicting demands) to mold themselves to fit the needs of their principals; to subordinate identity and ego sufficiently to merge with, and become strengthening extensions of, the personalities and talents of their presidents. They also had the energy to perform such service around the clock if necessary.[13] Very few older, more independently established people will have the uncluttered personal lives, the new-worshipful devotion, the malleability or the vitality needed to meet such all-encompassing demands.

Not every president will require such extensive sacrifices from their closest aides, but many have developed youthful alter-egos and protégés, and most presidents have been old men, weighted down with the burdens of office. It would not be surprising for people in such circumstances to experience the zeal, idealism, dedication and enthusiasm characteristic of not-yet-cynical, not-yet-selfish youth as a refreshing counterpoint to the more wizened and jaded veterans who are the president's age peers' simply more enlivening, inspirational and otherwise pleasant to be around, whatever the particular duties performed.

Organizational Options

If the foregoing has provided adequate accounts of the generic demands of the presidency, the types of assistance presidents need and the kinds of people generally summoned to offer it, the next questions to emerge are, how will (or should) the president divide up the work, deploy the hired talent, structure the interactions of people, functions and problems, and allocate his own energies? Put more simply, how will he use his people and himself to push his agenda and cope with the unexpected?

Until quite recently no standardized organization model had been put forward as theoretically or practically the best choice for presidents-in-general.[14] The consensus was that there is no "one best way" to organize the presidency. Instead, the management system had to be fitted to the operating style of the central figure, and would thus necessarily vary. As Alexander George, perhaps the leading exponent of the diversity perspective, notes, all president-watchers have emphasized that the incumbent's personality will shape the formal structure of the policy making system he creates around himself, and it will decisively affect how the formal design actually works in practice. This point was taken a step further in the first section of this article, where it was argued that one major *purpose* of the organizational system is precisely to accommodate the idiosyncrasies of the president.

George defines personality in terms of three variables, each of which can be expected to influence organizational choices.[15] *Cognitive style* is the way the president defines his informational needs, his preferred ways of acquiring and using information, and his preferences regarding advisers and ways of using them in making decisions. Such styles vary significantly among presidents, and "it simply will not work to try to impose on a new president a policymaking system or a management model that is uncongenial to his cognitive style."[16] *The sense of efficacy and competence;* the tasks at which a president feels particularly adept or inadequate will influence how he uses himself and others, as will his *orientation toward political conflict.* Thus, some presidents enjoy and profit from observing heated policy confrontations among their advisors in preparation for decisions, while others find confrontation or the struggle for political influence distasteful, and are likely to install systems which minimize or sequester such activities. These three personality variables, together with the nature of any prior experience in executive decision-making, will determine how the policy making system will be structured. As people differ in these terms, so too will the systems they establish.

The major alternative organizational systems established by presidents since Franklin D. Roosevelt have been described by Alexander George, Richard Tanner Johnson, and Colin Campbell, among others.[17] Although their characteristics are quite familiar to students of presidential management, they are summarized again here for convenient reference. Each pattern of management is associated with certain costs and benefits that predictably surface when a given approach is used. As Greenstein notes, it is rare to discover strict adherence to the pure form of any management system in practice. Also, some presidents have used different modes in different policy areas.[18] These complexities notwithstanding, comparative strengths and weaknesses become clearer if the alternative systems are presented in oversimplified model form.

1. **Formalistic Model**   The formalistic model, variants of which can be found in the administrations of Truman, Eisenhower, Nixon, and Reagan, emphasizes structure, order, and adherence to procedure. It generally features a clear-cut division of labor, with particular duties—carefully defined and circumscribed—assigned to specialists. Also featured are hierarchical lines of communication and formally specified reporting relationships. Presidential responsibility and authority are delegated to a comparatively greater extent in this than other models. Issues and problems earmarked for presidential decision tend to be 'staffed out;' that is, subjected to careful prior analysis and review by well-qualified technical specialists. Specialized staff inputs on a policy problem may be synthesized and distilled into decision options by the president himself, as with Harry Truman, or by an advisor near the president who specializes in such work, often a Chief of Staff, such as Eisenhower's Sherman Adams or Nixon's Bob Haldeman. A strong chief of staff is unlikely to be found in any but a formalistic system, although not all formalistic systems have employed a single strong chief.

The advantages of the formalistic model are numerous, and closely parallel the superiority of bureaucratic forms of organization over others detailed by Max Weber. There is first the likelihood that the model's emphasis on orderly employment of specialized expertise on more or less permanent assignment will yield more thorough, and higher quality analysis than less disciplined procedures. There is next the fact that, comparatively speaking, the formalistic system affords greater presidential flexibility and freedom of choice concerning how to allocate his time and energy. He may involve himself in the policy process to a fairly large extent, as with Truman, or he may distance himself from all but an irreducible minimum of decision making, as with Reagan. Formalistic presidents see as many or as few other people as they wish. Other systems, featuring greater and less formalized access to the president, gain whatever advantage this affords at a significant cost: relative loss of presidential control over time and schedule. Along with the formalistic system's greater potential for presidential self-determination comes the opportunity to specialize—Nixon in foreign policy, for example, or Reagan in the arts of communication and persuasion. Finally, the formalist system has the potential of affording political distance, deniability, personal insularity, and other forms of protection against public attributions of responsibility for problems and failures to the president. The Eisenhower and (pre-Iran crisis) Reagan cases suggest that a public conditioned to expect other high administration officials to share responsibility with the president seems less inclined to hold the president to strict, exclusive personal account for administration mistakes or problems, more inclined to perceive others inside the administration as primarily or at least jointly responsible, and thus somewhat less prone to withdraw support from the president when the news is bad.[19] These are among the strengths that account for the claim of the 1986 San Diego conferees that a hierarchical system under the direction of a strong chief of staff is the optimal pattern for the modern presidency.

As we would expect, the presidents who employed formalistic systems did so in significant degree because they found them personally congenial. Truman's variant expressed his distaste for bureaucratic politics, his pride in supporting those to whom he delegated authority, and his desire to suppress political and personal considerations in an orderly search for quality decisions. Eisenhower's reflected his sense of personal efficacy as one who stood above politics to moderate conflict and promote unity. Eisenhower contributed most significantly to the institutional presidency and made the fullest use of the Cabinet and the National Security Council. Nixon's system expressed his very analytic cognitive style, his penchant for privacy and a strong distaste for face-to-face conflict.[20] And Reagan's formalistic system shielded him from the conflict and overwork which depressed and taxed him, while enabling him to nurture and express his communicative skills, which were at the center of his personal sense of political efficacy.[21]

The potential disadvantages of formalistic systems can be noted briefly.[22] Perhaps most obvious is their tendency toward slow, cumbersome operation. Careful, time-consuming procedures may be ideal when circumstances permit, but they tend to respond slowly, inappropriately, or break down altogether in the face of the unexpected, unprogrammed problems which beset all presidencies. The indications are that they are simply not often used in the crunch, being displaced by less formal discussion groups. Another problem which led both presidents Ford and Carter to avoid the formalistic system in the wake of Watergate and Vietnam, is the tendency toward presidential isolation from external currents of opinion and criticism which the system encourages.[23] Related to this is the problem of accountability. Is it consistent with democratic and constitutional principles for a president to delegate to unelected others potentially fateful decisions which the constitution clearly vests in the president? To be sure, all presidents must delegate, despite the fact that the Constitution "states emphatically that all authority exercised (within the executive branch) emanates from the president."[24]

But it is a matter of degree. How much is too much? The formalistic system, with its tendency toward greater presidential isolation and delegation, increases the number of actions taken by others in the president's name, and therefore the likelihood that some of them will cross the line of Constitutional propriety.

Last among the potential drawbacks is the distortion potential of formalistic hierarchy. Unless special provisions exist (and are followed) to counteract it, the system which emphasizes careful, high-quality substantive analysis of policy options by technical experts may be insensitive to issues of political feasibility, notably the prospects for Congressional and public acceptance of whatever decision the analysis system ends up recommending to the president. This is largely because the system tends to concentrate on substance and to be relatively impermeable to informal input by politically attuned outsiders, particularly in the early stages of generating options.

2. *The Competitive Model*   This approach to presidential organization and management will get short shrift here because while it is in some respects ideally suited to the unpredictability and politically tumultuous dimensions of the presidency, it suffers from certain fatal flaws that make it extremely unlikely to serve as the dominant organizational mode of any future administration. Indeed only one president—Franklin D. Roosevelt—has actually employed it, and the case can be made that its burdens and demands hastened the end of his life. Still, an advantage of considering it here is the sharp contrast it provides to the formalistic system. Unlike the latter, the competitive model is deliberately open, uninhibited, and informal, seeking to avoid the stultifying effects of bureaucratic procedure, specialization and cumbersomeness. It thrives on diversity, is thus highly permeable and solicitous of outside input, both political and technical. It deliberately seeks to provoke conflict, both by encouraging heated policy debate and by instilling competitiveness through organizational ambiguity, overlapping jurisdictions, and multiple channels of access and communication to the president. One beneficial result is creative tension, productive of new and unusual ideas. Another is a greater likelihood that the impracticality or political infeasibility of a prospective policy or action will be discovered well in advance of its implementation. Still another is a situation in which the only source of resolution for the conflict and competition the system instigates is the president himself; a fact which keeps him involved and in control of the entire operation.

All this, of course, is just the way Roosevelt wanted it, and the system is indeed a faithful reflection of the temperament of its author. FDR revelled in politics, felt entirely equal to the demands of the presidency, and did not seek to avoid or moderate any of them, had little respect for jurisdictional boundaries, was personally comfortable with conflict, even to the point of enjoyment, had an insatiable appetite for information and was extraordinarily adept at manipulating the competitive relationships among his subordinates. He was boundlessly energetic and optimistic, and was moved neither to anxiety nor depression in the face of the bitterness and tension his system engendered. His apparent indifference to the suffering his style inflicted on subordinates has led some biographers to speak of a mean streak.

Roosevelt's operational style was then of a piece with his personal disposi-tions, and well-suited to the early years of his administration, with its emphasis on the search for new ways of applying governmental machinery to increase the economic well-being of a depression-crippled America. As suggested, the com-petitive model, with its accessibility and permeability, its extraordinary opera-tional flexibility, its acute political sensitivity and propensity toward surveillance of outside currents of opinion and information, and its tactical mobility may be an inherently better mode than the formalistic of contending with the chaotic, unpre-dictable side of the presidency.

As the formalistic model well serves the steady state features of the presidency, the conflictual is nicely configured to respond to the pressures of domestic poli-tics and policy processes in particular. Too, it avoids problems of delegation and accountability by keeping the president directly involved and in charge. Its biggest drawback—the fatal flaw that will probably prevent its reappearance—is the fact that it makes nearly unmeetable demands on the slender resources of a single human being. Although such devices as forcing competing subordinates to settle their own disputes can be used to reduce the presidential workload, the fact is that the competitive model virtually guarantees overload. Few human beings will want or be able to be as accessible, as vigilant, as knowledgeable or as emotionally resilient as successful operation of this model requires. The inabil-ity of even FDR to be consistently equal to the system's voracious demands accounts for the other drawbacks identified by Richard Tanner Johnson: the dan-ger that an informal, ad hoc search for information and intelligence spearheaded by a single individual, a non-specialist at that, will more often yield sloppy or inaccurate analytic results than a competently staffed formal policy analysis pro-cedure. It led Gordon Gray to refer to Roosevelt's ad hoc decision making process as the "yo-yo" method, by contrast with Eisenhower's formally structured process, which Gray, his security advisor, favored. There is also the fact, as the Roosevelt experience showed, that deliberately aggravating staff competition undermines loyalty and dedication, and the motivation to perform, even as it increases presidential control. The upshot is occasional sabotage, and more fre-quently high staff turnover, with accompanying loss of experience and expertise.

3. *The Collegial Model* Is it possible to obtain some of the advantages of both the competitive and the formalistic models while avoiding their worst draw-backs? Such is the aim of the collegial model, first installed in the recent items by John F. Kennedy, and used since in variant form by Presidents Ford and Carter.

Presidents who have opted for this approach have sought more active involve-ment in the policy process—and at earlier stages before the system has produced options or a single recommended policy—than formalistic presidents. In "spokes of a wheel" fashion, they have been directly accessible to a number of advisers, resisting "gatekeeper" chief of staff arrangements often found in formalistic sys-tems. Such presidents have typically shared the responsibility for generating information, and like FDR, have been willing to go outside official channels and reporting relationships to obtain it, personally consulting those in and outside government whose expertise was perceived as relevant. This has offered partial protection against the de-emphasis on functional specialization among advisers, and against the absence of highly formalized policy analysis and option generating procedures. And the potentially stultifying affects of such bureaucratized decision making (and the narrowly parochial perspectives and interests often displayed by departments and agencies which participate in formalistic processes) are counteracted by the creative potential of brainstorming generalists, conditioned to seeing the world from the president's point of view, (yet free to solicit technical, or specialized information from non-group members in or outside the government as needed) who form the collegial team engaged in group problem-solving. When an effectively staffed collegial system is functioning at its peak potential, it may represent the optimal response to the unprogrammed, unexpected, problems and crises which comprise so significant a proportion of presidential responsibilities. The prime example of a successful collegial process is the Kennedy Administration's handling of the Cuban Missile Crisis.[25]

Why, then, have analysts like Alexander George cautioned against the potential dangers of the collegial system? And why did a number of the former top presidential aides at the San Diego Conference argue so vehemently against a "spokes of a wheel" system as a general mode of organizing the presidency? Because, argues Richard Tanner Johnson, the system places substantial demands on the president's time and attention; demands not every chief executive will want or be able to meet. Also because the successful operation of a collegial group—which entails maintaining group commitment to and enthusiasm for the presidential perspective, sustaining the informal norms that lead to meaningful discussion, and preserving a collegial atmosphere—demands extraordinary interpersonal skills of the group leader; skills few people possess. For example, the lack of formally designated responsibilities within the group invites conflict, confusion and uncertainty about who is responsible for what, which the leader must continuously monitor and be prepared to address. The group's necessary emphasis on informal collegiality may operate to suppress, in the interests of interpersonal harmony, major policy disagreements which should be confronted, a possibility to which the leader must remain acutely sensitive. Too, the informality so crucial to creative give and take carries the risk of inconsistency; the structural requirement for disciplined, thorough analytic procedure built into the formalistic system is absent from the collegial. The leader (or someone else) must therefore constantly press for uniformly thorough, fully adequate analysis and synthesis of problem components and decision priorities across the range of issues and meetings. And because even carefully managed, well orchestrated collegial groups can disintegrate and split irretrievably into factions on some issues, thereby forcing the president to improvise an alternative approach, even effective use of the model carries with it no guarantees of success.[26]

Because of the consensus that emerged in favor of a strong, formalistic chief of staff approach, and because the strongest critics had served under presidents who attempted to use the "spokes of wheel" collegial approach, the criticisms of the collegial model offered by former top White House aides are especially interesting. One source of dissatisfaction, expressed by Ford Chief of Staff Richard

Cheney, concerns the tendency of a president who is informally accessible via multiple 'spokes,' and not committed to formal decision-making procedures to reach hasty, ill-conceived decisions.[27]

Cheney's complaint is echoed and illustrated by his predecessor as chief of staff in the Ford Administration, Donald Rumsfeld, who offers the following example:

> Secretary of Labor John Dunlop comes in to see the president; wants to see him alone . . . they came to some understanding as to what John Dunlop would negotiate with respect to situs picketing, as I recall. And Dunlop went out of the office and proceeded to do exactly what he believed the president wanted. (Ford) didn't tell me, didn't tell Dick (Cheney), didn't tell anybody else what was going on . . . and pretty soon, John Dunlop comes back in and reports, "I've done it." And the president (who had since become aware that Republican constituencies were strongly opposed to what Ford had authorized Dunlop to do earlier) says "My gosh, I can't do that, John, and I'm very sorry." Obviously it wasn't what he (Ford) had intended. Events had intervened and there was no way he could agree to what John had done, and John said, "Well, I can appreciate that, but if you don't do it, I can't stay. My credibility is gone." So you lose a Secretary of Labor unnecessarily . . . Ford didn't want Dunlop to leave. Dunlop didn't want to leave, but there was no way [he] could stay because of this spokes-of-the-wheel nonsense.[28]

Complaints expressed by three former chiefs of staff who served two of the three presidents who employed some form of collegial management model, underlay an emerging consensus that neither competitive nor collegial management models can any longer adequately serve the modern presidency. The more plentiful and complex White House operations become, the greater the pressure for hierarchy, standard operating procedures, and strong, disciplined management. At least since the Nixon administration, sufficient complexity has emerged to warrant the most hierarchical of systems. As the institution continues to grow in scope and complexity, only orderly, systematic procedures can be expected to contend successfully with the increasing workload. Who is best equipped to direct and control these expanded White House operations? Increasingly, experts and practitioners agree that the answer is not the president, but instead a kind of professional manager; a strong chief of staff. Let us consider the argument in detail.

The Case for a Strong Chief

As Stephen Hess puts it:

> My contention is that Presidents have made a serious mistake, starting with Roosevelt, in asserting that they are the chief managers of the federal government . . . . Rather than the chief manager, the President is the chief political officer of the United States. His major responsibility, in my judgment, is to annually make a relatively small number of highly significant political decisions—among them, setting national priorities, which he does through the budget and his legislative proposals, and devising policy to ensure the security of the country, with special attention to those situations which could involve the nation in war.[29]

Not only should presidents avoid any management role for the government as a whole, goes this argument, they should also avoid such a role within their own organizations: The White House Office and the Executive Office of the President. In simpler times, it might have been possible for presidents to function as both leaders and managers without doing injustice to either duty. After Sherman Adams' departure Eisenhower virtually became his own chief of staff. ". . . because we had a small enough staff that he could serve in that role" says Theodore Sorensen, "Jack Kennedy was his own chief of staff."[30] "Conceivably in Eisenhower's era, conceivably in Kennedy's era, the nature of the world and the size of the White House staff and the nature of the problems, you could have a different arrangement," allows Donald Rumsfeld. "Today, I do think you need a chief of staff."[31]

These are the theoretical and practical arguments for separating the president from the operation of his own management system. He can no longer spare the time, energy and attention to do the refereeing required by a competitive system, or the interpersonal handholding demanded by the collegial, or even the supervisory or intellectual synthesis work required by a formalistic model, (as Truman once did) because to do so is to risk neglecting the political and moral leadership that only he can offer in order to deal with tasks easily left to others.

But if others must do the organizational maintenance work, why must it be done in a bureaucratic, hierarchical manner? The first reason, already noted in foregoing quotations, is the ever-increasing *size* of the White House staff. Bradley H. Patterson, Jr., who has written a comprehensive historical analysis of the development of the White House staff, estimates that there may be as many as 3,000 people on the White House staff apart from the Executive Office of the President.[32] Many of these individuals are on payrolls other than the White House, most are in technical, security, household maintenance and other non-polity related support functions, but they are present. Their work must be allocated, organized, supervised and evaluated. All this poses management and control problems on a scale that rules out casual, informal non-hierarchical styles of operation.

But supervising large numbers of tertiary employees is not the only problem for which a disciplined managerial capacity is needed. Proponents would have the central management (headed by a strong chief) in distant charge of the thousands engaged in peripheral support functions, but much more centrally involved in the "real" work of the presidency. For even when attention is restricted to core presidential staff roles and units, such as the National Security Council, domestic and economic policy staff, political and press advisers, speechwriters, media specialists, and the like, the number of individuals involved has burgeoned, such that the 'size' argument retains validity. Planning, organizing, staffing, directing, coordinating, synthesizing and scheduling the work of these multifarious units in support of presidential initiatives and other needs is an increasingly forbidding management problem. Such work not only requires the attention of managerial specialists, but also demands reliance on systematic routines, not ad hoc, "if I remember to think of it" styles of management, to be effectively discharged.

There are simply too many things to think of, remember, and integrate, to rely solely on the creative, 'wing it' approach to operations management. The greater the number and complexity of organizational units and problems to be integrated into presidential operations, the greater the need for specialized process management, and the greater the need for standard operating procedures which can compensate for human limitations of memory, consistency, energy and creativity.

The foregoing explains why specialized management competence, focused on staff coordination and integration in the service of the president's needs, and reliant to a significant extent on formalistic procedures, are requisites of the modern presidency. But why must the manager be 'strong?' And why must he or she be a single individual? Why not a group? The strength requirement, it seems, stems from the need to secure the respect and cooperation of what are usually strong, tough, willful, egotistical and ambitious people (a not unreasonable characterization of most White House senior staffs and cabinet officials). If coordination, work, deadlines, restrictions, denials, and other potentially unpleasant outcomes are to be imposed on such people, the officer doing the imposing must have the formal clout to make it stick. This is why Chiefs of Staff have often been second in rank only to the president himself.

That the Chief of Staff function is best performed by a single individual is left implicit rather than explicitly argued by those who endorse the strong chief system.[33] Still, we might assume that proponents feel as they do for the same reasons that the framers chose a unitary rather than a plural executive—in the interests of energy, unity and dispatch. The coordination and control of policy analysis and decision-making processes is arguably simpler, less contentious, and subject to fewer miscommunications and other snafus, in a single pair of hands. This position becomes more understandable as we consider in greater detail just what it is that a chief of staff does for a president.

The Functions of the Chief of Staff

Perhaps the best source of information and insight into the subtleties of staff operation near the top is former White House chiefs of staff themselves. Conveniently, a group of them met recently to discuss the nature of their responsibilities. A careful reading of the transcript of their discussion, together with similar commentary drawn from other sources, suggests three broad categories of function: *decision-manager, representative,* and *protector.*[34] As we will see, each function embraces considerable variety and detail.

Decision Manager   Virtually all the former chiefs agree that presidents require a high level staffer whose job is to establish and maintain a process by which relevant, high quality information—both substantive and political[35] in content—is systematically obtained from all available sources, distilled into genuine decision options, and conveyed to the president in a form and manner he finds congenial (memos, informal discussion, formal briefings, etc.) prior to decision.

The process must be disciplined and the information search broad in order to reduce the possibility of impulsive decision-making and neglect of pertinent information, which less routinized procedures often yield. The objective, says Jack Watson, Carter's able final-year chief of staff, "is to do everything within your power to see that the president is fully briefed before he does make a decision."[36] This is accomplished by "staffing out" important problems or questions; that is, seeking the counsel of the people in and outside the administration who have significant political or substantive input to contribute, prior to presidential decision or speeches.[37]

Such procedures also increase the confidence of administration members like technical advisors or cabinet officers that their views will receive a full and fair hearing whenever they are relevant. Otherwise, argues Jack Watson, you will not build the trust of cabinet officers and others, with the result that "they are not going to come to you, and you are not going to play."[38]

Yet the top staff does have a sifting and editing role, as Nixon's H.R. Haldeman explains: ". . . in the sense of eliminating or bringing together repetitive material . . . and organizing the material in an orderly manner so that the president can proceed through it. The president shouldn't have ten piles of irrelevant or unrelated paper that he's got to wade through, sort out, and figure out what to do with. That's the staff's function."[39] Does this not invite the top staff to 'cook' the information to support its own preferences? "I don't think you have a situation where a chief of staff survives very long if he, in effect, warps the flow of information to suit his own bias with respect to policy" answers Dick Cheney. "Then he's not serving the interest of the president. It's very easily found out after two or three times, and it seems to me that anybody who did that would quickly find himself going down the road."[40] Haldeman continues: "[The chief of staff] functions as an honest broker [in the information sifting process by] making sure that opposing material is also available when one side of an issue is presented."[41]

This "honest brokering," plus genuine concern with careful thoroughness in the search for information and formulation of options, is apparently what Ford's Donald Rumsfeld has in mind when he says: ". . . call it professionalism, altruism, desire to see the president succeed for political reasons or desire to see the country do well, people in these jobs end up knowing that the staff system has to have integrity and it is their job to bring that balance and integrity to the job."[42]

Sometimes insuring the integrity of the process may involve reining in the president. H.R. Haldeman: "It's the obligation of the staff and the function of the staff to pose the alternatives. [Moreover, the senior staff should not] carry out [any presidential] order until it has been at least reviewed once and then reordered by the president on the basis of making the right decision for the right reasons [careful, dispassionate weighing of options] instead of the wrong reasons [presidential impulse or irritation]. The staff function . . . [is] to get the proper information to the president, and then the president (makes) the decision. Once the president has made the decision on the proper basis, then it does have to be carried out."[43]

At other times, presidents may need to be prodded to interact with people whose views they ought to hear, but whom they tend to avoid. Haldeman was apparently concerned, for example, that Richard Nixon not be unduly influenced by his close friend Treasury Secretary John B. Connaly at the expense of the views of others less personally close to Nixon, like his OMB director and the chair of the Council of Economic Advisers.[44] Donald Rumsfeld, describing President Ford's personal discomfiture with his first Secretary of Defense, James Schlesinger, asks: ". . . does that mean that the Defense views and Jim Schlesinger's views ought to be cut out of [the option reviewing] process? Of course not. They had to be put into the process, and the job of the chief of staff during that period was to assure that, in fact, Defense input got into the foreign policy and national security decision-making process."[45]

As these examples suggest, the essence of decision management is quality control: coordinating and directing a process aimed at avoiding threats to decision quality posed by inadequate or incomplete information, unbalanced or one-sided interpersonal influence, poorly framed choices, and presidential impulse.

Representative   Increasingly, the former chiefs agree, the top aide has functioned as the president's representative or surrogate: to the other members of his staff in the White House or the Executive Office, to the members of his cabinet, to other formal and informal participants in the governmental process (e.g., Congress and media) and occasionally, to the American people.

Most members of the White House staff rarely see the president personally. Although speaking of the Ford presidential campaign organization, Richard Cheney could have been describing the workaday White House when he characterized his role: "You are . . . the reflection of the president for people down in the organization. Everybody in the organization sees a lot more of the chief of staff than they do of the president, and you set the whole tone for the organization."[46] Prior to the public disclosure of the Iranian arms for hostages policy, it was chief of staff Donald Regan, arguably the most powerful chief yet to serve an American president, who was perceived as "the man we work for" by most presidential aides. Only after the controversy erupted, and critics began to clamor for Regan's resignation, did staffers take pains to identify President Reagan as the man for whom they worked, and to stress their direct reporting relationships to the president.[47]

A large portion of the surrogate function as it pertains to members of the cabinet has to do with mediating disputes. Cheney again: "[Another] problem . . . is when you have a major conflict between two willful cabinet members. I can't count the number of times I would get a phone call . . . and it would be a situation in which Pat Moynihan [then U.S. Ambassador to the United Nations] was calling threatening to resign or Henry Kissinger [then Secretary of State] was threatening to resign because they didn't like each other." (Moynihan accused Kissinger of interfering in his U.N. work; Kissinger contended Moynihan was posturing to enhance his prospects for election to the Senate).[48] General Andrew Goodpaster describes Eisenhower chief of staff, Sherman Adams' role in forging agreement on economic policy when the Treasury Secretary and Council of Economic Advisers chair were at odds: ". . . I recall that Governor Adams had the task of seeing what could be done to define the issue and . . . to resolve it . . . And Adams, in his careful and thoughtful and firm way, had this discussed between the people involved, found out what the issue was, and was able finally to work it out in a way that they then took to the president and that satisfied the requirement."[49]

Conveying bad news, dispensing discipline, or even wielding the axe are tasks frequently undertaken by chiefs in the name of the president. It was, for example, initial Ford staff chief Rumsfeld, and later Dick Cheney, who thwarted many of Vice President Nelson Rockefeller's domestic policy proposals, but as surrogates for the president and with his clear blessing.[50] Despite news releases to the contrary, it was first Reagan staff chief James Baker, and not Reagan himself, who "took David Stockman to the woodshed" over his indiscreet disclosure of his lack of faith in administration economic policy.[51] And it was Reagan's second chief of staff, Donald Regan, who reportedly pressed Health and Human Services Secretary Margaret Heckler to resign that post and accept the position of Ambassador to Ireland.[52]

Jack Watson describes a somewhat different dimension of the representative function: being, in effect, the president's ears. This meant becoming sufficiently trusted by members of the cabinet so that they perceived that communicating with Watson was tantamount to communicating with the president (i.e., they believed Watson would deliver and would not distort their messages) but without the need for direct personal contact with Carter: "They wanted to tell the president something but they didn't want to call him, for whatever reason . . . Maybe they just didn't think he needed to be bothered, that it didn't rise to the level of a personal call to the president by a cabinet secretary."[53] But as Watson makes clear, being a communication link to the president does not mean acting as an advocate for cabinet members when their wishes collide with presidential interests. In persuading a reluctant Housing and Urban Development secretary Moon Landrieu to accept a high level subordinate selected by Carter for his HUD staff, for example, Watson succeeded in exercising power in the president's interest without need for the personal involvement of Jimmy Carter.[54]

Last among the representative tasks of recent chiefs of staff is an increasing tendency to deal with the media, both on background (i.e., off the record) and on camera. Camera exposure takes place in the name of the president and his programs, but it inescapably makes the chief a public figure in his own right. The former chiefs who participated in the San Diego conference were unanimous in deploring such publicity, and in cleaving to Brownlow's "passion for anonymity" as the appropriate dictum for all presidential staff. Still, most of them ventured at least once onto network public affairs programs, and all were regular objects of media and press attention.

The exposure increased dramatically during the Reagan administration, with various presidential aides openly engaging in the political debate—a key component of a deliberate strategy of distancing the president from controversy in order to protect his high public standing.[55] Thus, former White House communications director Patrick Buchanan, one of the Reagan administration's most vociferous conservative ideologists, frequently mounted strident verbal attacks on the president's political opponents. His early 1987 departure from the administration was front-page news.[56] And second term chief of staff Donald Regan, a high-profile spokesman for the administration prior to the Iranian arms for hostages affair, served more as a deputy president than an anonymous coordinator.[57] The Reagan staff sought publicity, but future staffers may no longer be able to avoid it. Argues Dom Bonafede: The "Brownlow Committee's concept [of passionately anonymous staffers], may be impossible in today's environment in which the White House staff undergoes careful scrutiny by the news media, and has, in effect, been totally abandoned by contemporary White House staffs."[58] Adds Samuel Kernell: "The discreet aide steeped in neutral competence and honest brokerage has [necessarily] been succeeded by celebrity politicians who actively pursue the president's policy goals with other politicians in the executive branch and beyond."[59]

The growth of this function has increased both the visibility and power of the chief of staff, as he speaks authoritatively on behalf of the president to ever-wider audiences, thus entrenching his image as presidential surrogate and wielder of presidential power. Yet, paradoxically, it has also increased the chief's vulnerability, as he is pulled involuntarily into the limelight by becoming the target for antagonists who do not wish to confront the president directly. In this, and in other ways to be considered next, the chief of staff has become a protector as well as a surrogate.

Protector In representing their presidents, the chiefs are relieving them of duties that do not constitute the most profitable use of presidential time, so that such time may be devoted to the things others cannot do. As decision managers, the chiefs are professionally concerned with maintaining the quality and integrity of a core policymaking process. Although personal concern for the success and well-being of the president may underlay the performance of either of these functions, both have more of the flavor of 'neutral competence' in the service of a viable presidency. One can imagine these jobs being done well on the basis of professionalism alone, without need of strong personal affection and loyalty to the president.

The protector function is different. Here motives of fealty, loyalty, respect and affection assume clearer relevance. Though alluding to other matters, Bob Haldeman voices the sentiments most likely to underlay the kind of self-sacrifice often demanded by the protector function: "I had had management experience [before becoming Nixon's first chief of staff] but more importantly I had had an extremely strong and intimate working relationship with the president himself. That's the absolute vital factor in the chief of staff's role . . . [to operate successfully the staff must have] a strong loyalty to the president and commitment to the president and a recognition that they serve him first, and through him the country. . . ."[60] Such loyalty is necessary because, in the process of protecting a president, unpleasant duties, of the sort not easily done for another toward whom one is indifferent, may be required. Too, the chief must *want* to help if he is to feel impelled to move in circumstances when the president needs protection but cannot or won't ask for it, or less often, doesn't even know it.

From what must a president be protected? Often from the consequences of his own mistakes. One such mistake, for example, was made by President Ford, when, against the unanimous advice of his staff, he placed vice president Nelson Rockefeller in charge of the Domestic Council, with control over all domestic policy making and staffing. The result, says Ford chief Dick Cheney, was a series of

policy proposals "totally inconsistent with the basic policy of the Ford administration," a message given to Rockefeller by the staff, not the president. There ensued
"great personal hostility between . . . myself and the vice president, and Don
[Rumsfeld] before that . . . . I was the SOB, and on a number of occasions, got
involved in shouting matches with the vice president . . . . If you ask President
Ford today why that relationship was strained, it was always the staff problem with
the vice president . . . . But the problem, in fact, was created by the president."[61]
By protecting Ford from the consequences of his mistake, Cheney made it possible for Ford to maintain an excellent relationship with Rockefeller, and also to
avoid a leftward turn in administration domestic policy. Ford seems to have been
unaware of this protective service, and also unaware that the enmity of the vice
president was a personal price Cheney had to pay in order to provide it.

Presidents occasionally need shielding from the potential consequences of
their own conceptions, which, if left uncorrected, can yield significant mistakes.
General Andrew Goodpaster, who held the then new post of staff secretary, created to manage the work flow into the White House,[62] illustrates this situation
with an anecdote from the Eisenhower administration. When the president
insisted that action be taken to implement the U.S. policy of reducing forces in
Europe, Goodpaster responded that the policy that had been established required
that the Europeans first be able to fill the troop gap before American forces were
withdrawn. Eisenhower insisted that such was not the case, and was persuaded
to yield only after his secretary of state, John Foster Dulles, reiterated Goodpaster's position. Goodpaster implies that Eisenhower was not pleased by this situation, but concludes: "He was just sounding off, and that was part of our role in
life, to let him relieve some of the pressure, but make sure that he didn't make
that kind of a mistake."[63]

Last, presidents occasionally need to be protected from themselves; notably
their own ill-advised emotional impulses. The most recent case in point, perhaps,
was Ronald Reagan's understandable if impolitic desire to exchange arms for
hostages; overwrought as he was said to be with the grief of victim's families.
Diplomatically asserting that presidents need people with whom they can
"explore" potentially "damn fool things," H.R. Haldeman describes an order issued
by President Nixon, in heated reaction to leaks which threatened the Vietnam
negotiations: "The order . . . was that every member of the State Department staff
worldwide was to be submitted *immediately* to lie detector tests." After stalling an
impatient Nixon for a period of time, Haldeman finally confronted him: "Mr. President, this really is a mistake. There are other ways of dealing with this problem.
. . . We came back in a few days with a plan, and he said at that point 'I didn't
think you would do it.' But it was fairly clear at the time I was supposed to."[64]

Enabling the president to use his own power without paying the price for
doing so can mean representing the chief aide as considerably more powerful
and autonomous than he in fact is. This is what Gerald Warren, former Nixon
press aide and conference organizer, is telling us when he says: "[I hope that] the
American press understands that when Bob Hartmann leaks to Evans and Novak
that Haig is keeping all those Nixon folks in the White House, he's doing that

because he doesn't want to attack Jerry Ford. It's Jerry Ford who's doing it, not Al Haig. It was Richard Nixon who didn't want to see the transportation secretary, not Bob Haldeman."[65] With a chief or other surrogate to protect him, the president may indirectly wield his own power, yet escape the unpleasant or otherwise costly consequence. Since presidential power is ephemeral, and tends to diminish with use, such a service can be valuable indeed.

A Critique and an Alternative

We come finally to the question, answered implicitly in the negative by the former top aides to recent presidents, of whether it is any longer realistic for a president to seek alternatives to a hierarchically organized, single chief of staff arrangement. Following a brief examination of the problems likely to be associated with the strong chief model, a management system is described, that of the first Reagan administration, which did not employ the unitary strong chief system, yet still somehow managed to provide the necessary decision management, representational and protective services most of the time. If nothing else, this experience demonstrates that it is possible to get by without a single dominant chief of staff. Other lessons of the first Reagan model are considered, along with some propositions relevant to the design of future presidential management systems.

What's Wrong with the Strong Chief? In principle, it may seem plausible that a single, dominant White House coordinator other than the president himself could orchestrate and direct the varied staff needs of the contemporary presidency, as the San Diego conferees maintained. Yet a fair question is why [before Bush] have only two modern presidents, Eisenhower and Reagan, employed such a system?[66] The likely answer is that, in practice, individuals with the range of talents needed just to direct, let alone operate personally in all facets of such a complex assignment are not plentiful. The odds against a single person adequately discharging decision management, representational and protective functions simultaneously are great. For one thing, the roles conflict. Could Rumsfeld, for example, once he had alienated vice president Rockefeller in president Ford's behalf, any longer expect Rockefeller to perceive him as an honest broker, a neutral, fair channel of access to the president? For another thing, the different functions seem to attract, and each to be best performed by, persons of strikingly different talents and temperaments. Thus, the honest broker needs to be genuinely and dispassionately able to see and comprehend the merits in opposing views and to articulate them even-handedly, perhaps more of a scholarly than a political or an organizational talent. For his part, the process manager needs to be disciplined, well organized and forceful, capable of cracking the whip when necessary to suppress palace intrigue, sustain order, and meet deadlines, but also temperamentally able and willing to let relevant information—whether supportive or disturbing to presidential preferences—enter into the analytic, option-forming process. The representative is most effective who is interpersonally competent, well-spoken, politically sensitive, and able to elicit the respect and trust even of those to whom he must convey bad news. And the protector must be at once intuitive, selfless and able to see and forecast what the president himself may not perceive, and willing to pay a larger price than most would be willing to pay, all in order to shield the principal from unpleasant consequences. All this is a lot to ask of a single person.

Even when a single chief does not attempt to do it all himself, but instead is placed in charge of others who do most of it in response to his direction, the all-too-human tendency, as displayed by such prominent and controversial figures as Zbigniew Brzezinski and Donald Regan, is to let egotism and/or policy preference[67] creep into the performance of the functions, the selection and deployment of others, and regulating access—of people and information—to the president. Thus, Brzezinski, who was to have operated as President Carter's 'custodian manager' of National Security Council procedures, (a kind of chief of staff for foreign policy decision making in the White House), did not adopt the impartial, low profile stance generally thought best suited to the collection, clarification and presentation of available decision options, but instead became a vigorous public advocate for specific policies, often in widely publicized disagreement with the Secretary of State.[68] And Donald Regan, a strong personality with a firm conviction of his status as 'chief chief executive officer' in the Reagan White House, is said to have "forgotten" to convey the deep reservations of such cabinet officers as Secretary of State George Shultz about the clandestine sale of arms to Iran to President Reagan, thereby displaying a serious abuse of his role as the main channel through whom all others had to pass to reach the president.[69]

Still another criticism of the Reagan approach—expressed by Norman J. Ornstein in a *New York Times* op ed piece—emerges from displeasure with his 'management philosophy.'[70] It is worth summarizing here because the Regan philosophy is largely equivalent to the strong chief philosophy as espoused by the participants in the San Diego conference. It amounts, says Ornstein, to the same approach Regan took while running Merrill Lynch: a tight, hierarchical, corporate model, with the president as chief executive officer, the chief of staff as chief operating officer, and all others serving as subordinates without independent roles:

> The flow of command was unidirectional: the President would indicate his policy desires, the chief of staff would direct his team to find the appropriate ways to implement them. Feedback followed an equally constrained path. Telephone calls to the President and appointments with him were routed through Mr. Regan. Feedback did not take the form of debating with the President or taking issue with his broad policy desires.[71]

The upshot, argues Ornstein, was a loss of senior advisory talent, dangerous presidential insulation from the political process and alienation from Capitol Hill, mitigated only by occasional counsel from Mr. Reagan's personal friends in the Senate when they managed to circumvent the gatekeeper. Though the agreeable president willingly accepted the situation, Ornstein contends it denied Reagan the kind of information he needed to do what he does best: choose from among clearly and fairly presented alternatives on the basis of his own finely honed, pragmatic political instincts as tempered by his entrenched sense of ideological direction. Only continuous unvarnished political feedback, able to bypass administrative filters and bottlenecks, can prevent the oval office from becoming a cocoon in which unrealistic thinking prevails. In defense of Regan, seasoned *New York Times* journalist William Safire calls the attribution a myth. Safire asserts Reagan was well aware of Shultz's views, but chose other advice.[72]

"Great" chiefs of staff—those who can either do it all themselves or effectively and impartially direct others who do it—may be no less difficult to locate than great presidents. Sherman Adams had seemed indispensable. Yet in many ways Eisenhower's accomplishments were the most significant after Adams's departure when Eisenhower virtually became his own chief of staff. Though it does not seem prudent to institutionalize a need for greatness in the chief of staff, the presidency is another matter. The constitution requires that the executive function be vested in the hands of a single individual. Given the highly unusual constellation of talents needed to operate effectively in that role during the present era, and given the lack of such extraordinary talent in the general run of flawed human beings, we are already forced into a never-ending and frequently unrequited search for the elusive "right stuff." There is no good reason to impose the same kind of limitation on the search for those who can ably serve at the top of the staff system. It can be, and in light of the unitary executive ought to be, designed to function adequately by mixing and matching the expectable uneven talents and shortcomings of a variety of support personnel.

The First Term Reagan System   Veteran journalist Steven V. Roberts tells us that "there is wide agreement that in his first term, Mr. Reagan was well-served in the White House by a 'troika' of top aides, James A. Baker 3d [chief of staff], Edwin Meese 3d [counselor to the president], and Michael K. Deaver [deputy chief of staff]." Continues Roberts: "While Mr. Reagan was not interested in details, these aides kept the President reasonably well informed and presented him with a diversity of viewpoints."[73] Roberts, and the conventional wisdom he summarizes, overlooks the turbulent, conflict-ridden history of the troika, and does not mention that it lasted only a single year in cohesive form and effectiveness, becoming a quartet (the "big four"), that did not operate as a unit, in 1982 (with the addition of William Clark as national security advisor), and a kind of "big three" from November, 1983 (by which time Clark had departed to become Secretary of the Interior. Moreover the Meese role lessened although he continued as Counsellor until 1985 when he was confirmed as Attorney General. However, beginning in 1984 he was preoccupied with the protracted hearings for the Attorney General post, effectively leaving the field to Baker and Deaver) until the 1985 staff reorganization creating a unitary chief of staff arrangement under Regan. Still, for most of that first term, the evolving Reagan staff arrangements counted more successes than failures, which invites those of us made uneasy by strong chief arrangements to wonder if there are transferable lessons there to be learned.

What system of management did these varying groups employ? One which: a) evolved over time, but which generally featured a division of labor among two to four nearly equal top aides with different skills and easy access to the president; b) made frequent use of discussion groups—whose membership varied according to needed expertise—to prepare the president for decisions; c) had a special commitment to strategic planning evinced by the early emergence (in February, 1981) of the Legislative Strategy Group (LSG); d) conducted policy analysis and coordination by authoritative committees such as cabinet councils or senior interagency groups (SIGs), and e) mobilized ad hoc task forces to address emergent issues and problems (such as was assembled to deal with the Japanese auto import problem).

The strength and the success of the original triumvirate, as they called themselves, was in part the product of necessity—brought on by the March 30, 1981 attempt on Reagan's life—which forged among the three a degree of personal compatibility, coordination and cooperation not usually observed in the competitively charged atmosphere of palace politics.[74] This would however, be short-lived; in evidence primarily during the period immediately following the assassination attempt. Conflict would ensue, but it would only occasionally—as in the case of foreign policy—undermine effectiveness. There would be numerous mistakes: But for the most part, as in legislative and media relations, the projection of a favorable presidential image, and the containment of various kinds of political damage—the system worked throughout the first term.

Interviews conducted by John H. Kessel in 1982, whose findings are corroborated by parallel media accounts, offer a snapshot of how the staff functioned in the early going.[75] In these and other interviews given during the second year of the first term, various staff members describe one another's unique roles and skills in glowing terms. One major ingredient in sustaining the cumbersome system of power sharing, for example, is alleged by his colleagues to have been the intuitive insight and interpersonal skills of Michael Deaver. Ever-sensitive to personal tensions on the staff, remarked then-communications director David Gergen: "Deaver has the reputation in my book for being the person who really holds this thing together."[76] Said staff chief James Baker about Deaver, whose most important skill was his awareness of and his ability to handle the personal needs of Ronald and Nancy Reagan, "[Deaver] has the closest relationship of any of us. He's the one they trust and that gives him the greatest overall influence. I think that if they ever got in a box, they'd pick up the phone and call him."[77] Deaver's special responsibility was the cultivation and protection of the Reagan image, which meant that he would involve himself in any issue or substantive arena that could threaten or enhance it. Thus, when the president's standing began to weaken at the end of the first year, it was Deaver who organized a new informal planning group to determine how to ration Reagan's time for maximum yield. When relations with black groups worsened, it was Deaver who managed the salvage operation. When Reagan's image as a foreign policy president was tarnished by the disarray and conflict in the NSC and State Department, Deaver would involve himself in the ouster of the national security adviser and would help to expedite the secretary of state's resignation.[78]

Chief of Staff Baker, who was political and process manager and who controlled the staff, would gradually accrue greater power than his initial equal, policy analyst and formulator of options, Meese, and would make an ally of his nominal subordinate, but defacto equal, schedule manager and first family confidant, Deaver. But with the arrival of William Clark there would be in effect four seniors with free access to the president and only limited coordination among themselves. Even when Clark left in 1983, Baker would be unable to consolidate power. By then he had become the target of ultra conservatives who, because of such moves as his strategically motivated efforts to delay action on the conservative social agenda, and his public advocacy of cuts in defense spending, considered him an "infidel defiling Reaganism."[79] In part because of the chronic diffusion of power among the top staff, and in part because he had been made a controversial and distract-ing issue in his own right by hostile conservatives, Baker would never wield by himself the kind of power wielded by Sherman Adams or H.R. Haldeman, let alone Donald Regan. The power wielded by the first term Reagan top staff was unprecedented because of the president's unprecedented disengagement. But for the most part it was collective—not individual power.[80] Nevertheless, Baker remained *primus inter pares* throughout the first term; because of his administra-tive acumen, his strategic savvy and the support of Reagan intimate Mike Deaver. Said Deaver about Baker's exceptional administrative skill: ". . . he just thrives on solving problems. He refuses to let anything fester. If there is a problem anywhere in the White House, either with the three or four of us or with other people . . . it is on his desk being taken care of and he (is) . . . on to the next thing. That is a tremendous asset in any kind of organization, particularly one that has the kind of intrigues and turf problems and all the quirks that people concern themselves about in the White House."[81] Baker's other strength was strategic planning, notable in the early legislative success enjoyed by the administration (the Economic Recovery Tax Act of 1981, plus substantial reductions in the growth rate of spending on entitlements and other social services). The instru-ment for Baker's management of legislative and other political tactics was the Legislative Strategy group, the February, 1981 brainchild of Baker's gifted chief aide, Richard Darman. As the only non-Californian outsider close to Reagan, and as a former political opponent of the president with enemies in the conservative wing of the Reagan constituency, the cautious Baker felt himself to be in a per-petually delicate situation which did not conduce to grabs for power. He reveals some of the discomfort which led him to trade jobs with Donald Regan in 1985, in the following comment to Laurence I. Barrett: "You might say I'm not a tradi-tional Chief of Staff in the sense that I'm not *the* closest person to the President. No, I'm not, and I never will be. But I'll tell you this. I'm a lot closer to him now (mid 1982) than when I came in, and I think that says something."[82]

Baker's description of the contribution of Meese is equally revealing: "[His] strength is that he is a very good synthesizer of policy options for the President, a very good ear for the President to sound off to . . . [his] skill is isolating the crit-ical issues from the mass of surrounding detail."[83] Adds an unidentified staffer: "(Meese) manages . . . to reconcile very different views and temperamentally opposing proposals in quite a common sense way. That's a very important func-tion."[84] And Deaver: "[Meese has an] ability to distill a lot of information and suc-cinctly give it back to the President, to regurgitate it and give him the three or four major points. It is a very strong resource for the President."[85] Meese was also a loyalist, utterly committed to the Reagan agenda, viewed by conservatives as the protector of their trust amidst pragmatists willing to compromise it away, yet also someone whom the president had learned he could rely on to be cool and sensible in difficult situations and to fairly present contrary views. But despite the favorable commentary cited above, Meese would come to be viewed, by Baker, Clark, and others, as the weak link in the system. His failure to wake the president when U.S. fighter planes downed Lybian jets over the Gulf of Sidra in August, 1981 would diminish his standing and eventually cost him control over the development of administration foreign policy. He would be blamed for the politically untenable stand the administration would take on tax exemptions for racists schools in January of 1982. He developed a reputation as a poor administrator and bureaucratic pettifogger who had difficulty making decisions. David Stockman, describing his own rise to the point on economic strategy, sheds light on these Meese traits as well as those of the other members of the triumvirate:

> (Baker knew) he wouldn't get any policy ideas from others in the inner circle. Meese had by now entombed himself beneath a pyramid of paper and disorganization. He never met a committee he didn't like. Mike Deaver had never even feigned an interest in policy. But then he was busy stage-managing the upcoming inaugural—hiring elephants and Frank Sinatra. So when Baker saw that his new colleague from the congressional back benches was eager and organized and had a script almost ready to go, he was relieved.[86]

Meese would make other mistakes, but Reagan refused to cut him out completely. The president's abiding loyalty to Meese had been a source of admiration to conservatives but a subject of wonderment to reporters.[87]

William Clark's January 1982 installation as national security advisor, is said to have provoked a major change in the operation of the senior staff.[88] With Clark's arrival the NSA position was elevated from its second tier status during Richard Allen's tenure, to the highest level. Clark assumed administrative control of the National Security Council staff. Unlike his predecessor, who communicated with the president indirectly through Meese's policy office, Clark reported directly to Reagan, and became the independent foreign policy power in the White House, as well as a major rival to Baker. Clark's contributions to the system were numerous. He would reorganize and revitalize the National Security Council staff. He would set about educating the president in foreign policy, literally running seminars for Reagan in which outside experts participated. And he would reassert the president's control over his own foreign policy apparatus and direction, bringing the secretaries of state and defense under closer White House supervision. As a former chief of staff to Reagan while Governor of California, he had displayed some of the organizational acumen of a Baker. He was thus well equipped to contend with the organizational problems in foreign policy which had emerged under Meese and Allen. More importantly, perhaps, he combined the strong points of the other two Californians closest to Reagan. Like Meese, he knew how to formulate and synthesize Reagan's ideas. Like Deaver, he had sensitivity for the ways in which Reagan operated and the ways in which he could be influenced.[89]

Unlike his colleagues, he would rarely advance his own policy preferences, but he was assertive in reminding the other foreign policy players in the government that Reagan's ideals were paramount.[90] Clark was able to situate the president at the helm of a more smoothly operating foreign policy apparatus, but he lacked the expertise needed to assist in the development of a sophisticated foreign policy direction. This, plus his weariness at the skirmishing for position and power, led him to turn the NSA job over to his deputy, Robert McFarlane, and escape to the Secretaryship of the Interior recently vacated by James Watt, in November, 1983. The National Security Council system was most effective during the last two years of the Reagan administration with Colin Powell as the Assistant for National Security Affairs.

Conclusion

The foregoing, while not a complete reckoning of the staff's operation, reveals enough to make it clear that the initial Reagan system was not perfect. The unremitting competition and tension engendered by power diffusion and the difficulties of coordinating equals eventually wore the major players down and drove them away. Yet it was worth describing here because it contains the elements of a viable alternative to the strong chief system, at least for those presidents who are temperamentally able to endure its rigors.

What the first term Reagan staff managed to do that few others have consistently done as well, was to remain in control—"out in front"—of the flow of events and problems. This was what accounts for the favorable reputation reported by former *New York Times* reporter Roberts (see note 73). For the most part they sustained the *proactive,* and avoided being forced into the reactive mode by circumstantial pressure. Their planfulness, itself a distinctive characteristic, bought them time and a measure of protection from adversity. During the initial year the LSG was able to seize the initiative and generate legislative victories which created momentum for the administration, put the media and other critics on the defensive and garnered operating control of the political agenda. This cushion, plus their tendency to attack emergent problems with ad hoc strategy groups, enabled them to avoid consumption by mistakes no less serious or numerous than those which have beset other administrations which fared less well.

Of course the staff operation was not solely responsible for the first term track record. Circumstances, fortune, and the persuasive skills of the president played as large or larger roles. But the staff was undeniably a factor, and the 'secret' which made it such appears to have been organizational structures and procedures which required *thoughtful review by many minds.* Atop the organization were always two to four equals, each able to command the attention of the president and, because of their essential equality in the president's eyes, each other. Equality created interdependence: if things were to proceed smoothly, as they knew the president wanted, a great deal of informal interaction, coordination and communication among them was necessary. By all accounts, the top staff found the arrangement time consuming, tedious and draining. The tensions were revealed in the press leaks of their subordinates, criticizing their superior's competitors, and in the eagerness with which each top staffer sought eventual escape from the White House. But though its costs were significant power-sharing insured that no single individual or perspective would come to dominate the presentation of information and options to the president.[91] Coalitions were formed and power ebbed and flowed. But owing largely to the president, a working comity was sustained among the varying membership of the top group most of the time. The central procedural routine, which both enhanced the quality of decision management and reinforced the atmosphere of civility at the top was a carry-over from the way Reagan had used his cabinet while governor of California.[92] Called "roundtabling," it involved group discussions in which the top staff, the president and relevant outside experts would identify and debate presidential decisions options. In addition to educating the president, such meetings also give him the opportunity to work his charm on the staff, making it abundantly clear with his optimism and good humored affability that he expected everyone to avoid animosity and pull together.[93] Roundtabling procedures, with and without presidential participation, were duplicated throughout the organization in cabinet subcouncils, ad hoc strategy groups and coordination committees.

Can power-sharing, planfulness, roundtabling, and problem-centered ad hocracy at the top, grafted onto a formalistic superstructure integrating the Cabinet and the White House staff in more stable organizational routines, be forged into a credible alternative to a strong chief system by presidents other than Reagan?[94] Is such a system transferable? In principle, as much so as any other system. But like any other system, it must be staffed with persons able to make it work. In this case, the system requires a president who, like Reagan or Kennedy, will welcome the diversity of opinion it generates, adhere to procedures which enhance its effectiveness (e.g., changing personnel, fine-tuning the mix of people and interactions, etc.) and who can tolerate or reduce the tensions power sharing creates. The system also requires actors in the key staff roles who are substantively and temperamentally complementary and compatible with one another. Any system can be defeated by poor choice of personnel. And no system, however well designed and staffed, is guaranteed to succeed. Every management model must meet difficult requirements of one sort or another, and is subject to malfunctioning.[95]

But the margin for error is likely to be greater in a system like that described and endorsed here, where no one staffer is organizationally crucial, and top staff may enter and depart, like Clark or Meese, without forcing the defacto collapse and redefinition of the entire system. That, after all, is precisely what is required following the departure of an individual who in his person, embodies the system, like Donald Regan or any other strong chief. Too, the predictable problems of a plural staff: conflicts, power struggles, internal stalemates, and bickering, are more readily corrected (via presidential influence and/or selective replacement of staff) and thus potentially less devastating to the quality of a president's work than those of a unitary system, which include the pride and egotism of the strong chief of staff, yielding presidential isolation and/or distorted exposure to information and options. The orderly, formalistic procedure the San Diego conferees saw as the best protection against damage due to human impulse, weakness and inconsistence is certainly not the exclusive province of the strong chief system. Such procedures are as or more likely to emerge under the auspices of a wary, self-policing committee like Reagan's 'big four' than under a dominant chief of staff. By the same token, such protean figures as Henry Kissinger or Zbigniew Brzezinski are not the only source of creativity available to a president. Ad hoc groups such as those that studded the organizational landscape of the first Reagan White House showed themselves quite capable of injecting the flexibility needed to avoid consumption by sterile, unresponsive routine.

NOTES

1. Emmette S. Redford and Richard T. McCully, in their 1986 book on Lyndon B. Johnson's presidential management style, put the problem this way: "While law does not prescribe duties or status, there is much constancy from president to president in roles of White House aides. In general, every president needs similar kinds of service as he operates as chief of state and chief of government, in the wide span of foreign and domestic affairs, in policy deliberation and political strategy, and in regular events or crisis situations." See Redford and McCully. 1986. *White House Operations: The Johnson Presidency.* Austin, Texas: University of Texas Press, 1986, p. 3.

2. Samuel Kernell and Samuel L. Popkin, *Chief of Staff: Twenty-Five Years of Managing the Presidency.* Berkeley, California: University of California Press, 1986, p. 32.

3. Tower Committee televised press conference, February 26, 1987.

4. One example of the kind of highly personal support an advisor may provide a president is found in the relationship between Lyndon Johnson and Bill Moyers. Said Moyers: "I knew far more about Johnson that I ever knew about my own father. My father never talked to me about his sexuality. My father never talked to me about his wife, my mother. My father never talked to me about his failures. Johnson would talk about everything—about his relationship with Lady Bird, about his worries with his daughters growing up, even about his own problems with his girlfriends. And I won't discuss that even now, because he trusted me." (Michael Medved, *The Shadow Presidents: The Secret History of the Chief Executives and their Top Aides.* New York: Times Books, 1979, p. 289).

5. Lou Cannon, *Reagan.* New York: G. P. Putnam's Sons, p. 306.

6. George J. Church, "How Reagan Decides," *Time,* December 13, 1982, pp. 12–17.

7. Another instance of personal accommodation is found in the special relationship between John F. Kennedy and Theodore Sorensen. JFK had the personal presence and the rhetorical skills, but lacked the eloquence needed to exploit his own talents to the fullest. The eloquence was supplied by Sorensen. Argues Michael Medved: "There is little question that the lofty style of speaking and writing that became so finely identified with JFK was more Sorensen's doing than Kennedy's . . . [Sorensen], according to one of his friends, saw Kennedy as his 'work of art'." Medved, *op. cit.,* pp. 261–2.

8. This typology borrows heavily from a similar discussion under the heading of "Three Sorts of Personal Servants" in Matthew Holden, Jr., *Bargaining and Command in the Administrative Process,* Part I: Chief Executives and the Executive

Entourage. Institute of Government, University of Virginia, Working Papers in Public Administration, No. 2, 1986, p. 23.

9. Richard E. Neustadt, "Foreword," in Kernell and Popkin, *op, cit.* p. ix.

10. "Typically," argues Ford and Reagan economic adviser Roger B. Porter, "political advice arrives relatively late in the process of developing a policy initiative." See R.B. Porter, "Advising the President." *PS.* 19, Fall, 1986, p. 868. If true, this circumstance represents an enduring problem in the management of presidential advice.

11. For an intelligent discussion of how much knowledge is enough for a president, see Paul Quirk, "Presidential Competence," in Michael Nelson, (ed.) *The Presidency and the Political System.* Washington, D.C.: CQ Press, 1985.

12. Holden, *op. cit.,* p. 25.

13. For description of the extraordinary relationships between Sorensen, Moyers and their presidents, see the relevant chapter of Medved, *op. cit.*

14. That would change to some extent with the emergence—at a conference of former top White House aides at the University of California-San Diego—of a consensus that the modern presidency requires a standard doctrine of presidential management. The proceedings are reproduced in Kernell and Popkin *op. cit.* Said political columnist David Broder, an observer of the discussions: ". . . striking was the degree of consensus two days of talks produced about how the work of the modern presidency should be organized. After saying at the outset that each White House staff must be tailored to the needs and style of a particular president, it turned out that they really agreed among themselves that some ways will work better than others, no matter who is sitting at the President's desk. What they endorsed was essentially the strong chief-of-staff system now being operated by Donald Regan . . ." David Broder, "The White House 'Javelin Catchers'" *Austin American Statesman,* January 22, 1986, A8.

15. Alexander L. George, *Presidential Decisionmaking in Foreign Policy: The Effective Use of Information and Advice.* Boulder, Colorado: Westview Press, 1980, pp. 147–148.

16. *Ibid.,* p. 147.

17. Cf., Richard Tanner Johnson. *Managing the White House.* New York, Harper and Row, 1974; Colin Campbell, *Managing the Presidency: Carter, Reagan, and the Search for Executive Harmony.* Pittsburgh: University of Pittsburgh Press, 1986, pp. 83–112; George, op. cit., 145–168; Stephen Hess. *Organizing the Presidency.* Washington, D.C.: Brookings, 1976.

18. Fred I. Greenstein. *The Reagan Presidency: An Early Assessment.* Baltimore: Johns Hopkins University Press, 1983, p. 62.

19. For a discussion of the political value to Reagan of the phenomenon of 'distancing,' see Bruce Buchanan, *The Citizen's Presidency.* Washington, D.C.: CQ Press, 1987, p. 128.

20. George, *op. cit.,* pp. 145–166.

21. Buchanan, *op. cit.,* pp. 166–169.

22. This discussion of the disadvantages of formalistic presidential systems, and the discussion of disadvantages of other systems later in the text, are drawn from Richard T. Johnson "Management Styles of Three U.S. Presidents," *Stanford Alumni Bulletin.* Fall, 1973, p. 35.

23. President Reagan's difficulties with the Iranian arms deal, orchestrated by mid-level aides in the National Security Council, have been increasingly attributed to Reagan's isolated, minimalist involvement in the details of his presidency. Political

columnist David Broder cites his colleague Lou Cannon, who wrote prophetically at the beginning of 1986: "Increasingly, the Reagan administration functions reflexively, with most of the work done by mid-level aides . . . (Mr. Reagan's) government often runs on automatic pilot, and he seems too distant from his subordinates' deliberations or the outside world's concerns to notice. Eventually, isolation is likely to extract a price." Broder concludes that the price Reagan's management style extracted was the Iranian crisis: "Virtually every reporter in Washington—and politicians too—knew Mr. Reagan had only a fleeting interest in the day-to-day policies and operations of government. But too many of us convinced ourselves that it made no difference; that it was enough to be lucky and popular." (David Broder, "Paying the Price of Reagan's Isolation," *Austin American-Statesman,* December 31, 1986, A6).

24. Colin Campbell, *op. cit.,* p. 4.
25. For a detailed discussion of the group decision-making characteristics that contributed to the successful resolution of the Cuban Missile Crisis, see George, *op. cit.* pp. 212–215.
26. George, *op. cit.,* p. 215.
27. Kernell and Popkin, *op. cit.,* pp. 20–21. After a brief period during which Donald Rumsfeld served as Chief of Staff in the Ford administration, Richard Cheney assumed the position and operated a more disciplined, formalistic system than Rumsfeld had. See Medved, *op. cit.,* pp. 338–339.
28. Kernell and Popkin, *op. cit.,* pp. 74–75.
29. Hess, *op. cit.,* pp. 10–11.
30. Kernell and Popkin, *op. cit.,* p. 27.
31. Rumsfeld, in Kernell and Popkin, p. 75.
32. Bradley H. Patterson, Jr., *The Ring of Power: The White House Staff and Its Expanding Role in Government* (New York: Basic Books, Inc., 1988).
33. For example, none of the former chiefs of staff who participated in the San Diego discussions of White House management made the case for a unitary as opposed to plural chief, but all of the conference participants (except for Richard Neustadt, who suggested that there has usually been a "big three to five" advisory body; see p. 143) spoke of the role in unitary terms. See Kernell and Popkin, *op. cit., passim.*
34. Kernell and Popkin, *passim.*
35. Meeting at the American Political Science Association annual meeting for 1986, another group of presidential advisers, including former Reagan national security adviser Robert C. McFarlane, Carter domestic policy adviser Stuart E. Eizenstat, Reagan economic policy adviser Roger B. Porter and Reagan political pollster and adviser Richard B. Wirthlin reached the following conclusion, recorded by Porter: "Presidents inevitably are faced with the need to have advice both about the substantive effects of their policy choices and about the political implications of these alternatives. There was broad consensus that *both strands of advice are important,* that bringing them forward in parallel is difficult, and that *a strong White House Chief of Staff is the best place to lodge responsibility for ensuring that these two streams of advice are well coordinated.* Typically, political advice arrives relatively late in the process of developing a policy initiative." (emphasis mine). See Roger B. Porter, "Advising the President" *PS* 19; 867–869. (Fall, 1986). Porter is a major staff advisor in the Bush administration.
36. Kernell and Popkin, p. 26.

37. The preparation of presidential speeches offers an interesting illustration of the need for a carefully managed 'staffing out' process, as described by Donald Rumsfeld. Acknowledging that speechwriters are correct in believing that speeches sound better if not 'written by a committee,' Rumsfeld nonetheless argues that the 'substantive people must comment on it' before the president gets the speech; something the speechwriter will often seek to prevent, by submitting the speech late, in order to preserve his own language. What is the chief of staff to do? ". . . heave his body in the middle and try to figure out a way for the substantive portions of the speech to finally reach the substantive people so they have a chance to look at it. . . ." Kernell and Popkin, pp. 172–173.
38. Kernell and Popkin, pp. 164–165.
39. Kernell and Popkin, p. 129.
40. Kernell and Popkin, p.128.
41. Kernell and Popkin, p. 129.
42. Kernell and Popkin, p. 170.
43. Kernell and Popkin, pp. 21–22.
44. This situation is described by Rumsfeld rather than Haldeman, but Haldeman, who was present at the discussion, did not deny it. See Kernell and Popkin, p. 171.
45. Kernell and Popkin, p. 170.
46. Kernell and Popkin, p. 135.
47. Dick Kirschten, "White House Vacancies Go Begging . . . As Don Regan Waits Out the Storm," *National Journal,* January 24, 1987, pp. 214–215.
48. Kernell and Popkin, p. 149.
49. Kernell and Popkin, pp. 176–177.
50. Kernell and Popkin, p. 174.
51. Stockman recounts the stern warning issued him by James Baker, and the innocuous, friendly chat he had with the president, in his book, *The Triumph of Politics: Why the Reagan Revolution Failed.* (New York: Harper and Row, 1986). The 'confessions' that led to his dressing down appeared in William Greider, "The Education of David Stockman" *Atlantic Monthly,* December, 1981, pp. 27–54.
52. Kernell and Popkin, p. 155, note 6.
53. Kernell and Popkin, p. 165.
54. Kernell and Popkin, pp. 166–167.
55. For a discussion of the Reagan distancing strategy, see Buchanan, *op. cit.,* pp. 125–129.
56. Gerald M. Boyd, "Buchanan Joins Those Leaving President's Side," *The New York Times,* February 4, 1987, p. 1.
57. Bernard Weinraub, "How Donald Regan Runs the White House," *The New York Times Magazine,* January 5, 1986.
58. For a discussion of the special circumstances of Howard Baker, perhaps the only top presidential aide ever selected *because* of his independent public reputation, see the *National Journal,* May 23, 1987, p. 1332.
59. Samuel Kernell, "The Creed and Reality of Modern White House Management," In Kernell and Popkin, p. 198.
60. Kernell and Popkin, pp. 186–187.
61. Kernell and Popkin, pp. 174–176.
62. See Sherman Adams, *First Hand Report: The Story of the Eisenhower Administration.* (New York: Harper and Brothers, 1961, p. 53).
63. Kernell and Popkin, pp. 24–25.

64. Kernell and Popkin, pp. 22–23.

65. Kernell and Popkin, pp. 190–191.

66. Elspeth Rostow writes: "Only two recent presidents have abandoned the concept of an array of advisors, usually a "Big Three" team, in favor of a single chief of staff. In neither case was the experiment successful." *Austin American-Statesman,* March 9, 1987, p. A10.

67. Brent Scowcroft, in the press conference which presented the Tower Commission Report, argued that key foreign policy advisers should do both; that is, both lay out credible options and present a policy recommendation. In fact, however, human beings find it difficult not to downgrade those options they do not support.

68. George, *Presidential Decisionmaking in Foreign Policy,* p. 200.

69. For an analysis of Donald Regan's status as perhaps the most powerful chief of staff ever to serve a president, plus commentary on Regan's assertive will to power, see Bernard Weinraub, "How Donald Regan Runs the White House," *The New York Times Magazine,* January 5, 1986, p. 12. For an assessment of Regan's dissembling and his flawed character, see David Broder, "President Must Show Regan the Door," *Austin American-Statesman,* January 28, 1987, p. A6.

70. Norman J. Ornstein, "Regan's Mismanagement Style," *The New York Times,* February 25, 1987, p. 23.

71. *Ibid.*

72. There is some dispute, hard to resolve without access to official records, concerning just how insulated the Regan system left President Reagan. For example, David R. Gergen, who was Ronald Reagan's director of communications from 1981 to 1983, said that after the president's landslide reelection, the staff began to treat Reagan "like a sort of living national treasure" instead of challenging him. "They no longer actively engaged him in a dialogue about options and about what possibilities and what consequences might flow from certain policy decisions" (Quoted in Matthew L. Wald, "Reagan's Staff Depicted as Failing Him," *The New York Times,* March 4, 1987, p. 9). Gergen thus endorses the conventional view expressed by Ornstein in the text. Yet in a discussion of the most damaging consequence usually attributed to Reagan's second-term management system, the Iran debacle, William Safire calls the attribution a myth: "The President slid into error, but did not lack for experienced political advice." Reagan was well aware of disaffection about the Iran adventure on the part of Secretary of State Shultz and Secretary of Defense Weinberger, but simply chose to heed the advice of another seasoned advisor: CIA Director William Casey. For Casey, the opening to Iran and return of the hostages was to be the ultimate achievement, tying in closely with covert support of the Afghan resistance, aid to the Angolan rebels and the reversal of the arch of Communism in Central America. Safire acknowledges that secrecy prevented repeated challenge to a policy gone awry, but contends that at the time, the Iran venture was not regarded as political foolishness by most members of the NSC. Nor was the president ill-informed: "Ronald Reagan knew all he needed to know to decide to trade arms for hostages. Selling those arms was his decision, nobody else's . . . he stayed in touch with it, cutting out of meetings Secretary Shultz and others who were on record as opposing the decision." William Safire, "Ten Myths about the Reagan Debacle" *The New York Times Magazine,* March 22, 1987, p. 20.

73. Steven V. Roberts, "Did the Reagan Style of Management Fail Him?" *The New York Times,* March 6, 1987, p. 12.

74. Lou Cannon and Lee Lescaze, "The Triumvirate—3 Men Who Speak and Act of the President," *Houston Chronicle,* June 21, 1981, section 1, p. 16.

75. John H. Kessel, "The Structure of the Reagan White House," paper presented at the annual meeting of the American Political Science Association, Chicago, Illinois, 1983, pp. 34–36.

76. Kessel, *ibid.,* p. 36.

77. Kessel, p. 35, The Reagans did call Deaver in the midst of the Iran/contra controversy, along with Stuart Spencer and other close confidants.

78. Laurence I. Barrett, *Gambling with History: Reagan in the White House.* New York: Penguin Books, 1983, pp. 252–253.

79. Ibid., p. 384.

80. Cannon, *op, cit.,* p. 382.

81. Kessel, *op cit.,* p. 35.

82. Barrett, *op. cit.,* pp. 385–386.

83. Kessel, *op. cit.,* p. 36.

84. Kessel, p. 36.

85. Kessel, p. 36.

86. David A. Stockman, *The Triumph of Politics: How the Reagan Revolution Failed.* New York: Harper and Row, 1986, p. 83.

87. See for example, *Time* magazine White House correspondent Laurence I. Barrett's discussion of Meese in Barrett, *op. cit.,* p. 100.

88. Kessel, p. 35.

89. Canon, p. 397.

90. Barrett, *op cit.,* p. 234.

91. Baker's aide Richard Darman was responsible for preparing the briefing materials for Reagan's use in making decisions, but Deaver, Clark and Meese all had input in the preparation of materials and the opportunity to observe the use the president made of them when they gathered to discuss decision options.

92. See Gary G. Hamilton and Nicole Woolsey Biggard, *Governor Reagan, Governor Brown.* (New York: Columbia University Press, 1984), p. 192.

93. Hamilton and Biggard, *op. cit.,* p. 46.

94. In some respects, the first Reagan system can be seen as a more structured and otherwise improved version of the collegial system of John F. Kennedy. As practiced by Reagan, the system featured greater emphasis on anticipatory strategic planning, clearer division of labor among group discussants, much more restricted access to the president by persons outside the top group, much less presidential involvement and direction, and greater adherence to standard operating routines and procedures during noncrisis periods. It was as if a collegial system had been grafted onto a formalistic system at the top of the hierarchy only.

95. Organizational structures are assessed in James P. Pfiffner and R. Gordon Hoxie (eds.), *The Presidency in Transition* (New York: Center for the Study of the Presidency, 1989). This includes essays by Reagan's final Chief of Staff, Kenneth M. Duberstein and his final security advisor, Colin Powell, also Edwin Meese, Bradley Patterson and Donald Rumsfeld.

The President's Chief of Staff in Historical and Institutional Perspective

Ted Jones
Washington State University

The position of White House chief of staff is a relatively new one in the history of the presidency. The position was created in 1952 with the appointment of Sherman Adams by President Eisenhower (even though Adams was officially a "special assistant," he is widely regarded to be the first presidential chief of staff). However, the position did not become a regular part of the White House staff until the late 1970s and early 1980s when President Carter finally appointed Hamilton Jordan, followed by Jack Watson, and President Reagan continued the office throughout his two terms. No president since Carter has tried to manage the White House without the help of a chief of staff. This raises an obvious question: why? Why is it that James Pfiffner (1993) can accurately claim, "No president has successfully run the White House without a chief of staff since 1968, and since 1979 no President has tried?" (78)

Why a Chief of Staff? And Why Now?

The answers to these questions are found in the remarkable changes that occurred in the White House, the executive branch and the national government in the final two-thirds of the 20th Century.

1) *The Overall Growth and Composition of the Executive Office and the White House Staff* The Executive Office of the President (EOP) was created by Congress in 1939, but the growth of the White House staff can be traced back even further. In 1929, Congress increased the number of presidential secretaries from one to three. This allowed the aides to specialize, and President Hoover designated George Akerson the first press secretary. Aside from these three "secretaries," the White House staff included thirty clerical staff assigned to the White House and a varying number borrowed (or "detailed") from outside agencies, as had been done since Andrew Jackson (Hart, 1987).

The growth in presidential staff accelerated after 1939. President Roosevelt in 1936 appointed three leading public administration scholars—Louis Brownlow, Charles Merriam, and Luther Gulick—to study ways the executive branch could be reorganized to improve management. The report of the President's Committee on Administrative Management (or "The Brownlow Committee"), issued in January 1937, recommended a sweeping overhaul of the executive branch. Part of their overall reorganization plan was a recommendation for a significant increase in the White House staff, both high level aides and lower level clerical staff. These new staff were not supposed to implement policy, but were instead supposed to help the president deal with the increasing difficulties of coordination and management that accompanied the changing roles of the national government and the presidency in the early part of the 20th Century. The committee went to great lengths to stress that these new high level aides were to be presidential assistants, not "assistant presidents." In addition to being competent and energetic in their work, they were to be possessed with a "passion for anonymity." They should not draw attention to themselves, either through their actions or their public statements (Hart, 1987).

The Brownlow Committee's recommendations were only partially implemented, and not for more than two years, but in 1939, Congress passed the Reorganization Act. This bill gave the president six high level assistants and allowed him to submit plans to Congress for the reorganization of the executive branch. Pursuant to this authorization, President Roosevelt formally created the Executive Office of the President with five divisions: the White House Office (WHO), the Bureau of the Budget (BOB—it had been located in the Department of the Treasury since its creation in 1924 and later became the Office of Management and Budget, or OMB), the National Resources Planning Board, the Liaison Office for Personal Management, and the Office of Government Reports. The president's personal staff is formally housed in the White House Office—though they are not likely to have their offices physically located in the White House building. Many are housed next door in the Old Executive Office Building (OEOB).

Since the creation of the EOP, the number of divisions within it have varied, as has the number of staff. Some have been added or removed by presidents, like the Office of Economic Opportunity. It was created by President Johnson and subsequently disbanded by President Nixon. Others have been added by Congress, like the Council of Economic Advisors and the National Security Council. The increases in divisions and staff of the EOP began almost immediately. During President Truman's administration, six new divisions were created. Johnson added three. Nixon added six. Kennedy added none. Ford abolished some but added six. Eisenhower, Carter, and Reagan were the only presidents to leave office with fewer divisions of the EOP than when they entered (Hart, 1987).

The number of staff has varied as well, with the general trend to more staff relative to the 1940s and 1950s, as can be seen in Figure 1. Much like the number of divisions within the EOP, the amount of staff assigned to the EOP increased rapidly in the late 1950s, leveled off and decreased in the mid 1960s, increased rapidly in the late 1960s and early 1970s, and has declined or remained roughly stable since the mid- to late-1970s.[1] An accurate accounting of the exact number of staff in the EOP is a difficult task due in large part to the detailing of executive branch agency or department staff to the EOP. However, by one estimate, the Executive Office staff expanded to as many as 5751 in 1974, and it has fluctuated between 1514 and 1910 since.

---

[1]Wartime EOP staffing figures are grossly misleading because they include temporary, but labor intensive, units created specifically to help manage the war. In 1939 and 1940, there were 631 and 647 EOP staff members, respectively. In 1941, there were 21,482. By 1943, the number had swelled to 194,194. In 1948, the number was back to "normal": 1,118. For this reason, pre-1948 figures have been excluded.

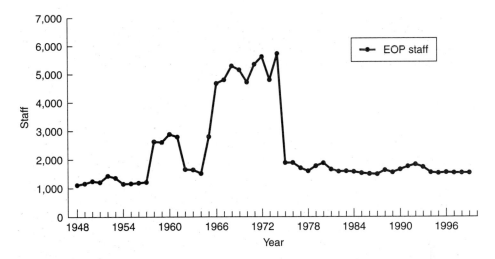

FIGURE 1
EOP Staff: 1948–1998
Source: The Budget of the United States, 1924–2000 (Washington, D.C.; Government Printing Office, 1924–2000.)

The staff figures for the White House Office have fluctuated as well, but they have not followed the same path as the overall EOP numbers. As Figure 2 demonstrates, there were sharp increases in 1950, 1956–1963, and 1971, and declines from 1964–1968 and 1976–1978. The size of the staff of the WHO was relatively stable from 1938–1946 and 1979 to the present.

It is notable that the staff figures for both the EOP and WHO have stabilized since the late 1970s and at levels higher than those of the 1940s and 1950s. This is coincident with the institutionalization of the presidency identified by Ragsdale and Theis (1997). Using a variety of measures, Ragsdale and Theis concluded that the presidency became institutionalized in the 1970s. They concluded that it was during this time that the combination of features of the Executive Office of the President—the relative autonomy of the presidency and its constituent units, the relative adaptability of the organization (measured in part by the longevity of EOP units), the complexity of the EOP (the number and size of EOP unit staff), and its coherence (the EOP's ability to manage its workload)—attained levels high enough to be considered "institutionalized." Of the three possible causes identified by Ragsdale and Theis—national government activity, congressional activity, and individual presidential variation—the primary reason they identified was the growth in national government activity, measured by social welfare and defense expenditures. As the national government grew in size, the EOP became larger and more complex and eventually became a stable institution.

The increased size and complexity of the national government and the presidency required that someone other than the president be responsible for coordinating the activities of the many offices within the EOP and the White House. The research of Ragsdale and Theis suggests that it is not a coincidence that the chief

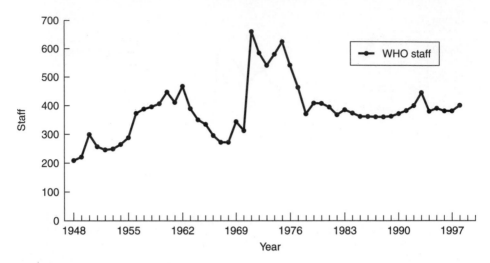

FIGURE 2
WHO Staff: 1948–1998
Source: The Budget of the United States, 1924–2000 (Washington, D.C.; Government Printing Office, 1924–2000.)

of staff has become a permanent fixture in the White House at the same time the sizes of the EOP and WHO have both stabilized at levels too large for a president to coordinate and manage without substantial assistance.

2) ***The Trend to Bring More Policy Making and Implementation into the White House at the Expense of the Executive Branch Bureaucracy (Line Agencies) and Congress***   Presidents have long desired and attempted to attain more direct control over the policies whose implementation is their constitutional responsibility. These attempts have qualitatively and quantitatively altered the presidency and the executive branch.

Terry Moe (1985), in his influential work "The Politicized Presidency," puts this historical trend into perspective. He noted that both Presidents Kennedy and Johnson had continued a trend accelerated by President Roosevelt in the 1930s by "seeking to centralize the policy process more fully in the White House." (252) Both were frustrated by the existing agency bureaucracies that preferred stable routines and were resistant to change. However, "neither president really pushed its [policy centralization] potential as a control mechanism." (255) It was President Nixon, however, who "frustrated in achieving his social goals through legislative action, put this structure to distinctly presidential use in a dedicated attempt to achieve programmatic ends through bureaucratic control." (256) The result was the "administrative strategy."

In 1970, the BOB moved into the EOP and [was] renamed the Office of Management and Budget (OMB). More political appointees were added, and its funding was increased. The Domestic Policy Council was created. Political appointments to the bureaucracy became more formalized and stressed political loyalty and ideology.

This emphasis on loyalty from agency appointees is key to the administrative strategy. In the wake of Watergate, Presidents Ford and Carter did not so openly emphasize ideology and presidential loyalty as President Nixon, but neither ignored these qualities either. However, it was President Reagan who pushed the administrative strategy to its fullest expression.

Emphasizing political and ideological loyalty, the Reagan Administration appointed partisans in as many positions as possible. This included the OMB, which was used by the Reagan Administration to gain budgetary control over the federal bureaucracy. As a result, "the OMB quickly became a central participant in policymaking and political action." (Moe, 1985, 261)

All of these efforts illustrate an important balance which must be struck by presidents if they are to adequately carry out their legal and constitutional responsibilities to execute the laws of the United States. Presidents seek responsiveness from the bureaucracy. After all, it is the president who must answer to all of the nation's voters if their desires are not translated into public policy. On the other hand, presidents also need competence. Bureaucracies tend to promote neutral competence, however, not responsive competence. And they tend to resist change. As Moe put it:

> Since the Roosevelt years, there has been a continuing tension between the competing values of neutral competence and executive leadership, the latter gaining in importance with modern growth in the complexity of social problems, the size and fragmentation of government, and expectations surrounding presidential performance. This tension has never been resolved, but it has maintained a characteristic balance in favor of neutral competence, which is clearly the core value. (265)

This tension has produced a noticeable effect on the management of the modern White House. The attempts to bring policy development and implementation more directly under the control of the president have made management both easier and more difficult at the same time. It is easier in the sense that presidents are now more directly in control of their fates through the added resources of the OMB and their efforts at stocking the bureaucracy with loyalists. On the other hand, it creates managerial problems within the White House. In spite of the formalization and routinization of the appointments process relative to the 1940s and 1950s, each president must develop his own system. This creates a management problem, and the chief of staff position is one specifically charged with alleviating management problems.

3) *The More Active Role of the National Government*   All of the above is a byproduct of the expansion in the role of the national government. This expansion accelerated in the 1930s and has since become a fixture in the American political environment. A more massive national government needed more people to run it. With more people to coordinate and monitor and more responsibility focused on the president, the president needed more staff. More staff required more attention. Attention means time, and time is a commodity that presidents have precious little to spare.

Each of these three factors contributed to the development and "institutionalization" of the position of the presidential chief of staff. The increased size and complexity of the presidency, as seen in the number of units and staff in the EOP and the staff of the WHO, the desire of presidents to exert more direct control over policy making, and the expanded role of the national government that made presidential coordination and oversight more unwieldy all helped to make the chief of staff position an indispensable one in the modern White House.

Chief of Staff: Responsibilities[2]

It is not enough to claim that the chief of staff helps the president manage the White House. It is necessary to understanding the importance of the chief of staff to have a reasonably clear grasp of the tasks and responsibilities that compose the role of chief of staff. For many years, scholars largely ignored this important issue. However, a number of recent efforts have taken the first steps to identifying just what it is that chiefs of staff are expected to do (see esp., Kernell and Popkin, 1986; Buchanan, 1991; Pfiffner, 1991 and 1993; Patterson, 1988 and 2000; White House 2001 Project, 2000). The following discussion is based on their efforts.

In many ways, the position of chief of staff today is remarkably similar to the original conception. Many of the responsibilities described further were part of the job description for Sherman Adams in the 1950s and are expected of the current occupants of the position. That is not to suggest that the role is identical to the one President Eisenhower and Mr. Adams conceived and executed. There have been a few relatively small changes over the years. The rest of this section will be devoted to a discussion of these tasks and responsibilities of presidential chiefs of staff. They are listed in a rough chronology of the order in which they appeared. That is, the tasks which have defined the position from the beginning are first, and more recent additions come last.

1) ***Coordinate Staff Activities***   It is here, in the oldest and most fundamental responsibility of the chief of staff, that the management styles of the president and chief of staff interact to define the basic shape of a given president's White House operations. At the beginning of each chief of staff's tenure, he must establish how the president wants the staff managed, what are his specific powers and limitations, and the extent to which the White House advisory and administrative structure is hierarchical or resembles the "spokes-of-a-wheel" (an approach which allows considerable access to the president with very few filters and gatekeepers). In doing so, the chief of staff works with the president to establish the organizational chart of the White House, and then he is expected to manage that organization with a minimum of disruptions which would require the president's attention. This is not to suggest that the White House is then on auto-pilot after the initial work of the president and chief of staff. Organizational structures can and

---

[2]For the reader's reference, Table 1 provides a list [of] presidential chiefs of staff (from Ragsdale, 1998; modified by the author).

TABLE 1
CHIEFS OF STAFF

President	Chief of Staff	Tenure
Eisenhower	Sherman Adams	1952–58
	Wilton "Jerry" Persons	1958–61
Kennedy	None	—
Johnson	None	—
Nixon	H. R. Haldeman	1969–73
	Alexander Haig	1973–74
Ford	Donald Rumsfeld	1974–75
	Richard Cheney	1975–77
Carter	Hamilton Jordan	1979–80
	Jack Watson	1980–81
Reagan	James Baker	1981–84
	Donald Regan	1985–87
	Howard Baker	1987–88
	Kenneth Duberstein	1988–89
Bush	John Sununu	1989–91
	Mike Skinner	1991–92
	James Baker	1992–93
Clinton	Thomas "Mack" McClarty	1993–94
	Leon Panetta	1994–96
	Erskine Bowles	1997–99
	John Podesta	1999–2000
Bush	Andrew Card	2000–

do change throughout a chief of staff's tenure, but it is the initial understanding reached by the president and chief of staff that defines its basic structure and provides a base-line from which future variations in White House operations flow.

Research by David Cohen and George Krause (2000) suggests that there are a number of important variables that determine how much hierarchy exists under a given president and chief of staff. These include the management style of the president, the management style of the chief of staff, and the quality of their "working relationship." Their research, based on data obtained through a survey of former White House staffers under Presidents Reagan and Bush, asked respondents to characterize on a seven-point scale the organizational structure of the White House in which they served (spokes-of-the-wheel to hierarchical), their president's management style (delegating to hands-on), the chief of staff's management style (delegating to hands-on), and the president-chief of staff general working relationship (poor to excellent). Cohen and Krause's models suggest that "as the president's management style becomes less active, the more hierarchical the organizational structure will become in practice. Conversely, as a chief of staff's management style becomes more active, the structure of the White House as an organization behaves in a more hierarchical fashion and less like a spokes-of-the-wheel structure." (429) In addition, "the better the general working relationship between the president and the chief of staff, the more hierarchical the organizational structure of the White House will operate as presidents become more willing to function in a "vertically" structured White House." (429)

Presidents Carter and Reagan illustrate the influence a president's management style can have on the organizational structure of the White House. President Carter's management style was very active, and he clung tenaciously to the belief that he could serve as his own chief of staff and employ a "spokes-of-the-wheel" approach to managing the White House (this adds weight to Cohen and Kraus' conclusions). Eventually, after two and a half years, Carter acceded to political and logistical reality and appointed Hamilton Jordan then Jack Watson as his chiefs of staff. By then, it was too late. His White House had acquired an inescapable reputation for disorganization. In addition, Carter was unwilling to cede much power to his chiefs of staff or dramatically revise the organization of the White House. This made Jordan's and Watson's tasks more difficult and undermined Carter's efforts at getting the White House under control (Ayres, 1984).

In contrast, President Reagan took very little interest in management issues, preferring instead to give his chiefs of staff broad grants of authority and allow them to fill in the details (Rockman, 1988). This approach allowed the management styles of his chiefs of staff to manifest themselves more fully than they might have otherwise. This led to more hierarchy than that found in the Carter White House and dramatically different levels of success enjoyed by Reagan's chiefs of staff.

James Baker served as chief of staff throughout President Reagan's first term. He was one third, along with Michael Deaver and Ed Meese, of the "troika" which led the White House during this period. He was praised for instituting a system that was hierarchical enough to allow for the efficient operation of the White House, but not so hierarchical that it choked off information flowing to and from the president (see #2 . . .). In addition, Baker drew upon his Washington, D.C. experience in dealing with people both in the White House and out to earn the nickname "The Velvet Hammer," which was an indication of his combination of toughness and personal sensitivity. The result was that Baker was the first man to serve as chief of staff for a long period of time and leave with his reputation not only intact but enhanced (to the point that he was considered a serious possibility to succeed President Reagan in 1988).

Donald Regan assumed the reins from Baker at the start of Reagan's second term after serving as Secretary of the Treasury in the first term. He met a very different fate than that of Baker. Using the authority granted him by President Reagan, Regan immediately instituted a more hierarchical system than that of Baker. This reflected the training he had received in his many years with Merrill, Lynch before coming to Washington. Regan was a very active manager. He dramatically reduced access to the president and was involved in virtually every aspect of presidential activities (Pfiffner, 1993). He also was not as gifted in interpersonal relations as Baker, and he was eventually forced out of his job in 1987. Fairly or not, few White House staffers were sad to see him leave.

With respect to White House management, Reagan and Carter were direct opposites. Whereas Carter would not surrender authority over management of the White House and employed a "spokes-of-the-wheel" approach, Reagan took little interest in management issues. Instead, he gave his aides broad goals and expected them to figure out how to carry them out. In doing so, the management styles of his chiefs of staff manifested themselves more fully in the organization of the White House, and both employed more hierarchical structures than any used by President Carter.

2) ***Guard the President's Door but See to it That Information Reaches the President When He Needs It to Make Decisions***   This is where the rubber meets the road in White House operations. White House staff exists in large part to allow the president to focus his attention on decision making, and the chief of staff walks a narrow line between protecting the president's time and energy and choking off the vital flow of information to the president.

In order to successfully manage this balancing act, the chief of staff must have control of the paper flow in the White House and access to the president. In order to control paper flow without isolating the president, chiefs of staff work closely with the staff secretaries to see that decision memoranda are circulated to all relevant actors so that their input can be obtained and all of the president's options can be described to their satisfaction (White House 2001 Project, 2000, 9).

In general, more hierarchical structures will more severely limit personal access to the president. The greatest danger of such a system is that the president will not be exposed to the wide range of views that would allow him to make decisions with full knowledge of the consequences. President Nixon's experience is illustrative. His staff grew increasingly hierarchical as his administration aged. In fact, the ability of Nixon's top aides (Haldeman, Erlichman, and Kissinger) to keep people away from the president earned them the nickname "The Berlin Wall." The hierarchical structure that developed in the Nixon White House and the growing isolation which overtook the president reinforced the worst aspects of Nixon's personality and decision making abilities. The president slowly became more isolated and withdrawn, and this contributed to the problems which would bring down his presidency.

3) ***Serve as an "Honest Broker" in Internal White House Policy Debates*** A chief of staff cannot effectively guard the president's time and attention if others in the policy process do not believe their views are being fairly presented to the president by the chief of staff. If this becomes the case, they will attempt to find ways around the process the chief of staff and president have established (in other words, to "end run" the chief of staff). As Bradley Patterson (2000) wrote, "Presidents expect their chiefs of staff to hold, and to express, their own independent judgments about any issue in the Oval Office neighborhood. They must do so, however, without using their stature and their proximity to give their own arguments an edge over competing contentions from other staffers or cabinet disputants." (353)

James Baker (White House 2001 Project, 2000, 9) put it this way: "You have to make sure you have an orderly system, that you have a system that's fair. Otherwise, you start the leaking in the press, one against the other. You have to have a system that lets the President hear all sides. And you have to have one, that if you're going to be running the White House, you have to know what's going on."

It should be apparent to the reader that the first three responsibilities of the chief of staff are closely intertwined, and success or failure in one aspect can have serious consequences for others. Failure to be perceived as an honest broker will undermine a chief of staff's ability to guard the president's door. Failure to guard the president's door will undermine the chief of staff's ability to implement the agreed-upon organizational structure. Failure to implement this structure makes staff coordination difficult, if not impossible. A lack of staff coordination makes effective presidential decision making less likely. Successfully carrying out these three duties is a necessary, but insufficient, precondition to success as a chief of staff.

4) *Fire People/Bear Bad News/Play the Heavy*   Jack Watson, President Carter's second chief of staff, semi-jokingly described the chief of staff position as the president's "javelin catcher." (Kernell and Popkin, 1986, 182) If there's a tough job to be done, it is often the chief of staff's responsibility to carry it out. This allows the chief of staff to draw anger over tough decisions away from the president. The drawback to this is that chiefs of staff can make many enemies and few friends. Chiefs of staff can often be the targets of a "shoot the messenger" sentiment. This can undermine their support among the rest of the White House staff if it is not carefully managed by the president and chief of staff. Part of the downfall of Sherman Adams, H.R. Haldeman, Donald Regan, and John Sununu can be attributed to the fact that when they got into trouble, they had few friends willing to stand by them publicly or privately.

5) *Protect the President from Mistakes and Allow Him to "Blow Off Steam"*   Presidents are human and sometimes react emotionally or make poor decisions. They also occasionally feel the need to say what's on their minds without fear of consequences. Chiefs of staff often serve their presidents by *not* immediately implementing presidential orders. Effectiveness on this score requires a knowledge of the president and thick skin.

This may mean that a chief of staff will come to believe that in certain circumstances he is best serving the president by disobeying orders, even direct orders. H.R. Haldeman (1978) wrote that there were times when President Nixon "had to be protected from himself." (58) Haldeman believed that it was part of his responsibility to ignore "petty vindictive orders" (58) that would occasionally come from Nixon and which, if carried out, would damage the president legally or politically. In fact, Haldeman placed much of the blame for the Watergate scandal on his belief that Chuck Colson "encouraged the dark impulses in Nixon's mind, and *acted* on those impulses instead of ignoring them and letting them die." (59)

Exercising the power to occasionally disobey the president has obvious dangers. Not only is such authority ripe for abuse, it could occur simply through misunderstanding. Haldeman felt he could ignore some of Nixon's orders because he had known the president for several years. Not all chiefs of staff have such extensive experience with their president. Therefore, they should employ this approach only with great caution, and, for the most part, chiefs of staff have done just that.

6) *Soothe Egos and "Manage" Staff Personalities*   In spite of their common interests and desires, presidential aides occasionally come in conflict, both

personally and politically. It can often fall on the chief of staff to see to it that these conflicts remain limited and do not unnecessarily interfere with White House operations or take up the president's time and attention. Some conflicts, like the Brzezinski-Vance conflict of the Carter Administration (Kernell and Popkin, 1986) or the Kissinger-Rogers conflict of the Nixon Administration (Haldeman, 1994), are too large or too important for the chief of staff to handle alone, but others can be managed to a large extent without requiring the president's attention, and these are the chief of staff's responsibility.

The ability to perform this task adroitly has become increasingly valued in recent White Houses. Early chiefs of staff were not known for their personal sensitivity. They had to deal with these internal conflicts, just as later chiefs of staff have done, but they were typically less subtle in their approaches. However, in the wake of the successes of James Baker and Leon Panetta and the failures of Adams, Haldeman, Regan, and Sununu, look for future presidents to display a greater appreciation for interpersonal skills when making their choice of chief of staff.

7) *Occasionally Take the President's Case to the American People* Samuel Kernell (1986) perceptively noted the tendency of recent presidents to take their cases to the people more often than in the past. As presidents have increasingly made arguments directly to the American people, they have expected their staffs to aid in this endeavor by representing the president in the media. As a result, chiefs of staff have become increasingly visible media figures. Recent chiefs of staff appear more frequently on public affairs talk shows and are more likely to be quoted in magazine and newspaper articles, especially "on background," than their predecessors.

While contrary to the Brownlowian "passion for anonymity," this increased public exposure appears to have become an unavoidable part of the job, but it can be a double-edged sword. The increased visibility of the chief of staff has increased the position's power, but it also has made him more vulnerable to attacks by those unwilling to attack the president directly.

Conclusion

The office of White House chief of staff is a relatively new position in the White House. It has only been around for a half century. Its responsibilities include: coordinating the activities of various White House units and staff; guarding the president's time; serving as an "honest broker" in policy debates; bearing bad news and playing the heavy; managing the egos and personalities of the White House; protecting the president, both from others and from himself; and occasionally speaking publicly for the president. The development of the position of chief of staff was precipitated by the rapid growth in the Institutional Presidency, the increased implementation capacity of the White House, and the general expansion in the role of the national government in modern American society.

The result of all these changes is that the chief of staff position is one of considerable power in the modern White House, and that worries many students of the presidency (and a seemingly endless number of Hollywood screenwriters who

concoct the most fanciful Machiavellian scenarios involving the chief of staff—
"The West Wing" excepted). Pfiffner (1993) argued that the strong or "domineering" chief of staff is potentially the most dangerous incarnation of the position. He
contended that there are two lessons to be learned from the experiences of recent
presidents. First, "a chief of staff is essential in the modern White House." (77) Second, "a domineering chief of staff will almost certainly lead to trouble." (77)

Buchanan (1991) examined the experience of one recent "strong" chief of
staff, Donald Regan. His experience led Buchanan to several conclusions. First, a
strong chief of staff will inevitably alienate other participants in the policy process
and this will undermine his credibility as an honest broker. More broadly, the
chief of staff's responsibilities call for a man or woman with many skills. This suggests to Buchanan that it may be asking too much to find one person to carry out
all of these tasks. According to Buchanan, "'great' chiefs of staff—those who can
either do it all themselves or effectively and impartially direct others who do it—
may be no less difficult to locate than great presidents." (98)

However, the experiences of President Carter's chiefs of staff, Hamilton Jordan
and Jack Watson, and President Clinton's first chief of staff, "Mack" McClarty, argue
the opposite conclusion. Weak chiefs of staff cannot bring order and coherence to
White House operations and, therefore, can seriously undermine presidential
efforts, perhaps to the same degree or even worse than strong chiefs of staff.

This paradox suggests that it is incumbent upon presidents to do a number of
things. First, they must give their chiefs of staff enough authority to carry out their
considerable responsibilities. Second, they must take great care in appointing to
the position of chief of staff a person of considerable skill. Finally, presidents
must take an active role in the management of the White House but not so active
as to undermine the chief of staff's ability to carry out his duties.

The astute reader will identify a great irony in this. The chief of staff position
was created to help relieve the burden on presidents of managing the White
House. For the most part, chiefs of staff have done exactly that. However, presidents still must actively involve themselves in the management of the White
House because their fates are in many ways linked to the fortunes of their chiefs
of staff. In the minds of many observers, a failing chief of staff is a failing White
House. A failing White House is a failing president. And a failing president will
have great difficulty getting reelected. Thus, it is fair to conclude that the Brownlow Committee was partially correct. It warned high presidential aides that they
were "assistants to the president," not "assistant presidents," but they forgot to
warn presidents that assistants to the president were no substitute for the president the American people elected.

WORKS CITED

Ayres, Q. Whitfield (1984) "The Carter White House Staff." In Abernathy, Hill, and
Williams (eds.), *The Carter Years*. Frances Pinter Publishers. London.

Buchanan, Bruce (1991) In *The Managerial Presidency*. J. Pfiffner (ed.) Brooks/Cole
Publishing Company. Pacific Grove, CA.

Cohen, David B. and George A. Krause (2000) "Presidents, Chiefs of Staff, and White House Organizational Behavior: Survey Evidence from the Reagan and Bush Administrations." *Presidential Studies Quarterly;* 30:3. 421–442.

_____ (1978) *The Ends of Power.* With Joseph Dimona. NY Times Book Company, Inc. New York.

Haldeman, H. Robert (1994) *The Haldeman Diaries: Inside the Nixon White House.* G.P. Putnam's Sons. New York.

Hart, John (1987) The Presidential Branch. Pergamon Press. New York.

Kernell, Samuel (1986) *Going Public: New Strategies of Presidential Leadership.* CQ Press. Washington, D.C.

Kernell, Samuel and Samuel L. Popkin (eds.) (1986) *Chief of Staff: Twenty-Five Years of Managing the Presidency.* University of California Press. Berkeley, CA.

Moe, Terry (1985) "The Politicized Presidency." In *The New Direction in American Politics.* J. Chubb and P. Peterson (eds.) The Brookings Institution. Washington, D.C.

Patterson, Bradley (1988) *The Ring of Power.* Basic: New York.

Patterson, Bradley (2000) *The White House Staff.* The Brookings Institution. Washington, D.C.

Pfiffner, James P. (1991) *The Managerial Presidency.* Brooks/Cole Publishing Company. Pacific Grove, CA.

_____ (1993) "The President's Chief of Staff: Lessons Learned." *Presidential Studies Quarterly;* Winter 1993, 77–102.

Ragsdale, Lyn (1998) *Vital Statistics on the Presidency: Washington to Clinton.* Congressional Quarterly, Inc. Washington, D.C.

Ragsdale, Lyn and John J. Theis, III (1997) "The Institutionalization of the American Presidency, 1924–92" *American Journal of Political Science;* 41:4. 1280–1318.

Rockman, Bert. (1988) "The Style and Organization of the Reagan Presidency." In Jones (ed.), *The Reagan Legacy.* Chatham House. New Jersey.

White House 2001 Project: The White House Interview Program: Report No. 21 (2000) "The Chief of Staff" C. Walcott, S.A. Warshaw, and S. Wayne. Released Dec. 17, 2000 (see http://whitehouse2001.org).

10

THE PRESIDENT
AND CONGRESS

The President in a More Partisan Legislative Arena

Richard Fleisher,
Fordham University

Jon R. Bond,
Texas A&M University

This article updates our previous analysis of presidential success from 1953 to 1984 (Bond and Fleisher 1990) to see how increased partisanship in the House since 1985 has altered presidential-congressional relations. We analyze support from the four party factions in Congress (liberal Democrats, conservative Democrats, liberal Republicans, and conservative Republicans) and the types of coalitions that formed on presidential votes in the House. The results present a mixed picture of how elevated partisanship altered the nature of presidential-congressional relations. We found an increase in the tendency for partisan coalitions to form under recent minority presidents. This tendency, however, did not continue under unified government in the 103rd Congress. The analysis of presidential success rates under different coalitional structures provides more evidence that increased partisanship has altered presidential-congressional relations. Reagan in his second term and Bush lost more often than previous minority presidents when partisan coalitions formed. In contrast, Clinton won more party votes than previous majority presidents. Although the literature leads us to expect minority presidents to be more successful with ideological and bipartisan coalitions, we find that Reagan and Bush lost more often than previous minority presidents when the House divided on the basis of ideology or when the party bases acted in a bipartisan fashion.

Note: We wish to thank the Department of Political Science and the Center for Presidential Studies at Texas A&M University, and the Graduate School of Arts and Sciences at Fordham University for the support provided for this study. The data for 1985 through 1994 are from LEGI-SLATE. None of these organizations bears responsibility for the interpretations and conclusions reported here. We owe special thanks to Stephen Hanna for his indefatigable assistance in retrieving the information we needed from LEGI-SLATE and for constructing the data sets in a way that we could use them. We are also grateful to Glen Krutz, Jeff Talbert, Frank Baumgartner, and Asgar Zardkoohi for advice at various stages of this project.

A previous analysis of presidential-congressional relations found that, even after controlling for the ideological diversity of American parties, party discipline on presidential issues fell far short of that in disciplined party systems (Bond and Fleisher 1990: chap. 4). The evidence supporting this finding is based on an analysis of presidential success on roll-call votes from 1953 through 1984. During the mid-1980s, about the time that analysis ended, Congress—especially the House—became a more partisan institution. This article extends the analysis of presidential success through the end of 1994 (to include Reagan's second term, Bush, and the first two years of Clinton's term) to see how elevated partisanship in the House affected presidential-congressional relations. In particular, we seek to determine if there have been shifts in the types of coalitions that form on presidential votes, and how different coalitional structures affect the success of majority and minority party presidents.

The next section summarizes our predispositions model of presidential-congressional relations, discusses the causes of increased partisanship in Congress, and offers hypotheses about the effects of increased partisanship. The second section describes the research design and measures. The third section reports findings on trends in presidential success, the size and behavior of the four party factions (liberal Democrats, conservative Democrats, liberal Republicans, and conservative Republicans), changes in the types of coalitions that formed on presidential roll calls, and levels of success associated with various coalitions. To see the effects of increased partisanship, we compare patterns in the less partisan period from 1953–84 with those in the more partisan period after 1985. The final section offers conclusions.

Literature and Theory

A Predispositions Model Our theory of presidential-congressional relations is based on a predispositions model of congressional behavior. On any conflictual issue, members of Congress are predisposed to take one side or the other. Although each member's political predispositions vary along a number of dimensions, party and ideology have been shown to be among the most important (Kingdon 1981). When the president takes a position, the coalition that forms reflects choices made by members with different partisan and ideological predispositions.

When members cast roll-call votes on controversial issues, they are motivated by (1) their own partisan and ideological predispositions; (2) constituency interests; and (3) other actors both in and out of government, including party leaders, committee leaders, staff, state delegations, interest groups, bureaucrats, and the president's position and his activities to influence their vote. Note that the president's position is only one of several competing cues, and the president is seldom the dominant influence in members' decision-making calculus. Research on congressional behavior clearly establishes party, ideology, and constituency as the dominant forces (Jackson 1974; Matthews and Stimson 1975; Kingdon 1981).

On most issues, members do not experience conflict between constituency interests and their own predispositions because they share constituency values or the constituency is indifferent. But some members do experience frequent conflict between party and ideology. Both parties in Congress are characterized by ideological diversity. The interaction of party and ideology fragments each party into two factions: the Democratic party has a mainstream faction of liberals and a smaller cross-pressured faction of conservatives; the Republican party has a mainstream faction of conservatives and a small cross-pressured faction of liberals. Because partisan and ideological values are reinforcing for some members and conflicting for others, the strength of predispositions vary across members.

The effects of predispositions show up clearly on presidential issues. With few exceptions, presidents are selected from the ideological mainstream of their party; presidential positions are generally compatible with the preferences of the mainstream faction of their party in Congress. Hence, in analyzing presidential-congressional relations, it is useful to orient the party factions in terms of how the interaction of party and ideology affects members' predisposition to support or oppose the president. The president's party base is the mainstream faction of his party; these members have the greatest predisposition to support presidential positions because they share with the president both a party affiliation and an ideological outlook. Cross-pressured members—conservative Democrats and liberal Republicans—have ideological orientations outside their party mainstreams; these members are often cross-pressured on presidential roll calls because party pushes them in one direction while ideology pulls in the other. The opposition party base is the other party's mainstream faction; these members have the least predisposition to support presidential positions because they share neither a party affiliation nor an ideological orientation with the president.

A presidential position occupies a point in a partisan-ideological space. Members' partisan and ideological predispositions determine how close they are to the president's position in that space. Hence, the coalition that forms on a presidential vote reflects choices made by members with different partisan and ideological predispositions that vary not only in content (Democrat vs. Republican, liberal vs. conservative) but also in strength (mainstream predispositions vs. cross-pressured predispositions). Because presidential positions are typically closest to the preferences of their party's mainstream, support from the president's party base is the highest and most consistent; support from the opposition base is the lowest and least consistent; and support from cross-pressured members of both parties is in between the two bases (Bond and Fleisher 1990: chap. 4).

Presidents, however, often cannot win with votes only from their base. The president's base seldom constitutes a majority. Moreover, because members of Congress have different institutional perspectives, even members who are predisposed to support the president may fail to do so. To win, the president typically needs votes from members who are less inclined to support him. The dilemma is that there are trade-offs: if the president takes positions that appeal to factions outside his base, he risks alienating his core supporters.

Predispositions in a More Partisan Congress   Congress, especially the House, became a more partisan institution in the mid-1980s. The new-found party unity resulted from changes within the institution and in the electoral arena.

First, congressional reforms in the mid-1970s gave the party mainstreams the tools to foster party unity. Both Republicans and Democrats adopted reforms between 1971 and 1973 that made committee leaders subject to a vote of the party caucus. The defeat of several senior House committee chairs in the 1970s and 1980s demonstrated that the Democratic caucus would use its power to hold unresponsive committee chairs accountable. These reforms weakened the seniority system and obliged committee chairs to be more responsive to the wishes of the Democratic caucus (Rohde 1991).

Second, electoral forces in the states and districts reduced the differences between the constituencies of southern and northern Democrats. With more similar electoral interests, the ideological heterogeneity of congressional Democrats decreased (Rohde 1991; Fleisher, 1993). Congressional Republicans, pushed by extremely conservative presidents and a new generation of obdurate congressional leaders, shifted to the right and became less willing to compromise on the Republican agenda.

Evidence of increased partisanship in the House appeared after the 1982 midterm elections. By the start of Reagan's second term in 1985, the trend toward greater partisanship was clearly established (Ornstein, Mann, and Malbin 1994: 191, 200). Hence, we use 1985 as the cut point between the less partisan and more partisan periods.[1]

Hypotheses The heightened partisan atmosphere in the House leads us to expect some changes in presidential-congressional relations:

1. Minority presidents who served after 1985 (i.e., Reagan in his second term and Bush) should have lower success rates than minority presidents who faced a less partisan House; majority presidents, in contrast, benefit from increased partisanship, so Clinton's success rate in 1993–94 should be higher than other majority presidents.

2. Elevated partisanship suggests that the number of cross-pressured members in both parties should shrink in the period after 1985.

3. As congressional behavior becomes more partisan, presidential support from both factions of the president's party should increase, while support from both factions of the opposition should decrease.

4. The level of partisanship in Congress might affect the trade-offs the president faces, and hence, the types of coalitions that form. In less partisan Congresses, we expect more bipartisan, ideological, and reverse-partisan coalitions; as partisan predispositions strengthened after 1985, party coalitions should be more prevalent.

Research Design

Units of Analysis We analyze presidential victories and defeats on roll-call votes in Congress. The unit of analysis is the roll-call vote. The data base is all conflictual roll calls in the House on which the president expressed a position. A

---

[1]The results of a Chow test suggest that 1985 is the most appropriate cut point. The difference in trends before and after 1985 is significant at the .01 level (Chow's $F = 7.11$), while the trends before and after 1981 ($F = 2.98$) and 1983 ($F = 3.61$) are less distinctive.

conflictual roll call is defined as one on which less than 80 percent vote in agreement with the president's position. This research design allows us to analyze variation in presidential wins and losses, as well as variation in levels of presidential support from the four party factions across roll-call votes. Presidential positions on roll calls are identified by Congressional Quarterly (*Congressional Quarterly Almanac* 1953–95).

A floor vote, of course, is only one of several decision points in the legislative process. Although important interactions between the president and Congress occur earlier in the process, the floor vote is certainly one important point. The ebb and flow of presidential success on roll-call votes is a critical component of presidential-congressional relations.

Identification of Party Factions   To control for the ideological diversity of American parties, students of presidential-congressional relations often divide members along regional lines: many conservative Democrats are from the south; many liberal Republicans are from the northeast. Region, however, is an imprecise indicator of ideology. Furthermore, southern Democrats have become more like their northern colleagues (Rohde 1991; Fleisher 1993), and conservative Democrats are no longer exclusively from the south (Bond and Fleisher 1995). We have the ability to measure ideological predispositions more precisely to identify cross-pressured members regardless of the region from which they come.

Indexes calculated by the Americans for Democratic Action (a liberal group) and Americans for Constitutional Action or American Conservative Union (conservative groups) are frequently used indicators of general ideology. Although these indexes are generally reliable and valid proxies of members' ideology (Smith, Herrera, and Herrera 1990; Herrera, Epperlein, and Smith 1995), using them to analyze presidential-congressional relations is problematic because some votes used in the indexes are also presidential roll calls used to gauge presidential success. To minimize this circularity, we purged votes on which the president expressed a position from the list of ideological votes selected by ADA and ACA or ACU,[2] and recalculated liberalism scores for all members of Congress from 1953–94.

We use votes selected by two ideological groups to (1) identify a subset of roll calls that evoke a liberal/conservative division on the floor, and (2) determine a priori what the "liberal" position is. A liberal position is defined as voting in agreement with the ADA position or against the ACA/ACU position. Although each group selects between 10 and 20 votes per year in each chamber, eliminating those on which the president takes a position reduces the number of usable ideological votes. We use votes selected by two groups and calculate scores over the two years of each Congress to have enough votes on which to base a stable ideology score for members of Congress.[3]

---

[2]ADA votes are used for the entire time series. ACA votes are available from 1958 to 1984. After 1984, ACU votes are used.

[3]We adopted a standard of at least 10 votes. Only in the 87th (1961–62) and 88th (1963–64) Congresses were there less than 10 ADA and ACA votes on which the president did not express a position. In these Congresses, we had no choice but to supplement the list with Conservative Coalition votes on which the president did not take a position.

The mean liberalism score for each party defines the party mainstreams in the chamber. Cross-pressured members are defined as those who have liberalism scores closer to the mean of the opposition party than to the mean of their party.[4] For each presidential vote, we recorded the level of support from each party faction. Thus, we can observe differences in presidential support from each party faction across the sample of roll calls.

Coalitions on Presidential Votes   From the perspective of our predispositions model, different types of coalitions may form by combining two or more of the four factions. We adopt a majority threshold to define the behavior of a faction, and place each presidential vote into one of three general categories: (1) Partisan Coalitions; (2) Bipartisan Coalitions; and (3) Reverse-partisan Coalitions. The behavior of the party bases determines the basic nature of a coalition.

A Partisan Coalition is defined as a vote on which a majority of the president's base support his position, while a majority of opposition base oppose. The behavior of the cross-pressured factions modifies the degree to which a partisan coalition is purely partisan, purely ideological, or mixed. Hence, we identify four varieties of partisan coalitions:

1. Pure Partisan Coalition—a majority of members in each of the president's party factions support the president's position, while a majority of members in each of the opposing party factions oppose it.

2. Ideological Coalition—a majority of the president's base plus a majority of cross-pressured opponents vote with the president, while a majority of the opposition base and the cross-pressured members of the president's party vote against him.

3. Three-versus-one Coalition—the president's base and both cross-pressured factions support the president, while the opposition base stands alone against him.

4. One-versus-three Coalition—the president's base stands alone in support of the president, while the opposition base and both cross-pressured factions oppose him.

Bipartisan Coalitions occur when a majority of members in each party's base vote the same way—either in support of or against the president's position. Since the bases comprise the dominant faction of each party, we do not consider the behavior of the cross-pressured factions in defining bipartisanship: any time the party bases take the same position is evidence of bipartisan behavior even if the cross-pressured factions vote differently.[5]

---

[4]Some might prefer using the party medians. Either measure of central tendency produces similar classifications of members. The means and medians are close, and the mid-points between them similar (Bond and Fleisher 1990; 85). During the period from 1985 to 1994, for example, only 10 cases out of over 2000 (435 members X 5 Congresses) would have been classified differently using the median.

[5]It is important to distinguish between bipartisan and consensual or universal coalitions. We have excluded consensual votes from the analysis, because all but a small number of them involve routine or less important issues. The bipartisan coalitions in our analysis are those that involve some conflict—at least 20 percent of those voting oppose the president's position.

Finally, we observe some cases of Reverse-Partisan Coalitions in which a majority of the president's base oppose the president's position, while a majority of the opposition base support it. Although reverse-partisan coalitions could be divided into different types, the small number of such coalitions makes creating sub-categories problematic.

Findings

Presidential Success   Table 1 shows presidential success from 1953 to 1994. In the American system, majority presidents benefit from increased partisanship, but minority presidents do not. In the less partisan era from 1953 to 1984, majority pres-

TABLE 1
PRESIDENTIAL VICTORIES ON ROLL-CALL VOTES, 1953–1994

President and year	All votes				Conflictual votes			
	House		Senate		House		Senate	
	%	(N)	%	(N)	%	(N)	%	(N)
DDE								
1953	91.2	(34)	87.8	(49)	88.5	(26)	84.6	(39)
1954	78.9	(38)	77.9	(77)	61.9	(21)	72.1	(61)
1955	63.4	(41)	84.6	(52)	44.4	(27)	68.0	(25)
1956	73.5	(34)	67.7	(65)	55.0	(20)	61.1	(54)
1957	58.3	(60)	78.9	(57)	47.9	(48)	69.2	(39)
1958	74.0	(50)	76.5	(98)	65.8	(38)	69.3	(75)
1959	55.6	(54)	50.4	(121)	45.5	(44)	35.5	(93)
1960	65.1	(43)	65.1	(86)	61.5	(39)	55.9	(68)
Mean	68.4		70.7		57.4		61.0	
JFK								
1961	83.1	(65)	80.8	(125)	78.0	(50)	77.4	(106)
1962	85.0	(60)	84.9	(126)	79.1	(43)	79.6	(93)
1963	83.1	(71)	88.8	(116)	77.8	(54)	84.5	(84)
Mean	83.7		84.7		78.2		80.2	
LBJ								
1964	88.5	(52)	91.2	(203)	84.6	(39)	90.4	(167)
1965	93.8	(112)	91.9	(162)	90.7	(75)	89.4	(123)
1966	89.4	(104)	68.0	(125)	84.5	(71)	55.1	(89)
1967	75.6	(127)	81.4	(167)	62.2	(82)	71.0	(107)
1968	83.5	(103)	69.1	(165)	72.1	(61)	58.5	(123)
Mean	85.5		81.6		78.0		75.2	
RMN								
1969	72.3	(47)	74.6	(71)	61.8	(34)	64.7	(51)
1970	84.6	(65)	71.4	(91)	73.0	(37)	53.6	(56)
1971	82.1	(56)	69.5	(82)	77.8	(45)	60.3	(63)
1972	81.1	(37)	54.3	(46)	76.7	(30)	38.2	(34)
1973	48.0	(125)	52.4	(185)	38.7	(106)	30.7	(127)
1974	67.9	(53)	54.2	(83)	57.5	(40)	47.2	(72)
Mean	68.1		61.3		58.2		46.4	

(continued)

idents won an average of 75 percent of conflictual House votes, compared to Clinton's 84 percent success rate in the 103rd House. Minority presidents who served before 1985 won an average of 54 percent, whereas the average for Reagan's second term and Bush was only 33 percent. Thus, we have preliminary evidence that increased partisanship has affected presidential-congressional relations in expected ways. We now turn to the composition and behavior of the party factions.

Size of Party Factions   The predispositions model suggests that the relative size of the party factions determines whether the president will interact with a more or less favorable cast of actors in the legislative arena. As Congress becomes

TABLE 1
(concluded)

President	All votes				Conflictual votes			
	House		Senate		House		Senate	
and year	%	(N)	%	(N)	%	(N)	%	(N)
GRF								
1974	59.3	(54)	57.4	(68)	43.6	(39)	44.2	(52)
1975	50.6	(89)	71.6	(95)	43.6	(78)	57.8	(64)
1976	43.1	(51)	64.2	(53)	37.0	(46)	50.0	(38)
Mean	51.0		65.3		41.7		51.3	
JEC								
1977	74.7	(79)	76.4	(89)	66.1	(59)	65.0	(60)
1978	70.2	(114)	84.8	(151)	64.2	(95)	81.6	(125)
1979	71.7	(145)	81.4	(161)	66.4	(122)	75.4	(122)
1980	76.9	(117)	73.3	(116)	69.7	(89)	65.2	(89)
Mean	73.2		79.7		66.6		73.5	
RWR								
1981	72.4	(76)	88.3	(128)	66.7	(63)	82.1	(84)
1982	55.8	(77)	82.5	(120)	41.4	(58)	77.7	(94)
1983	47.6	(82)	85.7	(84)	46.3	(80)	82.6	(69)
1984	52.2	(113)	85.7	(77)	44.3	(97)	81.0	(58)
1985	45.0	(80)	71.6	(102)	43.4	(66)	65.5	(84)
1986	33.3	(90)	82.3	(79)	32.4	(71)	77.4	(62)
1987	33.3	(99)	56.4	(78)	28.3	(56)	30.0	(56)
1988	32.7	(104)	54.8	(88)	22.8	(91)	43.6	(55)
Mean	46.5		75.9		40.7		67.5	
GHWB								
1989	49.4	(85)	73.3	(101)	43.2	(74)	59.1	(66)
1990	33.3	(105)	66.3	(80)	30.0	(90)	58.9	(73)
1001	43.2	(111)	69.1	(81)	32.3	(93)	59.7	(62)
1992	37.1	(105)	54.2	(59)	33.3	(99)	45.8	(49)
Mean	40.8		65.7		34.7		55.9	
WJC								
1993	86.3	(102)	85.4	(89)	84.4	(90)	82.7	(76)
1994	87.2	(78)	85.5	(62)	83.3	(60)	80.4	(46)
Mean	86.7		85.5		83.9		81.0	

more partisan, we expect a decrease in the size of the cross-pressured factions. Table 2 shows the number of members in each of the four party factions in the House from the 83rd (1953–54) through the 103rd Congresses (1993–94).

We see that the cross-pressured faction in each party has diminished considerably since the end of Reagan's first term. Congresses from 1953 through 1984 contained an average of 61 conservative Democrats and 27 liberal Republicans. In the more partisan Congresses since 1985, the size of both cross-pressured factions has been cut by more than half: an average of 29 House Democrats and 12 House

TABLE 2
NUMBER OF MEMBERS IN THE PARTY FACTIONS IN THE HOUSE

President and Congress	President's base	Cross-pressured partisans	Cross-pressured opposition	Opposition base
DDE				
83rd	*201*	*19*	*43*	*170*
84th	129	74	74	157
85th	178	22	37	196
86th	141	12	33	248
JFK				
87th	*188*	*74*	*31*	*143*
88th	*166*	*90*	*32*	*146*
LBJ				
89th	*203*	*91*	*19*	*121*
90th	*180*	*65*	*16*	*173*
RMN				
91st	160	31	81	162
92nd	146	34	75	179
93rd	157	35	62	180
GRF				
94th	120	22	68	224
JEC				
95th	*223*	*66*	*21*	*124*
96th	*230*	*45*	*16*	*143*
RWR				
97th	168	24	51	191
98th	150	17	25	242
99th	164	18	29	224
100th	158	20	22	236
GHWB				
101st	163	15	37	223
102nd	159	8	20	248
WJC				
103rd	*222*	*36*	*1*	*176*

Note: Entries are number of members in each party faction. Numbers may not sum to the total for the chamber because of vacancies. Majority presidents [numbers] in italic.

Republicans had ideology scores closer to the mean of the opposite party. Indeed, the number of cross-pressured Republicans all but disappeared in the 103rd Congress, with only one Republican (Constance Morella of Maryland) having an ideology score closer to the Democratic mean than to that of her own party.

Another notable change is in the relative size of the Democratic majority base. In the less partisan era, the Democratic majority base rarely exceed 218 members, a majority of the chamber. From the 98th Congress to the 103rd Congress, the Democratic base, if it was unified, has been large enough to control the House floor.

The interaction of several forces altered the composition of the congressional parties. Changes in the type of Democrat elected to Congress, especially from the South, the resurgence of the Democratic caucus, a decade of increasingly acrimonious partisan conflict, and a marked shift in the ideological center of the Republican party all contributed to a much smaller number of cross-pressured members.[6]

Support from the Party Factions   Although the interaction of party and ideology creates different predispositions to support the president, American political parties are undisciplined. A previous analysis found that the party factions generally behaved as predicted by the predispositions model: the president's base was most supportive; the opposition base was least supportive; and both cross-pressured factions provided similar levels of support in between that of the bases. But except for the behavior of liberal Democrats under Kennedy and Johnson, support from the party bases fell far short of levels common in disciplined party systems (Bond and Fleisher 1990: chap. 4). In the more partisan period after 1985, we expect the party bases to behave more like responsible parties. And as party pressures increase, we expect higher levels of support from the president's cross-pressured partisans and less from the cross-pressured opposition.

Table 3 shows average levels of presidential support from each party faction. We see that levels of support are still broadly consistent with the predictions of the predispositions model, but there is only limited evidence of increased partisanship.

The behavior of House Democrats has become somewhat more partisan since 1985. Although support from the Democratic base is higher for Clinton than for Carter, it still falls far below the levels for Kennedy and Johnson. But liberal Democrats have become more partisan in opposition to Republican presidents since 1985: the average level of support from liberal Democrats during Reagan's second term and the Bush regime was only 20 percent compared to about 35 percent, for earlier Republican presidents. Conservative Democrats also have become somewhat

---

[6]The midpoint between the two party means was typically between 48 percent and 52 percent, but in the 103rd House (1993–94) the midpoint was 40 percent. We were concerned that this rightward shift in the midpoint might add additional error to the measure of party factions, because a lower liberal score is required to place Democrats in the mainstream faction and to place Republicans in the cross-pressured faction. If the lower cut point resulted in such systematic error, then relative to Congresses with higher cut points, there would be fewer cross-pressured Democrats and more cross-pressured Republicans. The shift in the midpoint, however, is not associated with such a change in the number of cross-pressured members. In fact, there were fewer cross-pressured Democrats and more cross-pressured Republicans in the 102nd Congress in which the midpoint between the party means was 51 percent.

TABLE 3
AVERAGE PERCENTAGE OF HOUSE PARTY FACTIONS SUPPORTING THE PRESIDENT

President	President's base	Cross-pressured partisans	Cross-pressured opposition	Opposition base	(N)
DDE I *(83rd)*	74	68	37	43	*(47)*
DDE I (84th)	57	67	30	42	*(47)*
DDE II	61	63	29	47	*(169)*
JFK	90	52	46	23	*(135)*
LBJ	87	42	57	23	*(340)*
RMN I	67	60	52	41	*(145)*
RMN II	66	49	50	27	*(146)*
GRF	64	49	48	28	*(161)*
JEC	69	38	56	26	*(363)*
RWR I	67	45	53	26	*(296)*
RWR II	65	36	44	19	*(339)*
GHWB	71	41	48	21	*(364)*
WJC *(103rd)*	76	66	71[a]	36	*(150)*

Note: Entries are the average percentage of faction members voting in agreement with the president's position on conflictual House roll-call votes. Majority president [initials] in bold.
[a]Only one member.

more partisan: Clinton received more support from conservative Democrats than any previous Democratic president, and conservative Democrats were slightly less supportive of Reagan in his second term and Bush than they were before 1985.

Evidence of increased partisanship among House Republicans is more limited. Although Bush received higher levels of support from conservative Republicans than any other minority president, the increase was modest: an average of 71 percent supported Bush compared to an average of 64 percent for other minority presidents. The Republican base gave Reagan only average support during his second term. Liberal Republicans became slightly less supportive of Republican presidents in the recent period than they were earlier. And in the role of opposition party base, conservative Republicans appear less partisan in the recent period: whereas Democratic presidents before 1985 typically got the support of about one-fourth of the Republican base, Clinton received an average of 36 percent in the 103rd Congress.

Looking at support from each faction individually, however, provides an incomplete picture of partisanship. Understanding partisan behavior requires analysis of the joint actions of the party factions as they form coalitions.

How Often Different Types of Coalitions Form   To see if coalition formation on presidential issues changed as the House became more partisan, we observed the type of coalition that appeared on each conflictual House vote from 1953 to 1994. Table 4 presents the percentage of votes on which each type of coalition formed during each presidential administration. Because majority and minority presidents face different opportunities and constraints, we compare the types of coalitions that appeared for majority and minority presidents before and after 1985.

TABLE 4

HOW OFTEN VARIOUS TYPES OF COALITIONS APPEARED

President	Partisan coalitions					Bipartisan	Reverse-partisan	(N)
	Pure party	Ideological	3 vs. 1	1 vs. 3	Total			
DDE (83rd)	30	11	9	0	50	38	13	47
DDE (84th)	34	0	2	4	40	28	32	47
DDE II	21	8	5	5	39	34	27	169
JFK	31	18	17	16	82	16	2	135
LBJ	19	35	10	14	78	19	2	340
RMN I	8	26	19	3	53	32	15	145
RMN II	8	25	19	8	60	30	10	146
GRF	7	21	20	12	60	25	16	161
JEC	7	38	12	14	71	22	9	363
RWR I	4	19	23	17	63	31	7	296
RWR II	4	18	19	24	65	29	6	339
GHWB	12	25	19	16	72	24	5	364
WJC (103rd)	48	18	NA[a]	NA[a]	66	19	15	150
MAJ (PRE 85)	17	32	12	13	74	21	5	885
MAJ (POST 85)	48	18	NA[a]	NA[a]	66	19	15	150
MIN (PRE 85)	10	18	17	10	55	30	15	963
MIN (POST 85)	8	22	19	20	69	27	5	703

Note: Entries are the percentage of conflictual votes on which each type of coalition formed. Majority presidents [numbers] in italic.

[a]NA means not appropriate. Because only one Republican member was cross-pressured in the 103rd Congress, we ignore this faction, and identify partisan coalitions based on the behavior of only three factions. If calculated with this one-person faction, the figures would be Pure Party = 11%; Ideological = 12%; 3 vs. 1 = 37%; 1 vs. 3 = 5%.

Looking first at majority party presidents, we find that partisan coalitions (of all varieties) were less likely to form under Clinton than under any other majority president except Eisenhower—66 percent of votes in the 103rd Congress were some type of partisan coalition, compared to an average of 74 percent for previous majority presidents.[7] The formation of partisan coalitions under Clinton lagged considerably below that of Kennedy or Johnson. And although the late 1970s are typically thought of as a less partisan period, partisan coalitions were more likely to form under Carter than under Clinton.

[7]Although it appears that pure party coalitions were considerably more likely to form under Clinton than under earlier majority presidents, interpretation of this result should be cautious. Since there was only one cross-pressured Republican in the 103rd Congress, identifying the different types of party coalitions is problematical. Regardless of how one treats this one-person faction, the results are distorted. The figures in the table ignore this one-member faction. With only three factions, we cannot identify three-versus-one and one-versus-three votes, which inflates the apparent percentage of pure party and ideological votes. But using the votes of this one liberal Republican as the cross-pressured Republican faction, inflates the percentage of three-versus-one votes. We report the results both ways for readers who are interested, but we rely more on the total of all types of partisan coalitions for interpretations of the 103rd Congress.

The data reveal a different picture of partisanship under minority presidents. Partisan coalitions (of all varieties) were more likely to form during Reagan's second term and Bush's administration than under previous minority presidents. Note, however, that the rise of partisan coalitions was gradual rather than an abrupt change in the mid-1980s: partisan coalitions increased from about 40 percent under Eisenhower, to 50 percent under Nixon, to 60 percent under Nixon/Ford, to 63 percent in Reagan's first term, to 65 percent in Reagan's second term, to 72 percent under Bush.

As noted . . . , the nature of partisan coalitions varies depending on the behavior of the cross-pressured factions. Ideological coalitions and those on which both cross-pressured factions oppose the president (columns two and four) provide an indication of factional disagreement in the president's party. Combining instances when the president failed to receive majority support from both factions of his party, we find signs of a decline in party splits in the Democratic party in recent years. Democratic presidents before Clinton failed to receive support from conservative Democrats on an average of 45 percent of votes; in 1993–94, Clinton failed to get support from conservative Democrats less than 20 percent of the time. This finding suggests that ideological conflict was much less likely to split House Democrats under Clinton than during previous Democratic administrations.

Looking at the Republican factions under Republican presidents, we find evidence of increasing disagreement between mainstream and cross-pressured Republicans. In the period before 1985, liberal Republicans voted against the Republican base on 28 percent of presidential roll calls; during Reagan's second term and under Bush, liberal Republicans split from the party on 42 percent of roll calls. It is important to keep in mind, however, that the number of cross-pressured Republicans dropped considerably during the mid-1980s (see Table 2).

Table 4 also shows how often bipartisan coalitions formed. Bipartisan coalitions form more often under divided government than under unified government. But bipartisanship was no more common before 1985 than after, for either majority or minority presidents.

Finally, we look at reverse-partisan coalitions. Although these are partisan votes, the president's position attracted support from the opposition base and lost most of his own party base. Here Clinton stands out from the other Democratic presidents. On 15 percent of conflictual roll calls, Clinton took positions that resulted in a reverse-partisan coalition, compared to 9 percent under Carter and 2 percent under Kennedy and Johnson.

Since Clinton's record of attracting reverse-partisan support in a more partisan House stands out, we decided to look at the types of issues on which such coalitions formed. Reverse-partisan coalitions were more likely to occur on foreign affairs, trade, and defense issues than on domestic issues: a reverse-partisan coalition formed on 36 percent (17 of 47) of Clinton foreign and defense votes, compared to only 6 percent (6 of 103) of domestic votes.

A possible explanation for this finding is that Clinton took more conservative positions on foreign and defense issues than on domestic issues. To test this possibility, we used ADA and ACU votes on which Clinton took a position to calculate a presidential ideology score.[8] Overall, Clinton took a liberal position (i.e., agreed with ADA or disagreed with ACU) 76 percent of the time in 1993–94. But the difference between Clinton's ideology score across policy categories is enormous: on domestic votes, Clinton took the liberal position 96 percent of the time (27 of 28); on foreign and defense issues, Clinton took the liberal position only 12.5 percent of the time (1 of 8). Clearly, the perception of Bill Clinton as a mainstream, liberal Democrat is accurate only to the water's edge.

Under divided government, the frequency of reverse-party coalitions declined over time. Compared to minority presidents who served before 1985, Reagan and Bush were less likely to support the position of liberal Democrats in opposition to conservative Republicans.

Looking at how often different coalitions form provides insights about the effects of increased partisanship on presidential-congressional relations. The more important question, however, is whether presidential success rates under different coalitions has changed.

Presidential Success under Different Coalitions   Table 5 shows presidential success rates when the various types of coalitions formed. Recall that recent minority presidents were defeated on the House floor at a much higher rate than was the case for previous minority presidents, while Clinton was more successful than the average majority president (see Table 1). The data in Table 5 permit us to see the types of coalitions associated with presidential success and failure in the House.

Not surprisingly, majority party presidents are usually successful when some type of partisan coalition emerges on the floor of the House, while such coalitions usually spell defeat for minority party presidents. Among minority party presidents, only Nixon in his first term won more often than he lost when the House divided along party lines. The number of cross-pressured conservative Democrats was relatively large during Nixon's first term, suggesting that many of these victories may have occurred on ideological votes on which conservatives prevailed. We will consider this possibility shortly.

Party coalitions seem to affect the success rates of both majority and minority presidents more after 1985. Clinton's success rate on party votes was 11 points higher than the mean for previous majority presidents; the success rate on party votes during Reagan's second term and Bush's time in office was 16 points lower than the mean for previous minority presidents.

Students of Congress frequently emphasize the importance of ideological coalitions. Some research suggests that minority Republican presidents can succeed with a conservative coalition, while Democratic presidents are often frustrated by the conservative coalition (Brady and Bullock 1980; Frymer 1994; Manley 1970; Shelley 1983).

---

[8]These are the votes eliminated from the lists used to calculate ideology scores for members of Congress.

TABLE 5

PRESIDENTIAL SUCCESS UNDER DIFFERENT COALITIONS

President	Pure party	Ideological	3 vs. 1	1 vs. 3	Total	Bipartisan	Reverse-partisan	(N)
			Partisan coalitions					
DDE *(83rd)*	79	100ª	100ª	—	87	83	17	47
DDE (84th)	19	—	100ª	0ª	21	54	80	47
DDE II	29	43	67	0	33	78	56	169
JFK	95	88	100	23	80	81	33	135
LBJ	89	78	94	52	78	74	57	340
RMN I	55	79	89	0ª	74	70	73	145
RMN II	27	35	89	8	48	33	60	146
GRF	27	29	59	11	35	35	76	161
JEC	88	76	100	43	75	42	68	363
RWR I	27	44	81	12	48	39	81	296
RWR II	8	21	73	9	31	20	52	339
GHWB	21	24	68	3	30	35	77	364
WJC *(103rd)*	94	74	NAᵇ	NAᵇ	89	75	74	150
MAJ *(PRE 85)*	90	78	98	43	78	62	57	885
MAJ *(POST 85)*	94	74	NAᵇ	NAᵇ	89	75	74	150
MIN (PRE 85)	30	46	79	10	47	51	69	963
MIN (POST 85)	18	23	71	6	31	27	63	703

Note: Entries are the percentage of presidential victories with each type of coalition. Majority presidents [numbers] in italic.

ᵃPercentages are based on less than five votes.

ᵇNA means not appropriate. Because only one Republican member was cross-pressured in the 103rd Congress, we ignore this faction, and identify partisan coalitions based on the behavior of only three factions. If calculated with this one-person faction, the figures would be Pure Party = 83%; Ideological = 79%; 3 vs. 1 = 98%; 1 vs. 3 = 63%.

The evidence presented in Table 5 suggests otherwise. Democratic presidents prevailed about three-fourths of the time when an ideological coalition formed. Democrats' success rate on ideological votes is not significantly different after 1985.[9]

Minority Republican presidents usually lose when the House divides along ideological lines. Only Nixon during his first term found himself on the winning side of an ideological coalition structure. The level of support Nixon received from conservative Democrats was about average for Republican presidents (see Table 3), but the number of conservative Democrats was relatively large (see Table 2). No other minority party president won as much as half the time when the House divided on the basis of ideology. Note that Reagan's 44 percent success rate on ideological

[9]We should note that our definition of an ideological coalition differs from Congressional Quarterly's "conservative coalition" used in the studies cited. Our definition requiring that a majority in each liberal faction vote against a majority in each conservative faction is more stringent than CQ's definition of a majority of Republicans and southern Democrats voting against a majority of non-southern Democrats. Some of CQ's conservative coalition votes would be three-versus-one and one-versus-three votes under our definition.

votes during his first term is about average for minority presidents who served before 1985. During Reagan's second term and continuing under Bush, ideological coalitions resulted in presidential victories on less than one vote in four.

The most successful partisan coalition for minority party presidents is the three-versus-one—i.e., when they took positions that kept both factions of their own party on board and attracted support from cross-pressured Democrats as well. But recall that such coalitions occur on less than one in five votes (see Table 4).

Although minority presidents do not benefit from ideological coalitions, perhaps bipartisanship might provide a path to victory. Bipartisanship does not guarantee victory, however, because a bipartisan coalition can form either to support or oppose the president. Indeed, we find that bipartisanship usually results in defeat for minority party presidents. Only Eisenhower and Nixon in his first term were successful when bipartisan coalitions formed. Before 1973, both majority and minority presidents won about three of four bipartisan votes. Since 1973, bipartisanship in the House usually meant that both dominant factions opposed a Republican president.

Majority presidents are more successful than minority presidents on bipartisan votes. But majority presidents win more with partisan coalitions. Although Clinton's success on bipartisan votes was higher than previous majority presidents, he was still most successful on partisan votes.

Finally, both minority and majority party presidents won more often than they lost when reverse-party coalitions formed. For minority presidents, supporting the position of the opposition base led to victory about two-thirds of the time in the partisan Congresses after 1985 as well as before. Two caveats temper this observation. First, the frequency that minority party presidents took positions consistent with the Democratic base dropped over time. Second, opposing the dominant faction of his party can lead to later political troubles, as President Bush learned when he sided with the Democratic base on the 1990 budget battle.

Conclusions

Over the past decade, a period spanning three presidencies, we have witnessed a sharp increase in the level of partisan conflict in Congress. Increased partisanship may be seen not only in roll-call voting patterns, but also in congressional deliberations with partisan attacks on the House floor becoming more common and more acrimonious in recent years. Against this backdrop, we investigated how increased partisanship changed the nature of presidential-congressional relations. We expected to find a significant increase in partisan coalitions, resulting in a greater tendency for majority presidents to win and minority presidents to lose.

The findings present a mixed picture. Although the trends in success rates are consistent with expectations, the analysis of coalition formation provides only limited evidence that elevated partisanship has altered presidential-congressional relations. We found an increase in the tendency for partisan coalitions to form under recent minority presidents. This tendency, however, did not continue under unified government in the 103rd Congress. But when partisan coalitions did form, they exerted stronger effects on the success of both majority and minority presidents after 1985, with Clinton being on the winning side of partisan divisions more often, and Reagan and Bush winning less often. Although it is not surprising that minority presidents typically lose party votes, we might expect minority presidents to be more successful with ideological and bipartisan coalitions. But we find that Reagan and Bush lost more often than previous minority presidents when the House divided on the basis of ideology or when the party bases coalesced in a bipartisan fashion.

Even in this era of heightened partisanship, congressional behavior on presidential issues still falls short of the disciplined parties in most parliamentary democracies. Nonetheless, parties have an increasingly important bearing on presidential-congressional relations. The limited ability of minority presidents to succeed was diminished further by the increased partisanship in Congress. Like Reagan and Bush, Clinton is learning the difficulties of being a minority president facing a partisan legislature. If the patterns observed here continue, Clinton could be the least successful minority president we've seen.

REFERENCES

Bond, Jon R. and Richard Fleisher, 1990. *The President in the Legislative Arena.* Chicago: University of Chicago Press.

———. 1995. "Clinton and Congress: A First Year Assessment." *American Politics Quarterly* 23: in press.

Brady, David W., and Charles S. Bullock III. 1980. "Is There a Conservative Coalition in the House?" *Journal of Politics* 42: 549–59.

Congressional Quarterly Almanac. Annually, 1953–95. Washington, DC: Congressional Quarterly.

Fleisher, Richard. 1993. "Explaining the Change in Roll-Call Voting Behavior of Southern Democrats." *Journal of Politics* 55: 327–41.

Frymer, Paul. 1994. "Ideological Consensus within Divided Party Government." *Political Science Quarterly* 109: 287–311.

Herrera, Richard, Thomas Epperlein, and Eric R. A. N. Smith. 1994. "The Stability of Congressional Roll-Call Indexes." *Political Research Quarterly* 48: 403–16.

Jackson, John E. 1974. *Constituencies and Leaders in Congress.* Cambridge, MA: Harvard University Press.

Kingdon, John W. 1981. *Congressmen's Voting Decisions.* 2nd ed. New York: Harper & Row.

Manley, John F. 1970. "The Conservative Coalition in Congress." *American Behavioral Scientist* 17: 223–47.

Matthews, Donald R., and James A. Stimson. 1975. *Yeas and Nays: Normal Decision Making in the U.S. House of Representatives.* New York: Wiley.

Ornstein, Norman J., Thomas E. Mann, and Michael J. Malbin. 1994. *Vital Statistics on Congress 1993–1994.* Washington, DC: Congressional Quarterly.

Rohde, David. 1991. *Parties and Leaders in the Postreform House.* Chicago: University of Chicago Press.

Shelley, Mack C. II. 1983. *The Permanent Majority: The Conservative Coalition in United States Congress.* University: University of Alabama Press.

Smith, Eric R. A. N., Richard Herrera, and Cheryl L. Herrera. 1990. "The Measurement Characteristics of Congressional Roll-Call Indexes." *Legislative Studies Quarterly*
15: 283–95.

Received: July 19, 1995
Accepted for Publication: January 2, 1996
Political Research Quarterly, Vol. 49, No. 4 (December 1996): pp. 729–48

Impeachment and the Post-Monica Presidency

Richard M. Pious
Barnard College

To understand the effect that Clinton's impeachment will have on the presidency and our system of governance, we need to examine the constitutional
law of impeachment and how it has changed as a result of the actions of the
House of Representatives and Senate. These actions rested largely on political
calculations, at the intersection of constitutional and popular law. It was what
the public supported that determined the limits of congressional power in the
Clinton impeachment. The president dominated public opinion and was able to
use the power of the plebiscitary presidency to blunt the Republican drive to
remove him. This facet of presidential power has implications for the long-term
development of the presidency.

——————— I ———————

The Law and Politics of Impeachment

The constitution is incomplete, ambiguous, and silent on most of the questions
involving presidential impeachment. This has led to a situation in which Democrats and Republicans define constitutional law as they see fit, according to whatever interpretation provides tactical advantage. It is no accident that every single
censure or impeachment crisis has involved a Congress controlled by one party
squaring off against a White House controlled by the other, and in each case the
parties differed over the meaning of the term "high crime and misdemeanor." It
should not surprise us that Democrats borrow prior Republican constitutional
arguments and vice versa—it all depends on which party defends the White
House incumbent and which party tries for a removal.

Defining High Crimes and Misdemeanors   Impeachment politics revolves
around the definition of the phrase "High crimes and misdemeanors," which is a
term of art in the Constitution. As such its meaning must be construed according
to what the Framers meant, but because the phrase is ambiguous, capable of
expansive and restrictive interpretations, the members of the House and Senate
can determine its meaning for themselves. Defenders of the president take the
restrictive position: a high crime and misdemeanor must involve a federal crime

defined by statutory law, with the restrictive "high" referring to the significance of the indictable crime. The Democratic Minority Report in 1867, during the impeachment of Andrew Johnson, argued that the Framers had not provided "the House with the right to ramble through all grades of crimes and misdemeanors, all instances of improper official conduct and improprieties of official life, grave and unimportant, harmful and harmless alike." Republicans made the same restrictive arguments a century later. "You don't have to be a constitutional lawyer to know that the Constitution is very precise in defining what is an impeachable offense," Nixon claimed at one of his press conferences. "A criminal offense on the part of the President is the requirement for impeachment."[1]

There is another, much broader view. One of the framers, Alexander Hamilton, described "high crimes and misdemeanors" in *Federalist 65* as "those offenses which proceed from the misconduct of public men, or, in other words, from the abuse or violation of some public trust. They are of a nature which may with peculiar propriety be denominated political, as they relate chiefly to injuries done immediately to the society itself." Until Clinton's case, those who wished to impeach a president took this *expansive* view of "high crimes and misdemeanors": abuses of power, which might or might not involve indictable crimes, were grounds for impeachment. To those who embraced the broad view, abuse or usurpation of power could be seen in a pattern of smaller actions, none of which in and of themselves might be criminal or unconstitutional, but which when taken in the aggregate might involve "high crimes and misdemeanors." In this expansive view impeachment was designed to punish crimes against the state, against the system of government itself. As a matter of abstract constitutional law the expansive rather than the restrictive construction of "high crimes and misdemeanors" is a more accurate reading of the Framers' intent, and is supported by historical precedent, analysis of the functioning of a system of separation of powers, past judicial acquiescence, and the weight of the opinion of constitutional lawyers with no political axes to grind. But that doesn't stop defenders of the president from arguing for the more strict interpretation.

Those who attack the president deploy both the strict and expansive views. In the fourteen American impeachment proceedings up to the Nixon case the grounds for impeachment of federal officials included specific felony offenses, but they also included the following more general charges: exceeding powers of office in derogation of those of another branch; behaving in a manner grossly incompatible with the proper function and purpose of the office; and employing the power of the office for an improper purpose or personal gain. In the Nixon impeachment proceedings the Democratic majority on the House Judiciary Committee took an expansive position, based on Nixon's course of conduct in office, even while fashioning a bipartisan majority around the more restrictive set of indictable crimes that several Republicans were willing to condemn. Thus our precedents include a combination of indictable and non-indictable "high crimes" based on the sense of the members of Congress as to what they will and will not tolerate. Just as justices claim to know pornography when they see it, legislators claim to know an impeachable offense when confronted with one.

The Clinton Impeachment   Clinton's impeachment lowered the bar, as the House Republican majority defined High Crimes and Misdemeanors down, succumbing to "an almost irresistible impulse to the vindictive passion of parties," as the French observer of American political life, Alexis de Tocqueville, had put it more than 150 years earlier.[2] The House's definitions of impeachable crimes were inconsistent, unclear, and not widely accepted.[3] The actions of the House echoed Tocqueville's observation about impeachment politics when he wrote: "There is nothing more terrifying than the vagueness of American laws when they are defining political crimes properly so called."[4]

House managers were not thinking ahead, nor did they understand their power stakes. If the House voted to impeach, developments would be out of its hands and into the hands of the Senate. Since two-thirds of the Senate was not likely to convict, the House might well face the repudiation of its prerogative power not only by the electorate, but also by its colleagues in the upper chamber, in a classic "backlash" situation. The Republican Party, demonstrated by its unprecedented loss of five seats in the midterm congressional elections in November 1998, already had paid significant costs. Alternatively, if the House had decided on censure or another form of rebuke, it would have controlled the language of its denunciation rather than turn matters over to the Senate. It would have been in tune with overall public opinion and with the results of the midterm election.

The House Republican leaders went for a riskier, but by their lights not an irrational decision, especially when viewed in partisan terms. Not only was the impeachment option favored by all the Republicans on the Judiciary Committee and a large proportion of the backbench, it was also approved by Republican primary voters and would have been the majority electoral sentiment in about 180 House districts held by the Republicans. Thus impeachment was the course of action that would preserve party unity for the 2000 elections. It would prevent conflict between those insisting on a drastic remedy and those inclined to more moderate positions.

Republicans also believed that an impeachment vote might set in motion events that would topple Clinton. Just before the House vote, a national poll was released that indicated that 58 percent of the public believed that Clinton should not "fight" impeachment but should resign if the House did vote to impeach.[5] (Unfortunately for Republicans, the poll wording was misleading: Americans don't like conflict, and when the wording was changed to "defend himself in a Senate trial" support for resignation dropped precipitously into the 30 percent range). As it turned out, the Republicans miscalculated the degree to which public sentiment was headed their way, and ultimately two-thirds of the public believed that the House impeached the president on political grounds. As the House approval rating sagged, Clinton's rose.[6]

The Weakness in the House Case   The referrals to the House Judiciary Committee brought by Independent Counsel Kenneth Starr and the charges reported by Republicans on the Judiciary Committee to the full House of Representatives both consisted of ordinary felonies defined by statutory law. Of the eleven counts discussed by Starr in his referral, the first four involved perjury and so did count eight. The prosecutors relied on the legal theory that an intentionally misleading statement constitutes perjury, which is the applicable common law definition in several federal circuits, including the Sixth Circuit. Clinton, however, had testified in the District of Columbia, where the key case interpreting the federal perjury statute is *Bronston v. U.S.* This is a case in which the Supreme Court held that the burden is on the questioner to frame the interrogation acutely to elicit the precise information sought, and that a witness who gives an answer "that is literally true but not responsive to the questions asked and arguably misleading by negative implication" has not committed perjury.[7] Subsequently a D.C. Circuit Court, in *U.S. v. Dean,* relied on *Bronston* to reverse one count of a perjury conviction that had been won by an Independent Counsel against HUD employee Deborah Gore Dean, on the grounds that "a statement that is literally true cannot support a perjury conviction."[8] Because the perjury case was so weak and the case law defining perjury would be on the side of the president, the House managers who brought this charge would be hampered in proving their case.

The referral also included several charges of obstruction of justice involving Clinton's testimony during the Paula Jones sexual harassment lawsuit. Under federal rules of civil procedure, the attorneys for Ms. Jones were able to question Clinton on past relationships, including his sexual relationship with Monica Lewinsky. Based on that testimony, the Independent Counsel and the House managers charged that Clinton helped Lewinsky conceal their affair, that he helped her conceal his gifts to her, and that he tried to ensure her silence with promises of help as she sought a job in the private sector, and that he coached his personal secretary Betty Currie to give misleading testimony. Two other charges of obstruction of justice were made: that the President lied to his aides who had to testify before the grand jury while trying to avoid testifying himself, and that he invoked executive privilege so his lies to the cabinet and the American people would not be uncovered.[9] Only the last two charges had no statutory foundation. Similarly, the preliminary fifteen counts drawn up by David P. Schippers, the Republican chief counsel for the House Judiciary Committee, consisted of conspiracy to obstruct justice, obstruction of justice, misprision of felonies, testifying falsely under oath, and witness tampering—all of which occurred either in the Paula Jones trial or in grand jury proceedings.[10] The main problem the House managers would have with these charges would be the difficulty of getting witnesses to corroborate these charges; the witnesses they intended to call were all sympathetic to Clinton.

The President and his defenders responded with a two-fold approach. First, the president's lawyers claimed that the president did not commit a crime: "The President did not commit perjury. He did not obstruct justice. He did not tamper with witnesses. And he did not abuse the power of the office of the Presidency."[11] Although the president went to great lengths in his legal briefs and public addresses to avoid admitting that he committed perjury or asked anyone to lie for him, his hairsplitting legalisms were so weak, and the public response so negative, that Democratic congressional leaders asked him to abandon them.[12] Congressional defenders of the president in this instance did not rest their case on the specious argument that Clinton did not commit perjury (even though they recognized the difficulty Republicans would have in "proving" that he did). Elected congressional Democrats argued that even if he had done these things, his actions did not rise to the level of an impeachable offense. They argued that the charges brought by the Independent Counsel were designed primarily as an excuse for a report containing "unnecessary graphic and salacious allegations" whose principle purpose was to damage the president.[13] They also claimed that no prosecutor in his right mind would bring criminal charges against someone for perjury or obstruction of justice in the absence of an underlying criminal offense, which Starr had not alleged in his report. Whatever crimes Clinton might have committed were low crimes and not *high* crimes, and at worst they were crimes involving testimony about private consensual behavior in a lawsuit involving a private dispute over alleged harassment—with no adverse consequences to the State and no obstruction of any justice that might have been due to Ms. Jones (since her case was dismissed on grounds unrelated to the president's testimony and while it was on appeal, was subsequently settled out of court). The entire scandal was a private matter about sex, Democrats claimed.[14]

The president's defenders argued that the House Judiciary Committee claimed that an impeachable offense must involve "wrongdoing directed against the state," "injury to the state," and offenses "against the system of government."[15] Democratic Minority Counsel Abbey Lowell argued that "Bill Clinton's alleged crimes are not those of an errant president, but that of an unfaithful husband." Representative John Conyers observed that "Impeachment was designed to rid this nation of traitors and tyrants, not attempts to cover up extramarital affairs." To become a high crime more than a mere statutory violation was needed. "While the President's conduct was reprehensible," Representative Rick Boucher pointed out, "it did not threaten the nation. It did not undermine the constitutional form and principles of our government. It did not disable the proper functioning of the constitutional duties of the Presidential Office."

House Republicans, by accepting the premise of Starr's referrals that these were impeachable offenses, originally had decided to impeach on *restrictive* grounds. Faced with Democratic criticism that the issue involved only private consensual behavior on the part of Clinton and Lewinsky, Republicans now broadened their grounds by transmuting common crimes into a larger constitutional principle. "If at the end of the day I were to conclude that the president lied under oath in deposition in the Paula Jones case with criminal intent and committed perjury," observed Republican Judiciary Committee member William McCollum, "I would vote to impeach him because if we don't do that, he will have broken the rule of law and undermined the rule of law and we would be setting a terrible precedent."[16] As Schippers put it, "this is not about sex or private conduct. It is about multiple obstructions of justice, perjury, false and misleading statements, witness tampering, abuses of power. . . ." Schippers argued that "there is no such thing as non-serious perjury—non-serious lying under oath."

Republicans argued that even a so-called private act *became* a public act because it involves the president. When Clinton lied under oath he turned the private sex act with Lewinsky into a High Crime because he violated his oath of office. "The oath constituted a solemn compact between the President and the American people," Judiciary Committee Chairman Henry Hyde argued. "That compact has been broken. The people's trust has been betrayed." He not only lied to the people and the courts, but also gave "false, misleading and perjurious testimony to the Congress as part of our inquiry," Representative Lindsey Graham argued, drawing a similarity to Nixon's abuse of authority and usurpation of House investigative powers during Watergate. Any transgression of law is serious if the president is involved, Republicans argued, because the president is the chief law enforcement officer of the land. "Perjury and obstruction of justice cannot be reconciled with the Office of the President of the United States," Hyde argued. And so, according to Schippers, these acts did constitute high crimes and misdemeanors in the broader meaning of the term: "The ultimate issue is whether the President's course of conduct is such as to affect adversely the office of the Presidency by bringing scandal and disrespect upon it, and also upon the administration of justice, and whether he has acted in a manner contrary to his trust as President, and subversive to the rule of law and to constitutional government." These were not private acts, minor acts, or transgressions against impossible moral standards, but touched fundamental issues. "This is not a question of perfection," Hyde argued. "It's a question of foundations. This isn't a matter of setting the bar too high. It's a matter of securing the basic structure of our freedom, which is the rule of law." And so even moderate House Republicans such as Nancy Johnson came around in the end, for as she concluded in casting her vote: "our democracy is far more capable of surviving a transition in power than surviving an erosion of fundamental obligations such as that to tell the truth under oath and to treat all citizens equally under the law. . . ."

The White House and the Democratic minority were on the receiving end of the Republican strategy of characterization of motives, and of inflating specific issues into broad statements of general principle—tactics that Clinton had excelled in over the years. The Democratic response was to attack the motives and conduct of the Republican majority. The impeachment wasn't about Clinton, Abbey Lowell argued, "It's about Congress's conduct." Democrats charged that it was a partisan witchhunt. "It should not be used as a club by a partisan majority that dislikes a particular President," cautioned Martin Frost. Maxine Waters charged that "Bill and Hillary Clinton are the real targets, and the Republicans are the vehicles being used by the right-wing Christian Coalition extremists to direct and control our culture." Democrats borrowed Republican rhetoric from the Iran-Contra affair and talked of the criminalization of political difference. "We are now at the height of a cycle of the politics of negative attacks, character assassination, personal smears of good people, decent people, worthy people," Minority Leader Dick Gephardt said. Democrats accused the majority of a rush to judgment, in pushing impeachment votes while American forces were engaged in hostilities against Iraq—a reference to a bombing campaign against Baghdad conducted during the impeachment inquiry. "Today we should have our men and women who stand in harm's way in the Persian Gulf in our thoughts and in our prayers, rather than trying to politically decapitate their commander in chief," Ike Skelton complained.

Democrats also used the techniques of hyperbolic characterization they had employed so successfully against Kenneth Starr. During the summer, when Starr had pursued his investigation and released several reports outlining Clinton's behavior in great detail, Democrats had responded by accusing Starr of having a salacious interest, of being a "peeping tom and a voyeur," of bringing the power of the prosecution down on the president to satisfy his own puritanical (or perverted) interests. They also accused Starr of seeking excessive penalties against Clinton, and of violating the president's due process rights, claiming that Starr had intimidated witnesses and gained evidence against Clinton in violation of Justice Department procedures. In short, the Clinton administration made Starr, rather than Clinton's own conduct, the main issue.

Now in late fall congressional Republicans were portrayed as ideological extremists attacking Clinton to pursue their moral agenda, as zealots who wished to impose an excessive penalty, and as violators themselves of due process of law. Democrats claimed that the "Rodino model" of inquiry was not being followed: In the Nixon impeachment the House Judiciary Committee kept evidence to itself and did not leak it to the media or do document dumps; Rodino negotiated bipartisan agreements on witnesses to call and evidence to gather, and did not engage in fishing expeditions; the Judiciary committee heard witnesses, assessed their credibility, and did not rely on the conclusions of the Special Prosecutor; the committee agreed on a standard of clear and convincing evidence of high crimes, and did not assume it was simply a grand jury that could hand off the charges to the Senate. In the Clinton impeachment Democrats charged that Republicans were denying the president his due process rights, by relying almost exclusively on Independent Counsel Kenneth Starr's referral, by not calling witnesses, by not establishing its own evidentiary record, by reversing the presumption of innocence (because Clinton did not testify or provide evidence), by entertaining vague, trivial, and unspecified counts that would be thrown out of any court, and by charging Clinton with obstruction of justice simply because he asserted his testimonial privileges against the Independent Counsel and Congress. The Republican majority on the Judiciary Committee seemed partisan, arbitrary, ad hoc (with rules and procedures developed not on the basis of principle), and it seemed to be disregarding fundamental notions of due process and fairness, giving the White House the opportunity to use the same kind of defenses it had employed against Starr in the months preceding impeachment. "No citizen should be treated below the law," Chet Edwards argued, not even the president. Democrats also complained that under Republican rules they could not vote their conscience on a censure vote. "You get to vote your vote of conscience, and I respect that right," House Minority Leader Dick Gephardt intoned. "All we're asking for is that we get to vote our conscience."

Republicans did what they could to counter the "fairness" issue, but with as little success as they usually have when Democrats raise the issue against them. Republicans claimed that they were acting on constitutional and not partisan grounds. They noted that perjury is not a trivial offense: it is treated more harshly in sentencing than is bribery under federal sentencing guidelines, and therefore should fall under the definition of "High Crime." House managers denied rushing to judgment, and claimed that they had accommodated Democratic concerns. The majority had been fair to the minority, giving it more time to present its case than it had given to the majority counsel. It had been fair to the president, inviting him to testify and tell the truth, giving him the privilege of responding to evidence received in testimony, and giving his lawyers one hour to question Starr, while Schippers got only 45 minutes. Democrats, not Republicans, had objected to calling witnesses and had called for abbreviated proceedings. As for the timing of the House vote, a former POW in Vietnam, Sam Johnson, told the House that the service personnel in the Gulf were "fighting to uphold the Constitution and the oath that we took and they took," rhetoric that demonstrated that in impeachment debates, patriotism is a refuge for both parties.

The two parties jousted over the impact this impeachment would have on the system of governance. Democrats argued that going forward with impeachment would establish a parliamentary system. "We are considering changing the balance of power and the proportionality of the branches of our Government," Gephardt warned. Steny Hoyer urged the House to reject impeachment and let the president face judgment in the courts. Democrats claimed that the House was acting improperly as a grand jury, and handing off its responsibilities to the Senate. The majority knew the Senate would not convict, and were using impeachment to stain Clinton's record. "Impeachment is not a form of rebuke or censure for the President's conduct," Lowell warned. Democrats also pointed to the polls, arguing that the will of the people, expressed in polls and the results of two elections, should be respected, charging that Republicans were trying to accomplish by impeachment what they had been unable to accomplish at the ballot box.

Republicans rejected these arguments. The House *should* act as a grand jury, Hyde claimed: "Our job is to decide if there is enough evidence to submit to the Senate for a trial." He argued that if the House did not impeach it would set the precedent that the president was above the law. It was absolute monarchy that was at stake here, not parliamentary government. Not to impeach would weaken the checks and balances and separation of powers system, according to Schippers: "The President mounted a direct assault upon the truth-seeking process, which is the very essence and foundation of the judicial branch. Not content with that, though, Mr. Clinton renewed his lies, half-truths and obstruction to this Congress when he filed his answers to simple requests to admit or deny. In doing so, he also demonstrated his lack of respect for the constitutional functioning of the legislative branch." It was also the authority of government itself. "How far can the standard be lowered without completely compromising the credibility of the office for all time?" David Shippers wondered. Republicans rejected the plebiscitary model, arguing that Congress should ignore the polls, because following them was what got Clinton into trouble in the first place. "Or will it be that you announce that there is no abiding standard and that public officials are answerable only to politics, polls and propaganda?" Schippers asked.

Democrats raised practical objections. Impeachment was too weighty a process for inconsequential issues. The trial would take forever. Lewinsky would have to testify to the tawdry details. Financial markets would come unglued. A weakened presidency would result in a weakened nation. Our leadership in world affairs would be weakened. Republicans dismissed these out of hand: The nation's business could go on, Lewinsky would not be asked to testify on details of the relationship; failure to impeach would weaken our position at home by weakening respect for the rule of law.

The House Precedents   The question of what constitutes a "high crime and misdemeanor" seems to have been settled by the House votes to impeach Clinton on two charges of perjury and obstruction of justice. In doing so, the House Republican majority established precedent, in the sense that it impeached Clinton for common federal crimes rather than for abuse of power. Its charges were more restrictive than those Andrew Johnson had faced, and more restrictive than the formulation used by the House Judiciary Committee when it had voted articles against Nixon. Even so, the Republican rhetoric indicates that abuse of power was bound up in the specific charges, in the sense that it provided the "High" measurement for the specific Crimes, and so the real "indictment" of Clinton seems to have been on broader grounds than those indicated in the technical language of the articles.

The House and Senate together also settled one issue of process definitively: impeachment by a lame duck House stands in the next Congress. Some constitutional law professors had argued to the contrary, claiming that the House is not a continuing body and that a lame-duck House (i.e. the House elected in 1996 and sitting in the fall of 1998, rather than the House elected in 1998 which would not take office until January 1999) lacks legitimacy to act, that its impeachment bill would violate democratic principles, that it would usurp the power of the newly elected House to consider the matter in January, and that it would be unconstitutional if the Senate took articles of impeachment up after the lame-duck House expired.[17] Nevertheless in January 1999, the newly convened House, still controlled by Republicans, did not seek to overturn the impeachment vote (which it could have done by refusing to appoint managers, for instance) and the Republican Senate in the 106th Congress that convened in January accepted the charges of impeachment which had been voted by the lame-duck 105th House. The Senate decision conformed with past precedents involving judicial impeachments, one-fifth of which (federal judges Pickering, Louderback and Hastings) had carried over from one session to another, as well as the rules of *Jefferson's Manual* in 1801, the conclusion of the Senate Rules Committee in 1988, and the opinion of the Congressional Research Service. As a practical matter, no other interpretation makes sense, since such an important non-legislative congressional check cannot remain in limbo in the inter-election period, particularly if one imagines a situation in which a president would have to be impeached and removed quickly—such as a case of treason or bribery by a foreign power.

The Clinton Impeachment Trial   When the impeachment articles were reported to the Senate, they were received by a chamber in which an extraordinary two-thirds majority would be required to convict. They also moved to a chamber that has always viewed itself as the upper house, as a judicious body that corrects the errors of the more impetuous House. As James McHenry described the Senate's impeachment role at the Maryland state ratifying convention in 1788: "The power of trying impeachments was lodged in this body [the senate] as more likely to be governed by cool and candid investigation, than by those heats that too often inflame and influence more populous Assemblies."[18]

More than two centuries later that formulation only partly applied: public opinion was intent on cooling down the House, as the midterm elections had indicated, and Senate Republicans knew that popular opinion was with the White House no matter how inflamed their House colleagues might have become in contemplating Clinton's crimes. They knew there was no way to obtain a two-thirds vote to convict, given the fact that public opinion backed the president (whose job approval rating remained in the high 60s) and the weak constitutional and factual case of the House managers. The best the Senate Republicans could do was manage the trial to preserve the institutional prestige of the chamber and their own political stakes, and do so in a way that would give their House colleagues at least a fighting chance to make their case. They understood their need to guard their reputation for acting judiciously and with bipartisanship, and their need to focus on perjury or obstruction of justice, not on Clinton's sexual conduct.

The Republican Senate leaders faced a dilemma if they went ahead with a vote: even if by some miracle the Senate voted to remove Clinton, the Democrats would get Vice President Al Gore, Jr. in the White House before the Year 2000 elections, giving him a chance for up to ten years in office; if the Republicans lost, Clinton could argue that he had been vindicated. Yet there was no way out of the dilemma, because if the Senate voted to do anything less than hold a trial and have a vote on articles of impeachment, that would be taken as a repudiation of their Republican House colleagues (particularly if the Senate voted for censure, the option that the House leadership had refused to allow to come to a vote), and it would split moderate from right-wing Republicans, imperiling party unity.

Republican leaders settled on a minimax strategy: avoid infighting, prevent a revolt of the right-wing backbenchers, allow the process to move forward, and "kick the can down the road" to placate the House managers and the conservative base of the party. Permit at least the semblance of a trial without letting it get out of hand, and minimize losses with the American people by trying to act judiciously and in accordance with the rule of law. Meanwhile, they could pray for a White House miscue, or for some new revelations about Clinton's misconduct that would be so egregious it would create a public groundswell of opinion for removal.

Understanding that their own careers were at stake, Republican Senators agreed with Democrats on rules granting the Senate maximum flexibility. The Senators would not be passive "jurors" but would make their own decisions on procedures, rather than leave these decisions to the Chief Justice of the United States.[19] Under the "Rules of Procedure and Practice in the Senate when Sitting on Impeachment Trials," which would have governed deliberations in the absence of the bipartisan agreement, all motions on evidence, including calling of witnesses, would have been decided by the chief justice as the presiding officer. Under the bipartisan agreement, the Senators themselves voted on deposing witnesses, on whether or not to call witnesses to the Senate floor, and on the admissibility of evidence. A final set of procedures, passed by a partisan Republican vote, allowed Minority Leader Daschle a "co-veto," along with Majority Leader Lott, over the witnesses and evidence. Members of the House were converted from managers into supplicants (Henry Hyde was reduced to begging them for a "pitiful three" witnesses), which is just the way the Senate likes dealing with Representatives. "I do know, what an annoyance we are in the bosom of this great body," Hyde said in frustration, "But we are a constitutional annoyance, and I remind you of that fact."[20] His pleas fell on deaf ears in the Senate.

Even with this minimax strategy, Republicans had great difficulty extricating themselves. The White House defended Clinton vigorously on the facts (denying perjury and obstruction of justice) and the law. His lawyers claimed that the charges did not constitute high crimes and misdemeanors, that the articles were vague and contained multiple offenses, and that therefore it would be impossible to comply with the constitutional standard that two-thirds of the Senate convict, since bare majorities could be aggregated in a single "logrolling" vote without meeting the standard.[21] Again, the White House and Democratic supporters were defeating Republicans on the fairness and due process issues. Democratic Senator Robert Byrd offered a motion to dismiss, which Orrin Hatch countered with a "motion to adjourn," which would have left the House impeachment standing rather than have the charges dismissed. But no bi-partisan group could form around any proposal to end before trial.[22] "They have more exit strategies than they have votes" Democratic Senator Patrick Leahy taunted Republicans.

The trial itself proved anti-climactic. The Senate insisted on a short trial, granted the managers only three witnesses, and at no point came near the extraordinary majority necessary to convict. House managers continued to wax eloquent along the same lines they had developed in their own chamber. The rejoinders by the president's counsel and the Democratic senators also followed predictable lines.[23] Not only did the articles of impeachment fail to win the two-thirds necessary to convict: they also did not gain even a simple majority, as several Republican senators defected on both the perjury and obstruction of justice counts, which were all that remained of the prosecution case by the time of the final votes.

Assessing the Results   One can look at the result of the impeachment process in two ways: either by considering the action of each chamber separately, or by assessing the entire process. House Republicans argued that their impeachment vote constituted an extreme form of censure and condemnation, which would serve as a deterrent for presidential misconduct, and which upheld the constitutional honor of the Congress because it followed the constitutional process. (Of course up until the time their managers lost in the Senate they argued that acquittal would imperil the nation.) Senate Republicans focused on the procedural fairness of the Senate. In their view the constitutional processes were safeguarded and the system worked, even though Democrats had prevented a just resolution of the issue. Democrats argued to the contrary: Clinton was not removed from office because the case against him was weak on facts and law. The House had acted irresponsibly in attempting to lower the bar. Senate failure to muster a two-thirds vote, or even a majority, vindicated the Democratic position that nothing Clinton had done rose to the level of High Crimes and Misdemeanors, and they congratulated themselves for thwarting a "constitutional coup d'état" by the Republicans.

Since the Senate acquitted on the charges, at least in part because all Democrats and a few Republican Senators did not believe the charges warranted the definition of High Crimes, this congressional "backlash" might be interpreted to mean that no future House will impeach on such frivolous grounds. One thing we do know: this partisan food fight settled nothing about the law of impeachment, except to demonstrate what was already known—a factually ambiguous case involving low crimes rather than a substantial abuse of public office will not win the necessary supermajority of Senators. The impeachment of Clinton was like one of those World War I battles, which consumed a generation; at its end the two sides held the same positions they had held prior to the carnage.

Why Not Censure?   Why was there no censure by the House or Senate? This was the preferred outcome for a majority of legislators, but none of the proposals to censure floated by respected members reached a vote. This was so because the language of a censure resolution could not be agreed upon. A censure resolution with strong language would get centrist and conservative Democrats and moderate Republicans off the hook, but the White House was opposed, because strong language would jeopardize the president's position in a subsequent prosecution if he signed onto it or apologized to the Senate. (If it involved watered down language the White House could accept, but there would be no Republican votes for it and it would fail passage.) Highly conservative Republicans had to maintain their credentials with their constituents, who strongly opposed censure and would not vote for a weak motion, or even one with the strongest possible language. Support for censure on the Republican side would be taken as a repudiation of the House Republican leadership, which in turn might alienate contributors and voters. Majority Leader Trent Lott had to let the trial run to maintain party cohesion and to avoid a leadership fight with his ambitious lieutenant and rival from the right-wing of the party, Don Nichols. There simply weren't enough votes in for any censure middle to end the impeachment muddle.

All sorts of proposals were shot down. There was the "two-step" proposed by moderate Republican Susan Collins of Maine: first the Senate would vote on whether the president was guilty of perjury and obstruction of justice, and then vote on whether to remove him from office. A large bipartisan majority would have been happy to accept the two-step but there was "no way to get from here to there," as the joke from Maine goes, because the leadership on both sides was against it. Democrat Robert Byrd, among others condemned this "convict but don't evict" vote, while Collins' own party's conservatives torpedoed it on the grounds that the Constitution provides for a single vote on removal. The White House opposed it because such a finding might later be used in judicial proceedings.[24]

This was not the only proposal out of Maine: Collins' colleague, Republican moderate Olympia Snowe sponsored the "finding of fact," which was designed to attract some "Clinton-critical" Democrats such as Joseph Lieberman. Without using the "p" (perjury) or "o" (obstruction) words, the resolution would have censured Clinton for engaging in a course of conduct designed to "alter, delay, impede, cover-up and conceal the existence of evidence and testimony" in the Paula Jones case. Republican conservative Orrin Hatch proposed a different kind of "finding," to wit, that the impeachment by the House constitutes the highest form of condemnation, and then end the proceedings without any other vote— this way there would be no vote for acquittal which could set a precedent encouraging wrongful conduct by public officials and reducing the deterrent for future acts.[25] These proposals did not attract Republican conservatives, and Democrats would not vote for them without bipartisan political cover.

After Clinton's acquittal, Democrat Dianne Feinstein and thirty-six other senators circulated a censure proposal designed to inoculate them from any voter backlash: it stated that Clinton gave "false and misleading testimony," that his actions "had the effect of impeding discovery of evidence in judicial proceedings," and he "remains subject to criminal actions in a court of law," and it called upon future Congresses not to rescind the resolution (as the Senate had once rescinded a resolution of censure against Andrew Jackson). "Whereas William Jefferson Clinton through his conduct in this matter has violated the trust of the American people, now therefore be it resolved that the United States Senate does hereby censure William Jefferson Clinton, president of the United States, and does condemn his wrongful conduct in the strongest terms." Nine Republicans endorsed it, and it might have won a majority vote, but conservative Phil Gramm objected, and the two-thirds vote necessary to overcome his objection could not be obtained.

In censure politics each party made a rational choice. In proposing "offers in compromise" the Democrats maintained their position as the reasonable party, characterized Republicans as partisan zealots, distanced themselves from Clinton (with condemnatory language), and put the onus on the Republicans in the next election to explain why they did not vote to condemn Clinton. They positioned themselves correctly, according to their lights, in terms of ideology (centrist), scale (moderate penalty), and morality (condemnation of Clinton). By spurning the chance to censure Clinton, the Republicans maintained party unity in terms of ideology (right-wing), scale (severe penalty) and morality (condemnation of Clinton) and they did not fall into the trap of alienating their right-wing, true-believer, anti-Clinton base—as they had sometimes done on other issues.

———— II ————

Plebiscitary Power

Why was Clinton acquitted? Why was there no censure? The attempts to answer these questions required a complex constitutional analysis and an equally complex power stakes analysis, but there is another and more simple answer, which is that public opinion as monitored by polls supported the president. In the Senate (though not the House), the constitutional law of impeachment became transmuted into a popular law of impeachment. Republican efforts to impugn and then impeach backfired, and Clinton won the battle for public opinion. The White House could not, given the proprieties, lobby legislators directly: "Don't tamper with this jury," Senator Robert Byrd warned the president sternly. But published polls had a greater impact on party cohesion than direct lobbying would have had. Democrats no longer in office were somewhat equivocal, with a few such as former Senator Sam Nunn, a leading southern moderate, calling for his resignation.[26] But Democrats who expected to face the voters again held firm, anticipating political gains. Meanwhile Republicans wavered, if not on their final votes, then on the procedures for impeachment and trial, and in doing so gave the White House further opportunities to make gains with the public, as Republicans played a version of the death spiral.

Clinton has always had a "Godzilla effect": you can hit the monster with an atomic bomb, but it turns out the monster *likes* radiation, and becomes even bigger and stronger after the attack. A day after the first news stories about the Lewinsky affair surfaced Clinton's "strong" approval rating rose seven points in the ABC/Washington News polls, from 24 to 31 percent; within the week, his approval rating dipped only slightly from the low sixties to 57 percent. After Clinton delivered his 1998 State of the Union address his poll ratings soared to 73 percent in a CBS poll—a sixteen point jump in one evening, and his ratings for his job performance remained in the low sixty to low seventy percent range through the remainder of the crisis. After Clinton's speech confessing his affair, 76 percent of the public wanted Clinton to finish his term.[27] Nothing Republicans could do affected these ratings: following the release of his videotaped grand jury testimony on September 21, overnight polls indicated that his approval rating had gone up 9 points, from 59 percent the day before to an astonishing 68 percent, fueled in large measure by sympathy for the invasion of Clinton's privacy and outrage at the tactics of what some were calling the "Special Pornographer."[28] After Starr's report was released, attitudes hardened into a national consensus that the investigation into the affair should be ended.[29]

Based on these poll results, Clinton believed he could survive the revelations in the Starr report. He told a news conference that he would not resign, appealing to the results of these polls: "I believe the right thing for the country and what I believe the people of the country want, is now that they know what happened, they want to put it behind them and they want to go and they want me to go on and do my job. And that is what I intend to do."[30] As the Judiciary Committee began consideration of Starr's report in late September, 58 percent of the public believed it should not hold impeachment hearings.[31] As the House voted to impeach in December, 60 percent did not think it should cost Clinton his job, and 64 percent did not want their representative to vote for impeachment.[32] As the Senate voted to have a trial, 56 percent felt the charges were not serious enough, and that impeachment and trial never should have happened.[33] The public wanted the Senate to terminate the trial—not Clinton.

The White House succeeded in making Starr and his conduct the issue, playing on deep seated suspicion of both prosecutorial transgressions and antipathy toward "sex police," and as they did so, they could tar the Republicans with guilt by association. After Starr issued his report, 56 percent of the public believed he was mainly interested in hurting Clinton rather than in finding the truth, 60 percent thought he was trying to embarrass Clinton rather than prove perjury, 59 percent opposed releasing all the details to the public that were contained in his report, and his approval rating was put at 23 percent. By a 78 to 18 margin, the public believed that the time, effort and money spent on the investigation by Starr was "not worth it."[34]

Republicans who pursued Starr's line of inquiry suffered as well. Eight months of the sex scandals had not enabled his congressional opponents to land telling blows, and their efforts to do so seemed to have backfired. After the Judiciary Committee approved the release of the deposition tapes, the approval rating of Congress dropped 12 points, from 56 to 44 percent.[35] Only 30 percent approved of the release of videotaped grand jury testimony by Clinton.[36] The release of the videotapes in addition to the report, was seen as unnecessary by 58 percent of Republicans, 80 percent of Democrats and 72 percent of independents.[37] Democrats played the unfairness theme and the prosecutorial abuse theme hard during the impeachment hearings in the House.

After Clinton's speech admitting the relationship, and later after the release of Starr's report, the public seemed almost evenly divided: if the president had perjured himself and obstructed justice, 49 percent wanted him to resign or be impeached, while 48 percent wanted him to remain in office and have the matter dropped after limited punishment.[38] Prior to impeachment hearings, the public did not believe that Clinton ought to be impeached or that he should resign. In a "split the difference" position, in late September 66 percent of the public thought Clinton should finish his term, and 59 percent believed he should be censured: this group seemed to correlate very strongly with those approving of Clinton's job performance.[39] Nothing the House Judiciary Committee could do changed these conclusions. Just after the House impeached Clinton, 65 percent of the public believed that Clinton should not be removed, while 33 percent believed that he should be and 2 percent had no opinion.[40] Though President Clinton was the second President to be impeached, his job approval rating rose six points from the prior week to 72 percent, one of his highest ratings ever.[41]

The reason for the abbreviated Senate trial, and ultimately for the verdict, had to do with these stable poll findings. Republicans continued to take the heat for going forward, and were unable to win over public opinion. By early January 55 percent of all polled believed that the Senate Republicans were handling the impeachment of President Clinton poorly, while only 37 percent of those polled felt that the Senate Democrats were handling the situation poorly.[42] When asked whether the Senate should hold a full trial, including witnesses and testimony 60 percent said no (37 percent, 75 percent, and 60 percent of Republicans, Democrats, and Independents, respectively), indicating the Republicans had lost the crucial independent voter.[43] When asked in early January whether or not important witnesses such as

Betty Currie, Monica Lewinsky, and Vernon Jordan should be heard in the Senate trial, 57 percent said that they should not be called, while 40 percent believed that they should, and 3 percent had no opinion.[44] Another poll found that 69 percent of those polled preferred a quick trial where no witnesses were called, to a long trial with witnesses, which 26 percent preferred.[45] The president's job approval ratings during the Senate trial fluctuated between 62 percent and 69 percent.[46]

Nor could Republicans win the constitutional arguments when they tried to explain their case. When asked to judge the seriousness of Clinton's actions, and whether they warranted his conviction by the Senate, 61 percent of those polled in early January as the trial was getting underway did not believe they were serious enough.[47] By February, with the trial in full swing, the public mood strongly favored acquittal: with only 29 or 33 percent favoring conviction and 65 or 66 percent acquittal, depending on the poll.[48] Once the Senate did acquit, the action was strongly supported by the public, with an *LA Times* Poll indicating that 65 percent agreed with Senate vote while only 30 percent thought Clinton should have been convicted.

Censure had been favored by a majority for much of the time: as of December it was favored by 61 percent with majorities across party lines.[49] By the time the trial ended, however, censure did not command a majority: 60 percent approved of the Senate vote not to convict, 39 percent disapproved, and censure was supported by 44 percent, with 54 percent wanting to drop the case entirely.[50] The proportion of Democrats favoring censure dropped from 52 percent before acquittal to only 23 percent afterwards.[51]

The results of the Senate action are consistent with the popular law of impeachment. The public gave Clinton high approval ratings for his performance in office while condemning him for his personal conduct; it believed that one could distinguish between private and public acts; it believed that Starr's inquiry had been unfair and that Republicans had acted in a partisan manner that tainted their investigation; it wanted a short trial with few if any witnesses; it wanted Clinton to remain in office; it eventually opposed censure and formal rebuke. The constitutional results of the impeachment process were consonant with these deeply felt public attitudes. The popular law of impeachment trumped the constitutional law as defined by the House.

——————— III ———————

Implications for Governance

"The Lewinsky-Clinton affair goes beyond petty politics and the elections to come," the highly respected French newspaper *Le Monde* commented after the president's acquittal, "It touches on the evolution of American society."[52] In political terms, it touches on the patterns of regime formation, maintenance, and dissolution. Dealignment theorists have suggested that stable patterns of two-party competition might be ending, given the instability of voting patterns, the lessening of voter and other political participation rates, the lack of political knowledge and attentiveness, and the weakening of party organizations. But the politics involved in the Clinton impeachment demonstrate the great significance of party politics in resolving constitutional issues. In turn, the resolution of the issue may contribute to a fundamental political realignment. Each party went to its base; partisan and ideological divisions hardened in Congress and in the electorate; and the "culture wars" that have energized party politics in the past decade (morally rigid Republicans against morally relative Democrats) became more salient.

Will the impeachment have an impact that goes beyond party realignment into a more fundamental regime change? Will the Clinton impeachment and its resolution affect our system of governance? After the Andrew Johnson impeachment the power of the presidency weakened and "congressional government" became dominant. After the Nixon impeachment Congress passed laws mandating "collaborative decisionmaking" in many areas, including war and budget decisions. The aftermath of the Clinton impeachment already has influenced American politics: scandal politics is now be so embedded in the Washington culture that anyone in high office will be vulnerable. A scandal-industrial complex serves up infotainment about politicians' peccadilloes, not only damaging Clinton, but also Speaker-designate Robert Livingston, Representatives Bob Barr and Henry Hyde (both accused of adultery) and Minority Whip Tom DeLay (accused of conflicts in testimony given under oath in a lawsuit settled in 1994).[53] Agents and publicists representing the principals market proposals for books, serializations, cable and network mini-series, cover spreads and photo shoots, exclusive interviews, and other projects. Sex-magazines offer bounties for the scalps of leading politicians. Private investigators hired by candidates dig up dirt on their rivals and feed that dirt to the media. In this scandal market, information and revelations fetch the most reward just at the point when a politician makes his or her move to high office. The result is an inversion of the traditional Washington norms: it used to be that those in high places were protected by the press from all inquiring minds who might have inquired about their past. Now the financial rewards are so high for exposing people that those who are most successful are those least protected. And the occupant of the Oval Office becomes the most tempting target of all.

The direst projections made by the president's defenders were that impeachment would lower the bar and conviction would usher in a new age of parliamentary government, in which presidents would serve at the pleasure of a majority of Congress, and were likely to be removed if their party could not sustain such a majority. Clinton was acquitted, so we cannot say what would have happened had he been removed. Even his acquittal, however, has damaged the institution of the presidency, even if not in a parliamentary sense. Rather, it has weakened the president's legal position in litigation against his conduct. Court cases for the most part went against the Clinton White House. These included decisions requiring high-level aides to testify and narrowing the scope of executive privilege, limiting attorney-client privilege, and requiring Secret Service agents to testify.[54] Yet a "backlash" against untrammeled congressional and judicial prerogatives seems to have set in. Congress has dismantled some checks and balances against the president, such as the Independent Counsel provisions of the *Ethics in Government Act,* which was allowed to expire in 1999. It is also likely that the court decision requiring the Secret Service to provide testimony in certain judicial proceedings will be overturned by Congress.

In the long run the greatest impact on American governance may involve the expansion of the influence of the plebiscitary presidency into the impeachment process. Clinton got off because the polls were with him, and the polls were with him because the White House spinmeisters succeeded in winning over public opinion. Democrats insisted in the congressional debates that the will of the people be heeded; Republicans responded that this was "a republic and not a democracy." The American people accepted the Democratic argument: by the time the House voted, sixty-two percent believed that its members should be listening to the public when deciding on whether or not to vote for impeachment.[55] These expectations of the American public (and of the polling industry) do, however, take us way beyond the original constitutional understandings about the impeachment process and into uncharted territory. They move us closer to both the "people out of doors" concept of direct democracy (now transmuted into the people indoors on the internet) and towards the parliamentary system of "confidence" or "no confidence" in the executive that we have rejected throughout our constitutional history.

Frank Newport, the editor-in-chief of the Gallup Poll argued that "Congress should listen to the public's response—much of it measured through polling."[56] But if representative institutions are discredited in favor of direct democracy (even if indirectly expressed by representative institutions), then governance by public opinion and prerogative power—the plebiscitary presidency—seems a viable alternative, at least in the short term, because fusing popularity with prerogative provides the incumbent with a way to boost presidential power and control events. But in the long run, political leaders who rely on public approval ratings but who lack moral authority cannot rally the nation for great challenges. And it is a dangerous turn of events when any political leader relies on popularity, rather than legal argument, as a shield against constitutional sanction. Presidents in the current American political culture have relied on their spinmeisters' arts to evade, stonewall, or brazen it out—and they can survive if they are lucky enough to have enemies less versed in these arts. As a matter of constitutional law, Clinton did not deserve to be removed from office, but much of his defense involve a plebiscitary trend that in the long run will be bad for the presidency and for the American people.

REFERENCES

1. *The Public Papers of the President, Richard M. Nixon,* Vol. V (Washington, D.C.: Government Printing Office, 1995), "News Conference of February 25, 1974."
2. Alexis De Tocqueville, *Democracy in America,* Vol. 1, ch. 7 "Political Jurisdiction in the United States" pp. 110–12 (New York: Vintage, 1945).
3. Lon Fuller, *The Morality of Law* (New Haven: Yale University Press, 1964).
4. De Tocqueville, *Democracy in America,* Vol. 1, ch. 7 "Political Jurisdiction in the United States" pp. 110–12.
5. ABC/*Washington Post,* December 12–14, 1998.
6. Pew Poll, December 19–21, 1998. Clinton's approval ratings jumped from 67 percent in early November to 75 percent as of December 20, 1998, according to *NYT*/CBS polls.
7. *Bronston v. U.S.* 409 U.S. 352 (1973).

8. *U.S. v. Deborah Gore Dean,* 55 F. 3d. 640 (1995).

9. Office of Independent Counsel, "Referral to the House of Representatives, September 9, 1998." (Washington, D.C.: Office of Independent Counsel). The Starr Report, as the referral is commonly called, is reprinted widely, including *The New York Times,* September 12, 1998, pp. B1–18.

10. "Fifteen Impeachment Counts Against the President," *The New York Times,* October 6, 1998, p. A20.

11. "Response of President's Lawyers to Independent Counsel's Report, September 12, 1998" reprinted in *The New York Times,* September 13, 1998, pp. 39–40 at 40.

12. After the trial Clinton himself seemed to have abandoned it. When asked at a news conference, "how important do you think it is to tell the truth, especially under oath," he responded, "what young people will learn from my experience is that even presidents have to do that, and that there are consequences when you don't." Federal News Service Transcript, reprinted in *The New York Times,* March 20, 1999, p. A7.

13. "Second White House Response to Starr," Williams and Connolly, and Office of the White House Counsel, September 12, 1998, p. 1, reproduced at www.Washingtonpost.com, "Special Report: Clinton Accused."

14. Lowell's statements are from the Statement of Judiciary Panel Minority Counsel, December 10, 1998, as reprinted in *The New York Times,* Dec. 11, 1998, p. A31. Schippers' statements are from the Statement of Judiciary Panel Majority Counsel, December 10, 1998, as reprinted in *The New York Times,* Dec. 11, 1998, pp. A32–33. Statements of members of the House are taken from House Debate of December 18, 1998, as reprinted in *The New York Times,* Dec. 19, 1998, pp. B6–9. See also Michael Beschloss, ed., *The Impeachment and Trial of President Clinton* (New York: Times Books, 1999), Parts I and II.

15. "Letter from White House Counsel to Chairman and Ranking Democrat, House Judiciary Committee," October 2, 1998, reprinted in *The New York Times,* October 3, 1998, p. A-11.

16. Quoted in Ruth Marcus and Juliet Eilperin, "What is an Impeachable Offense?" *The Washington Post National Weekly Edition,* Sept. 14, 1998, p. 8.

17. See the testimony of Bruce Ackerman, Committee on the Judiciary, *Hearing on Impeachment Inquiry Pursuant to H. Res. 581,* December 7, 1998.

18. Max Farrand, *The Records of the Federal Convention of 1787,* 1911, vol. III, p. 148.

19. Democratic Senator Paul Harkin even insisted that the House managers not refer to senators as jurors, an objection sustained by Chief Justice William Rehnquist who was presiding over the Senate trial.

20. Michael Beschloss, ed., *The Impeachment and Trial of President Clinton* (New York: Times Books, 1999) p. 367.

21. Beschloss, ed., *The Impeachment,* p. 358.

22. According to Hatch, Byrd would be saying that the charges didn't have merit, and it would be a precedent. Hatch would be simply admitting they didn't have the 67 votes, and no precedential value would be attached. Neither had the needed 51 votes to get a variant of the motions through.

23. For excerpts see *The New York Times,* February 9, 1999, pp. A17– 20.

24. Robert Byrd, "Don't Tinker with Impeachment," *The Washington Post National Weekly Edition,* Feb. 8, 1999, p. 27.

25. Orrin Hatch, "A Precedent the Senate Shouldn't Set" *The New York Times,* February 2, 1999, p. A19.

26. *Washington Post National Weekly Edition,* August 31, 1998, p. 27.

27. Pew Poll, August 27–Sept. 8.
28. CBS Poll, September 21, 1998. Gallup Polls of October 21–22 had it at 66 percent approval. On Sept. 20 a CBS Poll indicated that 69 percent of the public did not think the tape of the testimony should be released to the media, and 59 percent believed that it had more to do with embarrassing the president than letting the public judge him.
29. An ABC poll taken August 19, shortly after Clinton's speech indicated that 69 percent of the public wanted the investigation to end, a rise of 10 percent from the days before.
30. "Presidential News Conference with Vaclav Havel," September 16, 1998, in *The New York Times,* September 17, 1998, p. A26.
31. *New York Times*/CBS News Poll, Sept. 12–14, 1998.
32. ABC News/Nightline Poll, December 11, 1998; Times/CBS Poll, December 12, 1998.
33. ABC News Poll, Feb. 12, 1999.
34. ABC Poll, September 12, 1998; CBS Poll, September 12–14, 1998; CBS Poll September 15, 1998; *New York Times*/CBS Poll, September 21–22.
35. CBS News Poll, September 20, 1998.
36. *NYT*/CBS Poll, Sept. 12–14, 1998.
37. *New York Times*/CBS News Poll, September 12–14 and 15, 1998.
38. CNN Poll, August 18, 1998. On the other hand, the Pew August 27–Sept. 8 poll had it at 65 percent not wanting Clinton impeached if he did lie under oath. After Starr's report, ABC News Poll had it at 51 percent wanting impeachment for lying, up 8 points in a week.
39. CBS News Poll, September 12, 1998. A *NYT*/CBS Poll of September 12–14 had censure at 57 percent, while a Princeton Survey Associates Poll released September 21 had it at 66 percent.
40. ABC News/*Washington Post* Poll, January 8–10, 1999.
41. *New York Times*/CBS News Poll, December 20, 1998.
42. CNN/*Time* Poll, January 7, 1999.
43. CBS News Poll, January 10–11, 1999.
44. Gallup/CNN/*USA Today* Poll, January 6, 1999.
45. The Harris Poll, January 7–12, 1999.
46. Gallup/CNN/*USA Today,* January 8–10 & 15–17, 1999 and ABC News/*Washington Post* Poll January 8–10, 1999.
47. CBS News Poll, January 10–11, 1999.
48. CBS News Poll, February 7, 1999; ABC News Poll, February 6–7.
49. ABC News/*Nightline* Poll, December 11, 1998.
50. ABC News Poll, February 12, 1999.
51. *Washington Post* Survey, February 13–15.
52. *Le Monde,* February 14, 1999, p. 1.
53. Jock Friendly, "DeLay Skirted Truth in Lawsuit, Disclosures," *The Hill,* February 3, 1999, p. 1.
54. Richard Pious, "The Paradox of Clinton Winning and the Presidency Losing," *Political Science Quarterly,* Vol. 114, No. 4, Winter 1999–2000, pp. 569–94.
55. Times/CBS News Poll, December 12, 1998.
56. Frank Newport, "Power to the People," *The New York Times,* September 24, 1998, p. A27.

11

THE PRESIDENT
AND THE BUREAUCRACY

The 1993 John Gaus Lecture: Whose Bureaucracy Is This, Anyway? Congress, the President and Public Administration[*]

Francis E. Rourke
Johns Hopkins University

The title of my presentation defines its subject: the struggle for control over bureaucracy between Congress and the president. In talking about this struggle, which provides a major key to understanding how public policy is made in the United States, I want to rely on something of a question and answer format, more or less in the style of the catechism used for religious instruction at a parochial elementary school I attended some sixty odd years ago.

In my youthful eyes, the questions in this catechism always seemed more compelling or at least lasted longer in my memory than the answers. I once made this point, of which I was extremely proud, to the nun in charge of the school, the Mother Superior of an adjacent convent, and Sister Mary Ellen Joseph fixed me with a cold eye (as was her wont) and said, "Francis, have you ever considered a career in political science?"

Note:
[*]I would like to dedicate this lecture to the memory of William Anderson, my mentor at Minnesota, who was the perfect model of a scholar and the kindest of friends. Not least of all, he gave me my first opportunity to write in this field.

Editor's Note: Francis E. Rourke, the Benjamin H. Griswold III Professor of Public Policy Studies of The Johns Hopkins University, was designated the John Gaus Distinguished Lecturer at the Association's 1993 Annual Meeting held in Washington, D.C. The award honors his lifetime of exemplary scholarship in the joint tradition of political science and public administration, and more generally, recognizes achievement and encourages scholarship in public administration. Previous Gaus Lecturers have included: Herbert Kaufman (1986), C. Dwight Waldo (1987), James Fesler (1988), Aaron Wildavsky (1989), Frederick C. Mosher (posthumously, 1990), Norton E. Long (1991), and Martha Derthick (1992).

The 1993 Gaus Award Committee consisted of: Barbara Nelson, University of Minnesota, chair; Jeffrey Brudney, University of Georgia; and Dennis Judd, University of Missouri.

Well, you may think that I have embroidered the truth a little bit in telling this story, but I have always regarded embroidery as the best part of the truth. This is a characteristic that has also served me well in my life as a political scientist.

1. The initial question that I want to put in this little political catechism is the question I raised in my title. "Whose bureaucracy is this anyway?" This query has haunted the relationship between the president and Congress from the very beginning of their history together in the American political system. Which institution is to have real sovereignty over the activities and decisions of agencies in the executive branch?

At first glance the American Constitution seems to provide what Descartes might regard as a clear and distinct answer in favor of the president. One of the plainest of all constitutional clauses is the provision in Article II, section 1, which states with luminous clarity that "executive power shall be vested in a President of the United States." As Ross Perot might have said, if he had been there in Philadelphia, "case closed."

However, showing a certain penchant for surprises, the framers inserted some other provisions in the Constitution that plainly undermined the supreme executive authority they had just conferred on the president. They authorized Congress to establish and empower all the agencies that might thereafter lie within the domain of the White House, along with the right to determine how much financial support each of these organizations would receive.

Under this constitutional arrangement, the bureaucracy was to operate under a system of dual sovereignty, or to use the more homely and revealing phrase of our day, joint custody. The president would reign in solitary splendor as the bureaucracy's chief executive officer, to whom civil servants high and low would have to defer, but Congress rather than the White House would control both the extent of their power and the scope of their resources.

Putting this system of joint custody into modern parlance, it gives the president clear title to the position of the bureaucracy's CEO, although the sparse language of the Constitution leaves open the possibility that the title may only be ceremonial. Congress, on the other hand, is given the unmistakably important role of serving as a unique kind of cash cow. It is to be a source of power as well as pelf for the bureaucracy.

2. My second question tonight is to ask how this plan for joint control over the bureaucracy, as crafted by the framers, worked in the century following ratification of the Constitution. What were the early consequences of this decision by the framers, acting like judges in a family court, to put the bureaucracy under the joint custody of the president and Congress?

One of the first things that the legislature decided, as it met in its early sessions and began the task of creating a new state, was that while some of the bureaucratic organizations it was establishing belonged in the president's executive family, others lay more properly in the legislature's domain, and it would be Congress that would fix the boundaries between these two separate and distinct spheres.

Consider, for example, the description that Lloyd Short gives of Congress's efforts at the beginning of the republic to establish executive departments. As Short wrote in his history of the development of national administrative organization in the United States: "the Secretaries of War and Foreign Affairs were made solely responsible and subordinate to the President, and only a general indication was made as to the scope of their duties. On the contrary, the Secretary of the Treasury, although he was also responsible to the President, was more minutely controlled and directed in the discharge of the specific duties assigned to him by Congress" (1923, 100).

As you can see, Congress ignored the arrangement devised by the framers for joint custody and decided that there should in fact be two bureaucracies in the new republic—one belonging to the president, the other to the legislature. The president would have jurisdiction over bureaucratic organizations dealing with matters like foreign affairs and national defense, where executive primacy was firmly rooted in both constitutional law and historical practice. Congress, however, could take the lead in shaping the operation of organizations outside this limited sphere of presidential responsibility.

It was this conception of a dual bureaucracy that prompted members of Congress to claim, during the presidency of Andrew Jackson, that the national legislature had legal authority over the affairs and decisions of the Treasury Department, because Treasury did not—like the Department of State—perform functions that were inherently executive in character. Instead, it carried out administrative tasks made necessary by the legislature's exercise of its appropriations power.

This attempt to wrest control over the Treasury Department from the president did not, however, succeed. Andrew Jackson gave us an early demonstration of the strength that later presidents were to draw from their power of appointment. He removed the Treasury Secretary who was willing to comply with the legislature's views on the national bank and replaced him with an official who would dutifully submit to instructions from the White House.

But presidents were not alone in rejecting this notion that the Constitution created two separate bureaucracies—one executive and the other legislative. Many members of Congress felt the same way. Right off the bat, during the tenure of the country's first president, George Washington, legislators demanded access to the records of executive deliberations on a matter central to the conduct of foreign affairs, the negotiations leading up to the highly unpopular Jay treaty of 1794.

This was a request that President Washington stiffly denied, but, by making such a demand, Congress acknowledged that it was no more prepared to cede complete control over foreign affairs to the president than the White House was to yield sovereignty over fiscal matters to the legislature.

Unsuccessful in its attempt to establish control over part of the bureaucracy, the national legislature went another route during the period of congressional government that followed the Civil War. It tried to dominate all administrative activity. In his book, *The American Presidency,* Richard Pious gives us a vivid description of the extent to which the legislature achieved mastery over the

bureaucracy in the days when President Andrew Johnson was facing impeachment for defying congressional efforts to restrict his power of removal. As Pious
wrote: ". . . by the time the House voted its impeachment, control of the departments already rested in the hands of congressional leaders. They instituted a system of congressional supremacy, involving a close connection between
department secretaries and committee chairs, which remained in effect for the
remainder of the century" (1979, 74).

As this passage indicates, Congress had handed over power to its committees
by the latter half of the nineteenth century. The task of supervising executive
agencies was thus spread among many hands. Such a power-sharing arrangement
was very much in harmony with the decentralized character of this country's
political life at that stage of American history, but it had serious drawbacks as a
means of imparting coherence and direction to the increasingly complex array of
bureaucratic organizations that were then emerging on the national scene.

3. What factors brought about a resurgence of presidential authority, and a
restoration of the principle and practice of joint custody over bureaucracy in the
twentieth century?

One of the chief consequences of the system of congressional dominance over
bureaucracy, as it developed in the late nineteenth century, was that it clearly
defined a task that would preoccupy congressional and White House officials in
the century ahead: the search for more orderly arrangements in the structure and
operation of the national bureaucracy.

The founding fathers may have been aware of the need for such order when
they put nominal authority over bureaucracy in the president's hands. As we have
seen, however, they sowed the seeds of disorder through the provisions they
included in the Constitution on legislative power, where they made bureaucratic
organizations dependent on Congress for both their power and their resources.

As the nineteenth century neared its end, Congress itself began to see the need
for reform in the organization of executive agencies. It established the Dockery-
Cockrell Commission which undertook a study of the efficiency of the bureaucracy in the 1890s. At this point at least, Congress still saw itself as holding the
answer to administrative disorder, rather than being its source.

However, as the twentieth century unfolded, the emerging movement for
administrative reform in the Progressive era took a far different tack. It saw the
presidency as having a far better vantage point from which to promote and preserve organizational coherence in the executive branch. Accordingly, the Taft
Commission on Economy and Efficiency in 1905 and virtually all subsequent
studies of executive operations have recognized the need for presidential leadership in this area, especially the path-breaking reports of the President's Committee on Administrative Management and the two Hoover Commissions.

Throughout the twentieth century, therefore, administrative reform has sought
to breathe new life into the president's constitutional title as the nation's chief
executive officer. There was continuing resistance in Congress to this development, especially since the growing authority of presidents in the bureaucratic

sphere went hand and glove with the increasingly dominant position of the White House in American politics and policymaking.

Such opposition made its last significant stand in 1937, when conservatives in Congress, led by Senator Harry Byrd (D-Va.), commissioned a study of administrative organization by the Brookings Institution that was intended to offset the presidential orientation of the Brownlow Commission by making a case for a substantial congressional role in governing the bureaucracy.

Generally speaking, however, the most remarkable feature of this search for order in the country's administrative system is the extent to which Congress has gone along with the principle of presidential leadership over the day-to-day administrative operations of government. While no treaty was ever signed on the subject, Congress had surrendered primacy in this area to the president by the middle of this century.

4. A question naturally arises—why did Congress accept such a broad increase in presidential authority over a bureaucracy that it had so strenuously sought to bring under its own control for more than one hundred years?

One answer to this question may be that Congress had no viable alternative, given the changes that occurred in American society during the first half of the twentieth century. Slowly but surely, government in the United States began to be recognized as big business, and in this corporate sphere of activity chief executive officers were now a standard feature of organizational life. Here as elsewhere, congressional as well as public attitudes toward what is desirable in the organization and operation of the national bureaucracy took their cues from what was happening in the private sector.

It can also be argued that congressional willingness to accept a greater degree of presidential authority over bureaucracy reflected its dawning awareness that joint custody was not a zero-sum game. An expansion in the president's role would not necessarily mean a contraction in congressional influence in this area. Under joint custody the legislature could still retain a strong voice in all major decisions affecting the power and operation of the national bureaucratic establishment.

Consider, for example, the arrangement devised in modern times for carrying out organizational changes in the executive branch—an arrangement that exemplifies joint custody in one of its purest forms. The vast expansion in the bureaucracy that occurred in the 1930s led Congress to give the president wide-ranging authority to propose shifts in its organization and command structure, but it stipulated that these changes could only go into effect if the legislature did not subsequently pass a resolution disallowing the president's initiatives.

Up until then, such reorganization could only be accomplished by statutes, an arrangement that led to a great deal of organizational rigidity in the executive branch. These laws were difficult to pass because executive agencies and their supporters commonly used all the features of congressional procedures that favor the opposition to insure their defeat. The legislative veto system for achieving reorganization converted this liability into an asset. Now the roadblocks in congressional procedures that had long impeded reorganization bills were obstacles that opponents would have to surmount in order to defeat presidential proposals. As Peri Arnold (1986) has shown, a great deal of executive reorganization has been accomplished since this veto procedure was established.

Following its introduction in the area of administrative reorganization, the legislative veto was used extensively by Congress as a strategy for maintaining its share of joint custody, even though it also allowed presidents and their appointees to expand their power over bureaucracy. The role of the legislative veto in strengthening the process of joint custody received a setback in 1983, when the Supreme Court held against its constitutionality in *INS v. Chadha*. As Louis Fisher has cogently argued, the Court grievously misread both the purpose and the effect of the veto in this decision. Rather than weakening the presidency, as the Justices surmised, it has actually strengthened it (1987, 100-04).

The growing acceptance of joint custody by both the president and Congress has not been confined to areas in which this legislative veto device has been available. As noted earlier, congressional demands for information in executive files became a bone of contention as early as George Washington's tenure as president. After World War II, such requests became a source of high-profile conflict in relations between the two branches of government, reflecting the fact that the media have a natural affinity for this topic.

At first—during Dwight Eisenhower's presidency, for example—the two sides took intransigent positions, and their disputes were often taken to court—most famously, of course, in the case of the Watergate affair during President Nixon's tenure. More recently, however, these controversies are being settled by political bargains in which each side retreats from an extreme position it has initially taken. Congress surrenders its claim to have access to all the information it originally requested, while the White House discovers that some of the information it is trying to withhold is not so privileged after all.

Joint custody is not without its problems, of course. It opens the door very wide to what critics describe as legislative micro-management of the decisions and actions of executive agencies. There was persistent criticism of such micro-management throughout the Reagan administration, when it was commonly seen by Republicans as an instrument through which the Democratic Congress waged war on the White House.

But it needs always to be remembered that, whatever adverse consequences it may have, such legislative micro-management takes place in a context in which Congress has agreed to surrender to the president much of the authority it once claimed over macro-management of the state apparatus.

Old habits die hard, it is said, and, even at a time when joint custody seems ascendant, it is still possible to find residues of the past. Some might argue that the nineteenth century effort to separate bureaucracy into separate spheres of presidential and congressional authority still lives on today in the distinction sometimes drawn between the inner and outer Cabinet departments, with the inner departments primarily responsive to the president, and the outer more open to congressional influence.

There are, however, powerful forces at work in twentieth century American politics that make it impossible for either the president or Congress to accept any such division of responsibility for the affairs of inner and outer Cabinet departments. With the end of the Cold War, Congress is increasingly unwilling to cede jurisdiction over defense and foreign affairs to the president. In the future as in the past, legislative oversight can be expected to be as intense here as in other areas of bureaucracy.

Presidents, on the other hand, now find their fate as much dependent on decisions that the Department of the Interior makes on the use of public lands in the West as it is on any of the weighty international issues that the mandarins in the State Department are trying to resolve in the Middle East.

There is, however, another area in which even stronger evidence exists of the present imitating the past. In the 1970s and the 1980s determined attempts were made in both the Nixon and Reagan administrations to "presidentialize the bureaucracy," as these efforts were sometimes described. The White House sought to bring all executive decisions into line with administration objectives by saturating the bureaucracy with political appointees.

This effort was doomed to fail. For one thing it triggered an offsetting response in Congress in the form of a new wave of legislative micro-management. Moreover, the most successful political appointees of these presidents quickly discovered that power in Washington depended less on their obedient compliance with White House goals than it did on their ability to build strong congressional and public support by achieving a reputation for independent judgment on policy issues. This was something that Reagan's Surgeon General, Everett Koop, did with a vengeance.

These recent attempts of the White House to establish unilateral control over executive agencies bear a strong resemblance to the congressional effort to achieve total legislative dominance over bureaucracy in the aftermath of the Civil War. The failure of both of these efforts suggests that joint custody over bureaucracy represents a point of equilibrium from which the President and Congress may sometimes depart, but to which they invariably return. For both institutions the idea of total control lies in a field of dreams.

5. What has been the most significant effect that each of its two institutional custodians—Congress and the presidency—has had on the character of American bureaucracy?

Of the presidency, I think it can fairly be said that its sharpest impact on the national bureaucracy stems from its ability to act as a spur to action in the day-to-day operation of executive agencies. Especially since the emergence and development of a high-powered White House staff, the weight of the presidency has often been thrown against the inertia characteristic of bureaucracy.

This presidential role is reminiscent of Alexander Hamilton's celebrated dictum that "energy in the executive" is indispensable to effective government. To be sure, the concept of an energetic bureaucracy may seem to many people to be an oxymoron, on a par with thundering silence or friendly fire. Moreover, there have been times when presidents have been better served by bureaucratic inertia than by decisive action. Certainly President Clinton would have been when the Bureau of Alcohol, Tobacco and Firearms was contemplating its ill-fated invasion of the Branch Davidian compound in Texas last February.

It should also be noted that the White House often plays its action-forcing role for purely self-serving reasons. Facing election deadlines, presidents are constantly looking for quick action that will yield immediate political payoffs. Bureaucracies are usually inclined to the view that success in policy requires a long march—lasting for months or years rather than days or weeks.

The congressional impact on American bureaucracy has been quite different. It stems mainly from the enormous influence the legislature has exercised over "state-building" in the United States—an area of research in which Theda Skocpol (1992) and Stephen Skowronek (1982) have stirred a revival of interest. Since the beginning of American history, Congress has approved the establishment of a variety of bureaucratic organizations designed to give the American state the muscle needed to handle its expanding set of responsibilities.

The legislature has been criticized for the slowness with which it acted, but the most remarkable aspect of congressional activity in state-building is the extent to which it has served to keep the character of American bureaucracy in harmony with the democratic character of the country. The establishment of organizations like the Departments of Agriculture, Commerce and Labor occurred as a result not of needs originated or defined in highly-placed government circles, as has been the case in many other societies, but in response to pressures for empowerment from various sectors of the American population.

One of the surprising things I discovered in a study I undertook many years ago of the origins and early development of the Department of Labor was that the department was born in 1913 before the national government had itself assumed any significant responsibilities in this field. Like Agriculture and Commerce at an earlier date, and Housing and Urban Development since that time, Labor was a department created to assure a significant sector of the population that it too had a rightful voice in the affairs of government.

Moreover, when the merit system was established in 1883, Congress insisted that civil servants be recruited from all parts of the country, thus insuring, as Fred Riggs has noted, that this country would not have the elitist bureaucracy common in other industrialized nations, such as Great Britain, France and Japan. The eventual result of this congressional action was to create a corps of civil servants that "looks like America"—to borrow a phrase from President Clinton—rather than resembling its social or economic elite. In sum, while presidents fought for a more efficient bureaucracy, Congress sought a bureaucracy in tune with the nation it served.

Of course, in talking about the presidency and Congress as instruments of transformation in the development of American bureaucracy, it has to be recognized that in human affairs the presumed authors of change can themselves be transformed. Some years ago we set up a tutoring program at Johns Hopkins, under which our undergraduate students provided remedial teaching for inner-city children. In the end, we discovered, tutoring was a much more transforming experience for our students than it was for the inner-city children.

In the same way, the interaction of the presidency and Congress with bureaucracy has had a marked effect on each of these two institutions, possibly more significant than their impact on it. Instead of the singular office the framers designed, the White House has become pluralized. In good part because of its efforts to keep the bureaucracy at bay, the presidency has itself become a bureaucratic apparatus in which many men and women exercise power, some of whom, like Henry Kissinger as Nixon's National Security Council advisor, seem to tower over the president himself.

In the case of Congress, its custody of bureaucracy has helped to turn the national legislature into what Lawrence Dodd (1989) has described as an increasingly technocratic institution, hiring its own professional staff and enlarging its research capacities in a continuing effort to overcome the advantage in expertise that executive officials so long enjoyed. In these and other ways both the presidency and Congress have been re-molded by the bureaucratic organizations they sought to shape.

What have virtually disappeared from the American scene are the organizations that once operated under no apparent custody save their own, organizations like the Corps of Engineers and the FBI. In 1951, when Arthur Maass published his classic study of the Corps, *Muddy Waters,* the agency seemed to call all the shots in its sphere of water resource policy, a power that no longer exists. Of the FBI today we might well ask, "where have you gone, J. Edgar Hoover?" What happened to your glory days as FBI director, when you had both presidents and congressional committees dancing to your tune, even as you were off somewhere, apparently, dancing to a quite different melody?

The disappearance or erosion in power of such seemingly self-directing organizations points to the fact that American bureaucracy has been, in terms of democratic norms, on an upward curve in recent years. Thanks to Freedom of Information statutes and other "sunshine" legislation, it has become less secretive, and the weakening of iron triangles has made it much more responsive to broad constituencies and much less the creature of its own clients. The regime of joint custody cannot claim sole credit for these changes, but it has certainly played a role in their accomplishment.

Still, nothing lasts forever in politics. Congress and the President face a constant temptation to restructure the understandings on which joint custody rests. As noted already, this has been an unstable arrangement in the past, when the bureaucracy was a much smaller and less valuable prize. Today, control over administrative organizations has become considerably more important for both the White House and Congress, since political fortunes in each of these institutions are often at stake in the exercise of discretion by bureaucratic underlings. This fact alone insures that the question with which we began will never die: "Whose bureaucracy is this, anyway?"

REFERENCES

Arnold, Peri E. 1986. *Making the Managerial Presidency: Comprehensive Reorganization Planning, 1905–1980*. Princeton: Princeton University Press.

Dodd, Lawrence C. 1989. "The Rise of the Technocratic Congress: Congressional Reform in the 1970s," in *Remaking American Politics,* ed. Richard A. Harris and Sidney M. Milkis. Boulder, CO: Westview Press.

Fisher, Louis. 1987. *The Politics of Shared Power: Congress and the Executive,* 2nd ed. Washington, DC: Congressional Quarterly, Inc.

Maass, Arthur, 1951. *Muddy Waters*. Cambridge: Harvard University Press.

Pious, Richard M. 1979. *The American Presidency*. New York: Basic Books, Inc.

Short, Lloyd M. 1923. *The Development of National Administrative Organization in the United States*. Baltimore: The Johns Hopkins Press.

Skocpol, Theda. 1992. *Protecting Soldiers and Mothers: The Political Origins of Social Policy in the United States*. Cambridge, MA: Belknap Press of Harvard University Press.

Skowronek, Stephen. 1982. *Building a New American State: The Expansion of National Administrative Capacities, 1877–1920*. New York: Cambridge University Press.

12

THE PRESIDENT
AND THE JUDICIARY

You Can't Always Get What You Want: Reflections on the Ginsburg and Breyer Nominations

Mark Silverstein[*]

William Haltom[+]

At first glance, the confirmations of Justices Ginsburg and Breyer may have suggested a return to senatorial acquiescence in presidential appointments to the United States Supreme Court. In this second glance at the Breyer and Ginsburg nominations, we suggest that conflicts—relocated but nonetheless persistent—continue to define the modern politics of selecting and confirming Supreme Court personnel. We do not contest the proposition that sharp, public confirmation battles are more likely during periods of divided government. We do contend, however, that unified party rule in 1993–1994 did not eradicate contentious confirmation proceedings but merely displaced the conflict that still rules in the appointment of Supreme Court justices. Strife migrated from *confirmation* in the Senate to *nomination* within the executive branch. This migration of conflict explains why no president in the last century has found selecting a nominee—as opposed to confirming the nominee selected—as daunting as President Bill Clinton did in 1993 and 1994.[1]

I. What Mr. Clinton Wanted and What He Got

Justices Ginsburg and Breyer dramatize a gap between what Candidate Clinton said he wanted and what President Clinton found he could get. Candidate Clinton said that he would seek to appoint to the High Court lawyers of genuine political

---

[*]Associate Professor of Political Science, Boston University. Cornell, B.A. 1969; Columbia University Law School, J.D. 1972; Cornell, Ph.D. 1983.

[+]Associate Professor of Politics and Government, University of Puget Sound. University of Washington, B.A. 1975; Ph.D. 1984.

[1]Of course, President Clinton's difficulties could stem largely from his own foibles or the shortcomings of his White House. Below, we explore aspects of modern appointments and confirmations that may bedevil President Clinton's successors as well.

stature who had achieved prominence outside of service on state or national courts. President Clinton's first two appointments were, however, *techno-judges:* politically innocuous, federal appellate judges with impeccable legal credentials and little political experience.[2] The obvious disparity between these techno-justices and the President's unrealized ideal illuminates the latest developments in the politics of appointing and confirming Supreme Court justices. Please allow us to summarize this current history.

Before the 1992 Democratic National Convention, Bill Clinton, the presumptive Democratic candidate, announced on an MTV "town hall meeting" that Mario Cuomo would make an excellent choice for the Supreme Court because the New York Governor was someone who "understands the impact of the law on real people's lives." After the broadcast, Clinton explained that his statement did not constitute a commitment to Cuomo but exemplified ". . . the kind of person I would want on the Court."[3] While neither George Bush nor Bill Clinton during the 1992 campaign emphasized appointments to the federal judiciary, Clinton made no effort to back away from the idea that he favored prominent public figures like Cuomo. Professor Walter Dellinger, consultant to the Clinton campaign on judicial matters, asserted that the Democratic candidate believed that the current Court suffered from the lack of any member who had played a prominent role in the life of the nation prior to coming to the High Court.[4] In this regard the Court of the 1990s stood in stark contrast to the Court of the mid-1950s that decided *Brown v. Board of Education* and counted among its members former senators, governors and other public figures. Dellinger's message was obvious: if elected, Bill Clinton would transform the Court with appointments of extra-judicial stature and political experience.[5]

When Justice White announced his retirement in the spring of 1993, President Clinton made it clear that he was seeking a nominee with broad political experience, well known to people for a big heart, whose nomination would be met with cries of "Wow! A home run!"[6] Within weeks, however, Governor Cuomo removed himself from consideration and the administration appeared to carom from one candidate to another before Clinton selected Ruth Bader Ginsburg eighty-seven days after White's announcement.[7] Judge Ginsburg was an extremely competent appellate judge with an impressive intellect and record, but she was certainly not a political figure of great stature. Clinton had sacrificed his ideal justice to obtain a "techno-judge" certain to be confirmed.

---

[2]Consider Mark Silverstein, *Special Interests Produce Dull Court Nominees,* NAT'L L.J., July 11, 1994, at A21. The career pattern of the techno-judge often includes graduation from a prestigious national law school coupled with service on the law review, clerkship with a Supreme Court justice, academic appointment at a similar law school and perhaps service in the public sector with the Justice Department or the Solicitor General's office prior to appointment to the federal court. Despite acquiring a reputation as a highly skilled jurist within the legal community, the techno-judge is virtually unknown to the public at large until selected as a nominee to the Supreme Court.

[3]*See,* Sam Fulwood, *Clinton Sees Cuomo as Potential Justice,* L. A. TIMES, June 17, 1992, at A12.

[4]Timothy M. Phelps, *Campaign '92—High Court.,* N.Y. NEWSDAY, Oct. 30, 1992, at A17.

[5]*Id.*

[6]Thomas L. Friedman, *The 11th Hour Scramble,* N.Y. TIMES, June 14, 1993, at A1.

[7]*Id.*

A year later, Justice Blackmun announced his retirement and again the Clinton Administration began to search for a nominee.[8] Again the president made it clear he was looking for a candidate well-known to the nation at large, with real political experience and stature.[9] Once again, after great delay, he nominated a techno-judge of substantial legal skills but utterly wanting in the political and real-life experiences he sought. If Candidate Clinton in 1992 found the Court to be sadly lacking members with experience outside of the judicial arena, President Clinton in 1993 and 1994 failed to ameliorate that shortcoming in back-to-back opportunities.

How could a newly elected President with a working Democratic majority in the Senate be so obviously frustrated on his selection of nominees to the Court? Beyond the usual divergence of campaign rhetoric and presidential conduct and the Clinton Administration's difficulties with appointments in general, changed nomination politics to a large degree accounts for the rise of the techno-judge and the demise of the nominee with real-life experience and political stature. In the next section, we shall briefly review the most obvious developments that have altered modern confirmation politics. In subsequent sections, we shall then show how conflict conditioned Clinton's choices *before* he nominated Ginsburg and Breyer. Taken together, these developments in *confirmation* and *nomination* politics explain Clinton's inability to get what he said he wanted.

II. From Deference to Defiance

From 1895 through 1967, the United States Senate deferred to presidents regarding nominations to the Court.[10] Through those seventy-three years, only Judge John J. Parker in 1930 was rejected by the Senate.[11] Between Rufus Peckham in 1895 and Thurgood Marshall in 1967, thirty-one of forty-five nominees (69%) occasioned no recorded vote.[12] When votes were recorded, opposition was usually token or unspoken. From 1930 through 1967, during unified and divided party rule, not one nominee excited opposition from even one-fifth of the Senate.[13]

In 1968, however, the politics of acquiescence quickly became the politics of confrontation and judicial confirmations were transmogrified. The Senate rejected Justice Abraham Fortas for Chief Justice and Judges Haynsworth and Carswell for Associate Justice.[14] Since 1968, seven nominations have elicited more than

---

[8]Indeed, Justice Blackmun had made his intentions known to the White House long before his resignation was announced, but we find no evidence that Clinton or his advisors took advantage of their lead-time. We thank Professor Stephen L. Wasby for reminding us of this point.

[9]Neil A. Lewis, *Supreme Court Search Said to Narrow to 2,* N.Y. TIMES, May 6, 1994, at A18.

[10]The single best source on the history of appointments to the United States Supreme Court remains Henry J. ABRAHAM, JUSTICES AND PRESIDENTS: A POLITICAL HISTORY OF APPOINTMENTS TO THE SUPREME COURT (1992). Before 1894, highly partisan Senates had turned down one of every four presidential nominees to the High Court. *See* THE SUPREME COURT: JUSTICE AND THE LAW 177-179 (Cong. Q. ed., 3rd ed. 1983).

[11]Henry J. ABRAHAM, JUSTICES AND PRESIDENTS: A POLITICAL HISTORY OF APPOINTMENTS TO THE SUPREME COURT 42 (1992).

[12]*Id.*

[13]*Id.* at 13.

[14]*Id.* at 13, 15.

twenty-five negative votes in the Senate.[15] Including Fortas, four nominations have failed of Senate approval.[16] Two sitting justices—Thomas and Rehnquist—garnered more negative votes than any other successful nominees in two hundred years.[17] Supreme Court confirmation hearings before the Senate Judiciary Committee since 1981 have been televised and the Bork and Thomas confirmations proved that, with the right mix of personalities, issues, and titillation, hearings attract huge audiences and substantial media coverage. More, confrontations now consume far greater time and energy. In 1932, Republican President Herbert Hoover nominated Democrat Benjamin Cardozo and a Republican Senate confirmed in ten days.[18] In 1994, on the eve of a nomination, the Democratic Chair of the Judiciary Committee, Senator Joseph Biden, informed a Democratic White House that it would take at least six to eight weeks for his committee to *prepare* for hearings.[19]

What produced this politics of confrontation? First, fragmentation of the New Deal coalition during the 1960s split the Democratic Party between old-line party regulars and elite progressives who increasingly relied upon the federal judiciary to further their social and political goals. Successful litigation by these new Democrats during the 1960s and early 1970s riled conservatives who focused attention on an "imperial" federal judiciary as a primary source of unwanted social change.[20] Successive Republican presidents responded to these developments by linking the New Right and the Christian Right to the Republican Party through at least rhetorical support of traditional values coupled with repeated pledges to overthrow the imperial judiciary through the appointment of more restrained judges.[21] Consequently, potent political forces within both parties now scrutinize federal judicial appointments intensely, if not fiercely.

Second, changes in the nature of judicial power ratcheted the stakes in the confirmation process still higher. The willingness of the justices of the Warren Court to make the federal courts amenable to a wider range of litigants and issues than before prompted an expanding array of interests to pursue policy goals in federal courts.

Third, alterations in both the formal rules and institutional folkways of the Senate enhanced the influence of individual senators at the expense of institutional

[15]Included among these seven, of course, is the failed cloture vote on Justice Fortas. While Fortas probably would have been confirmed had the filibuster been stopped, he nonetheless would have elicited more than twenty-five nays.

[16]ABRAHAM, supra note 11, at 39.

[17]Thirty-three negative votes were registered when the Senate confirmed Justice Rehnquist as Chief Justice in 1986. Justice Thomas received 48 negative votes. (Justice Rehnquist also produced 26 negative votes in his initial confirmation in 1971). CONGRESSIONAL QUARTERLY, GUIDE TO THE SUPREME COURT 995-98 (1990).

[18]ABRAHAM, supra note 11, at 206.

[19]Gwen Ifill, *Clinton Style Means a Slow Process in Picking a Supreme Court Nominee,* N.Y. TIMES, May 5, 1994, at B10.

[20]Of course, scholarly demonstration that the "imperial judiciary" was more sound-bite than sound reasoning did nothing to undermine the resonance of the charge. *See* Stephen L. Wasby, *Arrogation of Power or Accountability: 'Judicial Imperialism' Revisited,* 65 JUDICATURE 209 (1981).

[21]MARK SILVERSTEIN, JUDICIOUS CHOICES: THE NEW POLITICS OF SUPREME COURT CONFIRMATIONS 116-23 (1994).

unity and party leadership. Behind-the-scenes deals cut by presidents and Senate leaders to assure an easy confirmation route no longer manage an increasingly independent Senate.

The period of confrontation also has been marked by a divided government and several commentators have observed that increased scrutiny of nominees to the Court—at least during the 1980s—was the product of a Democratic Senate rebelling against the heavy-handed efforts of Republican presidents to shift the Court to the Right.[22] When the election of Bill Clinton in 1992 unified government and Judges Ginsburg and Breyer advanced to the Supreme Court with apparent ease, the divided government argument appeared persuasive. After all, both nominees enjoyed widespread support and in both cases the hearings before the Judiciary Committee were certainly thorough but, at least for the modern era, rather desultory.[23] The recorded votes in the Senate provided overwhelming majorities for both Ginsburg and Breyer.[24]

While one would be hard-pressed to characterize either confirmation a "mess,"[25] both nominations show that confrontation endures, albeit not in the Judiciary Committee hearings or on the Senate floor. Transmogrification of confirmations has relocated conflict. Democratic control (however precarious) of Senate hearings and the Senate floor prompted potential opponents (and, indeed, proponents) of a Clinton nominee to redirect their efforts to the stages of judicial recruitment and selection. President Clinton retreated from Candidate Clinton's ideal appointees because the politics of confrontation circumscribed his choices *before* he named his nominees to succeed Justices White and Blackmun. While the unhurried pace of the President and his aides exacerbated his vulnerability at early stages of nomination, we must not let the particulars of 1993 and 1994 distract us from more general developments in nomination and confirmation politics, developments intensified by the combination of a Democratic president and Republican control of the Senate.

III. Mobilization Precedes Nomination

Mobilizing opposition has always played a critical role in contesting Supreme Court nominations *once presidents have named a candidate.*[26] During the presidencies of Ronald Reagan and George Bush, however, opponents organized before nominations or even openings were apparent. Beginning in 1984, the Alliance for Justice,

---

[22]*See, e.g.,* William G. Ross, *The Supreme Court Appointment Process: A Search for a Synthesis,* 57 ALB. L. REV. 993 (1994).

[23]Indeed, Judge Breyer may have become Justice Breyer because Senators passed over conflict of interest charges without any real scrutiny.

[24]Justice Ginsburg was confirmed by a 96-3 vote. *See,* 51 CONG. Q. 2193 (1993). Justice Breyer was confirmed by an 87-9 vote. *See,* 52 CONG. Q. 2294 (1994).

[25]STEPHEN CARTER, THE CONFIRMATION MESS: CLEANING UP THE FEDERAL APPOINTMENT PROCESS (1994). The same, however, cannot be said for the selection process.

[26]For a recent example, *see* MICHAEL PERTSCHUK & WENDY SCHAETZEL, THE PEOPLE RISING THE CAMPAIGN AGAINST THE BORK NOMINATION (1989).

a coalition of approximately twenty public interest groups, formed the Judicial Selection Project to coordinate efforts in the battle against Ronald Reagan's appointments.[27] Groups as diverse as the Consumers Union, the Children's Defense Fund, the National Wildlife Federation and People for the American Way dedicated staff and funds to establish a full time, continuing effort to monitor Reagan judicial appointments.[28] With the support of the traditional civil rights establishment, the Project maintained links with sympathetic senators and, particularly during the battle over the Bork nomination, developed the structure to facilitate grassroots mobilization.[29] Well financed and particularly skilled in the use of the media, the Judicial Selection Project proved a powerful and often effective force in efforts to challenge Reagan and Bush nominees.[30] Although the Selection Project exercised little influence over the choice of nominees, the emergence of an organization dedicated to monitoring judicial appointments and skilled in modern media politics dramatically altered confirmations in the late 1980s.[31]

The success of the Judicial Selection Project and the results of the 1992 election spurred conservatives to develop a similar means of challenging Clinton appointments. Close upon Clinton's election, erstwhile Judge Robert H. Bork warned of the dangers of Clinton appointments to the federal judiciary and sought funds to establish a Judicial Selection Monitoring Project even before the first Clinton nominee had been selected.[32] Headed by Thomas Jipping and run under the Free Congress Foundation, the monitoring project sought to unite New Right groups in preparation for anticipated battles over Clinton nominees.[33] Mirroring the tactics of its liberal counterpart, the conservative Monitoring Project maintained important links with key Republican senators and grassroots organizations as well as providing a steady stream of Op-Ed pieces challenging the judicial activism of proposed Clinton nominees. The modest efforts of liberal groups to dissuade Reagan from choosing Bork were now dwarfed by conservative groups' efforts to moderate Clinton's choices. In effect, organizations dedicated to playing effective *confirmation* politics were refocusing their attention on judicial *selection*. The politics of confrontation was drifting backward from conflictual confirmations to contested nominations.

[27]ETHAN BRONNER, BATTLE FOR JUSTICE: HOW THE BORK NOMINATION SHOOK AMERICA 119-20 (1989).

[28]Ross, *supra* note 22, at 1023 n. 124.

[29]The Alliance for Justice over a period of several years in effect perfected the technique of contesting judgeships. For example, during the battle of the appointment of Daniel Manion to the Seventh Circuit the Alliance proved particularly adept at reaching out to law schools for support, mobilizing numerous deans and professors in opposition. During the effort to deny Rehnquist confirmation as chief justice, the Alliance found that groups outside the traditional civil rights arena were interested in judicial appointments and could be conscripted as part of the opposition.

[30]For a description and account of the tactics of People for the American Way, *see* Philip Shenon, *Praise and Pillory for a Liberal Lobby Group,* N. Y. TIMES, Aug. 6, 1986, at A16. *See also,* R. H. Bork, Jr., *The Media, Special Interests, and the Bork Nomination, in,* NINTH JUSTICE: THE FIGHT FOR BORK 245 (Patrick B. McGuigan & Dawn M. Weirich eds., 1990).

[31]However, some groups tried to influence President Reagan's selection of Bork. *See* BRONNER, *supra* note 27 at 26-126; Bork, *supra* note 30, at 1-10.

[32]Neil A. Lewis, *Conservatives Set for Fight on Judicial Nominees,* N.Y. TIMES, Nov. 13, 1993, at B16.

[33]*Id*.

In the days immediately following Justice White's resignation, for example, the Monitoring Project prominently floated—in addition to Cuomo—Laurence Tribe, Marian Wright Edelman, and Eleanor Holmes Norton as potential nominees.[34] That, aside from Cuomo, there was virtually no evidence that the Clinton Administration was seriously considering any of these individuals was beside the point. Each was anathema to the Monitoring Project's supporters and useful for mobilizing opposition before a nominee was selected. Clint Bolick spoke frankly of the strategy:

> At the very least, even if our side can't defeat a nominee in a particular instance, we would force Clinton to expend enormous political capital by mobilizing activists at the grass-roots level. This is the issue that energizes conservatives more than others.[35]

In the last decade, monitoring of nominees to the federal courts by coalitions of interests on the Left and Right has bracketed presidential choice. Ongoing scrutiny of potential as well as actual nominees increases the level of conflict in the selection process whether government is divided or unified. The Clinton White House has felt the full impact of these developments, at times assailed by the Alliance for Justice for proposed appointments to the federal courts deemed insufficiently sympathetic to progressive causes while being attacked from the Right for considering proponents of judicial activism.[36]

Hence, Candidate Clinton had expressed support for a nominee of political stature without regard to the political realities that would direct President Clinton to safe nominations lest his judicial nominees join Zoë Baird, Kimba Wood, and Lani Guinier as casualties of confirmation "messes." When a defeated Judge Bork warned that the politics of electoral campaigns had been brought to bear on his nomination,[37] he accurately forecast constraints on the selection as well as the confirmation of high profile nominees to the Court. That the political activist Bork has played an important and enthusiastic role in fulfilling Judge Bork's dire prophecy is yet another indication of the ease with which the politics of confrontation has migrated from confirmation to selection.

IV. Beware the Filibuster!

If liberals, conservatives, and others have employed campaign-like rhetoric and public relations to shape Clinton's nominations, a more familiar Senate tactic favored techno-judges as well. Once we remember that Justice Fortas was defeated by a filibuster and probably would have been confirmed over fierce opposition had the matter made it to a vote, the importance of a more confrontational modern

---

[34]Ruth Shalit, *Borking Back: The Rights Gets Even*, NEW REPUBLIC, May 17, 1993, at 18.

[35]Ruth Marcus & Joan Biskupic, *Justice White to Retire After 31 Years*, WASH. POST, Mar. 20, 1993, at A1.

[36]*See, e.g.*, Daniel Klaidman, *Just Like Old Times? Liberals Challenge President on Some Judgeships*, LEGAL TIMES, Oct. 25, 1993, at 1. Conservative ire with a potential nomination of Peter Edelman to the D.C. Circuit is described in W. John Moore, *From Shoo-in to Shutout?*, NAT'L J., Dec. 17, 1994, at 2,998.

[37]ROBERT H. BORK, THE TEMPTING OF AMERICA 10 (1990).

Senate becomes obvious. President Clinton has had to anticipate and to avoid fili-busters, an anxiety of which Candidate Clinton was oblivious, perhaps.

In his pioneering study of the Senate of the 1950s, Professor Donald Matthews showed that senators, able to bring the whole house to a standstill, would refrain from such obstruction except in the most extraordinary situations.[38] Today, this norm has been supplanted, in the view of former senator Fred Harris, by the unabashed readiness of individual senators to employ the rules and traditions of the Senate to further personal rather than institutional goals.[39]

The increased use of the filibuster is one obvious manifestation of this devel-opment and its use has proceeded in at least two directions. The *personal* filibuster or threat of a personal filibuster is a frequently employed tactic of champions of constituents or powerful interest groups. Senators Howard Metzenbaum and Jesse Helms are well known for employing their individual powers to delay proceedings to further their agendas. More significant for understanding the politics of the modern confirmation process is the resurgence of the *party* filibuster.[40] Through the entire nineteenth century, for example, there were sixteen filibusters; in 1993–1994, there were twenty filibusters, seventy-two motions for cloture, and an untold number of threatened filibusters that substantially altered the legislative process.[41] Employed by the Republicans in varying degrees after their loss of the Senate in 1986, the party-backed filibuster reached a new degree of effectiveness in 1993 and the spring of 1994 as the Republicans stymied Democratic policy ini-tiatives.[42] So effective was the Republican use of the filibuster that the failure of an early cloture vote typically doomed controversial legislation.

The threat of a potential party-backed filibuster and the resultant need for sixty votes to invoke cloture conditioned the Clinton White House's search for a suc-cessor to Justice Blackmun.[43] Although filibusters had rarely figured in judicial confirmations, the administration had to anticipate a supermajority *before nomi-nation.*[44] As a result, even suggested opposition to a proposed nominee derailed candidates.[45] In the recent past, senators and interests opposed to a nominee for the Court prepared for battle in the structured setting of the Judiciary Committee or debate on the Senate floor. The Clinton Administration, fearful of the disrup-tive effect of contentious hearings or the reality of a filibuster when the nomina-tion reached the floor of the Senate, permitted friend and foe alike a virtual veto over potential candidates during the selection process.[46] Thus did President Clinton allow senators to deny him the nominees that as Candidate Clinton he had lauded.

[38]DONALD MATTHEWS, U.S. SENATORS AND THEIR WORLD (1960).

[39]FRED R. HARRIS, DEADLOCK OR DECISION: THE U.S. SENATE AND THE RISE OF NATIONAL POLITICS 118 (1993).

[40]Described in HARRIS, *supra* note 39, at 155-56.

[41]*See* Graeme Browning, *Freelancers,* NAT'L J., Sept. 24, 1994, at 2204.

[42]*Id.* at 2203-06.

[43]*Id.* at 2204.

[44]For a sense of the continuing impact of the filibuster threat on the Clinton Administration, *see* Neil A. Lewis, *At the Bar,* N.Y. TIMES, Dec. 9, 1994, at B7.

[45]*Id.*

[46]See *infra* text accompanying notes 66-76.

V. Partisans Supplant Evaluators and Validators

The Ginsburg and Breyer nominations may also suggest that, prior to the announcement of the nominee, senators as well as interest groups intervene *before nomination* to influence the roles that their senators are likely to play during the formal confirmation process. Professors George Watson and John Stookey have demonstrated that senators' roles in confirmations are greatly influenced by the controversy that nominations engender.[47] If senators and lobbyists can threaten to make some nominees controversial and others "shoo-ins," they may be able to induce the White House to select safe candidates in order to assure that senators will adopt more conciliatory roles. While we are extending Watson's and Stookey's model from the hearing to the pre-nomination stage, we believe that this shift explains some of Clinton's inability to deliver on his promised nominations.

For our purposes, the key roles are the evaluator, the validator, and the partisan.[48] Evaluators remain at least somewhat open-minded and expect to use the confirmation process to make up their minds.[49] Validators already lean for or against nominees and largely engage in marshaling evidence for the position toward which they lean.[50] In contrast to evaluators and validators, partisans have made up their minds.[51] The goal of partisans is to win. Partisans turn all efforts toward securing their preferred outcomes, often by any means available.[52] Much of the effort prior to the committee hearings goes into moving potential supporters into more aggressive roles (that is, making validators of evaluators and partisans of validators) while neutralizing potential opponents in relatively passive stances.[53]

Watson and Stookey showed that many senators come to the hearings with minds made up and thus are prone to more aggressive roles.[54] What we suggest here is that the same is true before nominations if an administration is susceptible to threats and easily enticed by promises of gentle treatment. Clinton and his staff knew that Ginsburg and Breyer would elicit little immediate opposition and much immediate support while a high visibility, political candidate would push key senators into aggressive roles.[55] Absent another "Stealth nominee,"[56] Clinton had few safe options.

---

[47]George L. Watson & John A. Stookey, *Supreme Court Confirmation Hearings: A View from the Senate,* 71 JUDICATURE 186-96 (1987–1988). For a more complete treatment that accounts for more recent developments, *see* GEORGE L. WATSON & JOHN A. STOOKEY, SHAPING AMERICA: THE POLITICS OF SUPREME COURT APPOINTMENTS 148-55 (1995).

[48]Watson and Stookey defined two other roles—the educator and the advertiser—that seem less directly relevant to the pre-nomination period than the other three.

[49]Watson & Stookey, *supra* note 47, at 148-55.

[50]*Id.*

[51]*Id.*

[52]*Id.*

[53]*Id.*

[54]*Id.*

[55]Witness the reaction, for example, to the prominent names floated by the Judicial Monitoring Project following Justice White's resignation. See *supra* text accompanying note 36.

[56]"Stealth nominees" may be more fanciful than many pundits presume. *See* Michael Comiskey, *The Real and Imagined Consequences of Senatorial Consent to Silent Supreme Court Nominees,* 11 J.L. & POL. 47-53 (1995).

This view sees in the absence of conflict during confirmations a result of successful threats and inducements before nominations. Senators could sublimate defiance and simulate deference at hearings and in floor debates because conflict—threatened and anticipated—had already winnowed Clinton's choice to politically acceptable techno-judges. Is it too facile to hypothesize that the Senate readily consents if it has already substantially advised?

VI. The Separated Presidency

A final reason that President Clinton could not get what he had said that he wanted was that his presidency quickly fell victim to "the separated presidency."[57] Although an important element in the Democratic drive to capture the presidency in 1992 was the promise to end the gridlock of divided rule, once in office Bill Clinton proved unable to unite with a permanent, cohesive governing majority.[58] Instead, he has been forced to assemble ad hoc coalitions to secure passage of his agenda.[59] Clinton, for example, relied exclusively on Democratic votes to secure passage of his initial budget proposals.[60] On the North America Free Trade Agreement, however, he was forced to ally himself with congressional Republicans against the forceful opposition of many within his own party.[61] He has at once promoted measures certain to delight the Democratic left—the BTU energy conservation tax and efforts to end discrimination against gays in the military—while pilfering the crime issue from Republicans by embracing a crime control bill that alienated the congressional Black Caucus.[62] Clinton found that the 1990's version of unified government demanded that he do whatever worked to maintain narrow majorities available to him.

Marooned in his White House, President Clinton had to weigh the desirability of nominating to the Supreme Court an individual of political stature and experience against the impact of the nomination on the ever-changing coalitions needed for tomorrow's political battles. Assessing potential nominees, consulting with senators of both parties and allowing even the suggestion of opposition to kill a potential nomination guaranteed a confirmation process free from conflict. On the other hand, it made the nomination of a person of political stature a virtual impossibility. President Clinton kept Candidate Clinton from trying to get what he once wanted.

---

[57]Charles Jones, *The Separated Presidency—Making it Work in Contemporary Politics, in* THE NEW AMERICAN POLITICAL SYSTEM (Anthony King ed., 1990). Professor Jones was writing during a period of divided government but his conclusions seem applicable as well to the Clinton Administration's first two years.

[58]Francis Mancini, *Why the Crime Bill Went Down,* PROVIDENCE J., Aug. 18, 1994, at 1A.

[59]*See* Burnham, *American Politics in the 1990s, in* THE AMERICAN PROSPECT: READER IN AMERICAN POLITICS (1995).

[60]Facts on File WORLD NEWS DIGEST. *Clinton Budget Plan Clears Congress, 1.96 Billion in Tax Hikes and Spending Cuts Set,* Aug. 12, 1993, at 588 A1.

[61]Keith Bradsher, *Trade Pact Involves Delicate Talks with Congress,* N.Y. TIMES, Aug. 15, 1993, at A14.

[62]Steve McGonigle, *House Rejects Debate on Crime Package, Defect Leaves Clinton Bitter,* DALLAS MORNING NEWS, Aug. 12, 1994, at 1A.

The rigors of sacrificing nominees to the High Court for votes for various policy initiatives may not be so much Clinton's problem as the Democrats' problem. Professor Walter Dean Burnham has written of the extent to which the modern Republican party is ideologically united while the Democrats are "more of a holding company of diverse and often warring interests."[63] Republicans occupy a defined position on the right but Democrats range from across the political spectrum. As a consequence, Democratic presidents—with or without the benefit of unified government—are in less of a position to secure "blockbuster" appointments to the Court than Republicans. Ronald Reagan could count on relatively little opposition from within Republican ranks for a nominee as controversial as Robert Bork. If the nominee failed to get the necessary votes, the effort, over the long haul, would scarcely affect the president's power to govern. The same cannot be said for Democrats. For Clinton, a controversial nominee would not only evoke a Republican response but defections within his own party. President Clinton, we conclude, has been even more "separated" with a unified government than President Reagan was with a divided government.

Consider, for example, the difficulty faced by the administration following Justice Blackmun's retirement announcement. After retiring Senator George Mitchell removed his name from consideration, the White House engaged in a prolonged period of leaking names and assessing reactions.[64] Attention fastened on District (now Circuit) Judge Jose Cabranes.[65] Clinton was reported to be intrigued with the idea of appointing the first Hispanic to the Supreme Court but the Puerto Rican native was considered too conservative by several groups that preferred a Mexican-American for the post.[66] Civil rights groups rallied behind Solicitor Drew Days but Days attracted the ire of New Right groups with his stand on a child pornography case currently before the Court and administration sources, nervous over any linkage with "kiddie porn," quickly dropped Days from consideration.[67] Women's groups opposed the nomination of Judge Richard Arnold because of his vote in several abortion cases[68] and when, for the second time in just a year, attention focused on Secretary of Interior Bruce Babbitt, the ranking Republican on the Judiciary Committee, Senator Orrin Hatch, declared that he could not support Babbitt because he was certain that he would be an activist judge who would legislate from the bench.[69]

[63]Burnham, *supra* note 59.

[64]Stuart Taylor, *Bursting Clinton's Trial-Balloon Tactics,* NEW JERSEY L.J., May 23, 1994, at 18.

[65]T.R. Goldman, *Hispanics want Blackmun's Seat But Can't Unite,* TEX. L., Apr. 25, 1994, at 8.

[66]It will be interesting to see if an additional opening on the High Court might not induce President Clinton, *qua* Candidate Clinton again, to attempt to curry favor with increasingly important electoral "groups" by promoting Cabranes after all.

[67]The case is Knox v. U.S., 63 U.S.L.W. 3316 (U.S. Oct 18, 1994) in which Days, in his capacity as Solicitor General, had signed a brief urging the Court to reverse a lower court's extraordinarily broad and novel reading of a federal child obscenity statute. Clint Bolick threatened a "messy fight" if Days were to be nominated because Days' position in the case "makes many of our sister organizations absolutely apoplectic" (quoted in John Aloysius Farrell, *Partisan Jockeying Besets Hunt for Justice,* BOSTON GLOBE, May 2, 1994, at 1).

[68]Neil Lewis, *Clinton Nears a Court Choice as Lobbying Becomes Intense,* N.Y. TIMES, May 10, 1994, at A21.

[69]Conservative groups promised a major battle over Babbitt and the White House was equally dismayed by the prospect of having to confirm a new Secretary of the Interior.

In the end, Judge Breyer was the sole survivor of a tortuous, public selection process designed to avoid even the appearance of conflict in the Senate. A non-candidate throughout—in 1994, unlike 1993, his name was rarely mentioned until the president's announcement of his selection—Breyer was the choice precisely because he posed few political problems.[70] The ease of his confirmation, however, should not obscure the degree to which his selection was the product of conflict and political weakness.

VII. Clinton Can't Get What He Wanted

Thus, the Clinton Administration's "Techno-Judge" strategy responds to conflicts displaced toward nominations. Confrontations that once would have taken place on the floor of the Senate (such as Fortas and Thomas), in hearings of the Senate Judiciary Committee (Rehnquist provides examples in 1971 and 1986), or in the media between nomination and hearings (as with Bork and Douglas Ginsburg in 1987) now dominate, to a far greater extent than before, the period between announcement of an opening and nomination.

This relocation of conflict to earlier stages explains Clinton's tardiness in naming successors. Cabinet confirmation messes induced Clinton to take his time in nominating federal judges. Unlike too many openings in lower federal courts, at least Clinton named Supreme Court nominees eventually. Table One shows just how casual Clinton's pace has been with regard to the selection of Supreme Court justices.

While Clinton's pace roughly matches that of President Nixon (excluding the months that it took Nixon to replace Chief Justice Earl Warren with Chief Justice Warren Burger), he has tarried far longer than his immediate predecessors. Even if we overlook the time that the Clinton Administration had between the day that Justice Blackmun told them that he planned to resign and the public announcement that he was stepping down, Clinton took three days longer to settle on Judge Breyer than Ronald Reagan took to select all six of those whom he nominated. President Bush took one week to name his two nominees; Clinton nearly eighteen weeks to name his pair. President Ford, like President Bush, confronted a Senate controlled by the other party but saw Justice John Paul Stevens confirmed thirty-seven days after Justice William O. Douglas announced his retirement, the same number of days it took Clinton to pick Breyer. The bottom rows of Table One show that Clinton has taken three times as long to nominate as all Republicans since Nixon.

We may use charts to track the regression of confrontation from later to earlier stages of the process. Chart One displays the mean days per president for each of four "stages" in the recruitment process: Stage One runs from an announced opening until nomination; Stage Two from nomination to the opening of Judiciary Committee hearings; Stage Three from the start of hearings through the

---

[70]Taylor, *supra* note 64, at 18.

TABLE ONE
RECENT CONFIRMATION "PERIODS"

Departing justice	Opening announced	Nominee	Days until nominee announced	Days until hearings started	Days until comm vote	Days until floor vote
Warren	6/21/68	Fortas	5	28[71]	88	101[72]
	10/2/68[73]	Burger	232	245	245	251
Fortas	5/15/69	Haynsworth	95	123	147	190
	11/21/69	Carswell	59	67	87	128
	4/8/70	Blackmun	6	21	27	34
Black	9/17/71	Powell	34	47[74]	67	80
Harlan	9/23/71	Rehnquist	28	40	61	74
Douglas	11/12/75	Stevens	16	26	29	37
Stewart	6/18/81	O'Connor	19	83	89	95
Burger	6/17/86	Rehnquist	0	42	58	92
Rehnquist	6/17/86	Scalia	0	49	58	92
Powell	6/26/87	Bork	5	81	102	117
	10/23/87	Ginsburg	6			
	11/7/87	Kennedy	4	37	81	88
Brennan	7/20/90	Souter	3	55	69	74
Marshall	6/27/91	Thomas	4	75	92	110
White	3/19/93	Ginsburg	87	153	162	167
Blackmun	4/6/94	Breyer	37	97	104	114
	G.O.P. Mean Days[75]		20	57	74	93
	Clinton Mean Days		62	125	133	141

[71]Opening of hearings before Senate Judiciary Committee postponed seven days at the request of Senator Sam Ervin.

[72]Cloture vote, not roll-call on nomination. Justice Fortas withdrew the day after.

[73]Re-opening of office of Chief Justice due to Justice Fortas's withdrawal. Nomination of Judge Warren Burger was delayed by presidential election.

[74]Formally presented to Judiciary Committee; questioning began four days later.

[75]Figures for Chief Justice Burger excluded as *sui generis*.

Judiciary Committee's recommendation and vote; and Stage Four from the Judiciary Committee's report through the Senate roll-call.[76]

During the Fortas nomination, the bulk of the time was consumed between the start of the Senate Judiciary Committee's hearings and the vote of the Committee—Stage Three. This represents a classic confrontation inside the Senate. No nominee since Fortas has spent even one-third as many days in the Judiciary Committee (excluding Justice Thomas's time answering Professor Hill's allegations). Beginning with President Reagan, the Senate Committee stretched out the period between nomination and the commencement of the hearings. That is, confrontation migrated "back" to Stage Two. Stage Two permitted lobbyists to mobilize support

[76]One distinction of modern, confrontational confirmations is the roll-call: no justice since Abe Fortas in 1965 has been confirmed without a roll-call.

CHART ONE
Mean Days in Stages of Nominations and Confirmations

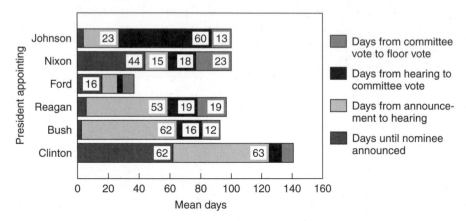

Chief Justice Burger Excluded
Judge Douglas Ginsburg Excluded

CHART TWO
Stages of Nominations and Confirmations

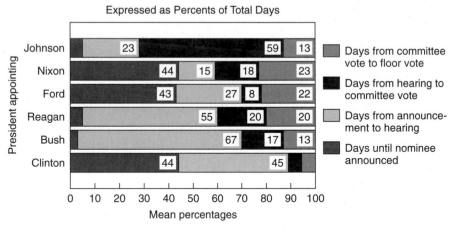

Chief Justice Burger Excluded
Judge Douglas Ginsburg Excluded

and opposition inside and outside the Senate. While President Clinton's nominees have endured similar lags between nomination and the beginning of the hearings, Clinton has taken as long, on average, in Stage One (between opening and nomination) as in Stage Two.

Chart Two displays the same data but measures each stage as a percentage of the total number of days that each nomination took. That is, each president's average number of days from announcement of an opening to roll-call vote becomes the denominator and the president's average number of days for each stage is the numerator. Thus, Clinton's two nominees averaged 140.5 days from opening to floor vote and, as Chart One showed, Clinton took sixty-two days to select a nominee (Stage One). As a result, Chart Two reports that Clinton's average first stage consumed 44% (sixty-two divided by 140.5) of the time between opening and roll-call.

Chart Two shows us that, like Presidents Nixon and Ford, Clinton has taken roughly 44% of the total time between announcement of an opening and the floor vote merely to select a nominee. This first stage took less than six days for the other three presidents, which translates to six percent or less. Represented in this way, the data reveal similarities between Clinton's situation and that of Nixon and Ford. In 1969 and 1970, President Nixon had to repay the South for his electoral victory and took his time to select Haynsworth and Carswell. Once their defeats released him from his promise, Nixon named successors far more quickly. Like Nixon, President Ford had to get his nominee past a Senate controlled by his opponents. We have seen that Clinton faced lobbying at Stage One and delayed his choices.[77]

However, Chart Two dramatizes the length of Stage Two for Clinton, Reagan, and Bush. Since 1981, nominees have moved from announcement to hearings in about fifty-seven days on average—about four days less for Reagan's nominees and about five days more for Bush's and Clinton's. Thus, Clinton's nominees have faced long second stages after long first stages.

Once we see that Clinton's nominees have faced the longest first two stages by far and the shortest last two stages (absolutely, as in Chart One, *and* relatively, as in Chart Two), we can appreciate the recent developments explained [previously]. For Ginsburg and Breyer, the first two stages of vetting accounted for fully 89% of the days before confirmation was secured. This represents an increase of nearly one-fifth over the next highest average (73% for Bush's nominees) and is nearly half again as long as for Reagan's nominees. Chart Two shows us, in sum, just how quickly Stages Three and Four may proceed, provided that conflict at Stage One has shaped nominations.

Taken together, the table and the charts expose President Clinton's particular vulnerability. Burned by inadequate screening when he was naming his cabinet[78] (and, as Ms. Guinier and Dr. Henry Foster have shown, since), Clinton has taken weeks to select a nominee. This period of vulnerability encourages interest groups (such as environmentalists concerned about Babbitt and conservatives sending up alarms about Marian Wright Edelman), Senators (such as Orrin Hatch,

---

[77]Of course, the relation between delay and lobbying is dialectic. The longer a president dawdles, the more vulnerable to pressure he becomes, but the more vulnerable he is to pressure, the more likely he is to temporize.

[78]Joel D. Aberbach, *The Federal Executive Under Clinton, in* THE CLINTON PRESIDENCY: FIRST APPRAISALS 163-187 (Colin Campbell & Bert A. Rockman eds., 1996).

troubled by Bruce Babbitt but thrilled by Stephen Breyer), and reporters (investigating "nanny problems" and pot-smoking) to boost or blast rumored nominees and otherwise try to influence the President's choice. Once such pressure arises, a safe course is to select a techno-judge.

Each of our answers to the Clinton puzzle bears on this earliest stage with particular force. "Separated" from power centers, President Clinton possessed few resources with which to compel or cajole support, so he chose safe candidates to preserve scarce resources that he wanted to devote elsewhere. Senators can commit early to more aggressive roles toward specific, anticipated nominees, so Clinton sought nominees who would restore troublesome senators to more passive stances. The ever-present threat of a filibuster meant that the president could not content himself with a candidate who would please the president's party, so Clinton had to nominate a woman and a man who would not excite much opposition from Republicans. Prior to nomination, groups could lobby the president with shows of opposition and promises of support, so Clinton had to stay within the bounds of counter-vailing lobbies. Transmogrification of confirmation politics has made nomination politics a race for the center.[79]

VIII. Conclusion and Implications

This second glance at the Ginsburg and Breyer nominations led us to the conclusion that conflicts over appointments to the United States Supreme Court have evolved along a spatial-temporal dimension. Battles to confirm Fortas, Haynsworth, and Carswell were joined predominantly in the District of Columbia and mostly in Stages Three and Four (from the start of committee hearings through the floor vote). Struggles to confirm Bork and Thomas pushed conflict "out" from the Beltway (through direct-mail and network coverage) and "back" into Stage Two (between naming and hearings). Most conflict over Clinton's nominees has preceded their naming, so confrontations have escalated both inside the Senate and out in the country *in Stage One*. Once early confrontations diverted Clinton from ideal appointees and toward confirmable techno-judges, later stages of the process seemed uncontroversial inside and outside the Senate. We cannot formulate current practice by stating that conflict in nominations and conflict in confirmations are inversely related, for presidents might resist pressures at Stage One and risk pressure at subsequent stages. We do conclude, however, that the 1993–1994 moments of unified government did little to obviate the conflict that has characterized Supreme Court confirmations for the last quarter-century.

This recent development tantalizes us with the possibility that senators will now actually advise as well as consent. Suppose that judicial activism, litigation for social change, and congressional reforms and changes have raised the actual and symbolic stakes of appointments to the Court as gridlock and divided government

---

[79]This movement toward the middle of the road recalls the "broad center" model of two-party competition, reinforcing Judge Bork's point that judicial appointments have come to resemble electoral politics in unsettling ways.

have dissipated congressional and presidential power. Under such conditions, elevated stakes insure that controversial appointees will face intensive vetting that will, in turn, overtax procedures designed more for consent than for advice or deliberation. In turn, we might expect confrontational confirmations to induce senators and other participants into more partisan, less open-minded roles in which they would strive to demonstrate the absence or presence of debilitating disqualifications rather than positive qualifications.[80] Presidents who cannot afford to abide a Senate confirmation fight might then seek nominees who exhibit technical, legal-formal skills but few clear principles or ideological attachments and senatorial and presidential staffs might negotiate in advance with interested parties inside and outside the Beltway to minimize conflicts. The foregoing sequence would account for how advice could precede consent almost as if the Constitution called for a genuine Senate role.

Please forgive one more implication. Messier nominations may now be leading to more orderly confirmations. That is, as senators and other interested parties participate more in Stage One—actual advice—they may feel less pressure to participate fully and fiercely in the consent stages. The net result may be the ascendancy of the techno-judge on the Supreme Court as intensified advice-stage activities fulfill a cycle: judicial activism and its consequences led to messy confirmations, democracy, and concomitant demagogy, which in turn produced greater pressure at Stage One that eliminated judicial activists left and right as potential nominees and over time produced a less activist and perhaps less political Supreme Court.

On "Let It Bleed," the Rolling Stones opined that "You can't always get what you want / But if you try sometime / You might find / You get what you need."[81] The challenge in 1995, at least with respect to Supreme Court nominations and confirmations, lies in determining precisely what we really do need. On the one hand, a compelling case can be made that the modern federal judiciary, overburdened by responsibilities and subject to frequent attack from both the Left and the Right, might indeed benefit from the quietude and the lower political profile that will inevitably follow the appointment of techno-judges.[82] On the other, there remains the nagging suspicion that Candidate Clinton had it right: the current Court *is* diminished by the fact that it lacks members with experience and stature gained from a life outside the classroom or the judge's chambers.

If Candidate Clinton was at all correct, then perhaps President Clinton or his successors should follow the Rolling Stones' advice. Even if he cannot always get what he wants, a president should try sometime. Absent such effort, we just may find that transforming the Supreme Court to simply a powerful appellate court is not what we need.

---

[80]CARTER, *supra* note 25.

[81]Jagger and Richards, *You Can't Always Get What You Want.*

[82]*See* LAURENCE TRIBE, GOD SAVE THIS HONORABLE COURT: HOW THE CHOICE OF SUPREME COURT JUSTICES SHAPES OUR HISTORY (1985); HERMAN SCHWARTZ, PACKING THE COURTS: THE CONSERVATIVE CAMPAIGN TO REWRITE THE CONSTITUTION (1988).

13

PRESIDENTIAL DOMESTIC POLICY

Social Policy and White House Politics: An Examination of the Presidency from Franklin D. Roosevelt to George W. Bush[1]

Byron W. Daynes
Brigham Young University

Glen Sussman
Old Dominion University

Over the years, American presidents have used their political resources to fulfill their domestic, economic, and foreign policies. Just as important, of course, are *social policies* defined here as "public policy that possesses legal authority having the potential of influencing or changing moral practices, individual standards of behavior as well as community values."[2] Specifically, social policies include death penalty, abortion, pornography, gun control, homosexuality, affirmative action, environmental policy, as well as other issues that evoke "moral questions" and direct our thoughts to "social concerns." Social issues, in particular, have proven difficult for presidents to handle over the years. The result has been that many presidents have devoted less attention to them than to economic or foreign policies, despite the fact that social issues can be more divisive to the polity.

Given the prominence of the presidency in the political system and the potential disruptiveness of social issues in American society, it is essential that we examine how presidents have responded to these types of issues.

The Presidents[3]

In this chapter we will consider those presidents who have served during the period when social issues have been most important to presidential politics,[4] namely, during the modern period covering the presidencies of Franklin Roosevelt through George W. Bush.[5] Our examination of these twelve presidents, not all of them have had to confront the vast array of social issues, nor have social issues been a major part of the social agendas of all of these presidents. After all, presidents recognize that political involvement with socially divisive issues can at times be uncomfortable and result in "no-win" situations since in taking a policy position a president may lose as many supporters as he gains. Nevertheless, all of these presidents have at least confronted, or been confronted by, one or more of these issues as a result of the social conditions of the time, including periods of crisis. When the Supreme Court decided *Engle v. Vitale* (1962), a case forbidding school prayer, for example, it forced a reluctant John Kennedy, a Catholic, to take a position opposing school prayer. Kennedy let it be known that while he supported the Court's position against prayer, at the same time, he encouraged Americans who opposed the Court's decision to continue to pray in their homes and in their churches.[6]

The Social Issues

So what are the social issues we will examine? As we limit our analysis to the modern presidents, we will focus on the following six social issues: *abortion, pornography, gun control, homosexuality, affirmative action, and environmental policy.* These issues have all generated a great deal of interest within the political system, and have led to actions taken within the Congress, between interest groups, in the courts, and among the modern presidents as they have encouraged issue adoption or rejection.

Abortion   As an issue of importance to presidents, abortion only became prominent in the 1970s, after the Supreme Court's decision in *Roe v. Wade,*[7] which made Richard Nixon the first president to have to confront the issue. It was a divisive issue from the beginning, and has remained a source of social and political conflict ever since.

Presidents have found abortion to be the sort of issue they try to avoid altogether, given the political dangers and intense emotions it generates. But most have been unsuccessful in turning away from it completely, given the public's interest in it. The pro-life position found strong support during the Reagan-Bush years while the pro-choice movement came into its own during the Clinton years. With George W. Bush now in office, and with his selection of John Ashcroft—a longtime pro-life supporter—as his Attorney General, the pro-life movement once again has something to celebrate. In short, abortion has managed to touch, in one way or another, each of the presidents since 1973.

Pornography   Unlike abortion, pornography and/or obscenity has been an issue that has created bipartisan disdain. Among Democratic and Republican presidents and those who have run for the office, all have found it much easier to come out against it than, in any way, to support a First Amendment position favoring freedom of expression. This has particularly been the case with regard to child pornography. Because "child porn" is so universally disapproved, a president can take a stance against it without having to prove the more difficult question as to whether the material is actually obscene or not.

Gun control   Presidents have found themselves on both sides of the gun control issue, finding it easiest to hold the same position taken by their own political party. From the 1930s to the 1960s, very little effort was made by presidents to secure gun control legislation. It was not until the late 1960s that modest gun control legislation was passed in Congress at the urging of President Lyndon Johnson, immediately after the assassinations of Martin Luther King, Jr. and Democratic presidential candidate, Robert Kennedy.

Republicans like Ronald Reagan, on the other hand, have generally supported free access to guns and have opposed any gun restrictions. Yet, as Robert Spitzer has suggested, few presidents have become involved with gun control beyond the "symbolic level."[8]

Homosexuality   This has been the latest social issue that has emerged as a controversial concern for presidents. It was during the 1980 campaign that homosexuality first became an electoral issue of importance for presidents. It has proven to be an issue that has divided one party against the other, and separated the membership of both parties. Thus far, Democrats have appeared more likely to support the homosexual agenda than have Republicans. The first major presidential effort for and in behalf of homosexuals, did not take place until the 1992 presidential campaign. Bill Clinton indicated that he would change military policy by issuing an executive order that dropped the ban against homosexuals serving in the armed forces—a policy that had been in effect since 1982.

Affirmative Action/Equal Opportunity   While affirmative action has been with us throughout the modern period,[9] direct presidential involvement has been rather limited. Most presidents, Democrats and Republicans alike, with some exceptions, have followed Franklin Roosevelt's lead in encouraging fair employment and fair labor practices in the work place. Lyndon Johnson, Jimmy Carter, and Bill Clinton demonstrated their commitment to expanding equal employment opportunities by engaging in more vigorous efforts to ensure fairness in the hiring process. And with the exception of Ronald Reagan, most presidents have moved in rather incremental ways to expand equal opportunity practices. George H. W. Bush, to a lesser degree, followed in Reagan's footsteps in opposing quotas as a means to improve the status of women and minorities.[10]

The Environment   The environment is one social issue that presidents find hard to avoid. Some presidents have treated the issue more seriously than others, however. Franklin Roosevelt was the president considered to have introduced the so-called "Golden Age of Conservation" to America.[11] Much of his interest was tied to the critical concerns of the time related to the Depression. For example, Roosevelt's Civilian Conservation Corps (C.C.C.) put people to work and served the purpose of conservation as millions of trees were planted.

The period from Roosevelt through Nixon has been looked to as one of the most productive times for the protection of the environment and its natural resources.[12] Ronald Reagan was the first president to limit White House efforts to protect the environment, preferring, instead, developmental goals over the environment, despite the public and Congressional opposition to his stance. George W. Bush shows all the signs of following Reagan's policy example in his early efforts in office. His most controversial recommendations have been oil drilling in the Arctic National Wildlife Refuge in Alaska, repealing restrictive limits for arsenic in drinking water, and opposing the Kyoto Protocol, an agreement limiting greenhouse gas emissions. Public opinion and Congressional opposition to the Bush proposals may, however, prevail.[13]

Presidential Roles

In an effort to analyze presidential responses to these issues, we will examine presidential action through a series of behavioral roles. A role here will be defined as a ". . . set of expectations by political elites and the citizenry that define(s) the scope of presidential responsibilities within a given policy area."[14] We will consider five roles that encompass the major foreign and domestic activities of a president. Specifically, they include: (1) *Commander-in-Chief*—a constitutional role, that grants military powers to the president; (2) *Chief Diplomat*—a role that views the president as he interacts with other nations; (3) *Chief Executive*—a role that treats a president's relationship with staff and bureaucracy; (4) *Legislative Leader*—a role that looks to the president's relationship with Congress; and (5) *Opinion/Party Leader*—a combined role that assesses the president's relationship to the public through political party and public opinion.[15]

The two roles that focus a president's attention on foreign policy are *Commander-in-Chief* and *Chief Diplomat*. These are a president's strongest roles in terms of authority and resources. However, they are also the roles that probably have the least to do with social policy. Thus, we will combine them for our analysis. In the future, however, a president may have to more frequently use these roles as the issues of abortion, gun importation, transnational environmental issues, and pornography become increasingly susceptible to regional and international pressures.

The *chief executive* may seem quite a powerful role for the president since the Framers' determined that a chief executive should not share power with any advisory body. Despite the fact that appointment power is key to a president's success in the role, the president is often frustrated in supporting social issues using this role since the Constitution fragments control over the bureaucracy.

Success as a *legislative leader* is important to a president since his overall accomplishments in office are quite often determined by the legislation he has been able to influence. For a president to be an effective Legislative Leader, he must assertively use all his individual skills as a negotiator and persuader, since a president has little real authority to exert, while Congress has substantial advantages.[16] Most presidents have thus enjoyed rather modest records of legislative achievement regarding social policy.

Opinion/Party Leader—This role is a combined role that attempts to generate public support for the president's program, administration, and party. Of all the roles, this is perhaps the president's weakest since there are few resources available to call upon. Thus, a president who is successful in this role will, of necessity, have to rely on personal skills and influence rather than established authority. Franklin Roosevelt, John Kennedy, and Ronald Reagan were three of these presidents who were able to use this role impressively.

TABLE 1
SOCIAL ISSUES AND PRESIDENTIAL ROLES

Roles of the President	Social Issues					
	Abortion	Affirmative Action	Environment	Gun Control	Homo-Sexuality	Pornography
Opinion/ Party Leader	x	x	x	x	—	—
Legislative Leader	x	x	x	x	—	x
Chief Executive	x	x	x	x	—	x
Chief Diplomat/ Comm. in Chief	x	x	x	x/—	x/—	(x)[1]

"x" = presidential assertiveness
"—" = presidential passivity
"x/—" = moderate action exhibited by a president.
[1]Future public concern with transnational cyberporn will certainly involve these roles.

Summary of the Roles   Table 1 indicates the potential importance of these five roles in considering each of these issues. Some roles have encouraged more political involvement in an issue area than have other roles. Moreover, with the exception of the chief diplomat/commander in chief role, most of the roles presidents have relied on to secure their social agendas have been those considered to be moderate to weak. As Table 1 suggests, presidents have been assertive in each of the roles when it has come to dealing with abortion, affirmative action/equal opportunity, the environment, and gun control. But when it has come to pornography and homosexuality, presidents have, overall, been rather passive. More often than not, when presidents have decided to act on the issue of pornography, they have relied upon their legislative leadership, their role as chief executive, or their opinion/party leader role to stop the production and distribution of pornographic literature.

Homosexuality has been the quintessential controversial issue in American society and most presidents have chosen to remain uninvolved with the issue. Until Bill Clinton, in his role as Commander in Chief, took on the issue of open access to military service, nothing of substance had been done by any president for the gay community.

Observations about Presidential Behavior

In the remainder of this chapter, we will propose several observations that will sum up our assessment of presidents and their approach to social policy over the last seven decades.

TABLE 2
PRESIDENTIAL TYPES AND THE SOCIAL AGENDA

Presidential Types		Policy Outcomes
Activist	⟶	substantive
Symbolic-plus	⟶	nominal/to none
Evasive	⟶	substantive
Aloof	⟶	nominal/to none

Observation #1   **Social issues are divisive, and the public and presidents respond to them in different ways:**

Social policy both divides and politicizes society. Presidents, when they have been involved with social policy, have been either quite *assertive* in their responses to these issues, or somewhat *passive* in their involvement with social issues (Table 2). Ronald Reagan, when he dealt with the abortion issue, for example, frequently spoke about the "unborn" child and the need to add a Human Life Amendment to the U.S. Constitution. Bill Clinton also strongly supported gun restrictions in encouraging the passage of the Brady Bill in an effort to reduce the violence associated with firearms. Other presidents have been less involved with these issues.

As a result of presidential involvement, social policy may either elicit *substantive* results or more *nominal* consequences, or, in fact, no results at all for their efforts. Harry Truman, for instance, issued an executive order in 1948 to integrate United States armed forces encouraging equal minority access to the military services. This action did produce a tangible policy change. By contrast, despite Ronald Reagan's very outspoken position against abortion, and his efforts to attach an amendment to the Constitution, no amendment resulted, nor probably will it result during the presidency of another outspoken anti-abortion president, George W. Bush.

From observing the way presidents have responded to social policy, then, one can classify them, as we have in Table 2, as either (1) *activist* presidents, achieving substantive results; (2) *symbolic-plus* presidents, who, while actively supporting social policy, fail to achieve substantive outcomes; (3) *evasive* presidents, who refuse to become involved with the issue, yet see substantive policy results come about because of the involvement of other political decision makers; and (4) politically *aloof* presidents, who have no interest in getting involved with the issue, and, not surprisingly, see no substantive outcomes.

Observation #2   **Presidents do not take the lead in responding to social issues:**

Although the president is a primary political actor in American politics, frequently other decision makers become the major players with regard to social policy. Once issues become politicized, however, presidents have a more difficult time avoiding involvement. The assassination of John Kennedy, for example, turned the attention of the nation to the consequences of gun violence and made the public aware that even the most visible figure in the country was vulnerable.

This encouraged Lyndon Johnson, JFK's vice president, who became our 36th president, to lobby Congress unceasingly for gun control legislation in 1968.

As far as abortion policy was concerned, it was the Supreme Court that nationalized abortion with its 1973 *Roe v. Wade* decision. It was only after this occurred that presidents became increasingly involved with the issue. However, presidential involvement varied from the activity of Richard Nixon, Ronald Reagan, and George W. Bush, who have embraced the pro-life position on abortion arguing against abortion rights, to Bill Clinton, who used his presidency to support the pro-choice position. Other presidents including Gerald Ford, Jimmy Carter and George H. W. Bush took a less than firm stand on the issue.

Contrasted with abortion, the president has been more visible on environmental issues. Richard Nixon ensured that the 1970s would be the decade for environmental awareness when he used his office to support passage of the National Environmental Protection Act, and other environmental legislation which made Nixon the president with more environmental legislation to his credit than any other modern-day president. Yet he was not thought to be a bold innovator but, instead, could best be described as an astute politician in seeing this as an issue he could capitalize on. Some presidents like Eisenhower and Ford, however, despite their support for environmental protection, viewed it as a responsibility of state and local governments. Yet with few exceptions, it has been the Congress, over the years, that has protected the environment.

Indeed, the nature of these issues raises the question as to why any president would decide to spend political capital on issues which lack consensus and sometimes threaten domestic tranquility. For example, when Bill Clinton decided to change policy direction by lifting the ban on gays in the military, he was confronted with much opposition from within as well as outside of his own party; from the gay community, who felt he had not done enough for them; and from the military itself. As a result, he was forced to compromise on the issue, coming up with his now famous guideline of "don't ask, don't tell" policy.

Lyndon Johnson, as chief executive, played a key role in encouraging the passage of civil rights legislation and in stressing the importance of affirmative action/equal opportunity. For Johnson, the struggle for social justice and racial equality came to the forefront of his administration. He issued the executive order establishing affirmative action in support of equal opportunity that shaped social policy for the next three decades.

For those presidential scholars who have taken social policy seriously, a common conclusion seems to prevail: that the *"politics"* that attends social policy places the president in a less than commanding position vis-à-vis other political institutions. Both Theodore J. Lowi, in describing *regulatory policy,*[17] and Raymond Tatalovich and Byron W. Daynes, in examining *social regulatory policies,* indicated that the president would more than likely play a less dominant role in fashioning these sorts of policies than one might expect of the Congress or the Court.[18] Of course, this has not been the case for all presidents. Bill Clinton and Ronald Reagan felt quite comfortable in strongly asserting views on abortion, for example, while Gerald Ford and Jimmy Carter preferred that other institutions lead out on this policy. Ford and Carter, on the other hand, attempted to straddle this issue. While Ford opposed abortion, he preferred that states deal with it. Carter also personally opposed abortion but supported the right of women to choose in opposing any constitutional amendment that would overturn the *Roe* decision. The public was not persuaded by either of these presidents' positions.

It is safe to say that while presidents have not always had a major affect on social policies, given the important position a president plays in the political system, even a subtle influence of a president may bear important political and social consequences. Further, we can also say that social policies have had an affect on presidential policies, politics, and administrations, even if only indirectly.

Observation #3 **Presidents have used the opinion/party role to explain their positions on social policy:**

As opinion/party leader, the president can build bridges between the presidency and the electorate through direct and indirect personal contact. Yet this role lacks formal authority and has few built-in resources. Modern presidents have tried a number of ways to engage the public in an effort to make their case regarding social issues. Presidents have delivered major policy speeches like the State of the Union message to emphasize their position on social policy allowing them to reach out to a national audience. Both Truman and Eisenhower used this message to discuss their views on conservation. Kennedy and Johnson emphasized their commitment to affirmative action/equal opportunity in communication with the public and Congress. Minor speeches have likewise played a role as each president has addressed the public and interest groups about affirmative action/equal opportunity and the environment.

Presidents Nixon, Carter, and Ford used a variety of media appearances in expressing themselves on the abortion issue, but their activity was constrained when compared to Ronald Reagan and George H. W. Bush who spoke frequently in support of the pro-life position, and Bill Clinton, who bolstered the pro-choice constituencies whenever he spoke on the issue.

Lyndon Johnson, Ronald Reagan, George H. W. Bush and Bill Clinton also relied on their access to the public to inform and educate the citizenry about their own positions on gun control. While Reagan and Bush presented their opposition to gun restrictions, Johnson and Clinton made their case to the American public in favor of more firearm restrictions.

Observation #4 **Presidents have largely been ineffective as legislative leaders regarding social issues:**

While the presidential veto can be a powerful tool in this role, it must not be used too frequently since it is then viewed as a sign of presidential weakness. John Kennedy and Lyndon Johnson used the veto to protect the free flow of information in light of anti-pornography legislation. Ronald Reagan and George H. W. Bush employed the veto to prohibit the expenditure of public funds for abortions, while Bill Clinton used the veto on several occasions to protect the environment from what he saw as Republican assaults.

Roosevelt and Clinton frequently used national addresses to focus congresspersons efforts on environmental priorities. Lyndon Johnson did the same for affirmative action/equal opportunity. Presidents Nixon and Reagan used speeches before joint sessions of the Congress to mobilize national opinion against pornography.

The personal skills of presidents, in this role, can make or break their efforts to shape social policy. Lyndon Johnson, as a result of his many years in the Senate, serving six years as Senate majority leader, understood the legislative process and knew which leaders in the Senate and House needed to be courted. By contrast, Jimmy Carter, whose personal relationship with members of Congress was rare, preferred to speak to a televised audience in his efforts to influence legislators. Carter's more removed approach failed more often than it succeeded with congresspersons. It is unclear how successful George W. Bush will be, with a closely divided Congress, in stressing his position on social policy.

Most presidents would prefer to work with a Congress with their own party in control; yet as Carter proved, having his party control the Congress is no guarantee that the Congress will work with the president. When Carter decided to terminate nineteen water projects in several western states, those in greatest opposition to his proposals were his fellow Democrats in the North and the South.[19]

Observation #5 **Presidents have modestly exercised their staffing role of chief executive in an effort to strengthen their social agenda:**

The size and complexity of the federal government makes it increasingly difficult for the president to manage the bureaucracy. As chief executive, the president has the power of appointment which allows him to staff and shape policy. A president's social agenda can be enhanced or undercut by the people he appoints to important positions. Lyndon Johnson showed his interest in affirmative action by appointing Thurgood Marshall, the first African-American to the United States Supreme Court, whereas two decades later, Ronald Reagan broke precedent and selected Sandra Day O'Connor as the first woman associate justice to the Supreme Court.

Ronald Reagan's appointment of development-sympathizer James Watt, as the Secretary of the Interior, stood in stark contrast to Bill Clinton's selection of environmentalist, Bruce Babbitt, to be his Secretary of Interior. Babbitt was as active in protecting the environment as Watt was in undercutting it. Moreover, Clinton's selection of Al Gore as Vice President and the appointment of Carol Browner as Administrator of the Environmental Protection Agency was a positive signal to the environmental community that this president felt the environment was a worthwhile social issue on which to focus. By contrast George W. Bush's appointment of Dick Cheney as Vice President, a former oil CEO of Halliburton, an oilfield service company, his selection of Commerce Secretary Don Evans, chair of Tom Brown oil, and his appointment of Condoleezza Rice, a director of Chevron,[20] pleased the oil industry but did not please environmentalists. In addition, Bush's appointment of Christie Todd Whitman as administrator of the Environmental Protection Agency, and Gale Norton—a person who had worked with James Watt during the Reagan Administration—as his Interior Secretary set a particular tone favorable to development over environmental priorities.

Observation #6 **Social Policy has been established less frequently by the president's commander-in-chief/chief diplomat role:**

These two roles have a strong authoritative base in the Constitution, in statutory law, in custom, and in tradition, which provide substantial resources for the president *if* he chooses to use this role. Both Presidents Reagan and Bush used this role as they determined to cease granting contributions to the United Nations Population Fund fearing that the funds might be used for abortions. They also used their influence to prevent abortions from being used as a service for women in military hospitals. These same two presidents also prevented government support for private family planning organizations fearing, again, that funding might be used for abortions.

The environment has been an important area for the president in this role when he has had to engage in both environmental diplomacy and with issues related to national security and environmental protection. Every president, beginning with Franklin Roosevelt through Bill Clinton, has signed some important bilateral or multilateral agreements in support of environmental measures. At the same time, there have been disappointments for environmentalists when presidents have refused to sign important environmental agreements as happened when George H. W. Bush refused to sign the Biodiversity Treaty during the 1992 Earth Summit and when his son, George W. Bush, refused, in March 2001, to approve of the Kyoto Protocol, a basic agreement among nations that would bind them to controlling carbon dioxide emissions to combat global warming.

Observation #7 **Increasing global connections may force presidents to address social policies internationally:**

When presidents have chosen to be assertive regarding social policy, it has usually been on domestic social policy. Presidents Roosevelt, Truman, Kennedy, Johnson, Carter, and Clinton all responded to race relations in the domestic sense by using resources and skills to improve equal access and equal opportunity for all Americans. Gun control encouraged an essential national focus in the 1990s.

Similarly, the modern environmental movement has also initially had a domestic focus. Yet many of these issues easily can have a transnational effect with an increasingly international impact such as our concern with acid rain that transcends the international border between the United States and Canada. This situation may constitute new challenges for the president as chief diplomat and commander in chief as global environmental issues could quite possibly dominate the twenty-first century.

The international flow of firearms has also become a concern to some presidents as commander in chief/chief diplomat. Given the debate over gun control within the United States, the NRA and other gun organizations have appealed to the outside world in their effort to prevent further restrictions on firearms. Although Presidents George H. W. Bush and Bill Clinton used executive orders to stop the flow of weapons across national borders, bilateral agreements and multilateral conventions which have already occurred may serve as models for presidential involvement with this issue in the international community.

Presidential actions with regard to restricting pornography between nations has usually been of domestic importance. However, pornography is an international industry and Americans are major consumers of the product. Public concern over this country's "moral standards" compared with the standards of other countries, can put pressure on a president to settle such a concern with international agreements.

Observation #8 **The climate of the times must be accommodating to presidents who are assertive in their approach to social policy:**

Where party, ideology, Congress, and public opinion have been supportive of a president's actions, several presidents have exerted both activist as well as symbolic leadership on social policy. Lyndon Johnson, with the backing of a Democratically-controlled Congress, for example, used his influence to secure passage of the 1968 gun control act. The assassinations of political figures in the 1960s, and a new Democratically-controlled Congress in 1964, as well as a supportive public for environmental protection, enabled Johnson to assert himself as legislative leader regarding social policy.

Richard Nixon as chief executive, chief legislator, and opinion/party leader became the strongest modern "environmental" Republican president. His impressive legislative record along with the establishment of important executive agencies and his declaration of the 1970s as the "decade of the environment," was fully supported by the public climate of the times including public opinion and the establishment of the first Earth Day in April 1970.

Even though Nixon and Reagan had to contend with a Democratic Congress (for Reagan, a Democratic Senate during his last two years), conditions appeared right for these presidents to maximize their leadership on the issue of pornography.

Observation #9 **The twelve presidents in this study have represented different responses to social policy:**

Table 3 presents an overall assessment of Presidents Roosevelt to George W. Bush. In some instances, presidents were activists using the power of the presidency to shape social policy. In other instances, presidents found that, despite their efforts, they failed to achieve tangible results. At other times, presidents avoided the issues all together.

Presidents Reagan, George H. W. Bush, and Clinton were active partisan presidents on the abortion issue. Reagan and Bush were conservatives who used their power as opinion/party leader, chief executive, and legislative leader to support the pro-life position. By contrast, Bill Clinton was a liberal activist strongly in support of a woman's right to choose abortion as an option in family planning. As opinion/party leader, he used the bully pulpit in support of this position; as legislator leader, he lobbied the Congress in support of abortion clinic safety; and as chief diplomat he reversed the Reagan-Bush ban on the funding of abortion for the United Nations Population Fund.

Seven of the eleven presidents were activists on affirmative action/equal opportunity. Although Lyndon Johnson has been characterized as the president most committed to creating a society where all citizens enjoyed equal opportunity, Franklin Roosevelt, Truman, and Kennedy before him, used their power as chief executive and/or legislative leader to begin the process of institutionalizing affirmative action/equal opportunity in American society.

Among the early modern presidents, Franklin Roosevelt was an activist on environmental issues. As opinion/party leader, he included environmental priorities in his State of the Union message. As legislative leader, he included environmental funding in his budgets, and as chief executive, he created several offices which

TABLE 3
PRESIDENTS AND SOCIAL ISSUES IN THEIR SOCIAL AGENDA

	Social Issues					
Presidents	Abortion	Affirmative Action	Environment	Gun Control	Homo-Sexuality	Pornography
Democrats:						
FDR	–	+	+	–	–	–
HST	–	+	+/–	–	–	–
JFK	–	+/–	+/–	–	–	+/–
LBJ	–	+	+/–	+	–	+
Carter	+/–	+	+	–	–	–
Clinton	+	+	+	+	+	+/–
Republicans:						
IKE	–	+/–	+/–	–	–	+/–
Nixon	+/–	+/–	+	–	–	+
Ford	+/–	–	+/–	–	–	–
Reagan	+	+	+	+	–	+
Bush (GHW)	+	+/–	+	+	–	+/–
Bush (GW)[1]	+	+/–	+	+	?	?

"+" = assertive approach to the social issue
"–" = avoidance of the issue
"+/–" = where some action is taken with no tangible results
[1]Early Assessment

fostered environmental protection. Among the late modern presidents, Richard Nixon was the most successful president in promoting environmental priorities. Nixon relied on all of the presidential roles to advance his environmental interests.

Others who followed Nixon—namely, Carter, Reagan, Bush and Clinton, to a lesser degree—also used their power to shape environmental policy. Jimmy Carter, for example, set aside vast tracks of land in Alaska. As a result he became the record holder in terms of setting aside more public land than any other president. Reagan was also an activist, but used his power as chief executive to reverse environmental progress in favor of development. As legislative leader, George H. W. Bush assisted Congress in passing the 1990 Clean Air Act, but then reversed his position on the environment after feeling pressures from business and fellow Republicans in the Congress. As chief executive, Bill Clinton appointed several "environmentalists" to important positions including the Administrator of the Environmental Protection Agency and the Department of the Interior. In addition, Bill Clinton established 22 national monuments, which included 6 million acres. He also created 42 wildlife refuges and preserved 84 million acres underwater in the Hawaiian Islands.[21] Clinton finally prevented the building of roads on more than 58 million acres of forest land in 39 states, protecting the forest land from development. By these actions, Clinton established his public land legacy.

Most presidents have avoided the gun issue. Although two bills were passed during the Roosevelt administration, the bills had in mind "gangster" weapons and the enforcement of the legislation was, thus, problematic. As legislative leader, Johnson took action in 1968, subsequent to three political assassinations, to oppose access to guns, whereas his successor, Ronald Reagan, represented an anti-gun control position. After leaving office, he made exceptions to this position by supporting the Brady Bill, and also the ban on foreign semi-automatic weapons imports.

Observation #10   **Presidential Action Matters:**

By becoming involved with a social policy, the president instantly becomes a focus of attention and is seen by the public as challenging the preserve of the Congress, as someone mobilizing organized interests, and as a leader trying to educate and inform the public. Presidential involvement with the social agenda is important for several reasons. First, social policies affect the linkage between presidents and constituencies. Lyndon Johnson's support for equal opportunity, for example, strengthened his relationship with African-Americans but weakened his support among southern whites. In Ronald Reagan's case, he found that advocacy of an anti-abortion stance increased his support among pro-lifers, but weakened it among women of various political persuasions. Social policies have also influenced presidential action indirectly as constituency groups pressure the Congress which in turn support, constrain, or modify the president's agenda.

Presidents and the roles they assume in shaping social policy can make a difference in public policy making. The role assumed by the president can lead to the pursuit or avoidance of particular social policies and these can have a profound impact on the exercise of presidential power. The environment was addressed quite differently by Republicans Nixon, Reagan, and George W. Bush. Where Nixon saw a political opportunity in supporting environmental initiatives, Reagan pursued a developmentalist, anti-environment approach. George W. Bush seems headed in the same anti-environmentalist direction traveled by Reagan. Both Richard Nixon and Ronald Reagan used the chief executive and legislative leader roles, for example, but in contrasting ways. Nixon used the executive order and legislation he signed to promote environmentalism, while Reagan used budget and appointment powers and the veto to thwart environmentalism.

The president has, at times, been forced to respond to social issues due to the emergence of "culture conflict," which is what Jeffrey Davison Hunter calls "political and social hostility rooted in different systems of moral understanding. . . . It is the commitment to different and opposing bases of moral authority and the world views that derive from them that creates the deep cleavages between antagonists in the contemporary culture wars."[22] In describing the opposing sides as cultural conservatives or moral traditionalists versus cultural progressives or liberals, Hunter argues that "[o]n political matters one can compromise; on matters of ultimate moral truth, one cannot."[23]

Conclusion

The social issues discussed in this chapter can be viewed within the context of the larger social movements affecting American politics and society including the women's movement, the right-to-life movement, the gay rights movement, the

Christian Coalition among others which have imposed new demands on the political system and on presidents. Additionally, the social change taking place in post-industrial America suggests continuing political conflict over social issues between contending forces. For some, the conflict has arisen due to the public's shift from a materialist to postmaterialist value orientation which places greater emphasis on non-economic issues (world peace, environmental protection).[24] On the other hand, political conflict might be characterized by ideological social cleavages where a liberal agenda (pro-choice on abortion, support for gay and women's rights) confronts a conservative agenda which emphasizes a pro-life, anti-gay, and anti-women's rights orientation.[25]

As we have seen, activist presidents have shaped social policy in many ways. At the same time, not all presidents have chosen to be activists with regard to social policy. Still, when the president used the power resources of their office, either actively or symbolically, the social agenda has been strengthened. While the activist president seeks results, the symbolic president has taken action which is significant in various sectors of the political system even if the results have been nominal.

The president occupies an important position within this complex federal system. Elections are never clear enough so that the president knows ahead of his own election whether he will be asked to lead a divided or unified government. He does know, regardless of party dominance, that he will be working with a decentralized Congress, and, as chief executive, with a fragmented bureaucracy. As opinion/party leader, he can inform and educate the voters, although he lacks formal authority to do so. As chief diplomat/commander in chief, the president has an authoritative base and more resources at his control, but is less likely to rely on this role in order to shape social policy.

In order for a president to maximize his position vis-à-vis social issues, he must use the authority and resources available in each of his roles. He must also use his personal skills and be assertive and creative. Most importantly, he must be supported by a social and political ambiance which is favorable to him. In such a climate, his social agenda will be secured. Unfortunately, such a situation occurs only rarely.

ENDNOTES

1. This chapter is based on the findings from the authors' book: Byron W. Daynes and Glen Sussman, *The American Presidency and the Social Agenda* (Upper Saddle River, New Jersey: Prentice Hall, 2001), with some updating to take account of the new presidency.
2. Daynes and Sussman, *The American Presidency and the Social Agenda* (Upper Saddle River, New Jersey: Prentice Hall, 2001), 1.
3. Since all of our presidents have been men, the masculine pronoun is used throughout the chapter. In addition, references to the presidency and presidents in general also use the masculine pronoun. This usage, of course, in no way excludes the possibility or anticipation that in the future women will occupy this position.

4. George Gallup Jr. maintained in 1996, that moral values were more important then, than at any other time in his 60 years of public opinion polling. See Patricia Edmunds and Ann Oldenburg, "Morality Issues Matter More," *USA TODAY,* August 6, 1996, 4A. In addition, a July 18–22, 1996 *USA TODAY*/CNN/*Gallup* poll, found that nine of ten voters, questioned before the 1996 presidential election, indicated that a candidate's "stand on moral values" would be important to the candidate's winning their vote. Ann Oldenburg and Patricia Edmunds, "Morals and Mixed Signals," *USA TODAY,* August 7, 1996, 4A.

5. While George W. Bush is less than a year into his presidency at this writing—we will, nevertheless, make an effort to consider some of his views that he has made known regarding social policy.

6. "The President's News Conference," June 27, 1962, in *Public Papers of the Presidents* (Washington, D.C.: Government Printing Office, 1963), 511.

7. 410 U.S. 113, 93 S. Ct. 705 (1973).

8. Robert J. Spitzer, "Gun Control: Constitutional Mandate or Myth?" in Raymond Tatalovich and Byron W. Daynes, eds., *Social Regulatory Policy: Moral Controversies in American Politics* (Boulder, Colorado: Westview Press, 1988), 126.

9. In responding to the Depression's unemployment, Franklin Roosevelt in a series of executive orders barred defense contractors from discriminating in their hiring practices; in addition, the Federal Employment Practices Committee (FEPC) was created by executive order on September 8, 1939, to implement these orders. See Executive Order 8242, September 8, 1939, in U.S. President, *The Public Papers and Addresses of Franklin D. Roosevelt* (New York: Russell & Russell, 1941), 490–509.

10. Paul J. Quirk, "Domestic Policy: Divided Government and Cooperative Presidential Leadership," in Colin Campbell and Bert A. Rockman, eds. *The Bush Presidency: First Appraisals* (Chatham, NJ: Chatham House Publishers, 1991), 75.

11. See Richard Lowitt, "Conservation, Policy On," Leonard W. Levy and Louis Fisher, eds. in *Encyclopedia of the American Presidency,* 4 Vols. (New York: Simon & Schuster, 1994), 1:289.

12. See Michael E. Kraft, *Environmental Policy and Politics* (New York: HarperCollins, 1996), 71.

13. Katharine Q. Seelye, "Bush Endorses Rule on Lead Emission Proposed by Clinton," *New York Times,* April 18, 2001 @ *www.nytimes.com/2001/04/18/politics/18ENVI.html?pagewanted=print.* Retrieved April 20, 2001.

14. This definition was first proposed by Raymond Tatalovich and Byron W. Daynes, in *Presidential Power in the United States* (Monterey, California: Brooks/Cole Publishing Co., 1984). It was later refined in Byron W. Daynes, Raymond Tatalovich and Dennis L. Soden, *To Govern a Nation: Presidential Power and Politics* (New York: St. Martin's Press, 1998), 2.

15. Daynes, Tatalovich and Soden, *To Govern a Nation: Presidential Power and Politics,* Chapter 1.

16. Two early studies that support this idea are: Lawrence H. Chamberlain, *The President, Congress and Legislation* (New York: Columbia University Press, 1946); and Ronald C. Moe and Steven C. Teal, "Congress as Policy-Maker: A Necessary Reappraisal," *Political Science Quarterly,* September 1970, 443–70.

17. Theodore J. Lowi, "Forward," in Raymond Tatalovich and Byron W. Daynes, *Social Regulatory Policy: Moral Controversies in American Politics,* 216–17.

18. Raymond Tatalovich and Byron W. Daynes, in considering the president's contribution to social regulatory policy, maintained that one could expect only ". . . modest leadership from the White House" in regard to these policies. See Tatalovich and Daynes, *Social Regulatory Policy: Moral Controversies in American Politics,* 216.

19. See James David Barber, *The Presidential Character: Predicting Performance in the White House,* 4th ed. (Englewood Cliffs, NJ: Prentice-Hall, 1992), 437–38; and Charles O. Jones, *Separate But Equal Branches: Congress and the Presidency* (Chatham, New Jersey: Chatham House Publishers, 1995), 153.

20. Molly Ivins, "Bush Going Backwards with Energy Policy," *Liberal Opinion Week,* January 22, 2001, 18.

21. See Charles Levendosky, "Clinton Left Us One of the Greatest Land Legacies," *Liberal Opinion Week,* February 5, 2001, 6.

22. Jeffrey Davison Hunter, *Culture Wars: The Struggle to Define America* (New York: Basic Books, 1991), 42–43.

23. Hunter, *Culture Wars: The Struggle to Define America,* 46.

24. Ronald Inglehart, *The Silent Revolution: Changing Values and Political Styles Among Western Publics* (Princeton, New Jersey: Princeton University Press, 1977).

25. Ronald Inglehart and Scott C. Flanagan, "Value Change in Industrial Societies," *American Political Science Review* (December 1987) 81: 1289–1319.

14

THE PRESIDENT
AND ECONOMIC
POLICY MAKING

Budgeting during the Clinton Presidency

Philip G. Joyce and Roy T. Meyers

Introduction

This article reviews the two-term Clinton administration record of budgeting, with the longer perspective enabling a better understanding of the most significant developments over eight budget cycles. Yet we offer this early summary of Clinton's fiscal performance with a consumer warning: some of what we have written will undoubtedly have to be revised as more primary documentation emerges. In addition, since eight years approaches an eternity in American politics (certainly it felt that long to many Republicans!), this article's short length forces us to ignore many interesting topics and events.

Competent social scientists learned long ago not to overidentify "eras" with individuals, and a president is not responsible for everything that happens during an administration. Nevertheless, it is understandable that many historians still focus their attention on how a president affected a period, for the simplest familiarity with American history shows that the chief executive's personality, style, skills, and knowledge typically have marked effects on government and society.

This was clearly the case with William Jefferson Clinton. Like most Presidents, he was an outsized and flawed character. His impressive intellect and his delight

Philip G. Joyce is Associate Professor of Public Administration at the George Washington University, Washington, DC 20052. E-mail address: *<pgjoyce@gwu.edu>*. Roy T. Meyers is Associate Professor of Political Science and Director of the Public Affairs Scholars Program at the University of Maryland, Baltimore County, Baltimore, MD 21250. E-mail address: *<meyers@umbc.edu>*.

This article assesses the Clinton administration record of budgeting. During President Clinton's two terms, the federal government moved from an era of large deficits to one of equally large surpluses. This turnaround was caused by both the strong economy and the deficit reduction deals of 1990, 1993, and 1997. Defense spending and interest declined as a percentage of the budget, whereas mandatory spending and nondefense discretionary spending increased. Acrimonious inter-branch budgetary relationships dominated, with Clinton ultimately winning far more fights than he lost. Executive branch budgetary and financial management capacity improved during the Clinton administration.

in analyzing the details of complex policy proposals quickly led the media to praise Clinton as a prototype "wonk," which caused some good budget analysts to think that a soulmate was running the country. On the other hand, as both budget analysts and Clinton have been known to bemuse, pop psychologists and partisan combatants were also quick to note Clinton's chameleon-like ability to shift positions for political advantage. The causes of this behavior were undoubtedly complex, including his supposed deep-seated craving for approval based on a difficult childhood, his sophisticated awareness of presidential history and his desire to adopt successful political techniques used by admired presidents, and the strong incentive to focus on self-preservation provided by the resurgence of the congressional Republican party.[1]

The contradictions in Clinton's behavior are matched by contradictions in budgeting during his eight years. This article is divided into four sections that sequentially reflect those contradictions: on macroeconomics and the budget; on microbudgetary policy; on presidential-congressional relations while budgeting; and on budgeting in the executive branch. Clinton's 1992 campaign managers gained fame with their mantra of "It's the economy, stupid," and the Clinton administration kept this focus to produce an incredibly successful macroeconomic and aggregate budgetary policy. Policy at the microbudgetary level was far less impressive; it often seemed that policy proposals were designed more for partisan posturing than for effectiveness and efficiency. The budgetary relationship between Clinton and the Congress was among the worst in American history, with Clinton winning far more fights than he lost. Yet though this conflict caused major shutdowns of agencies due to the lack of timely appropriations and stressed the many agencies that faced conflicting directives from the two branches, the Clinton years also saw marked improvements in the general budgetary and financial management capacity of the executive branch. We cover these developments in turn, incorporating a chronology of budgetary developments into a longer first section.[2] We conclude with some questions about budgeting during the next presidency.

Macrobudgetary Policy

In 1983, former Reagan budget director David Stockman projected $200 billion deficits "as far as the eye can see."[3] Ironically, the fiscal revolution that he led helped ensure the accuracy of this prophecy, as large deficits seemed to become a permanent part of the fiscal environment. Unified budget deficits averaged $204

[1]See Carl M. Cannon, "Judging Clinton," *National Journal* 32 (January 1, 2000): 14–25; Fred I. Greenstein, *The Presidential Difference: Leadership Style from FDR to Clinton* (New York: Free Press, 2000).
[2]See Daniel J. Parks, "A Legacy of Budget Surpluses and Thriving Markets," *Congressional Quarterly Weekly Report* 58 (February 5, 2000): 228–33; Allen Schick, "A Surplus. If We Can Keep It: How the Federal Budget Surplus Happened," *Brookings Review* 20 (Winter 2000): 36–39; Julie Kosterlitz, "The Economy: Luck and Skill," *National Journal* 32 (January 1, 2000), 26–28.
[3]"A Plea from David Stockman," *Washington Post* (April 20, 1983), A-20.

billion from fiscal year (FY) 1982 to FY 1994, exceeding $200 billion in eight of those 13 years. In fact, in 1997, when veteran budget reporters George Hager and Eric Pianin wrote a book on the deficit wars, its subtitle promised to explain "why neither Democrats nor Republicans can balance the budget, end the deficit, and satisfy the public."[4] They were not alone in their predictions. As the first of Bill Clinton's two terms came to a close, the Congressional Budget Office (CBO) continued to forecast deficits that averaged approximately $200 billion between FY 1997 and FY 2006.[5]

Perhaps we should consider it nothing short of remarkable, therefore, that as we write this article at the end of the second Clinton term, not only have Democrats and Republicans "balanced the budget and ended the deficit" (we'll leave a discussion of "satisfying the public" for another day), but CBO and the Office of Management and Budget (OMB) now project large unified budget *surpluses* as far as the eye can see.[6] How did this astonishing turnaround come about?

From 1990 Deal to the 1992 Campaign   Reducing the federal deficit had received major emphasis in the Bush administration, and a multiyear deficit reduction deal was enacted in the late fall of 1990. This law increased taxes, made targeted reductions in mandatory spending, and kept discretionary spending growth below the inflation rate for fiscal years 1991 through 1995. The latter savings were to be enforced by the new procedural control of statutory caps on discretionary spending; the caps were particularly tight in the later years of this period. Growth in new mandatory spending was to be controlled by PAYGO rules, which required offsets within the mandatory category for new entitlements and for revenue cuts. (These new procedures were part of the Budget Enforcement Act, or BEA.)[7] The expectation was that this deal would almost eliminate the federal deficit: a CBO analysis at the time projected a FY 1995 deficit of only $57 billion. However, the recession that started in the latter part of 1990 overwhelmed the effects of the policy changes, and by the time of the presidential campaign, CBO was projecting a FY 1995 deficit of $244 billion.[8]

The deficit took center stage in the 1992 presidential campaign in part because of the surprising appeal of third-party candidate H. Ross Perot, who made eliminating the deficit a centerpiece of his campaign. Since the voters who were most in tune with the Perot message were precisely the swing voters that both the Clinton and Bush campaigns needed to capture, Clinton pledged that he would cut the

---

[4]George Hager and Eric Pianin, *Mirage: Why Neither Democrats nor Republicans Can Balance the Budget, End the Deficit, and Satisfy the Public* (New York: Random House, 1997).

[5]Congressional Budget Office, *The Economic and Budget Outlook: FYs 1998–2007* (Washington, D.C.: Congressional Budget Office, January 1997), xviii.

[6]As long as the eye cannot see too far. Virtually all forecasters project that the budget will go back into deficit under current policies after about FY 2020.

[7]For more details on the 1990 deal, see James Edwin Kee and Scott Nystrom, "The 1990 Budget Package: Redefining the Debate," *Public Budgeting and Finance* 10, no. 1 (Spring 1991): 3–24.

[8]Congressional Budget Office, *The Economic and Budget Outlook: An Update* (Washington, D.C.: Congressional Budget Office, August 1992).

deficit in half by the end of his first term.[9] He also promised to enact a middle-class tax cut and to provide additional funding for the many public "investments" that were listed in his campaign manifesto, *Putting People First*.

The 1993 Deficit Reduction Package Having captured the presidency but with only 43 percent of the popular vote, Clinton needed to translate his budget pledges into practical and consistent proposals. Believing that his reelection depended on satisfying the Perot voters, for whom deficit reduction was the sine qua non of budgeting, Clinton abandoned the middle-class tax cut as being temporarily unaffordable. However, in February 1993, Clinton also called for immediate passage of a $19.5 billion "stimulus" package as a down payment on a larger $160 billion four-year effort to spend more money on physical infrastructure and human capital. Although originally expected by liberals to sail through Congress, the proposal met stiff opposition from Senate Republicans. Clinton lacked the 60 votes necessary to overcome a Senate filibuster, and eventually the plan was abandoned.

The defeat of the stimulus package marked the beginning of the first Clinton administration's focus on deficit reduction. This emphasis, championed by influential White House staffer Robert Rubin, by the Federal Reserve, and by the Treasury and OMB leadership, eventually led to a more conservative approach designed to reduce the deficit while placing very little emphasis on increasing public investment spending.[10] The mood at the time is perhaps best illustrated by the uncommon delay in passing a disaster relief supplemental appropriation for massive flooding on the Mississippi.[11]

A $500 billion, five-year deficit reduction package—the Omnibus Budget Reconciliation Act (OBRA) of 1993—was enacted into law in the first year of the Clinton administration. This effort was notable for the partisanship of its support and opposition. No Republican in either body voted for either the budget resolution that pledged deficit reductions or the reconciliation bill that codified the revenue increases and spending cuts necessary to make that pledge a reality. The Republicans were particularly opposed to the law's heavy reliance on tax increases, and especially the increase in the top marginal tax rate from 31 percent to 39.6 percent. OBRA 1993 also extended the discretionary spending caps and the PAYGO rules from the 1990 BEA. Therefore, by the end of Clinton's first year in office, a package roughly equivalent in magnitude to the 1990 deficit reductions was enacted, but unlike in that previous case, a downturn in the economy did not offset these savings.

Table 1 shows trend data on Clinton-era budgetary aggregates and related macroeconomic conditions. Receipts as a percentage of GDP grew steadily to a historic high, and outlays declined steadily in the opposite direction. Underlying these trends were an increase in economic growth rates and stable and low interest rates.

---

[9]Bob Woodward, *The Agenda* (New York: Simon and Shuster, 1994), 42.

[10]For an entertaining if not entirely credible description of the deficit hawks' victory—from the losing perspective—see Robert B. Reich. *Locked in the Cabinet* (New York: Knopf, 1997).

[11]Bob Benenson, "Members Seeking Budget Cuts Bottle up Flood Relief," *Congressional Quarterly Weekly Report* 25 (July 24, 1993): 1941–1943.

TABLE 1
CLINTON-ERA BUDGETARY AGGREGATES AND GDP

Fiscal Years	Receipts*	Outlays*	Deficit ( ) or Surplus*	Change in Real GDP	Interest Rate on 10-Year Treasuries
1992	17.5	22.2	(4.7)	3.3	7.0
1993	17.6	21.5	(3.9)	2.4	5.9
1994	18.1	21.0	(2.9)	4.0	7.1
1995	18.5	20.7	(2.2)	2.7	6.6
1996	18.9	20.3	(1.4)	3.7	6.4
1997	19.3	19.6	(0.3)	4.5	6.4
1998	19.9	19.1	0.8	4.3	5.3
1999	20.0	18.7	1.4	3.9	5.7
2000 est.	20.4	18.7	1.7	3.3	6.1
2001 est.	20.1	18.3	1.8	2.7	6.1
2002 est.	19.8	18.0	1.8	2.5	6.1

Sources: U.S. Budget for FY 2001: Historical tables: Economic Report of the President.
*As percentage of GDP.

Economic productivity and employment returned to levels not seen since the post–World War II era, but without causing an increase in inflation. The impression left by these numbers is one of calm and steady progress—the so-called glide path—toward fiscal responsibility and macroeconomic health. But although the end of the Clinton era may have featured a "soft landing," the flight that led to it was tremendously bumpy.

The Health Care Reform Detour The year 1994 was dominated by the administration's effort to pass comprehensive health care reform legislation. Its primary thrust was to provide nearly comprehensive access to health care. Clinton made what was later regarded as a major strategic mistake by putting his wife, Hillary Rodham Clinton, and White House aide Ira Magaziner in charge of the proposal's design and advocacy. Large task forces working behind closed doors produced a complicated plan that was derided by even some advocates of health care entitlements as a Rube Goldberg contraption, and a well-orchestrated campaign by the insurance industry then turned public opinion against the plan.

The health care plan was also criticized on budgetary grounds. The administration claimed that its plan would reduce the deficit by $59 billion between 1995 and 2000, but the CBO countered that the plan would *add* $74 billion to deficits in those six years. CBO also suggested that the proposed "health alliances" (conduits through which premiums would flow and benefits would be paid) were governmental in nature and that their transactions should probably be included in the budget; this enabled opponents to label these premiums as "taxes."[12] Some

---

[12]See CBO, *An Analysis of the Administration's Health Proposal* (Washington, D.C.: Congressional Budget Office, February 1994) for this analysis. See also Haynes Johnson and David Broder, *The System: The American Way of Politics at the Breaking Point* (Boston: Little, Brown and Company, 1996).

administration representatives blamed CBO's controversial rulings for the death of the plan, but this was sour grapes: political and economic conditions weren't exactly ripe for a nonincremental expansion of health spending.

Budgetary War and Uneasy Truce, 1995–1997   In part because Republicans convinced many voters that the 1993 deficit reduction law included "the largest tax increase in history,"[13] Republicans gained control of the House and Senate in the midterm election of 1994. The House's Republican revolutionaries then dominated the agenda with their campaign platform the "Contract with America," a poll-tested pledge to propose 10 groups of initiatives that included regulatory reform, reduced taxes, and a budget balanced through spending cuts.

Although little of the contract was eventually enacted into law, the Republicans made a strong start with passage of a budget resolution that would cut taxes and attack spending on Clinton's favorite programs. But the Republicans' momentum slowed during the summer and came to a crashing stop in the fall. Clinton vetoed the reconciliation bill that Republicans projected would balance the budget by FY 2002, citing in particular a cut of $270 billion from Medicare over a seven-year period. The Republican leadership countered by threatening to hold the appropriation bills hostage until the president capitulated on reconciliation. This was a massive miscalculation of Clinton's will and political savvy and of the public's support for the Republican approach.[14] Two separate government shutdowns, one six days (November 14 to 19, 1995) in length and the second lasting for three weeks (December 16, 1995, to January 8, 1996) paralyzed "nonessential" government services. Not until the spring of 1996 did the branches compromise on FY 96 appropriations, reducing discretionary spending, but not nearly as far as the Republicans would have liked.[15]

Reaching this compromise did not help the Republicans, for the tag of "extremist" still stuck to them, costing them seats in the 1996 congressional elections. Clinton also won a convincing 49–41% victory in the 1996 presidential elections over Senator Bob Dole, who had run on a tax-cutting platform that was inconsistent with his fiscal record as a senator and was not convincing to the voters.[16] The economy and associated revenue estimates were surging higher. Given these conditions, congressional Republicans understandably drew back from their confrontational strategy, and the reconciliation bill that passed in late 1997—the so-called Balanced Budget Act—had something in it for both sides. The Republicans did get a tax cut,

[13]This claim is not true, even if only increases since World War II are considered. On an annualized basis, the 1982 Reagan TEFRA bill raised taxes by a greater amount; the 1993 Clinton increase was in second place, however.

[14]George Hager, "Daring Budgets Would Create Vastly Smaller Government," *Congressional Quarterly Weekly Report* 53 (May 13, 1995): 1298–1303; idem, "Clinton Shifts Tactics, Proposes Erasing Deficit in 10 Years," *Congressional Quarterly Weekly Report* 53 (June 17, 1995): 1715–1720.

[15]For more on these shutdowns, see Roy T. Meyers, "Late Appropriations and Government Shutdowns: Frequency, Causes, Consequences, and Remedies," *Public Budgeting and Finance* 17 (Fall 1997): 25–38. For a journalistic account of the politics behind the government shutdowns, see Hager and Pianin, *Mirage,* particularly chaps. 8 and 9.

[16]Alissa J. Rubin, "Dole 'Bets the Country' on Tax Cut Package," *Congressional Quarterly Weekly Report* 54 (August 10, 1996): 2245–2249.

but a much smaller one than they had advocated two years earlier. Cuts in mandatory spending (emphasizing Medicare) coupled with a further extension of the discretionary caps through FY 2002 offset those revenue losses.[17]

Impeachment and Presidential Resurgence, 1998–2000   The period between 1998 and 2000 was an affirmation of the status quo: no major budget policy changes were enacted. Budget totals, however, changed dramatically. Although the goal of the Balanced Budget Act was to achieve a zero deficit by FY 2002, the holy grail of budget surplus actually arrived a full four years ahead of schedule. Continuing a trend that had begun with gradually declining deficits between 1992 and 1997, FY 1998 saw the first unified budget surplus ($69 billion) since FY 1969. The surplus for FY 1999 increased to $124 billion, and the surplus for FY 2000 exceeded $230 billion.

The politics of surpluses, surprisingly to many, proved as difficult as the politics of deficits. And as if the question of what to do with the surplus wasn't difficult enough, 1998 was dominated by talk—and later more than talk—of impeachment. The president was understandably weakened during this process, and the Republican Congress renewed its attempt to dictate appropriations to the president.

The level of discretionary caps enacted in 1997 was central to this dispute. The caps held fairly well in FY 1998, but as the years went on, the caps became progressively tighter. In FY 1999 and FY 2000, the Congress found itself in the difficult position of being unable to enact appropriation bills at the capped level while feeling politically bound to retain the caps. In this environment, the Congress began to "budget by gimmick."[18]

Although budget gimmicks are nothing new in the federal budget process,[19] the FY 1999 and FY 2000 appropriations processes practically elevated them to an art form. Chief among the gimmicks was the declaration of certain items as "emergency" spending. The emergency designation had been enacted in the 1990 BEA but was used in only a limited way between fiscal years 1991 and 1998, averaging a little over $7 billion per year. For fiscal years 1999 and 2000, however, designated emergencies averaged over $30 billion per year and included such nonemergency items as the decennial census, a constitutional requirement adopted 210 years earlier. Other gimmicks employed, particularly for FY 2000 appropriation bills, included advance appropriations (appropriations made in one fiscal year that do not become available until a future fiscal year), obligation and payment timing shifts (such as moving paydays from one fiscal year to another), and directed scoring (in effect, telling CBO that a particular bill costs less than CBO thinks it does).[20]

---

[17]George Hager, "Clinton, GOP Congress Strike Historic Budget Agreement," *Congressional Quarterly Weekly Report* 55 (May 3, 1997): 993–1006; Ronald D. Elving and Andrew Taylor, "A Balanced-Budget Deal Won, A Defining Issue Lost," *Congressional Quarterly Weekly Report* 55 (August 2, 1997): 1831–1846.

[18]Andrew Taylor, "Congress Wraps up and Heads Home on a Trail of Broken Budget Caps," *Congressional Quarterly Weekly Report* 56 (October 24, 1998): 2885–2889.

[19]See Roy T. Meyers, *Strategic Budgeting* (Ann Arbor: University of Michigan Press, 1994).

[20]CBO, *The Budget and Economic Outlook: Fiscal Years 2001–2010* (Washington, D.C.: Congressional Budget Office, January 2000), 12, 76.

The Republicans renewed their tax cut campaign, but the administration and congressional Democrats outmaneuvered them here as well. President Clinton was able to link the issues of tax cuts and Social Security, pledging that he would "save Social Security first" before agreeing to any reduction in taxes. Practically, this meant that the goal for budget balancing shifted from balancing the unified budget (which, a couple of years earlier, would have been seen as difficult enough) to "on-budget" balance (that is, balancing the budget without including the surpluses in the Social Security trust funds) and then eliminating the debt by some point in the future. This had the political effect of putting congressional Republicans on the defensive concerning tax cuts, and the Republicans were reduced to passing tax cut bills (involving, for example, marriage penalty and estate taxes) that were largely intended as 2000 campaign issues.

Although many Americans seem convinced that it would be desirable for the federal government to "pay down the debt," the president never explained clearly and simply the best justification for this policy: reducing the debt would enable the creation of more private capital and thus promote economic growth; it would also create more public debt capacity and private tax-bearing capacity in the future. Doing so would help the country prepare for the fiscal challenges presented by future Social Security and health care spending: the "ticking time bombs" in the budget. We lack the space in this article to detail how big those bombs are and when they will go off, but the consensus among fiscal experts is that by the 2030s (with health care spending contributing most of the risk), the borrowing required to maintain current policy could threaten economic prosperity. (This timetable is actually less worrisome than that which was projected before the more rapid growth of the mid- to late 1990s.)[21]

Now might be the best time to face up to these long-run threats, because funding would be available for transition costs and because changing policy now would provide individuals with more time to adjust their behaviors. On the other hand, perhaps it is never convenient for most politicians to advocate reforming programs that affect so many people in ways that can be portrayed negatively. The famous "third-rail" metaphor applied to Social Security and Medicare ("touch it and you die") was if anything given greater currency when Republicans bravely attempted to cut Medicare spending in 1995, for they were severely criticized and punished at the polls for doing so.[22] Since then, political debates over health policy have largely attacked the principle of managed care— understandable because of how managed care has been implemented, but also discouraging to those who believe that managed care is an inevitable part of the solution to rapid health care cost growth. Similarly, there has been very little serious discussion of reforming Social Security, despite the opportunity presented by the Advisory Council on Social Security's presentation of alternative reform approaches in 1997.[23]

[21]CBO, *The Long-Term Budget Outlook* (Washington, D.C.: Congressional Budget Office, October 2000).

[22]David Maraniss and Michael Weisskopf, *"Tell Newt to Shut Up"* (New York: Touchstone, 1996). See also Herbert Stein, "Don't Ask Alice," *Washington Post* (October 30, 1994): C5.

[23]For an alternative perspective, see Dean Baker and Mark Weisbrot, *Social Security: The Phony Crisis* (Chicago: University of Chicago Press, 1999).

Why Has the Budget Moved from Deficit to Surplus?   Consistent with the adage that "success has a thousand fathers, while failure is an orphan," both the Clinton administration and congressional Republicans sought acclaim for the 180-degree shift in fiscal results. Circumstantial evidence would credit the Clinton administration: the movement did happen on its watch, and certainly the 1993 budget agreement, which had no Republican support, was a significant contributor. But the ground was prepared for that law by the earlier 1990 budget agreement between President Bush and the Congress: in particular, that law established the BEA spending cap and PAYGO procedures, which were more likely to reduce the deficit than the Gramm-Rudman-Hollings sequestration empty threat that they replaced. This conclusion is ironic, because other Republicans maligned that agreement so much for Bush's abandonment of his "no new taxes" pledge that they helped Bush lose his reelection bid.

In a recent report, CBO noted that its January 1997 estimate of a $171 billion deficit in FY 2000 had changed by more than $400 billion in only three-and-one-half years, as a $232 billion surplus was forecast in July 2000. CBO then decomposed the causes of the government's vastly improved fiscal condition. Legislation during this period had almost no effect, and reductions in spending because of "technical factors" produced about a quarter of the change. The remaining three-quarters came from faster than expected growth in revenues. Significant increases in economic productivity meant higher profits, and these profits transformed into higher earned incomes and higher equity prices (to the point of an equity investment bubble?). Cashing in led to sharp increases into capital gains revenues, and as the numbers of taxpayers in upper income brackets increased, as did incomes within these brackets, the 1993 increases to marginal tax rates produced more revenues than anyone had expected.

Economists have long argued about how to explain changes in productivity. Certainly the information revolution contributed significantly to the recent spurt, illustrating the dynamism of a competitive economy. However, it would be a mistake to conclude, as some analysts have, that government played no supporting role: indeed, the web itself was invented by the government. Credit claimers from both parties can identify government actions that created the fundamental conditions for the 1990s' success: welfare reform increased labor flexibility, and deregulation and tax simplification reduced the effects of distorting incentives. The trade liberalization of the 1990s also promoted higher rates of economic growth. Nevertheless, the most widely admired governmental contribution to the virtuous cycle was the Federal Reserve's management of monetary policy under Chairman Alan Greenspan. The Clinton administration had a very cooperative relationship with Greenspan on a personal as well as a policy basis, allowing both to skillfully manage international crises in Mexico and then southeast Asia and to keep interest rates far below past "full employment" levels without stimulating inflation. Neither would have been possible had a tighter fiscal policy not been adopted first.

Our widely distributed praise must unfortunately be qualified. First, some of the impressive results of the 1990s were undoubtedly due to luck. The end of the Cold War came at a fortuitous time, allowing defense spending to be reduced at a rapid pace, and the energy markets were calm. One does not have to be an extreme pessimist to suspect that in the future, unexpected events will threaten our fiscal stability rather than improve it.

Second, although, in the short run, deficits may be behind us, we can easily project that they will return if the country's demographics and unselective technological innovation in health care continue as expected. As impressive as the progress on the deficit has been, the latter years of the 1990s may also be most remembered for squandering an opportunity to reform the largest entitlement programs.

Microbudgetary Policy

How did microbudgetary policy change during the Clinton era? Who won and who lost in the battle for budget allocations, and why? What do these results indicate about policy choices and the role of the budget process in affecting these choices?

Table 2 shows the shifts in BEA category allocations as a percentage of total outlays throughout the Clinton era. Allocations in two categories declined: net interest, as deficits were reduced, and defense discretionary, as the military downsized. The latter trend began in 1987, when defense discretionary spending accounted for 28.1 percent of total outlays. Nondefense discretionary and mandatory spending (excluding interest) increased during the Clinton years, the latter at a faster rate; at the end of the era, mandatory spending was a little more than three times the size of nondefense discretionary spending.

Table 3 shows budget allocations throughout this period by budget functions, and in this case, for budget authority as a percentage of the totals in even-numbered years. Some of the aforementioned winners and losers stand out: Social

---

TABLE 2
CLINTON-ERA SHIFTS IN BEA CATEGORY ALLOCATIONS
(OUTLAYS AS A PERCENTAGE OF TOTAL OUTLAYS)

	Defense Discretionary	Nondefense Discretionary	Mandatory Excluding Net Interest	Net Interest
1992	21.9	15.4	46.9	14.4
1993	20.7	16.1	47.5	14.1
1994	19.3	16.5	48.9	13.9
1995	18.0	16.6	48.7	15.3
1996	17.0	16.0	50.3	15.4
1997	17.0	16.1	50.5	15.2
1998	16.4	16.1	51.8	14.6
1999	16.2	16.4	52.7	13.5
2000 est.	16.3	17.0	53.2	12.3
2001 est.	15.9	17.3	54.1	11.4
2002 est.	15.8	17.4	55.2	10.5

TABLE 3
CLINTON-ERA ALLOCATIONS TO BUDGET FUNCTIONS, ALTERNATE FISCAL YEARS
(BUDGET AUTHORITY AS PERCENTAGE OF TOTAL)

	1992	1994	1996	1998	2000 (est.)
National Defense	20.1	17.2	16.8	16.0	16.3
International Affairs	1.4	1.2	1.0	0.9	1.1
Science, Space, and Technology	1.2	1.2	1.1	1.1	1.1
Energy	0.4	0.3	0.2	0.0	−0.1
Natural Resources and Environment	1.5	1.5	1.4	1.4	1.4
Agriculture	1.5	1.1	0.6	0.8	1.8
Commerce and Housing Credit	3.2	1.8	0.5	0.8	0.6
Transportation	2.5	2.8	2.3	2.7	3.0
Community and Regional Development	0.8	1.0	0.8	0.6	0.6
Education, Training, Employment, and Social Services	3.3	3.4	3.3	3.6	3.1
Health	6.3	7.6	7.0	8.0	8.8
Medicare	9.1	10.6	11.4	11.4	11.5
Income Security	13.7	14.2	14.0	13.7	13.5
Social Security	19.7	21.0	22.3	22.5	22.7
Veterans Benefits and Services	2.3	2.4	2.5	2.5	2.6
Administration of Justice	1.0	1.0	1.3	1.5	1.5
General Government	0.9	0.8	0.7	1.0	0.8
Net Interest	13.6	13.3	15.3	14.3	12.2
Undistributed Offsetting Receipts	−2.7	−2.5	−2.4	−2.8	−2.4

Source: U.S. Budget for FY2001, Historical Tables.

Security, Health, and Medicare in the first category, and National Defense (particularly military personnel) in the second. Other functions show stable patterns—Science, Space, and Technology and Veterans—whereas another, Agriculture, shows a significant down-then-up pattern. Yet another function—Education, Training, Employment, and Social Services—shows a surprisingly stable pattern, when knowledge of the politics of this period would cause one to expect a significant increase in funding (for Clinton was sometimes described as wanting to become "the nation's principal"). To begin to understand the real distribution of microbudgetary allocations during the period, we will have to go down to the subfunction level, consider tax expenditures as well as regular spending, and connect budget allocations to important authorizing legislation and other factors. We necessarily do this in a very selective fashion.

Starting with examples of successful advocacy of spending increases, one of the most interesting was for Ground Transportation—from $23.3 billion in FY 1992 to $38.6 billion in FY 2000 (all figures are in current dollars, and FY 2000 figures are estimates). The major cause was passage of the 1998 Transportation Equity Act for the 21st Century, which required that appropriations be no lower than the previous year's gasoline tax receipts. The extraordinary political skills of the House committee chair for the bill, Pennsylvania Representative Bud Shuster (R), were critical to its passage. By first threatening to take highway spending off-budget, then loading the bill with member set-asides, Shuster demonstrated that age-old legislative tactics could still work despite massive pressures to reduce spending.[24]

Another large increase in spending was in the Health Research and Training subfunction—from $10.7 billion in FY 1992 to $18.5 billion in FY 2000. Medical research advocates have long enjoyed widely dispersed geographic support and an understandable desire to cure terrible diseases; during the 1990s they successfully argued for more spending to take advantage of biotech's potential.

A third example of rapid spending growth was in the Administration of Justice function. The drug war's addiction to incarceration for lower-level dealers pushed Bureau of Prisons spending higher, and a tough-on-crime bidding war between the parties led to passage of the Violent Crime Control and Law Enforcement Act of 1994. The subfunction for Criminal Justice Assistance reflected the full menu of new grant programs, including Clinton's widely touted program to put "100,000 new cops on the streets": spending grew from $872 million in FY 1992 to $4.6 billion in FY 2000.

The start of an explanation for the apparent slow growth in education spending is that although budget authority for Elementary, Secondary and Vocational Education did increase from $14.2 to $17.2 billion, this was partially offset by Higher Education budget authority being stuck at around $12.2 billion. However, this masks a tremendous increase in federal financial support for higher education through tax preferences. By FY 2000, the government was expecting a revenue loss of $4.6 billion for the new Hope tax credit, $2.4 billion for the new lifetime learning tax credit, and additional losses for smaller higher education tax preferences.

The decline and increase in Agriculture spending is the result of what might be viewed as a "failed crop." After decades of academic critiques of price and income supports, with the Freedom to Farm Act (FTF) of 1996, the government finally agreed to wean the agricultural sector of these subsidies. The plan made sizeable transition payments at the beginning but was then to phase out subsidies and associated regulations over the next seven years. But bumper crops and plummeting international demand also weakened the resolve of many who voted for the FTF, and agriculture appropriations grew rapidly.

The other entitlement spending that was revised significantly was welfare. The long-standing Aid to Families with Dependent Children (AFDC) program was replaced in 1996 by Temporary Assistance to Needy Families (TANF). The distinctive word in the title was "temporary": the campaign pledge of "ending welfare as we know it" was operationalized by ending the entitlement status of welfare for current recipients through the mechanism of time limits; instead, each state became entitled to a block grant formula allocation. Many liberals criticized this welfare reform legislation, including some of Clinton's highest welfare administrators, who resigned in protest. They focused on the potential of the law to

[24]Kirk Victor, "Trust Me," *National Journal* (March 11, 1995): 607–11; Alan K. Ota, "Shuster Prepares for Onslaught Against Members' Projects," *Congressional Quarterly Weekly Report* 56 (March 21, 1998): 735–37.

encourage states to "race to the bottom" of benefit levels, particularly during a recession. Because of the strong economy, luckily that scenario has not yet come about. The threat of enforced time limits, and the new opportunities provided by expanded child care, job search and training funds made available to the states, jointly produced significant drops in state spending on welfare. The race then began in the federal government to recapture unspent funds held by the states, but the states successfully resisted. Although this area appears to be a success story, there remains significant uncertainty about the effect of the new policies on those who lost eligibility and on the depressing effect on take-up rates for the associated Medicaid program and the new State Children's Health Insurance Program. Advocates of a strong safety net also expressed their discontent about major cuts to food stamps spending and harsh limits on immigrants' eligibility for social services. Overall, federal spending on income security during the period remained quite stable (not counting the new child credit that was estimated to cost $20 billion in FY 2000, which was classified in the Education function). Poverty did decline, as the economic growth tide raised most boats, but the country's comparatively wide level of income disparity was not significantly changed.[25]

Although our limited discussion cannot determine who was responsible for these different budget allocations, it's generally safe to conclude that most were compromises between the parties and between the executive and legislative branches. Whether these compromises were in fact good budgetary policy is obviously a matter that is somewhat dependent on value perspectives. Defenders of adopted policies often rely on prime facie arguments, such as observing that the latter 1990's reduction in crime statistics was correlated with spending for increased incarceration and/or the explosion in grant funding for community policing. We are often skeptical about such arguments, despite being sympathetic to many of the Clinton administration's policy goals and to his "third-way" philosophy of considering innovative combinations of policy approaches. Our skepticism is generally based on a suspicion that the political leaders of this administration developed proposals primarily to produce positive focus group and opinion poll results (for example, "100,000 police officers") while at the same time spending insufficient amounts to have much chance of creating predicted impacts. Republicans often behaved similarly.

This problem is related to a question that may especially concern readers of this journal: did the formal rules and informal norms used to produce the 1990s' macrobudgetary success distort microbudgetary allocations? The BEA's different procedures for discretionary and mandatory spending were chosen because they matched existing committee jurisdictions; however, they hindered politicians from comparing approaches within budget functions or across policy tools. This artificial separation helped stimulate use of inefficient policy designs, particularly when combined with political pressures, such as when those who knew better argued

---

[25]R. Kent Weaver, *Ending Welfare as We Know It* (Washington, D.C.: Brookings, 2000); Rebecca M. Blank, *It Takes a Nation: A New Agenda for Fighting Poverty* (Princeton, N.J.: Princeton University Press, 1997).

that "targeted tax cuts" were not functionally equivalent to spending. A good example is the Clinton proposal to provide a tax exemption for income from municipal bonds that provide funds for school construction in disadvantaged areas.

Liberal strategists might argue that they rejected the obvious alternative—a targeted grant program—because the potential harshness of the discretionary caps prevented adequate funding. Using caps to generate most of the spending savings also created the incentive to carve spending out from this total by converting to quasi-mandatory status. An example is the crime bill's establishment of a pseudo-"trust fund" for criminal justice spending, which in effect set a floor on discretionary spending for this area. The cumulative effect of such conversions was to further reduce budgetary flexibility.

Presidential-Congressional Relations

Without meaning to diminish the seriousness of the transgression, Bill Clinton was not the first president to lie to protect his political career. That Bill Clinton was impeached for doing so indicates that his relationship with the Congress was extraordinarily bad. Conflicts over budgeting contributed significantly to that unhappy relationship.

One major explanation why is unrelated to the personalities of and the strategies used by Clinton and the various congressional leaders; rather, it is structural. According to presidential scholar Stephen Skowronek, one of the president's expected functions is to disrupt the existing order and legitimate a new one.[26] This was a dicey problem for Clinton. His fate was to begin his presidency when deficits were extremely high and worrisome to the public. However, cutting spending was counter to Clinton's predilection toward government spending; his 1995 State of the Union sound bite that "the era of big government is over" was surely an insincere tactical maneuver. For that matter, many citizens who wanted deficit reductions also disliked most cuts in spending or increases in taxes that would produce that result. Clinton therefore had to move back and forth between the need to reduce large deficits and the desire to use the fisc for many purposes.

His start in office was similar to that of most presidents—inexperience invites mistakes—and it was further hindered by the arteriosclerotic Democratic majority in the 103rd Congress.[27] The only major success of the first two years was OBRA 1993, but this helped the president's party lose the Congress. Paradoxically, the return of divided government made it easier for Clinton to deal with his structural dilemma, particularly because it provided him with weak opponents. Speaker Newt Gingrich had engineered an impressive electoral victory but had deluded himself that he could act like powerful 19th-century speaker Henry Clay. The

[26]Stephen Skowronek, *The Politics Presidents Make* (Cambridge: Harvard University Press, 1993); idem, "The Risks of 'Third-Way' Politics," *Society* 33 (September 1996): 32–36. See also Sidney M. Milkis and Michael Nelson, *The American Presidency: Origins and Development, 1776–1998,* 3d ed. (Washington, D.C.: Congressional Quarterly Press, 1999); Samuel Kernell, *Going Public: New Strategies of Presidential Leadership* (Washington, D.C.: Congressional Quarterly Press, 1997).

[27]Paul Charles Light, *The President's Agenda* (Baltimore: Johns Hopkins University Press, 1982).

Republicans had been a minority lost in the political wilderness for 40 years, and their actions in the first year of their congressional majority led many to conclude that the party was not yet ready for prime time. Their leadership's most critical mistake was forgetting that despite the constitutional assignment of the power of the purse to the Congress, the president is more than the political equal of the Congress. They learned as Clinton wielded the veto pen and spoke from the bully pulpit; at the same time they found out how difficult it is to convince a majority party to follow a coherent strategy.

The Republicans' problem was made even more difficult by Clinton's extraordinary skill at high-level bargaining. A major element of his approach was described by his political consultant Dick Morris as "triangulation": taking positions that would distinguish him from both congressional Republicans *and* Democrats.[28] The Democratic losses in 1994, which hurt moderates more than liberals and thus shifted the Democratic caucus to the left, led Clinton back to the "New Democrat" positions he had featured in his 1992 campaign. He returned to that campaign's "war room" approach of issuing frequent public statements within short media cycles, but he also gave his Republican opponents enough rope so that they exposed the contradictions in their own positions. During Clinton's second term, the Republicans would adopt budget resolutions with discretionary spending far below the president's budget requests, then hope that he would agree as the branches bargained over appropriations bills. They would also load down appropriations bills with numerous policy riders, particularly ones that countered actions by the Environmental Protection Agency and other regulatory and land use agencies. Why they did this repeatedly had most observers perplexed, for it was clear that the Republicans were mortally afraid to call Clinton's veto bluffs and go down the "shutdown" path again. By the end of Clinton's term, some Republicans publicly confessed that they didn't even want to negotiate with him! Each year, the Republicans searched for a new end-game strategy, but each year they caved to the administration's insistence on more funding for numerous nondefense discretionary programs.

The Republicans' credibility as fiscal conservatives was also hurt by their growing taste for the pork barrel. During their time in the minority, Republicans had vociferously criticized Democrats for appropriations set-asides, but after a year of self-denial, the attractions of majority power were apparently too strong to resist. And once most Republicans began loading up appropriations bills, they had a much harder time criticizing administration proposals.[29]

One brief instance of conflict over budgetary allocations came with the 1997 battles over President Clinton's use of the line-item veto. House Republicans, in their Contract with America, had pledged to give the president a statutory equivalent of

---

[28]William Schneider, "Triangulation's Budgetary Triumph," *National Journal* 27 (December 23, 1995): 3182.

[29]Senator John McCain's web page lists both Republican and Democratic set-asides: <*http://www.senate.gov/~mccain/porkbar.htm*>.

an item veto (actually, a change to the rescission process that tipped the presumption substantially in the president's favor). This promise became reality with passage of the Line Item Veto Act in 1996. The act took effect in 1997, and Clinton used it in a very limited way in the FY 1998 appropriations process to eliminate a small number of tax benefits and mandatory spending items. The president's discretionary cancellations totaled less than one-tenth of one percent ($477 million out of $526 billion) of the amount provided in appropriations bills; 60 percent of these cancellations were overturned by the Congress (especially in the Military Construction appropriations bill, a classic pork product). The line-item veto was reduced to a one-year experiment when the Supreme Court ruled it unconstitutional in June 1998, on *Chadha*-type grounds that this procedure did not conform with the constitutional requirements that legislation pass both House and Senate in identical form and be presented to the president for signature or veto.[30]

Budgeting in the Executive Branch

Budgeting occupied center stage during the Reagan and Bush presidencies; Reagan's first budget director, David Stockman, and Bush's only budget director, Richard Darman, were among the most easily identified members of those administrations. Early in the Clinton administration, it appeared that OMB's role would be diminished because of the president's decision to create a National Economic Council (NEC) as part of the White House staff and because OMB's career staff had been assisting Republican presidents for 12 years.[31] Yet the appointment of Leon Panetta as budget director brought almost immediate political credibility to OMB, and more generally, the professional qualifications and respect engendered by its directors throughout the administration ensured that OMB maintained its central policymaking position:

Leon Panetta (1993–1995) was the longtime chair of the House Budget Committee and a tireless advocate of deficit reduction when tapped by Clinton to be his first budget director. He fought successfully within the administration for an emphasis on the deficit over public investment spending, had a great deal of credibility on the Hill, and went on to be arguably the most successful of Clinton's White House chiefs of staff.

Alice Rivlin (1995–1996) took over for Panetta when the former was named Chief of Staff. A widely respected economist, she had been the founding director of the CBO. She had also been in the running to be the first Clinton OMB director but had settled for deputy director when Panetta was tapped for the job. She initially helped Panetta fight for deficit reduction, continued that effort on her own watch, and advocated attention to government performance issues during her time as director. She left OMB to become vice-chair of the Federal Reserve.

[30]Philip G. Joyce, "The Federal Line Item Veto Experiment: After the Supreme Court Ruling, What's Next?" *Public Budgeting and Finance* 18 (Winter 1998): 3–21.

[31]Paul Starobin, "The Broker," *National Journal* 26 (April 16, 1994): 878–83.

Franklin Raines (1996–1998) came to OMB from Fannie Mae, the giant government-sponsored housing enterprise. He was budget director in the early part of the second administration, playing an important role in negotiations between the White House and Congress associated with the 1997 reconciliation bill. He left OMB in 1998 to return to Fannie Mae, this time as its chairman.

Jacob Lew (1998–2001) had been an OMB official (serving as associate director for legislative affairs, executive associate director, and deputy director) since 1994 when he was selected to succeed Raines as OMB director midway through 1998. Lew was most heavily involved with negotiating with the Congress over administration priorities during his time in office.

In some contrast to our criticism of its apparent preference for symbolic policy proposals, the Clinton administration was exceptionally devoted to focusing attention on government performance. At first, the main role was played by Vice President Gore and his National Performance Review (later the National Partnership for Reinventing Government). Patterned after a state auditor's review of Texas government, the National Performance Review (or NPR) sought to identify both improvements in management practices ("works better") and new approaches for possible budgetary savings ("costs less"). The NPR in general advocated the empowerment of managers and accountability for results.[32] The NPR also championed a reduction in red tape in federal agencies. Part of this was to be brought about by a reduction of 272,900 middle managers, including many employees whom NPR believed existed only to keep an eye on other federal managers; an unspecified number of these were in agency budget shops. NPR was just as hostile to the annual review of agency budgets that was carried out by OMB and the Congress, and it proposed adoption of biennial budgeting and the availability of spending authority beyond one year. It was largely unsuccessful in implementing these and other budgeting reforms, particularly those that required legislative action.

A much more far-reaching reform was embodied in the Government Performance and Results Act (GPRA) of 1993. This legislation, which had been championed by Delaware Senator William Roth (R) since the late 1980s, required federal agencies to develop strategic plans and performance measures and to report on performance. OMB jump-started implementation of GPRA by requiring agencies to include more performance information with budget submissions with the FY 96 budget, earlier than GPRA required.[33] Further, an internal reorganization of OMB, called "OMB 2000," was designed to bring more review and attention to management and performance issues during budget review by merging "management" and "budget" sides of OMB to create new "resource management offices."[34]

---

[32]John Kamensky, "Role of the Reinventing Government Movement in Federal Management Reform," *Public Administration Review* 56, no. 3 (May/June 1996): 247–55. See also Peri E. Arnold, *Making the Managerial Presidency,* 2d rev. ed. (Lawrence: University Press of Kansas, 1998).

[33]Philip G. Joyce, "Performance-Based Budgeting," in *Handbook of Government Budgeting,* ed. Roy T. Meyers (San Francisco: Jossey-Bass, 1999), 597–619.

[34]Bernard H. Martin, Joseph S. Wholey, and Roy T. Meyers, "The New Equation at OMB: M + B = RMO," *Public Budgeting and Finance* 15 (Winter 1995): 86–96; Shelley Lynne Tomkin, *Inside OMB* (Armonk, N.Y.: M. E. Sharpe, 1998).

Although there is some evidence that OMB has used performance information in reviewing budgets for the president, the most significant effects of performance information have been seen at the agency level. This does not mean that performance information—for budgeting or anything else—is used uniformly across the federal government. For one thing, the federal government is a collection of agencies that do very dissimilar things, some of which are much easier to measure than others, and for another, some agencies simply have more experience measuring and managing performance than others do. The General Accounting Office's (GAO's) prediction in 1997, that implementation of GPRA would be "uneven" across the federal government has proven a prescient one.[35]

Still, the lack of any wholesale transformation of centralized budgeting processes masks a great deal of activity occurring in many agencies, where budget development and execution are increasingly becoming more informed by performance considerations. Consider the U.S. Coast Guard, which now makes wholesale use of performance information in budget formulation and implementation, allowing dollars to be allocated within the Marine Safety program in line with where they will have the greatest effect on preventing accidents.[36] The Veterans Health Administration has confronted a basic resource allocation problem—a disconnect between where veterans live (in the South and West) and where most hospitals are (in the East and Midwest)—by developing an allocation system based on where funding can best contribute to achieving health outcomes for veterans.[37] Our point is that it is in the management of resources by agencies that perhaps the greatest effect of this new performance orientation can be seen, an effect that would be missed if one focused only on how OMB used performance information.

GPRA also envisions that the Congress will prod agencies to develop a performance management orientation, requiring, for example, frequent consultation between the Congress and the agencies on the details of strategic plans and performance measures. That expectation has yet to be realized. The House Republican leadership quickly addressed the flaws in the initial strategic plans, issuing low grades to most, and kept GAO on the trail of other agencies' failures to comply with GPRA. Of course, full agency compliance would have been miraculous in light of confusing statutory directives and the tendency of members of Congress to put priority on the location of spending over other criteria, but the Congress has yet to look inward as an explanation for slow progress on GPRA.

Finally, a discussion of executive branch budgeting would be incomplete if it did not include implementation of the Chief Financial Officers Act (CFO Act) of 1990 and several amendments to this law, especially the Government Management Reform Act (GMRA) of 1994 and the Federal Financial Management Improvement Act (FFMIA) of 1996. The CFO Act was designed to battle some management

---

[35]GAO, *The Government Performance and Results Act: Governmentwide Implementation Will Be Uneven* (Washington, D.C.: Government Accounting Office, June 1997).

[36]For a description of the Coast Guard system, see Joyce, "Performance-Based Budgeting," 611. See also Anne Laurent, "The Curse of Can Do," *Government Executive* 32 (March 2000), 41–49.

[37]See "Healthy Accomplishments," *Government Executive* 31 (February 1999), 66–68.

failings that had been uncovered in the 1990s, perhaps best exemplified by the well-publicized scandals at the Department of Housing and Urban Development. The legislation required the establishment of chief financial officers in 24 executive branch agencies, the production of clean financial statements for agencies and the U.S. government as a whole, and a closer working relationship between federal financial management professionals, including chief financial officers, the OMB, and agency inspectors general. As expected, implementation uncovered financial management weaknesses in many agencies, such as failures in controlling property, plant, equipment, and cash. But because OMB and federal agencies have made "considerable investments of time, money and energy . . . to reengineer and refine agency accounting procedures and processes," according to L. R. Jones and Jerry McCaffery, some agencies have received unqualified opinions.[38]

Another Clinton-era financial management reform was the 1994 Federal Acquisition Streamlining Act, which required major capital purchases to be justified on the basis of cost, schedule, and performance, freeing the procurement process from excessive devotion to detailed specifications and low-bid awards.[39] The Information Technology Management Reform Act of 1996 (also known as Clinger-Cohen) required agencies to take a more performance-based approach to procuring information technology (IT) investments. This included a requirement to select and manage investments with a specific focus on the extent to which they assist the agency in fulfilling its mission, to establish measures for IT performance, and to report the results of these measures to OMB.[40]

Prospects for Budgeting During the Post-Clinton Presidency

In last year of the Clinton administration, news reports portrayed the president as being obsessed with his "legacy." Every aging president seems to become especially concerned about history's judgment, but perhaps Clinton was more so because of the embarrassment from his impeachment.

We would rather not make a definitive statement about Clinton's legacy, except for observing that there have been few great presidents in American history, and Clinton will join the large group with mixed records. Presidential historians will have much to debate, particularly because Clinton's record includes such extreme positives as his record on deficit reductions and such extreme negatives as the fact that he was "an unusually good liar," the capsule description offered by Nebraska Senator Robert Kerrey (D).[41] When we say that Clinton will be "a hard act to follow," we don't mean that to be a simplistic statement.[42]

---

[38]L. R. Jones and Jerry McCaffery, "Financial Management Reform in the Federal Government," in *Handbook of Government Budgeting*, ed. Roy T. Meyers (San Francisco: Jossey-Bass, 1999), 76–77.

[39]Suzannah Zak Figura, "Capital Considerations," *Government Executive* 31 (February 1999), 25–28.

[40]Nancy Ferris, "High-Tech Hurdles," *Government Executive* 31 (February 1999), 19–23.

[41]See Christopher Hitchens, *No One Left to Lie To* (New York: Verso, 1999).

[42]For comprehensive legacy assessments, see Colin Campbell and Bert A. Rockman, eds., *The Clinton Presidency: First Appraisals* (Chatham, N.J.: Chatham House, 1996); idem, *The Clinton Legacy* (New York: Chatham House, 2000).

Instead, we'd like to close by asking how budgeting might evolve in the post-Clinton presidency. We are leery of issuing formal predictions, because of the inherent unpredictability of some important variables, such as the balance of power between the major political parties. On the other hand, we consider it an absolute certainty that macroeconomic conditions will worsen, and probably sooner than most observers expect. When that happens, eliminating the debt won't appear to be as easy as it does today, nor as desirable. The days of reckoning for the major entitlements will be ever closer, and the cluttered tax code will beg for another attempt at revision. Can the budget process—as is or modified—live up to these challenges?

The experience of the past decade may justify some cautious optimism. The movement of the budget from deficit to surplus was an impressive and unexpected result, and it came about in part because of the acceptance of inconvenient budget process constraints. The easy symbolic outs of the balanced-budget constitutional amendment were repeatedly rejected. And improvements in the executive branch's capacity to integrate management and budgeting may serve as the basis for more selectivity among spending and taxing options.

On the other hand, the frequent breakdowns of the budget process indicate that it isn't very robust. Many observers have suggested that there is no reason to expect that a process that was created to deal with large deficits is up to the task of budgeting under large surpluses, and they cite the discretionary caps as a fine example. The caps temporarily answered the age-old question "How big a government do we want?" with the answer "no bigger for now." Under current law, the caps expire in FY 2002, but they most likely will not survive until then, because a bigger government is now more affordable. Recent events suggest that either the caps will have to be raised by large amounts or politicians will have to exercise more self-control in their advocacy and acceptance of the individual spending proposals that constitute discretionary spending. Reconciliation must also be revived, or a substitute invented, if mandatory spending is to be sufficiently controlled.

Another question is the future role of the congressional budget resolution. The main outlines of budget policy in the 1990s were set by occasional multiyear agreements between the branches. This practice is in stark contrast to that set out in the Congressional Budget Act, in which the budget resolution is the main means by which the Congress is to set fiscal policy *each* year. Perhaps the Congress will attempt to return to this approach, or it may decide that the vision of the Congressional Budget Act is an unrealistic one. If the latter is the case, it would behoove the branches to think about how they might better coordinate their budget processes, rather than rely on haphazard summit procedures.

In 2000, the House of Representatives debated and killed the proposed Comprehensive Budget Process Reform Act (H.R. 853), which would have converted to biennial budgeting and a joint budget resolution. Although this was not a perfect bill from our perspective, we also felt that it was often misunderstood and mischaracterized in the congressional debate concerning it. If the country is to address the fiscal challenges it faces, the Congress and the president will need to go beyond the day-to-day battle for partisan advantages and more seriously consider how to improve the country's budget process.

15

THE PRESIDENT
AND FOREIGN
POLICY MAKING

Crisis in the Balkans: The Road To War—
A Special Report; How a President, Distracted
by Scandal, Entered Balkan War

By Elaine Sciolino and Ethan Bronner

On Jan. 19, President Clinton's top aides met in the Situation Room in the White House basement to hear a fateful new plan for an autonomous Kosovo from Madeleine K. Albright, the Secretary of State. NATO, she urged, should use the threat of air strikes on Yugoslavia to force a peace agreement to be monitored by the alliance's ground troops.

The President, who had other matters on his mind, was not there. His lawyers were starting their arguments on the Senate floor against his removal from office. That night he was to deliver his State of the Union address.

Nearly 5,000 miles away, in Belgrade, Gen. Wesley K. Clark, the NATO commander, and Gen. Klaus Naumann, chairman of the NATO military council, were sitting with President Slobodan Milosevic of Yugoslavia. They came brandishing a plastic portfolio of color photographs documenting a massacre of Albanians three days earlier by Serbian security forces in the Kosovo town of Racak. They also came with threats of NATO air strikes.

This was far from their first encounter with the Serbian leader, but this time, they recalled, they found a newly hardened man with a bunker mentality.

"This was not a massacre," Mr. Milosevic shouted. "This was staged. These people are terrorists."

When General Clark warned him that NATO would "start telling me to move aircraft," Mr. Milosevic appeared infuriated by the prospect of bombings. He called the general a war criminal.

Jan. 19 is already seen as a pivotal day in the Clinton Presidency. But it may turn out to be so less for the Senate impeachment hearings and State of the Union address than for the moves toward war over Kosovo.

Kosovo would have presented a daunting foreign policy challenge even to a President whose powers of persuasion and moral authority had not been damaged by a year of sex scandal and impeachment.

It is unclear whether the President's decisions on Kosovo would have been any different if he had not been distracted by his own political and legal problems. But it is clear that his troubles gave him less maneuvering room to make his decisions. Diplomacy that came to rely heavily on military threats reduced the wiggle room even further.

Over the previous year, sharp criticism and questioning of Mr. Clinton's motives arose each time he did take military action, as with the strikes in December against Iraq when the House was poised to vote on his impeachment.

Now, Mr. Clinton is facing mounting criticism for not having acted earlier or more decisively on Kosovo. His critics say that had he done so, Mr. Milosevic would not have been able to move troops and equipment into Kosovo and carry out the massive "ethnic cleansing" of the past four weeks.

As the President viewed the situation, there were only "a bunch of bad options" confronting him, he said earlier this month.

Throughout, the NATO allies hoped, even assumed, that they were dealing with the Milosevic who negotiated the Bosnian peace at Dayton, Ohio, the man who lied and manipulated and ranted in all-night, Scotch-laden negotiations and then cut a deal in the morning when he saw that it was in his interest. Instead they were dealing with the Milosevic of Belgrade, who was willing to employ mass murder to assure his continued dominance of Serbia.

George J. Tenet, the Director of Central Intelligence, predicted in Congressional testimony in February that there would be a major spring offensive by the Serbs in Kosovo and huge refugee flows. But intelligence assessments presented to Mr. Clinton about how Mr. Milosevic would respond to NATO threats of military force were vague. These reports included speculation that the Yugoslav leader would back down in the face of air strikes.

One interagency intelligence report coordinated by the C.I.A. in January 1999, for example, concluded that "Milosevic doesn't want a war he can't win."

"After enough of a defense to sustain his honor and assuage his backers he will quickly sue for peace," the assessment went on. Another interagency report in February stated, "He doesn't believe NATO is going to bomb."

Prodded by such assessments and his advisers, the President pressed ahead with a strategy of threats coupled with negotiations, gambling that Mr. Milosevic would back down. These threats quickly became a test of NATO's credibility, with the added onus of the alliance's looming 50th anniversary, which is to be observed next weekend.

Last September, former Senator Bob Dole went to Kosovo to gather facts for an international refugee group of which he is chairman. On his return, he reported his findings to Mr. Clinton. Afterward Mr. Clinton sat with him alone in the Oval Office and asked for his help in lobbying his former Senate colleagues to vote against conviction in the impeachment trial.

In an interview, Mr. Dole said he thought "a lot of attention was diverted" from Yugoslavia and other foreign policy issues by the impeachment. It was "all consuming," he added, and Kosovo "may have been one of the casualties."

The Dangers:
A Balkan Firestorm That Slowly Spread

From the moment Yugoslavia fell apart in 1991, Kosovo—with its 90 percent ethnic Albanian population, and a Serbian minority that held its land sacred—was viewed as a place from which a wider war could erupt. The Bush Administration, which had adopted a hands-off policy on the killings in Croatia and Bosnia, warned Mr. Milosevic on Dec. 29, 1992, that the United States was prepared to take unilateral military action if the Serbs sparked a conflict in Kosovo.

The Clinton Administration reiterated the warning weeks after the inauguration. Three years later, when the Administration convened the conference in Dayton to end the Bosnia war, Kosovo was not on the agenda.

"Bosnia was then the emergency, and it had to be stopped," said Richard C. Holbrooke, the American envoy who negotiated the agreement at Dayton, in an interview. "Otherwise there would have been a real risk that Bosnia would merge with Kosovo into a huge firestorm that would destabilize the whole region." Over the next two years, younger, more confrontational ethnic Albanians began to build a ragtag army, supplied with weapons from neighboring Albania and financed largely by the Albanian disapora in Europe and the United States.

They faced serious obstacles. Mr. Milosevic, who had risen to power on the cause of protecting Kosovo's minority Serbs, took away Kosovo's broad autonomy in 1989 and was unlikely to give it back without a fight.

The killing in Kosovo began in earnest in February 1998, when the Serbs retaliated for rebel attacks on policemen with brutal operations of their own in the Drenica area. Members of the Kosovo Liberation Army and their families were slain.

The Administration sent Robert S. Gelbard, its envoy to the region, to confront Mr. Milosevic with horrific photographs of death and mutilation. A veteran State Department official respected for his tenacity but known for his temper, Mr. Gelbard had experience in Bosnia and Croatia. But he did not have much of a personal relationship with the Serbian leader, whom he castigated in unusually blunt language.

The Drenica killings, Mr. Gelbard felt, were the kind of ruthless act that would further radicalize the restive Albanian population and lead to an explosion that could affect the entire region.

"You have done more than anyone to increase the membership of the K.L.A.," Mr. Gelbard told Mr. Milosevic. "You are acting as if you were their secret membership chairman."

The meeting ended badly, American officials said. Mr. Milosevic was infuriated and would eventually refuse to meet with Mr. Gelbard at all.

The Distractions:
Foreign Policy Crisis Comes at a Bad Time

The eruption of violence in Kosovo in early 1998 could not have come at a more inopportune moment for the Clinton Administration.

The President and his aides were consumed by the Lewinsky affair. The Clinton foreign policy team was focused on Presidential visits to China and Africa and on Russia's economic implosion. Legislative electoral politics, especially with an incendiary sex scandal enveloping the White House, was never far from the President's concerns. And Kosovo did not register in any public opinion polls.

One of the President's political advisers said in an interview: "I hardly remember Kosovo in political discussions. It was all impeachment, impeachment, impeachment. There was nothing else."

Nonetheless, the spring of 1998 posed a question: Would the Administration, which had reaffirmed Mr. Bush's Christmas warning, take any action?

Weighing their options, officials said, they quickly ruled out unilateral military strikes, the very response Mr. Bush had promised. If anything was to be done, it would be in concert with the NATO allies, who along with America had troops on the ground as part of the international force in Bosnia. The United States could not start bombing while its allies were exposed in a neighboring country.

From then on, everything about Kosovo was subject to decisions by an alliance that worked by consensus and was soon to grow from 16 to 19 members.

Senior Administration officials who had lived through the years of delay and inaction in Bosnia believed they had learned a few things about how to deal with Mr. Milosevic. Diplomacy could work, but only if it was linked to the credible threat of force.

Ms. Albright began making the case for military action. At one key meeting in May, Mr. Gelbard argued that the time had come for air strikes.

Officials say Samuel R. Berger, the national security adviser, was opposed. The United States could not threaten without being prepared to follow up with a specific action.

Mr. Gelbard replied that he had already worked out some bombing targets with the NATO commander, General Clark. But Mr. Berger rejected the plan and no one else in the room supported Mr. Gelbard, who declined to discuss his role, saying only, "When I had the lead role on Kosovo issues I had complete support from the President and the Secretary of State."

The Administration then turned to Mr. Holbrooke. He pressed the Kosovo Albanians' main political leader, Ibrahim Rugova, who was becoming increasingly marginalized in his own camp, to meet with Mr. Milosevic. The payoff for Mr. Rugova was a meeting with Mr. Clinton in the Oval Office on May 27.

In a brief conversation with the President and Vice President Al Gore, Mr. Rugova warned that without direct American intervention, Kosovo was headed for all-out war. He pleaded for urgent American action and an increased American presence to halt the escalating violence.

"We will not allow another Bosnia to happen in Kosovo," a senior Administration official quoted Mr. Clinton as telling Mr. Rugova. The assurances were largely theoretical. Nothing concrete was promised.

After Mr. Rugova presented the President with a gift of a large piece of quartz mined from Kosovo, Mr. Clinton spent part of their time together telling him about similar minerals in his home state of Arkansas.

The two men posed for a photo. The meeting received little press coverage.

The Options:
From Cruise Missiles To a Force of 200,000

There was plenty of other news in Washington that spring. Kenneth W. Starr's sex-and-lies inquiry was still preoccupying the White House. There were drawn-out court battles between the President's lawyers and Mr. Starr over whether senior Administration aides, a few of whom were involved in foreign policy issues, should be forced to testify before Mr. Starr's grand jury.

In June, with the six-nation Contact Group on the Balkans warning Mr. Milosevic that he could not count on the West's dithering on Kosovo as it had on Bosnia, NATO was ordered to draw up plans for military action. Mr. Milosevic promised concessions.

The American strategy seemed to be working.

The situation on the ground, however, was far from stable. The Albanian guerrillas used the early summer to take control of some 40 percent of Kosovo, and Mr. Milosevic responded with a major offensive.

NATO's military planners began weighing their options. These ranged from an attack involving only the firing of cruise missiles to a phased air campaign to deployment of peacekeeping troops as part of a negotiated or imposed settlement. The planners also looked at what it would take to invade Yugoslavia. Western officials said the numbers were staggering: As many as 200,000 soldiers would be needed for a ground war.

In a few months in the spring and summer of 1992, Bosnian Serb forces expelled hundreds of thousands of non-Serbs from their homes in Bosnia. In 1995, the Croats in Croatia drove more than 100,000 Serbs from their homes in just a few days.

Seven years later, officials said, no one planned for the tactic of population expulsion that has been the currency of Balkan wars for more than a century and that Mr. Milosevic adopted in Kosovo: the expulsion, this time within weeks, of hundreds of thousands of people.

"There were a lot of Milosevic watchers who said a few bombs might do it," a senior NATO official said. "What was not assumed, and not postulated, was that he would try to empty the country of its ethnic majority."

NATO officials were wrestling with several legal and political hurdles, officials disclosed. Some NATO members were worried about imposing a peace without the approval of the United Nations Security Council.

Alexander Vershbow, the United States representative to NATO and a former National Security Council aide who had been deeply involved in Bosnia policy, suggested an answer in a classified cable titled "Kosovo: Time for Another Endgame Strategy."

Mr. Vershbow's plan, officials said, arrived with a heavy political price tag: The possible dispatch of NATO soldiers just before a midterm election and in the midst of the impeachment fight.

The cable spelled out a plan to impose a political settlement in Kosovo with the cooperation of the Russians, longtime allies of the Serbs. Moscow and Washington would then go together to the Security Council.

"Kosovo endgame initiative could become a model of NATO-Russian cooperation," Mr. Vershbow wrote. "No kidding."

The proposed deal called for creation of an international protectorate in Kosovo. The settlement would be policed by an international military presence, or ground force. If a peace settlement was negotiated in advance, as many as 30,000 troops might be required to enforce it. But Mr. Vershbow also left open the possibility that NATO might have to impose a settlement without Belgrade's consent, requiring 60,000 troops. To help sell the idea in Congress, Mr. Vershbow said, the American contribution could be limited.

"Sooner or later we are going to face the issue of deploying ground forces in Kosovo," he wrote in his cable. "We have too much at stake in the political stability of the south Balkans to permit the conflict to fester much longer."

Beyond concerns about the American ground troops in Bosnia, there were fears that a Kosovo war could spread, and even engulf Greece and Turkey, both NATO members.

The cable landed in Washington on Aug. 7, the day bombs exploded outside the American Embassies in Kenya and Tanzania. It was circulated as Mr. Clinton was preparing for his pivotal appearance before the grand jury investigating the Lewinsky affair and the White House was planning the cruise missile attack against Sudan and the Afghan bases of Osama bin Laden, the Saudi exile suspected of directing the attacks.

The plan generated some interest among midlevel officials in Washington. Senior officials agreed that it underscored the need to come up with a comprehensive strategy. In the end nothing came of it.

Mr. Clinton was under attack for his grand jury testimony and faced questions about whether his military decisions were motivated by domestic politics.

Jokes about the movie "Wag the Dog" became commonplace. Fittingly, the President in the movie seeking to distract attention from a sex scandal stages an ersatz conflict in, of all places, Albania.

The Politics:
No Will for Troops on Eve of Election

In Washington, impeachment was on Mr. Clinton's mind. Returning from a September visit to the region, Mr. Dole stopped in to see Mr. Clinton and Mr. Berger.

"The President listened carefully," Mr. Dole said in interview. "I don't recall him saying a great deal. He agreed it was terrible. Sandy Berger didn't say much, either." Then Mr. Berger left the room. "We discussed impeachment," Mr. Dole said. "This was a critical time in the Monica events."

Midterm elections were also at hand, and the Democrats were perceived to be on the run. Republicans fired another shot across Mr. Clinton's bow, warning against bombing Serbia.

"The Serbians have done what they wanted," Senator Trent Lott, the majority leader, said in an interview broadcast Oct. 4. "Now they're pulling back and now, only now what appears to be—will be—three weeks before an election, we're going to go in and bomb."

Senate Democrats were warning at the same time that they had little appetite for military involvement of any kind in Kosovo.

Senator Joseph R. Biden, the Delaware Democrat who favored action on Kosovo, said then that several Democratic colleagues approached him at a party caucus on Oct. 6 and said, "Don't count me in, Joe, don't count me in."

At the White House, the Democrats' leading Presidential contender for 2000, Vice President Gore, was keeping an eye on his own political future.

Officials say he supported air strikes in Kosovo but was careful to say little in meetings attended by large numbers of officials. His national security adviser, Leon Fuerth, prodded intelligence officials to scour the files for evidence that might implicate Mr. Milosevic in war crimes.

In October, the President outlined the plan for NATO air strikes in a letter to leading senators. The attacks, he said, would start out strong and "progressively expand in their scale and scope," especially if Mr. Milosevic and his forces remained in Kosovo.

"There will be no pinprick strikes," the President said in the letter.

NATO had agreed to the approach in a meeting of defense ministers in late September, in Vilamoura, Portugal. At the private meeting, William S. Cohen challenged his colleagues to embrace a new role for the alliance. If NATO could not muster a threat to Mr. Milosevic under these circumstances, he asked, what was the point of the alliance?

The Defense Secretary's toughened stance was striking. During the Bosnia crisis, he had assured his Congressional colleagues that American troops would be out of the region within 18 months.

There were limits. As Mr. Cohen made clear this week in Congressional testimony, his commitment was to air power, not the deployment of American soldiers on the battlefield. Questioned by the Senate Armed Services Committee as to why the United States did not field a credible ground threat last fall, he replied:

"At that time, you may recall there was great discontent up here on Capitol Hill. If I had come to you at that time and requested authorization to put a ground force in—U.S., unilaterally, acting alone—I can imagine the nature of the questions I would have received. You'd say, 'Well, No. 1, where are our allies? And No. 2, who's going to appropriate the money? No. 3, how long do you intend to be there? How many? How long? How much? And what's the exit strategy?'"

The Secretary concluded, "And that would have been the extent of the debate and probably would have received an overwhelming rejection from the committee."

The First Deal:
Bargain on Monitors Averts an Air Strike

Despite the harsh words and warning to Mr. Milosevic in the fall of 1998, no one, either in the Administration or in NATO, was eager to use force against the Serbs. So the White House turned again to Mr. Holbrooke to broker a deal that would push the issue into the next year.

It was a tall order.

For Dayton, Mr. Holbrooke had softened up Mr. Milosevic for months in advance and had sensed that the Serbian leader wanted a deal. In Ohio, Mr. Milosevic gave up territory in Bosnia, which was a separate country, and ended a war that was costing Belgrade huge sums of money.

When it came to Kosovo, the American envoy was pushing Mr. Milosevic to loosen his grip on land in his own country, a hallowed battlefield on which Serbian soldiers died trying to repel a Turkish invasion six centuries ago.

His only inducement was the threat of air strikes.

Mr. Milosevic and Mr. Holbrooke talked for nine days, and when it was over, the Serbian leader had made some concessions, perhaps significant, but they were only loosely outlined.

He agreed to withdraw the bulk of his forces from Kosovo. He said he would permit 1,800 unarmed international inspectors to monitor the deal and would allow overflights by NATO spy planes.

A token number of Yugoslav officers were to be sent to the NATO air base at Vicenza, Italy, with an equally small number of NATO officers stationed inside Serbia's Defense Ministry.

There was a catch. Mr. Milosevic wanted the lifting of the NATO order that gave authority to launch strikes immediately. Mr. Holbrooke made no promises. But he headed to Brussels, where he summoned NATO representatives to a meeting to report that a deal was nearly clinched.

The representatives voted to suspend the order, not remove it, angering Mr. Milosevic.

In Belgrade the next day, Mr. Milosevic told Mr. Holbrooke he was enraged that the order had not been entirely lifted. "He considered it a declaration of war," said one American involved in the discussions.

President Clinton praised the deal as a triumph of force-backed diplomacy, saying it was the basis for a lasting peace. Mr. Milosevic, he said, has "agreed to internationally supervised democratic elections in Kosovo, substantial self-government and a local police—in short, rights the Kosovars have been demanding since Mr. Milosevic stripped their autonomy a decade ago."

Within days, there were strong hints that Mr. Milosevic was not cowed. At a meeting in Belgrade to discuss implementing the agreement, General Clark asked him why some of the security forces covered by the agreement had not been withdrawn from Kosovo.

"That was not agreed," Mr. Milosevic shot back, according to an American official familiar with the conversation. "You call Holbrooke. He'll tell you what we agreed."

"No, I won't do that," replied General Clark, a veteran of hours of negotiations with Mr. Milosevic in Dayton. The general walked to a map to point out the locations of the brigades and battalions he wanted removed.

"We have no extra forces," Mr. Milosevic said. "NATO must do what it must do."

And then General Clark moved bluntly to the alliance's bottom line.

"Mr. President, get real," General Clark replied. "You don't really want to be bombed by NATO."

The Standoff:
Deal With Milosevic Is Quickly Unhinged

The October agreement quickly fell apart, and Western officials now acknowledge that the Serbs' preparations for a purge of Kosovo were evident in what they did and what they said.

According to NATO officials, the Serbs began infiltrating reinforcements and equipment in violation of the deal. Serbian officers bluntly told General Clark in October that they were just two weeks away from eliminating the Kosovo Liberation Army.

In January, the commander of the main military unit in Kosovo, Lieut. Gen. Dusan S. Smardzic, told local reporters that they could look forward to a "hot spring" in which the problems in the province would finally be resolved.

The Kosovo Albanian rebels were pushing ahead with their own war aims. Sensing that the deal essentially placed the world's most powerful military alliance on their side—despite NATO's continued assurances that it did not want to become the guerrilla army's "air force"—the rebels quickly reclaimed territory abandoned by the Serbian forces and mounted a continuous series of small-scale attacks. American intelligence officials warned Congress that the rebels were buying weapons, improving their training and becoming a more formidable force.

The unarmed observers, caught in the middle, could do little. William S. Walker, the American diplomat who headed the observer group, was threatened at one point by a belligerent drunken Serb wielding a gun and a hand grenade. Mr. Walker pleaded privately with old friends at the State Department for some security. The State Department was sympathetic but was struggling to cope with the aftermath of the embassy bombings.

American intelligence analysts struggled to read Mr. Milosevic's intentions. Was he playing for time or preparing for war? Were the troop movements in October a prelude to a major offensive in which the population would be displaced so that the Serbs could more easily root out the Albanian guerrillas?

"The October agreement," read a highly classified National Intelligence Estimate dated November 1998, "indicates Milosevic is susceptible to outside pressure." The estimate is a lengthy formal report drafted by the C.I.A. and vetted by all Government intelligence agencies.

It suggested that Mr. Milosevic "could accept a number of outcomes from autonomy to provisional status, with the final resolution to be determined, as long as he remained the undisputed leader in Belgrade."

Mr. Milosevic, this assessment added, would only accept "new status" for Kosovo "if he thinks he is in danger because the West is threatening to use sustained and decisive military power against his forces."

About the same time, NATO intelligence detected signs of a Serbian military buildup around Kosovo. Western intelligence officials, particularly the Germans, believed that these troops could form the backbone of a military operation to push hundreds of thousands of Albanians out of Kosovo.

Its code name was Potkova—in Serbian, Horseshoe.

American officials agreed that Jan. 16 of this year was a turning point. On that day, the bodies of at least 45 peasant farmers and their children were found on hillsides and courtyards in the village of Racak.

Most had been shot at close range in the head or neck with a single bullet, according to American officials. Some had been mutilated.

Witnesses said a small group of hooded men dressed in black and wearing gloves had carried out the killings. Mr. Walker arrived on the scene within hours, and accused the Serbian security forces of committing "a crime very much against humanity."

The Serbian Government declared him persona non grata and fiercely protested its innocence. The killings galvanized public opinion in the United States and Europe.

Three days after the bodies were discovered, Ms. Albright presented her new plan at a White House meeting.

It again threatened bombing if Mr. Milosevic did not go along with the West. But, for the first time, it demanded that he accept NATO troops in his own country to enforce a deal under which he would withdraw almost all his security forces and grant Kosovo broad autonomy.

Until then, the goal had been to stick to an agreement that had come to be known as "October plus"—the accord reached by Mr. Holbrooke plus some sort of protection for the observers. Mr. Berger was skeptical of going beyond that.

Mr. Cohen and Gen. Hugh Shelton, Chairman of the Joint Chiefs of Staff, had even greater reservations. They had wanted at all costs to avoid a troop presence that would require Americans.

But in the end the advisers embraced Ms. Albright's approach and sent it to the President, who accepted it.

Two days later, President Clinton was on the phone to Prime Minister Tony Blair of Britain describing the new approach.

The two leaders agreed that there were two options: to initiate an immediate bombing campaign in reprisal for Racak, or to fashion a diplomatic solution that included ground troops as peacekeepers in Kosovo, according to a White House aide who listened in on the conversation.

"Blair said that ground troops could not be used to fight a war, but only as part of a political strategy," the official said. "The President said, 'I completely agree with you on that. If we sent in a ground force without some sort of agreement beforehand, sooner or later they're sitting ducks for either side who is willing to provoke something.'"

Mr. Clinton said he would instruct his aides to try to bring Mr. Milosevic and the Kosovo Albanians to the bargaining table. "I will try to get Congress to go along with me," he promised Mr. Blair.

Meanwhile, General Clark and General Naumann were confronting Mr. Milosevic.

The two generals refused food and drink. This was to be a serious negotiating session in which they told Mr. Milosevic he was violating the October agreement.

"We figured we'd starve him out," General Clark told colleagues afterward.

Mr. Milosevic was, as General Clark later told reporters, "determined to go his own way."

His face red, his voice cracking, the Serbian leader described the Racak incident as provocation.

"This was not a massacre," Mr. Milosevic insisted, according to a NATO official familiar with the meeting. "It was staged. These people were terrorists. They do these things to people."

Mr. Clark warned that NATO is "going to start telling me to move aircraft" if Serbia did not live up to its agreement.

"You are a war criminal to be threatening Serbia," Mr. Milosevic replied.

Unquestionably, the meeting had gone badly. But General Clark, perhaps because he had lived through the stormy Dayton peace talks, reported to his superiors that he still saw some flexibility.

Two days after General Clark's meeting, two State Department veterans of the Dayton talks, James Pardew and Christopher Hill, delivered a similar message to the Yugoslav President.

This time Mr. Milosevic said that the killings had resulted from a firefight between rebels and the Serbian security forces.

The rebels, he continued, rearranged the bodies and dressed them to make them look like peasants and farmers, shooting the bodies through the heads and necks to make the incident look like a massacre.

Mr. Milosevic's behavior raised a crucial question for Western officials: What were his intentions? Were the troop movements into Kosovo saber-rattling, or preparations for war?

American intelligence agencies governmentwide were utterly divided on how to read the Serbian leader, classified reports show.

"Confronted with a take-it-or-leave-it deal, Milosevic may opt to risk a NATO bombing campaign rather than surrender control over Kosovo," read one late January report, according to a Government official. "He may assume he can absorb a limited attack and the allies will not support a long campaign."

A week later the prediction was the opposite. "Milosevic will seek to give just enough to avoid NATO bombing."

The day the bombing began, March 24, an intelligence report said Mr. Milosevic "would interrupt the offensive and sign the peace plan if he suffers or expects to suffer substantial damage to his armed forces and national level infrastructure from a bombing campaign."

Two days later, the analysts had changed their minds. "Air attacks," they wrote, "will not suffice to shake Milosevic's confidence."

In addition, while it was widely expected that NATO bombing would prompt retaliation against the Kosovo Albanians, officials said there had been no predictions that Mr. Milosevic would try to empty the province of them, as he has done.

After the Racak killings in January, some American officials favored air strikes. But there remained the delicate matter of NATO unity.

On Jan. 28, the NATO allies warned that they were ready to use force immediately, and Britain and France said they were prepared to send in ground troops to enforce a peace settlement. Two days later, after Kofi Annan, the United Nations Secretary General, said that the threat of force was justified to get the Serbs to the bargaining table, the allies decided they had justification enough under international law to authorize air strikes against Yugoslavia if it did not agree to negotiate a settlement.

To try to strike that deal, the Europeans wanted a conference that would be their equivalent of Dayton, Ms. Albright said in an interview on Friday.

The Negotiations:
Talks at a Castle Set Stage for War

But the gathering at Rambouillet, a former royal hunting lodge near Paris, was no Dayton.

The Americans approached the negotiations hoping to impose a solution on the Serbs and the Kosovo Albanians, but that attempt quickly broke down. Mr. Milosevic, who was a central figure at Dayton, did not even attend the meetings. The Albanians were balky, too, refusing to accept a three-year autonomy deal offered by NATO because it carried no guarantee of eventual independence.

If Dayton was a diplomatic triumph for the Clinton Administration and Mr. Holbrooke, Rambouillet was a debacle for Secretary Albright. She told friends it was one of the worst experiences of her career.

With the two-week deadline set for the talks almost expired, Ms. Albright went to Rambouillet and implored the Albanians to sign on to the deal. Ms. Albright failed to convince the hard-liners, the representatives of the Kosovo Liberation Army, who insisted on inserting language that held out promise of a referendum on independence after the three years of autonomy. But they also insisted that they needed a two-week pause to sell even that deal to their supporters.

That set the stage for the ultimate failure of diplomacy. By refusing to sign the deal, the Kosovo Albanians had taken the pressure off the Serbs, leaving NATO with no reason to order air strikes at that point. "If this fails because both sides say 'No,' there will be no bombing of Serbia," Ms. Albright said on Feb. 21, as the Rambouillet talks wound down.

Mr. Milosevic, for his part, concluded that there was not enough incentive for him to deal. While Ms. Albright had inserted language to satisfy the Albanian rebels, apparently none of the parties were negotiating any changes that the Serbs might have sought—particularly changes related to the deployment of NATO ground troops. Two days after Rambouillet ended, said the European Union envoy to the talks, Wolfgang Petritsch, the Yugoslav President decided that he was not going to accept NATO troops—and mustered his own forces and propaganda to prepare for the military showdown.

The standoff over Kosovo was growing more dire as President Clinton's political fortunes were rising and as the crisis drew more of his focus and energy. On Feb. 12, he was acquitted by the Senate. Only a few days later, on a trip to Mexico with Senator Biden, the President wanted to talk about the Kosovo crisis.

"All the way down on the plane I was reading a book about the Balkans and he saw me reading it," Mr. Biden recalled in an interview.

The book was "History of the Balkans," by Barbara Jelavich (Cambridge University Press). "And you know how he is," Mr. Biden added. "He asked me to give it to him to read. And I said, 'No, get your own copy.'

And I'll lay odds that he eventually got it and read it."

President Clinton believed war could still be averted, though he was prepared to undertake a short burst of bombings, if necessary.

In a meeting with Italy's new Prime Minister, Massimo D'Alema, in the Oval Office on March 5, Mr. Clinton said Mr. Milosevic had "accepted almost everything," according to Italian officials in Europe.

Mr. D'Alema, a rough-around-the-edges former Communist, was skeptical. He asked the President what the plan was if there was no deal and NATO air strikes failed to subdue the Serbian leader. The result, Mr. D'Alema said, would be 300,000 to 400,000 refugees passing into Albania and crossing the Adriatic into Italy.

"What will happen then?" Mr. D'Alema wanted to know, according to Italian officials.

Mr. Clinton looked to Mr. Berger for guidance. "NATO will keep bombing," Mr. Berger replied.

After Rambouillet fell apart, a followup conference was called in Paris three weeks later. While the world waited, Mr. Milosevic continued to build up his forces in and around Kosovo.

A defining moment came on March 18 at the International Conference Center on the Avenue Kleber in Paris. To polite applause, four ethnic Albanian delegates signed the peace plan that would give their people broad autonomy for a three-year interim period. The Serbs did not sign. That paved the way to air strikes.

Even though the United States and its NATO allies were now committed to war, three European Foreign Ministers—Robin Cook of Britain, Hubert Vedrine of France and Joschka Fischer of Germany—began murmuring about making a final appeal to Mr. Milosevic in Belgrade. Ms. Albright persuaded them to allow Mr. Holbrooke to go instead. But even as Mr. Holbrooke was en route to Belgrade, the situation grew more hopeless.

"The racial hatred was unleashed," said one senior Administration official. "Albanians began to kill Serbs; Serbs were shooting up villages."

Mr. Holbrooke has described his last meeting with Mr. Milosevic in Belgrade's Beli Dvor—White House—on March 22 as "unreal." Mr. Milosevic accused the Americans of "sitting at the Albania side of the table" at Rambouillet.

He insisted that there was no war in Kosovo, just a few terrorists who needed to be rooted out once and for all. Mr. Holbrooke later described parts of his conversation with Mr. Milosevic. "I said to him, 'Look, are you absolutely clear in your own mind what will happen when I get up and walk out of this palace that we're now sitting in?'"

"And he said, 'You're going to bomb us.'"

"And I said, 'That's right.'"

In the end it was Mr. Milosevic who was left to decide whether his country and NATO would go to war. "It was Milosevic who deliberately and consciously chose to trigger the bombing of his own country," Mr. Holbrooke said.

Ms. Albright said that setting up a deal signed by only one side was a crucial step forward. "Signing Rambouillet was crucial in getting the Europeans two things," she said. "Getting them to agree to the use of force and getting the Albanians on the side of this kind of a settlement."

The Serbs had already begun their offensive, she added, and if the signing had not been forced at that time, "we would be negotiating while they were carrying out their 'village a day keeps NATO away.'"

At 12:30 on the morning of March 25, hours after the first bombs fell, the President was wide awake. He had called his key counterparts in NATO and monitored the beginning of the air war that day. His foreign policy team had gone home and there was nothing left to do.

But the President apparently needed to assure and be reassured. So he called his Secretary of State and woke her up.

The President said, "We're doing the right thing here," Ms. Albright recalled. "We've got a long way to go. This is not going to be over quickly and we're all in this. I feel we've explored every option, that we're doing the right thing."

The Secretary said she replied: "I feel the same way. Nobody should ever think that we had gone into this without our eyes wide open."

The President's Dominance in Foreign Policy Making

Paul E. Peterson

In the fall of 1991, George Bush saw his own attorney-general defeated in an off-year Pennsylvania senatorial race. Richard Thornburgh, once a popular governor, fell victim to attacks by Harris Wofford, an aging, politically inexperienced, unabashedly liberal college professor. The Democrats succeeded in a state that had rejected their candidates in every Senate election since 1962.

Curiously, the defeat came after Bush had presided over the fall of the Berlin wall, the reunification of Germany, the democratization of Eastern Europe, and the resolution of the conflict in Nicaragua. If the voters had forgotten these early triumphs, Bush could brag that in the very year of the Pennsylvania election he had won a spectacular victory in the Persian Gulf War, negotiated a breathtaking arms control agreement with the Soviet Union, promised a further unilateral cut in nuclear weapons, supported Gorbachev in his final showdown with conservative forces within the Soviet Union, arranged the first international peace conference on the Middle East, helped achieve a settlement among contending forces within Cambodia, and facilitated a political settlement between blacks and whites in South Africa. Admittedly, history had not yet quite come to an end.[1] Disasters had struck the Philippines, the Serbs were fighting the Bosnians in Yugoslavia, and a military coup had reversed democratic tendencies in Haiti. But George Bush could tout foreign policy successes beyond the wildest imagination of his predecessors. Not surprisingly, Bush's standing in the polls reached levels that none of his postwar predecessors could match, achieving a spectacular 87 percent in February 1991.[2]

Harris Wofford ignored these accomplishments. The president, he said, was spending too much time on world affairs; more attention had to be given to domestic matters. Noting that the recovery from the 1990–1991 economic recession had petered out, Wofford emphasized how heartless George Bush had been in refusing to extend benefits to the unemployed. Health care costs were growing while millions of Americans were unable to secure medical insurance. Even some of Bush's foreign policy triumphs were dubious, Wofford claimed, alleging that the free trade negotiations with Mexico would cost Pennsylvania thousands of blue-collar jobs. By the end of the campaign, the president's travel abroad had actually become a political liability; Wofford's campaign workers wore teeshirts celebrating Bush's "Anywhere but America" world tour.

Paul E. Peterson, the Henry Lee Shattuck Professor of Government at Harvard University and director of its Center for American Political Studies, has written extensively on issues of American government and public policy. His most recent publication is the edited volume, *The President, the Congress, and the Making of Foreign Policy.*
    [1]Francis Fukuyama, *The End of History and the Last Man* (New York: Free Press, 1992).
    [2]"Presidential Job Ratings," *Cook Political Report*, 29 October 1991, 33.

The day after the election, the president announced that his Thanksgiving trip to the Far East had been canceled. On the day Americans celebrated their Pilgrim Fathers, Bush put Peking Duck and sashimi to one side and ate turkey (and crow) instead. By Thanksgiving Day, Bush's popularity rating had fallen to just 51 percent.[3] Quite clearly, George Bush, for all his foreign policy successes, was beginning to discover that the domestic front was quite another matter.

The denouement came within a year. George Bush was unable to transform his foreign policy achievements into a reelection victory. His opponent, Bill Clinton, eschewed foreign policy in favor of domestic and social policy themes. One of his key advisers was Harris Wofford's campaign manager, who placed a sign on his desk reminding him that the issue was "The Economy, Stupid!" Despite the fact that Clinton, a little known governor of a small, southern state, had avoided the draft by studying at Oxford, he defeated a commander-in-chief who could claim credit for having brought the cold war to an end.

Although the differences between the politics of foreign and domestic policy seldom reveal themselves this dramatically, they have been enduring features of American politics. At the same time, the distinctions between the foreign and domestic arenas faded during the years following the Vietnam war. The loss of Vietnam and the scandal named Watergate subverted executive authority. Control of the legislative and executive branches was usually divided between the two political parties. The parties themselves became internally more homogeneous and increasingly differentiated from one another. Foreign policy issues seemed to be completely absorbed into domestic disputes.

These changes raised key questions concerning the conduct of the nation's foreign policy. Had partisanship become so intense it no longer stopped at the water's edge? Had a prolonged period of almost continuous divided government handicapped the president's capacity to formulate foreign policy? Had the congressional role in the making of foreign policy been so enhanced that the differences between the making of foreign and domestic policy been all but obliterated?

It is the burden of my argument that the changes in American politics during the post-Vietnam era did not eliminate the distinction between foreign and domestic political arenas—primarily because the nature of the international system precludes it. To respond to external threats, the United States needs a relatively centralized, coordinated foreign policy-making system. Because of this international reality, presidents remain the most potent political force in the making of foreign policy.

Though Congress began to play a more important role in the years following the Vietnam war, especially when the executive's capacity to defend the national interest was diminished, the primary locus of decision making remained in presidential hands. As Bush's foreign policy triumphs illustrated, the presidency continued to be the dominant foreign policy-making institution. For all of Capitol Hill's increased involvement, it still remained a secondary political player. Conflict between the branches remained more contained than has been generally realized.

[3]*New York Times*, 26 November 1991.

A Hard Test

The United States is, in some respects, the last place one would look for international constraints on the making of foreign policy. According to a number of theorists, the international system is expected to have a greater effect on the foreign policy making of small nations compared to large ones, on the choices of weak nations compared to strong ones, and on economically dependent nations compared to economically self-sufficient ones.[4] Theorists also expect policy making to be centralized in the hands of the executive when external threats are immediate rather than distant.[5]

If these are correct estimates of the occasions when international constraints are greatest, then the postwar United States is a hard case, where external constraints are least likely to be controlling. As a large nation well endowed with natural resources enjoying the world's largest and most self-sufficient economy and containing the world's most powerful military arsenal, the United States was, of all nations, the one best able to compel others to act in accord with its wishes and the one least likely to be subject to constraints imposed by the external environment. If any nation-state can ignore external pressures, it was the richest and most powerful one. Thus, if one discovers that processes within the United States are constrained by external forces, then it is very likely that these constraints are quite general.

It is possible but unlikely that small countries have greater latitude on security questions than do large, powerful ones. It could be argued that they can do as they please and "free ride" on the more powerful. But free riders must be acquiescent riders; they can hardly let domestic politics interfere with the demands more powerful countries might place upon them.

Admittedly, the United States was not free of external threats during the cold war. Some may argue that it was particularly constrained by its need to protect the interests of the free world. Once the United States spread its economic, military, and nuclear umbrella, it was much more constrained than smaller nations who could free ride under U.S. protection. But if the cold war constrained U.S. choices, it was no more constrained than other countries. Had the United States not fulfilled its responsibilities, the impact on other nations would have been more devastating than on the United States itself. The threat posed by the Soviet Union to the United States was less direct and immediate than its threat to Europe, Asia, and almost any other country one can imagine.

Soviet expansion had to be contained, the possibility of sudden nuclear warfare was frightening, and revolutionary movements supported by the Soviet Union and motivated by communist ideology seemed threatening. Though the United States

[4]Peter J. Katzenstein, "The Small European States in the International Economy: Economic Dependence and Corporatist Politics" in John G. Ruggie, ed., *The Antinomies of Interdependence: National Welfare and the International Division of Labor* (New York: Columbia University Press, 1983); Guillermo O'Donnell, *Modernization and Bureaucratic Authoritarianism,* Politics of Modernization Series, no. 9 (Berkeley: University of California, Institute for International Studies, 1973).

[5]On the growth of executive power during World War I and World War II, see James L. Sundquist, *The Decline and Resurgence of Congress* (Washington, D.C.: Brookings Institution, 1981), chap. 6.

was the dominant figure in world politics, it hardly felt secure. But the precariousness of the international environment during the cold war was little different from the instabilities of earlier epochs. Thucydides, Machiavelli, and Bodin took a threatening international environment for granted. Wars and rumors of wars marked most of the twentieth century—though the United States sometimes pretended that it could ignore them. Indeed, the bipolar conflict of the cold war was more predictable and more manageable than the multipolar conflicts that preceded it.[6] Hardly before the cold war had come to an end, serious students of international relations became nostalgic about the regularities of bipolarity.[7]

Not only have the external constraints on the foreign policy choices of the United States been less than those facing other nations, but its constitutional framework makes it particularly difficult for U.S. foreign policy to be centrally led by a strong executive.[8] By separating the government into three branches, the Constitution insured that a wide variety of groups and interests would participate in decision-making processes. And by assigning most of the governing authority to a Congress divided between a Senate and a House, the Constitution further facilitated the intrusion of parochial considerations into the making of foreign policy.

The weakness of the presidency on issues of foreign policy within the U.S. constitutional framework is not always appreciated. The Constitution makes— and the courts have delineated—no clear distinction between foreign and domestic issues. The only powers given exclusively to the president are the powers to receive foreign ambassadors, grant pardons, and "execute" the laws of Congress. Admittedly, the president is also assigned the responsibility of commander-in-chief, but no specific powers are granted along with this responsibility and the Constitution quite specifically grants to Congress the authority to declare war, raise an army, and prepare for the common defense. The presidential powers to appoint ambassadors and make treaties are shared with the Senate. The president can veto congressional legislation, but this negative power can be overridden by a two-thirds vote in both Houses. Finally and ultimately, Congress can remove a president from office, but the reverse is not true. Thus, there is little in the U.S. constitutional framework that encourages executive dominance of the foreign policy-making system.

Over the past twenty-five years, the power of the presidency in foreign affairs has been especially weakened by two events that undermined executive branch credibility. The president and his advisers, who had in the decades since World

[6]Kenneth N. Waltz, *Theory of International Politics* (New York: McGraw Hill, 1979), chap. 9. The United States may have been the least constrained by the international system in the nineteenth century, when the country was protected from strong European powers by its isolation in the western hemisphere. This may account for the perpetuation of a relatively weak presidency throughout the nineteenth century. The power of the executive branch expanded with the increasing threat to the United States posed by the international system in the twentieth century.

[7]John J. Mearscheimer, "Back to the Future: Instability in Europe after the Cold War," *International Security* 15 (Summer 1990): 5–56.

[8]John E. Chubb and Paul E. Peterson, "American Political Institutions and the Problem of Governance" in John E. Chubb and Paul E. Peterson, eds., *Can the Government Govern?* (Washington, D.C.: Brookings Institution, 1989), 1–30.

War II enjoyed the enormous prestige that comes from winning a world war, were humiliated in Vietnam by their inability to resolve to their country's satisfaction a conflict with an underdeveloped nation. Simultaneously, a set of illegal and unconstitutional political practices by the executive were exposed as part of the Watergate scandal. For the first time in American history, a president was almost impeached and was forced to resign from office. Under the circumstances, Congress could no longer be expected to defer to executive expertise, the news media could be expected to hunt for presidential peccadillos, and the public could be expected to become distrustful of the country's political leadership.

Divided partisan control of the legislative and executive branches of government further undermined the basis for a consensual, executive-led foreign policy-making system. The Democratic party controlled the House of Representatives for all but four years during the postwar period and the Senate for all but ten of these years. Meanwhile, until the election of Bill Clinton, the Republican party had won the presidency in every election since 1968, save for the very close election of Jimmy Carter immediately after the Watergate crisis. The ethnic heterogeneity and decentralized internal structure of the Democratic party made it a very effective organization for winning congressional elections, while the more homogeneous, centrally directed Republican party made it more suitable for electing presidents. The Democratic party had the advantage of holding the more popular position on economic and social issues that tended to influence the outcome of congressional elections, while the Republican party had the political advantage on foreign policy and cultural issues that often played an important role in presidential politics.[9] The leaders of each party—presidential in the Republican case, congressional in the Democratic—had a vested interest in perpetuating the institutional structure and issue orientation that helped it remain in power within its institutional domain. And each party was able to use the political resources of the branch it controlled to facilitate the reelection chances of incumbents.

Consequently, both political parties have developed a set of partisan interests in the institutional power of a particular branch of government. The Democrats, after once having been the party of strong presidents (Andrew Jackson, Woodrow Wilson, Franklin D. Roosevelt, and Lyndon B. Johnson), became the defenders of congressional prerogatives. And Republicans, once the congressionally-based party (Whiggism, radical Republicans, Henry Lodge, interwar isolationists, anti-New Dealers, and Robert Taft), championed the prerogatives of the executive.

Partisan Politics and Foreign Policy

Given these political realities, it is not surprising that foreign policy making became more partisan. Party differences existed long before the early 1970s, of course.[10] Harry Truman was accused by Republicans of having lost China and

---

[9]Gary C. Jacobson, *The Electoral Origins of Divided Government: Competition in U.S. House Elections, 1946–1988* (Boulder, CO: Westview Press, 1990), chap. 6.

[10]Paul E. Peterson and Jay P. Greene, "Why Executive-Legislative Conflict in the United States is Dwindling," *British Journal of Political Science* 24 (1964): 1–24.

harboring communists within the State Department. Dwight Eisenhower scored heavily in the 1952 election when he announced that he would "go to Korea." John Kennedy "discovered" a missile gap as he was launching his presidential campaign in 1960. Republicans attacked Kennedy for the disaster in the Bay of Pigs, and in the months leading up to the Cuban missile crisis, New York Republican Senator Kenneth Keating attacked President Kennedy for his inability to identify missiles ninety miles from the Florida coast. Debates over Central and Latin America have divided the two parties at least since the Kennedy administration.[11]

But if parties are endemic to American politics, their role was enhanced after Vietnam. Congressional oversight of intelligence operations intensified.[12] Within the foreign policy committees, critical questioning of administrative witnesses became an increasingly partisan affair.[13] Party unity increased and partisan conflict intensified on foreign and defense roll calls cast in the House of Representatives.[14] Party leaders became increasingly active on foreign policy questions.[15] Many, if not most Democrats on Capitol Hill opposed the bombing of Cambodia in 1970, resisted the Reagan defense build-up of the 1980s,[16] and withheld support for the contras in Nicaragua.[17] Nor was partisan opposition simply a matter of Democratic legislators opposing Republican presidents. During the few years that Jimmy Carter was in office, he encountered strong Republican resistance to the Panama Canal and the SALT II treaties.

The apotheosis of partisanship may have occurred in the mid-1980s in the debate over the strategic defense initiative and the strains it placed on the interpretation of the antiballistic missile treaty negotiated by Richard Nixon and Leonid Brezhnev. The Republican administration headed by Ronald Reagan interpreted the treaty without reference to the debates taking place in Congress at the time of ratification, while a Democratic Congress refused to allow the strategic defense initiative to proceed beyond its understanding of the correct interpretation of that treaty.[18]

This increase in partisan conflict might be thought to have grave implications for the capacity of the executive to conduct foreign policy. For one thing, partisan opposition is effective opposition. While nonpartisan factions and special interests come and go, parties have an identity and a continuity that makes their involvement of more long-lasting significance.[19] Members of Congress are usually loyal members of their party, and if possible, they will support their partisan colleagues

[11]Robert Pastor, "Disagreeing on Latin America" in Peterson, *The President, the Congress, and the Making of Foreign Policy* (Norman, OK: University of Oklahoma Press, 1994), 204–27.

[12]Loch Johnson, "Playing Hardball with the CIA" in ibid., 49–73.

[13]Paul E. Peterson and Jay P. Greene, "Questioning by the Foreign Policy Committee" in ibid., 74–97.

[14]David W. Rohde, "Presidential Support in the House of Representatives," in ibid., 101–28.

[15]Steven S. Smith, "Congressional Party Leaders," in ibid., 129–57.

[16]Ralph Carter, "Budgeting for Defense," in ibid., 161–78.

[17]Pastor, "Disagreeing on Latin America."

[18]Alton Frye, "Searching for Arms Control" in Peterson, *The President, the Congress,* 179–203.

[19]Perhaps the best discussion of this point is to be found in V. O. Key, *Southern Politics* (New York: Random House, 1949), who argued that it was the absence of parties in the South that made opposition to dominant economic elites episodic and ineffective.

in institutional or policy struggles. Also, members of the interest group community and the policy elite often have partisan ties and connections, however much they may wish to appear separate and apart from partisan fracases. Partisan conflict, moreover, is portable. It can move from the legislative arena to the electoral arena quickly and decisively. Presidents cannot simply ignore with impunity the demands and complaints of their partisan opponents.

Executive Direction of U.S. Foreign Policy

But even though partisanship intensified after the Vietnam war, the fundamental responsibility for conducting the nation's foreign policy remained in the hands of presidents and their executive-branch advisers. Jimmy Carter negotiated the SALT II agreement, which took practical effect despite the Senate's refusal to ratify it. Carter reversed a policy of détente with the Soviet Union, once the Soviet invasion of Afghanistan had taken place. He canceled participation in the Olympic Games, imposed a grain embargo, and instituted a major increase in defense expenditures. The Carter administration facilitated the Camp David agreement between Israel and Egypt. And the Carter administration failed to anticipate the consequences of the Iranian revolution for U.S. interests, undertook a misbegotten rescue attempt, and finally negotiated the release of U.S. hostages.

Next the Reagan administration continued the defense build-up and successfully concluded the START and INF arms negotiations. Finally, the Bush administration invaded Panama, defined the U.S. response to the democratization of Eastern Europe and the collapse of the Soviet empire, and committed troops to Saudi Arabia, forcing congressional acquiescence to the Gulf war.

If one turns to international economic policy, the story is much the same. The crucial decision to leave the gold standard and float the dollar was made by the Nixon administration. Congress played only a marginal role on decisions concerning U.S. participation in the international monetary fund and the World Bank. The U.S. commitment to free trade was articulated and defended by the executive, with Congress left to complain and carp from the sidelines.[20]

One can find only a few examples in which, arguably, Congress participated in resolving issues of comparable import. When the Ford administration chose not to commit U.S. forces to Vietnam, even after the North failed to abide by the terms of the 1973 peace agreement, it may have been due to the congressional ban on expenditures for such purposes (though Ford very likely took into account public as well as congressional opposition to renewed conflict in Southeast Asia). Congressional opposition is sometimes used as a euphemism for more broadly based public opposition. This is understandable as political rhetoric, but analysts need to keep clear the distinction when assessing the relative power of Congress and the presidency as institutions.

When the Bush Administration negotiated an agreement with the Nicaraguan government, its decision was in all probability influenced by the strong congres-

[20]I. S. Destler, "Delegating Trade Policy" in Peterson, *The President, the Congress,* 228–45.

sional opposition to continued aid to the contras. Strong congressional support for Israel has complicated State Department efforts to encourage a resolution of the Palestinian question.

Although interest-group pressures account for some cases of significant congressional impact, in others Congress was influential because in retrospect it seems to have assessed more correctly the national interest than did the executive. Congress refused to appropriate development funds for Reagan's strategic defense initiative, because such expenditures violated an antiballistic missile treaty. Similarly, Congress cut defense expenditure in the mid-1980s, because the executive's assessment of the international danger seemed unusually extreme. The failure of the Soviet offensive in Afghanistan, the deterioration of the Soviet economy, and the growing pressures for democratization within the Soviet Union all indicated a weakening, not an intensification, of the international threat to the United States.[21]

The comparison with trade is instructive. More economists have concluded that the United States has little to gain from a protectionist trade policy, no matter how popular such a policy might be with certain industries and constituents in some congressional districts. By adhering to free trade policies and using the threat of protection mainly to open up foreign markets, the executive branch has chosen a course of action that most disinterested observers regard as in the long-run interest of the country. In this context, protectionist sentiments on Capitol Hill, though loudly expressed, have had only a modest policy impact.[22]

When the executive has steered a mainstream course considered by policy elites to be in the best interest of the country, congressional pressures have been more of a nuisance than a policy determinant. If Congress has exercised somewhat more influence than in the past, its increased role hardly seems to have been dangerous. Instead, the relative openness of the American political system seems to have facilitated an adjustment of policy when executive leadership was misjudging the national interest.

These instances of congressional involvement have not been so frequent as to indicate a major shift in power from the White House to Capitol Hill. Quite aside from the resolution of specific controversies, the authority of the executive to conduct foreign policy remains largely intact. The president can still reach executive agreements with foreign countries on almost any and all issues, thereby avoiding the necessity of winning consent of two-thirds of the Senate. Also, the courts have been increasingly willing to uphold executive interpretations of congressional intent. Unless the congressional delegation of power is exceedingly detailed, limited, and explicit, members find it very difficult to challenge in court an executive interpretation of that delegation.[23] Congressional delegations of authority, moreover, can no longer be hedged by a legislative veto.[24]

[21]Frye, "Searching for Arms Control."

[22]Destler, "Delegating Trade Policy."

[23]Gordon Silverstein, "Judicial Enhancement of Executive Power," in Peterson, *The President, the Congress,* 23–45.

[24]But Congress still has the power to ask the executive departments to report implementing decisions to congressional committees for their advance review, a power that often is as effective as the legislative veto. Jessica Korn, "Separation of Powers in Practice: The Limits of the Legislative Veto and the Impact of Chadha" (Ph.D. diss., Harvard University, 1993).

But if executive control over foreign policy has remained largely intact, even in the most partisan moments of the post-Vietnam era, it is worth considering theoretically the conditions that make this likely. To understand the relations between the branches, we must appreciate the extent to which day-to-day politics are constrained by the workings of the international system.

The Two Presidencies

The distinction between foreign and domestic issues has long been noticed. Two decades ago, in a classic essay written under the fetching title, "The Two Presidencies," political scientist Aaron Wildavsky argued that modern presidencies were fraternal—but hardly identical—twins. The one—domestic policy president—was subject to the debate, pressure politics, and congressional infighting that is a concomitant of the ordinary workings of democratic processes. The other—the foreign policy president—enjoyed an independence, respect, and prestige that enabled him to manage the external relations of the country quite autonomously. Wildavsky identified several factors that differentiated domestic from foreign policy:

• Since foreign policy questions often require "fast action," they are more appropriate for executive than legislative decision making.
• Presidents have vast "formal powers to commit resources in foreign affairs," and they have "far greater ability than anyone else to obtain information on developments abroad."
• Since voters know little about foreign policy issues, they "expect the president to act in foreign affairs and reward him with their confidence."
• On foreign policy questions, "the interest group structure is weak, unstable, and thin."
• Members of Congress follow a "self-denying ordinance. They do not think it is their job to determine the nation's defense policies."[25]

Wildavsky's analysis was not so much an original statement as a summary of a more generally held scholarly perception. Robert Dahl had put forth much the same argument more than a decade earlier: "In foreign policy the President proposes, the Congress disposes," Dahl wrote, adding that "in a very large number of highly important decisions about foreign policy, the Congress does not even have the opportunity to dispose."[26] Samuel Huntington similarly concluded that "strategic programs are determined in the executive rather than the Congress." "Just as power to legislate strategic programs was at one time, at least in theory, shared by President and Congress, so it is now, very much in practice, shared by the President and a variety of agencies within the executive branch."[27] Richard

[25]Aaron Wildavsky, "The Two Presidencies" in Steven A. Shull, *The Two Presidencies: A Quarter Century Assessment* (Chicago: Nelson-Hall, 1991), 11–25, esp. 14–17.
[26]Robert Dahl, *Congress and American Foreign Policy* (New York: W. W. Norton, 1964), 58.
[27]Samuel Huntington, *The Common Defense* (New York: Columbia University Press, 1961), 127–28, 146.

Fenno's views were little different: "Foreign Affairs members . . . help make policy in an environment strongly dominated by the President. . . . [They] have been hard put to develop any strategic posture other than one calling for responsiveness to executive branch expectations."[28]

As mainstream a statement as the two presidency theory originally was, it became the subject of steady criticism in subsequent decades. Wildavsky's own empirical test of his generalizations—a comparison of a limited number of roll calls—was woefully inadequate. Subsequent efforts to replicate his results on a wider set of data produced inconsistent and uncertain results.[29] Some of these studies suggested that the two presidency theory, though accurate enough for the Eisenhower era, did not explain the politics of foreign policy making in the years following the Vietnam war.[30] Writing with Duane Oldfield, Wildavsky himself concluded that "as ideological and partisan divisions have come to reinforce each other . . . foreign policy has become more like domestic policy—a realm marked by serious partisan divisions in which the president cannot count on a free ride."[31] Finally, two presidency "theory" was not much of a theory at all. It was only a set of observations about certain tendencies in American politics at a particular point in time. The structural underpinnings that might produce such a tendency were given little attention in either Wildavsky's essay or subsequent critiques.

But if two presidency theory is in disrepair, nothing very substantial has arisen to take its place. Instead, analysts of American politics are drawing few if any distinctions between foreign and domestic affairs. Instead, it is claimed that both arenas are equally likely to be the subject of partisan debate, voter interest, group activity, and legislative involvement. The president has as much—or as little—control over the one as the other. Within both arenas, the nature of the times, the skill of the participants, and the contingencies of the moment determine outcomes.

When generalizations are made about the making of foreign policy, they mainly chronicle changes that have occurred in the last quarter of a century. Congress is said to be more involved in foreign policy decisions, the process is more partisan than it used to be, the public is more attentive to and polarized by foreign policy questions, and interest groups with foreign policy concerns use the congressional channel more efficaciously than they once did.[32] It was the new Wildavsky, writing with Oldfield, who once again best expressed the now revised conventional wisdom: "If members of Congress disagree with the basic objectives of a president's foreign policy, deference is much less likely. . . . The press has

[28]Richard F. Fenno, Jr., *Congressmen in Committees* (Boston: Little, Brown, 1973), 212–13.
[29]Detailed discussions of various methodological problems associated with roll call analysis are contained in the articles included in Shull, *The Two Presidencies.*
[30]George C. Edwards III, "The Two Presidencies: A Reevaluation" in Shull, *The Two Presidencies,* 101–16; Lee Sigelman, "A Reassessment of the Two Presidencies Thesis," in ibid., 63–72; Donald A. Peppers, "The 'Two Presidencies' Thesis: Eight Years Later," in ibid., 26–35.
[31]Duane M. Oldfield and Aaron Wildavsky, "Reconsidering the Two Presidencies," in ibid., 181–90.
[32]Barry M. Blechman, *The Politics of National Security: Congress and U.S. Defense Policy* (New York: Oxford, 1990); Thomas Franck and Edward Weisband, *Foreign Policy by Congress* (New York: Oxford University Press, 1979); Thomas E. Mann, ed., *A Question of Balance* (Washington, D.C.: Brookings, 1990).

[also] grown less deferential. . . . Ideologically oriented interest groups have come to play a greater role. . . . There are also more domestic groups with foreign policy agendas. . . . All of these changes have added to the difficulty of keeping foreign policy isolated from public scrutiny and pressure."[33]

International Relations Theory and Domestic Politics

Nor has the theoretical vacuum been filled by students of international relations. Theories of international politics typically treat individual nation-states as unitary systems whose internal politics can be safely ignored.[34] "A systems theory of international politics deals with the forces that are in play at the international, and not at the national level," writes Kenneth Waltz. "An international-political theory does not imply or require a theory of foreign policy any more than a market theory implies or requires a theory of the firm."[35] Instead, each nation-state can be assumed to be governed by a single leader who considers the country's interests within the international system.

In traditional political theory, this point is cast in normative categories. Though Aristotle preferred a mixed constitution, he recognized a need for "the general with powers delegated for war." Less restrained in his recognition of the necessity of strong leadership, Machiavelli praised "the Roman practice of creating a dictator in emergencies." Not only was the "dictator very useful . . . when the Roman republic was threatened from without but also . . . 'in the increase of the empire.'"[36]

In contemporary international relations theory, the stance is analytical but the theme hardly changes. To explain foreign policy decisions, says Hans J. Morgenthau,

we put ourselves in the position of a statesman who must meet a certain problem of foreign policy, . . . and we ask ourselves what the rational alternatives are from which a statesman may choose . . . and which of these rational alternatives this particular statesman . . . is likely to choose. It is the testing of this rational hypothesis . . . that . . . makes a theory of politics possible.[37]

That Morgenthau uses the appellation "statesman" rather than "politician" indicates that it is the international, not the domestic political context, that provides the context in which choices are made.

Although Kenneth Waltz's analysis is internally more consistent than Morgenthau's, its point of departure is quite similar. Waltz defines the essential characteristic of the international system as anarchic, a Hobbesian state of nature in which each nation needs to guard its autonomy and security from external threat.

[33]Oldfield and Wildavsky, "Reconsidering the Two Presidencies," 188.
[34]But see Robert Putnam, "Diplomacy and Domestic Politics: The Logic of Two-Level Games," *International Organization* 42 (Summer 1988): 427–60.
[35]Waltz, *Theory of International Politics,* 71–72.
[36]Harvey C. Mansfield, Jr., *Taming the Prince: The Ambivalence of Modern Executive Power* (New York: Free Press, 1989), 135.
[37]As quoted in Robert Keohane, *After Hegemony: Cooperation and Discord in the World Political Economy* (Princeton, N.J.: Princeton University Press, 1984), 66.

This threat is so great—"war may at any time break out"—that individual countries must "worry about their survival, and the worry conditions their behavior."[38] The external constraints are so great that it is not necessary to understand the way in which responses to these constraints are chosen. On the contrary, trying to explain relations among countries by studying the making of foreign policy within them makes as much sense as trying to understand the fall of the Niagara River by examining the shape of a drop in its spray.

The mutual deterrence theory that guided the United States and the Soviet Union through the cold war relied almost exclusively on the assumption that the nation-state was guided by a single, rational leadership. But it is not only the members of the realist school, represented here by Morgenthau and Waltz, who have given short shrift to internal foreign policy-making processes. The assumption that nation-states are unitary actors acting rationally on behalf of the national interest has been no less important to the political economy school of thought.[39] These scholars suggest that the nation-state may not be as concerned about maximizing its security as its wealth. Since the international system has become more stable, nations can—indeed, must—concentrate on maximizing their economic development. Those that fail endanger not just their external security but even their political coherence, as the collapse of the Soviet Union reveals. These theorists are more optimistic about the possibilities for international cooperation. They expect that countries will respect international principles and rules designed for their common, long-term good and not cheat when it seems to be in their immediate interest to do so. The leading industrialized countries of the world have learned to respect one another's borders, coordinate their fiscal and monetary policies, are eliminating many tariff and other trade barriers, consult one another when altering the value of their currencies, and draw upon a common pool of funds to assist nations in temporary financial difficulty.

It is too soon to tell whether such coordination can continue over the long run, especially now that the threat of international communism has disappeared. Many analysts believe that current, fragmentary arrangements are only a precursor to a more stable world order in the future. Yet even the enthusiastic proponents of a "new world order" do not ground their expectations in the workings of the foreign policy system of key countries. Instead, they try to show that cooperation is possible among the rational statesman of whom Morgenthau spoke. In Robert Keohane's words, "rational-egoist models [that assume rational, unitary decision making] do not necessarily predict that discord will prevail in relations among independent actors in a situation of anarchy. On the contrary, . . . if the egoists monitor each other's behavior and if enough of them are willing to cooperate on condition that others cooperate as well, they may be able to adjust their behavior to reduce discord."[40]

---

[38]Waltz, *Theory of International Politics,* 102, 105.

[39]Stephen D. Krasner, *Defending the National Interest: Raw Materials Investments and U.S. Foreign Policy* (Princeton, N.J.: Princeton University Press, 1978).

[40]Keohane, *After Hegemony,* 83–84.

In short, there is considerable agreement among the various strains of international relations theory that states can be treated as unitary actors.[41] Still, international relations theorists have, for the most part, yet to work out their theoretical argument to its logical conclusion. If the international system constrains the policies of nations, so also it must influence the way in which nation-states deliberate upon and decide these policies. On this topic, research has barely begun.

Waltz even imposes upon himself a self-denying ordinance, making the peculiar claim that international theory is no more relevant to a theory of foreign policy making than a theory of markets is relevant to an understanding of the behavior of a firm. But, certainly, economists regularly use market theory to analyze—and prescribe—firm behavior. If a firm gave no attention to the bottom line, it would not survive for long. Since it necessarily follows that most firms pay attention to the bottom line, it then becomes a question of understanding the ways in which firms attend to this objective. It may be that information costs, costs of negotiation, and costs of changing practices all limit the success with which the firm can maximize profits. But that hardly makes market theory irrelevant; it only requires a sophisticated elaboration when applying the theory to specific firms.[42]

What Waltz declares inadmissible, Peter Goerevitch attempts. In a lengthy review of a wide literature, he shows that the international system has often influenced the internal politics of a country. Britain's insular position necessitated a navy but made a standing army pointless; Prussia's permeable border in the middle of the European continent had the opposite consequence. Without the presence of a standing army, a parliament independent of the monarch was more easily established in Britain than Germany.[43] It may be added that nations also learn from one another ways of best organizing their politics in order to protect their interests in a hostile world. Not only do they copy the military technology of more advanced countries, but they adopt and adapt those political structures that seem to work for competitors. For example, Britain, France, and, later, Japan created public bureaucracies that were capable of large-scale, organized activity, once the Prussians had demonstrated the potency of this organizational structure. The American executive began to model itself on European models when the United States acquired increasing international responsibilities. In short, international theory clearly implies that the executive is likely to dominate the making of foreign policy. The role played by the executive in foreign affairs is not due to transient factors such as the vagaries of public opinion or the momentary absence of interest group pressures. Instead, it is rooted in the requirements imposed on the

[41]This same point is made in Graham Allison, *Essence of Decision* (Boston: Little, Brown, 1971). Allison said that most international theorists assumed the state was a rational, unitary actor. The advantages and limitations of the unitary actor model are discussed in Paul E. Peterson, *School Politics Chicago Style* (Chicago: University of Chicago Press, 1976).

[42]Organizational theories of the firm can be reconciled with sophisticated restatements of market theory. Terry Moe, "The New Economics of Organization," *American Journal of Political Science* 28 (November 1984): 739–77.

[43]Peter Goerevitch, "The Second Image Reversed: The International Sources of Domestic Politics," *International Organization* 32 (Autumn 1978): 896.

nation-state by the potentially anarchic quality of the international system. Wildavsky hinted at these international sources of executive power in his original essay on the two presidencies: "Compared with domestic affairs," he wrote, "presidents engaged in world politics are immensely more concerned with meeting problems on their own terms. Who supports and opposes a policy [at home] . . . does not assume the crucial importance that it does in domestic affairs. The best policy presidents can find is also the best politics."[44] Policy takes precedence over politics because the international system both severely limits the sensible choices a country can make and shapes the processes by which these decisions are reached. International relations theory thus explains not only the policy choices of nations but also the existence of two presidencies.

Apart from encouraging the rise of a strong executive, what exactly are the requirements that the international system imposes on the domestic policy-making processes of a nation-state? Peter Katzenstein provides a useful point of departure for answering this question in his study of the small nations of Europe. Katzenstein points out that small countries are particularly vulnerable to changes in the international environment. Because international trade constitutes a higher percentage of their gross national product, policies must be designed carefully so that they do not adversely affect the countries' place in the international system. As a result, he says, "domestic quarrels are a luxury not tolerated in such adverse circumstances." Pointing out that "political metaphors [used by politicians in these countries] often emphasiz[e] . . . that all members of society sit in the same small boat, that the waves are high, and that all must pull on the same oar," he finds that "groups are held together by the pragmatic bargains struck by a handful of political leaders at the summit. Political compromise across the main social cleavages assures political quiescence and . . . reinforces political control within each camp. The greater the degree of segmentation dividing these societies, the more pronounced are . . . arrangements which defuse conflict."[45] In short, Katzenstein finds that in those countries where the international system places the greatest constraints on policy choice, there are strong pressures for elite consensus and centralized decision making.

In short, if the international system constrains the choices of the United States government, there are likely to be two presidencies. On foreign policy questions, the executive is dominant, Congress follows a "self-denying ordinance," interest group influence is weak and episodic, and voters look to the president for guidance and action.

International Constraints on the Making of Foreign Policy

The external constraints that differentiate foreign from domestic policy making are evident even in the years of partisan politics and divided government that characterized the post-Vietnam years. The capacity to formulate foreign policy

---

[44]Wildavsky, "The Two Presidencies," 24.
[45]Katzenstein, "Small European States," 118–19.

remained concentrated in the hands of the executive branch. Even the notable instances when Congress played a significant role do not necessarily demonstrate that external constraints are irrelevant to the foreign policy-making process. In many of these cases, the president's policy proposals constituted a dubious assessment of the country's long-term interest within the international system. Should the United States unilaterally reinterpret an international treaty in a way inconsistent with statements that were made at the time of its signing and ratification? Congress decisively argued against the position taken by the president, and in retrospect it seems warranted in doing so. Congress also moderated the defense build-up in the 1980s; once again, its decisions hardly seem to have done much harm. On the contrary, when Congress intervened into areas in which the executive branch traditionally exercised its prerogative, the actions seemed as appropriate as they were unusual.

It may even be argued that the need for the executive to defend its foreign policy positions before Congress helps to insure that foreign policy decisions are carefully reasoned. The sharing of information between key congressional committees and key executive branch agencies, and the close cooperation between these institutions may strengthen the influence of those who are best able to articulate the long-range interests of the country within the framework imposed by the international system. If a country is going to be led by people who take into account the long-term interest of the nation, then policy must be rooted in accurate assessments of the international situation, not based on myths or ideologies. To the extent that one branch or another indulges in fanciful myths or ideological thinking, the other branch should—and often does—become a more influential participant. Congress becomes more influential on defense and arms control policies when executive branch proposals seem unreal and fanciful. But when Congress ignores the interdependence of the United States and international economies, as it tends to do in the case of trade policy, the executive assumes a dominant role. As Morgenthau observed, to explain policy choice "we put ourselves in the position of a statesman who must meet a certain problem of foreign policy, . . . and we ask ourselves what the rational alternatives are from which a statesman may choose. . . . It is the testing of this rational hypothesis . . . that . . . makes a theory of politics possible."[46] And, it might be added, if a leader is not to be found in the executive branch of government, one will emerge in the legislative.*

[46]As quoted in Keohane, *After Hegemony,* 66.
*This article is a revised version of "The International System and Foreign Policy" in Paul E. Peterson, ed., *The President, the Congress, and the Making of Foreign Policy* (Norman, OK: University of Oklahoma Press, 1994), 3–22.

CREDITS

Selection 1.1
Selection 1.2
Selection 2.1
Selection 2.2
Selection 2.3
Selection 3.1
Selection 3.2, Selection 3.3 Reprinted with the permission of The Free Press, a Division of Simon & Schuster, Inc., from Presidential Power and the Modern Presidents: The Politics of Leadership from Roosevelt to Reagan by Richard E. Neustadt. Copyright © 1990 by Richard E. Neustadt.
Selection 4.1 Paul R. Abramson, John H. Aldrich, and David W. Rohde, "Progressive Ambition Among United States Senators," Journal of Politics, 49, 1987 (February): 3–35. Copyright Southern Political Science Association. Reprinted with permission.
Selection 4.2 Robert S. Erikson, "The 2000 Presidential Election in Historical Perspective." Reprinted with permission from Political Science Quarterly, 116 (Spring 2001): 29–52.
Selection 5.1
Selection 5.2 Arthur M. Schlesinger, Jr., "Rating the Presidents: Washington to Clinton." Reprinted with permission from Political Science Quarterly, 112 (Summer 1997): 179–90.
Selection 6.1 Mike Allen and Ruth Marcus, "GOP Missteps Helped Prompt Jeffords to Leave the Party," Washington Post, May 24, 2001. Copyright © 2001 The Washington Post. Reprinted with permission.
Selection 7.1 Mark J. Rozell, "Presidential Image-Makers on the Limits of Spin Control," Presidential Studies Quarterly, 1995, 25 (Winter): 67–90. Copyright © 1995 Center for the Study of the Presidency. Reprinted by permission of Sage Publications Inc.

INDEX

Van Buren, Martin, 88
Vandenberg, Arthur H., 31–33
Vedrine, Hubert, 342
Vershbow, Alexander, 335
Voter News Service (VNS) exit polls, 61
Voting patterns, 75–76

Walker, William S., 338, 339
Wallace, George C., 39
Waltz, Kenneth, 354, 356
Warren, Gerald, 117, 202–203
Washington, George, 88, 90
Watergate scandal, 82, 108, 109, 136, 144, 272
Waters, Maxine, 252
Watson, George, 285
Watson, Jack, 198, 200, 226, 228
Watt, James, 121, 209, 302
Webb, James, 33
Weber, Max, 190

Weiss, Juleanna Glover, 176
Whigs, 142, 144
White, Leonard, 140
White House Office (WHO), 218–220
Whitman, Christie Todd, 302
Wildavsky, Aaron, 352, 353, 357
Wilson, Woodrow
    campaign address of, 18–20
    mandate and, 143–144
    rankings of, 90, 93
    speeches and, 152
Wirthlin, Richard, 168–169
Wlezien, Christopher, 66
Wlezien-Erikson model, 66
Wofford, Harris, 344
Wolfowitz, Paul, 178
Wood, Kimba, 283
Woodward, Bob, 108
Wurfel, Walt, 118